RUSSIAN PEASANTS GO TO COURT

RUSSIAN PEASANTS GO TO COURT

Legal Culture in the Countryside, 1905–1917

Jane Burbank

INDIANA UNIVERSITY PRESS
BLOOMINGTON & INDIANAPOLIS

Publication of this book is made possible in part with the assistance of a Challenge Grant from the National Endowment for the Humanities, a federal agency that supports research, education, and public programming in the humanities.

This book is a publication of

Indiana University Press
601 North Morton Street
Bloomington, IN 47404-3797 USA

http://iupress.indiana.edu

Telephone orders 800-842-6796
Fax orders 812-855-7931
Orders by e-mail iuporder@indiana.edu

The paper used in this publication meets the minimum requirements of American National Standard for Information Sciences—Permanence of Paper for Printed Library Materials, ANSI Z39.48-1984.

Manufactured in the United States of America

Library of Congress Cataloging-in-Publication Data

Burbank, Jane.
Russian peasants go to court : legal culture in the countryside, 1905–1917 / Jane Burbank.
p. cm.
Includes bibliographical references and index.
ISBN 0-253-34426-3 (cloth : alk. paper)
1. Justice, Administration of—Russia—History—20th century. 2. Peasantry—Legal status, laws, etc.—Russia—History—20th century. 3. Russia—Social conditions—1801–1917. 4. Russia—Rural conditions. I. Title.
KLA1572.B87 2004
347.47'02—dc22 2004002133

1 2 3 4 5 09 08 07 06 05 04

TO MY PARENTS,

Jack and Helen Burbank,

WHO LOVE THE COUNTRYSIDE AND BOOKS.

CONTENTS

Illustrations

FIGURES

CHARTS

MAPS

Tables

Preface

I did not set out to write about a massive usage of courts in Russia by peasants. I was looking, in the beginning, for what I assumed would be a distinctly popular, distinctly peasant, non-Western manner of enforcing collective norms—a justice without regard for law or state. The archives confronted me with something else. Thousands of handwritten records of cases at the empire's township courts set me on a course of sustained interrogation and ultimately a rejection of the categories of analysis used by Russian elites for more than a century to describe, and gain at least intellectual control over, people known as peasants.

My earlier work on the Russian intelligentsia during and after the Revolution of 1917 revealed what I then thought of as their enduring, even endearing, populism. Engaged intellectuals of different political outlooks appeared convinced that "the people" did, or would, support their—the intellectuals'—ideals and political goals. This ascription of elite beliefs to others has its attractive aspects; a democratic illusion is more generous in spirit than an autocratic one. But the assumption that people think alike, share one's values, and will respond predictably to opportunities and constraints is disrespectful of the many ways that humans have made their lives and formed their minds.

Populism from above can become a formidable, self-sustaining obstacle to the creation of inclusionary polities. During the years of revolution and civil war, claims to know what Russian people were and what they wanted were made from different and conflicting positions. Not all these proclamations could have been right all of the time, and the assertion that the people supported one's own ideas was no recipe for winning and controlling the state. Russian elites have paid a high price for their refusal to engage, rather than speak for, the population.

As I began my work on law in the imperial period, I gradually uncovered one of the building blocks of the intelligentsia's habitually unreflective representation of the people's will. This was the widely shared conviction—among intellectuals—that peasants, the vast majority of the empire's population, had to be guided into civilization. The "peasant question" that became acute for

Russian elites after the emancipation had many answers before 1917, but most of these presumed that peasants had a distinctive set of values and that uplifting institutions—like the reformed legal system—were incomprehensible to them. Trained specialists and other educated people had to be intermediaries if peasants were to become real citizens of the better polities to which elites aspired. This way of thinking was well established by the late nineteenth century, and elites held fast to it later, through their frightening encounters with peasant agency during the 1905–1906 revolution and the subsequent, baffling period of electoral politics. It was an easy, if not logical, step in the years of civil war and revolution to imagine that "the people" would support the various visions of a new Russia proposed by Bolsheviks and their challengers.

The notion that peasants had a legal culture did not enter into theories of Russian society produced by intellectuals and activists in the revolutionary years. Only the National Bolsheviks saw a statist potential in the population; they suggested that Russian people, though primitive and crude, nonetheless wanted to belong to a great power and would respect a brutish, imperialist Russian government. Most intellectuals in most parties were terrified of the peasant anarchism that elites had come to believe in long before 1917. Even the violent and organized campaigns of peasants against the Bolsheviks were seen then not as civil war or a demand for a different kind of state but as a rebellion against all authority. That is what elites feared most.

Was this peasant anarchism a real threat or just a nightmare rising from the subconscious and conscious anxieties of leaders and would-be leaders of the Russian polity? As I proceeded with my research, I found my own sixties' romance with peasant anarchism and collectivism under siege. Not only were peasants in court, they were there as plaintiffs, seeking justice from the state's representatives on the bench. And they were not a "they." Court records revealed individuals with a variety of notions of how to live, in a profusion of conflicts with their neighbors, families, and business partners. These individuals were not content with custom; they had to have the law.

When I first presented my research—once with a title, "Law without the State?" where my residual suspicions are visible—I used the abstraction "peasant legal culture" to describe what I had encountered in the archives. The concept was regarded as oxymoronic or anathema or both. I found myself forced to clarify my assumptions against fixed ideas about "the peasants" and their beliefs. Hardest to shake were the interlocking notions that the collective peasantry had a collective mentality and that this mentality was anti-state.

I formulated four rules that guided my work on this project. First, I would try to represent activities and imaginaries of Russian peasants without presuming their collectivity. Second, I would ignore the grand opposition between state and society that underlies most historiography on Russia, and discard the premise of peasants' hostility and resistance to the state. Third, I would examine legal practices of Russian peasants without assuming that their usage of institutions organized by the state, such as the township courts, meant that peasants were for or against tsarism. One can have a statist culture and not be engaged in judgment—for or against—of the extant government. One can oppose the government's policies in principle or in practice, and still use the state's courts for one's own good. Finally, I rejected the widespread practice of making arguments about Russian peasants based on studies of peasants in other times and places. Peasants—defined by their legal status—in late imperial Russia existed in particular discursive, political, and economic circumstances. There is no good reason to presume that they engaged their opportunities in the same ways as did agriculturalists living in different polities, on other continents, in other climates, or even a few generations earlier in Russia.

To be fair to the individuality of peasant litigators, to respect the particular context of their activities, as they made their ways within the shifting constraints and possibilities of the Russian polity from 1905 to 1917, and yet not to lose sight of the larger social significance of their myriad choices made at township courts—this became the challenge of my project. Analysis of isolated court cases, rich in personality and local context, answered one part of my question about peasants' legal culture. Some peasants clearly had it. But to discover common concerns that inspired peasants to use the courts and reveal the values protected and enhanced by their court actions, it was essential to go beyond arguments based on perhaps singular cases or on selections of cases for a particular "peasant" issue. Encouraged by some colleagues, I embarked on the enterprise, novel for me, of quantitative analysis. After long hours of coding and data entry—115 characteristics for more than 900 cases—I am still enormously grateful to those who pushed me in this direction. As I explain in the first chapter, my interpretations are based in part on the exploration of more than 4,500 cases at a less detailed level, but it is the analysis of those hard-earned 907 cases that allowed me to see who went to court and why and when and where, and how decisions were made by judges. By watching the ebb and flow—mostly flow—of cases from 1905 to 1917, I witnessed the responsiveness of this modest, local peasant-led institution to the changing needs of rural people as they made their way through peacetime, war, and revolution.

This study views local life from the standpoint of a single legal instance, and does not claim to represent the whole range of legal activities in which peasants engaged. By choosing the township courts with their records of individual cases, I was able to hear peasants' stories one by one. I see my work as part of a shared project of democratizing a historiography that hyper-individualizes leaders, be they tsars or general secretaries or presidents, but collectivizes "the people," peasants, Russians, and others. Still, to give individuals voice is not to forget that they are always linked and in part formed by social relations, and that their manifold actions can reshape those relationships over time. The book does not avoid the question of social transformation, but it starts from rural people, in their courts, and looks out from there.

Acknowledgments

This book has had several homes, where many people helped me in fundamental ways. Let me start with Russia, and the people who made my project possible and my life there a continuing, fascinating adventure. First, I thank my dear friends, Sergei Romaniuk and Galina Ovchinnikova. Sergei generously shared with me his vast knowledge of Moscow, its surrounding settlements, and its archives, and kept me from many a silly error; Galina provided comfort, companionship, and feasts, even in hard times. I am grateful to others who fed my curiosity and spirits in Moscow, St. Petersburg, and Vyborg, especially in Soviet days, when we did not know whether we would see one another again—Marina Vekhova and Mikhail Sergeev, Vladimir Erokhin and Raia Gershzon, Elena Zakharova, Frida Avrunina, Galina Dozmarova, Natalia Serova, and Tatiana Smorodinskaia, and their many friends. I deeply miss my Russian mentor, Natalia Mikhailova Pirumova, who taught me more than history. Having Russian colleagues has been a privilege and has made a difference to this book. I thank Galina Ul'ianova, Efim Pivovar, Ekaterina Zhukova, Nikita Lomagin, Ekaterina Pravilova, Sergei Kazantsev, and Andrei Il'in for their help along the way.

Another pleasure has been working with two historians who share my enthusiasm for peasant legal culture—Cathy Frierson, whose comments vastly improved this book, and Gareth Popkins, who is providing even more numbers to make our case. Alessandro Stanziani, Elise Wirtschafter, William Wagner, Yanni Kotsonis, Nancy Kollmann, and Fred Cooper read the entire manuscript at various points and made their insightful criticisms and suggestions in thoughtful ways. Valerie Kivelson, colleague and fabulous critic, continues to expand my horizons in time, space, and otherwise. Natalia Zharinova, a political scientist trained in Russian law, was an ideal collaborator and made sure my statistics had significance.

A number of other scholars gave me various kinds of assistance: encouragement, patience, involvement in collective projects, citations, advice on methods and sources, an off-hand idea they hardly remember. For these kindnesses I thank Joseph Bradley, Barbara Engel, Jack Kollmann, Brian Porter, David

Ransel, Yuri Slezkine, Peter Solomon, Nikolai Ssorin-Chaikov, and Mark von Hagen. Jeffrey Brooks stepped in at a critical moment to help me with the title. Tamara Kondrat'eva translated rowdy peasant slang. John Burbank consulted on Finnish names. Maris Vinovskis encouraged me to take the plunge into statistical analysis. Steven Hoch offered appropriate cautions.

I am deeply grateful for the generous help extended to me by the personnel of many archives and libraries. I started research on this book in the foreigners' reading room in Moscow in 1987, to which files had to be hauled through rain and snow for my supervised use. What a pleasure it was in 1995—after the archives in Moscow were opened to all scholars—to meet the people who had transported these materials for me. I would like to express my thanks to the staffs of the Central Historical Archive of Moscow, the Central State Archive of Moscow Region, the Russian State Historical Archive, and the Central State Historical Archive of St. Petersburg, the Russian State Library and the State Public Historical Library in Moscow, and the National Library of Russia in St. Petersburg. I am particularly grateful to Irina Andreevna Guseeva who guided me through the local history of Moscow townships. In the United States I used the University of Michigan and Stanford University libraries extensively. Elena Danielson, Molly Molloy, and Olga Katz of the Hoover Institution and Library provided me with superb assistance during the last stages of writing.

In my search for materials, and in organizing them, I have been aided by assistants in Ann Arbor, New York, and Moscow. Several of them were graduate students, and some became professors while I finished this book. I am happy to have worked with Mary Cavender, Daniella Doron, Stuart Finkel, Rebecca Friedman, Lauren Kaminsky, Anna Kuxhausen, Ian Mladjov, Brigid O'Keeffe, Jim Reische, Jeanne Sklar, Olga Virakhovskaia, Christopher Wendt, and Martha Young. In Moscow Sergei Dundin located many sources for me. Mikhail Zolotarev searched for photographs of real peasants—not stereotypes—who lived in the townships of Moscow Province in the early twentieth century. His selections are reproduced in the book.

As publication became a reality, I began working with the editorial team at Indiana University Press. I want to thank my historian-editor, Janet Rabinowitch, for believing me about peasants and law, Jane Lyle for dealing with charts, tables, and other complexities of the manuscript, and Rita Bernhard for attentive copyediting.

I worked on this book in Santa Barbara, Ann Arbor, Moscow, St. Petersburg, Paris, New York, and Stanford, and in several institutional settings. The Russian State University for the Humanities, directed by Iurii Afanas'ev, assisted me in several research stays. I particularly remember the gracious help of Tatiana Shemakhanskaia and Irina Karapetianz, and the companionship of Natalia Basovskaia and Oksana Beidina, when we were together at this path-breaking institution. For most of the years of my research and writing I was on the faculty at the University of Michigan. There I profited immensely from the resources of the Center for Russian and Eastern European Studies and from Information Technology Services. Hannah D'Arcey was a patient and superb tutor in data collection and analysis. In 2002 I joined the faculty of New York University, where Lorna Hughes and Nicola Monat-Jacobs helped me produce a website. Edward Kasinec guided me to marvelous resources in the New York Public Library; Matthew Knutzen located elusive villages on his fine maps. During the academic year, 2002–2003, I was a Fellow at the Center for Advanced Research in the Behavioral Sciences. Lynn Gale helped me to make my tables presentable, and Kathleen Much deftly wielded the blue pencil as I cut the manuscript down to size.

My research was supported by fellowships from the International Research and Exchanges Board, the Hoover Institution, the University of Michigan, the American Council of Learned Societies/Soviet Academy of Sciences Exchange, Fulbright-Hays Faculty Research Abroad Awards, the National Endowment for the Humanities, the Center for Advanced Study in the Behavioral Sciences, and New York University. I am grateful to them all.

The circle is one of the best traditions of the Russian intelligentsia. Two groups had a strong impact on this book. I want to thank my former colleagues—Laura Downs, Sueann Caulfield, Susan Juster, Valerie Kivelson, and Sonya Rose for their readings of my work—and Kathleen Canning, Susan Crowell, Carol Dickerman, Marysia Ostafin, and Hitomi Tonomura for their companionship in Ann Arbor and elsewhere. A second friendly circle was formed by my fellows at the Center for Advanced Study in the Behavioral Sciences at Stanford. I particularly want to thank the Center's law group—Frank Dobbin, Peter Gourevitch, Jim McPherson, Deborah Post, Robert Sampson, Beth Simmons, and Mark Suchman. These wide-ranging intellectuals gave me confidence that my social reading of litigation at peasant courts was productive and even normal.

I have dedicated this book to my parents, whose sixtieth wedding anniversary we celebrated last year. I want to say a special thank you to my sister Cilla as well. Last, of course the best, I thank Fred Cooper, who ventured beyond Africa to Moscow in 1988 and almost starved. Fred does not live like a peasant, but he understands the practical side of life as well as the aesthetics of a wonderful marriage.

Note on Transliteration

I have used the Library of Congress system without diacritical marks to transliterate Russian names and words, with some modifications. I chose to simplify first names in the narrative by deleting apostrophes indicating soft signs and making a few other changes where exact transliteration would produce exotic or comical results in English. I use Maria instead of Mariia, Praskovia instead of Praskov'ia, Semyon, and so forth. Full transliteration is used in the notes and bibliography.

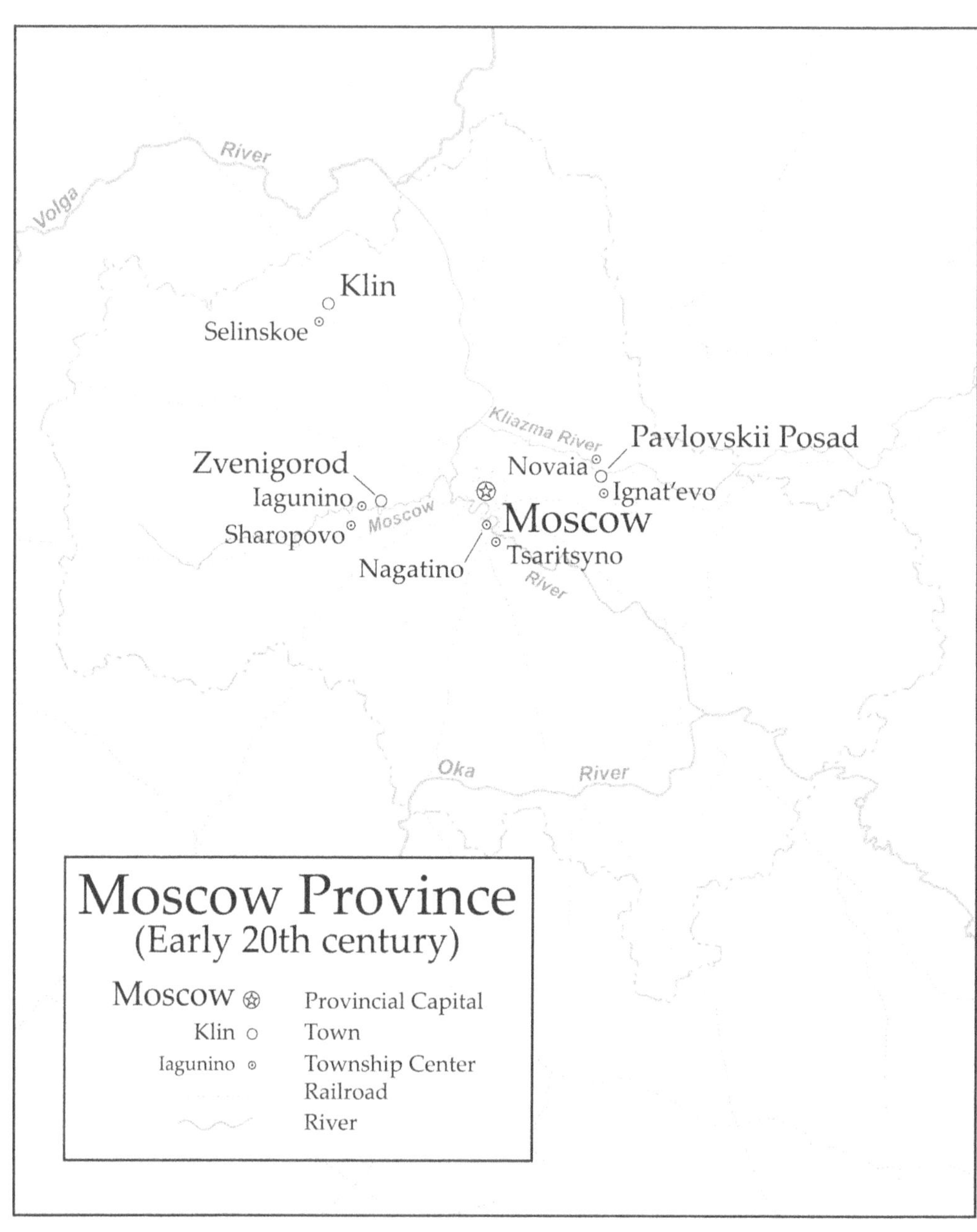

Moscow Province, Early Twentieth Century

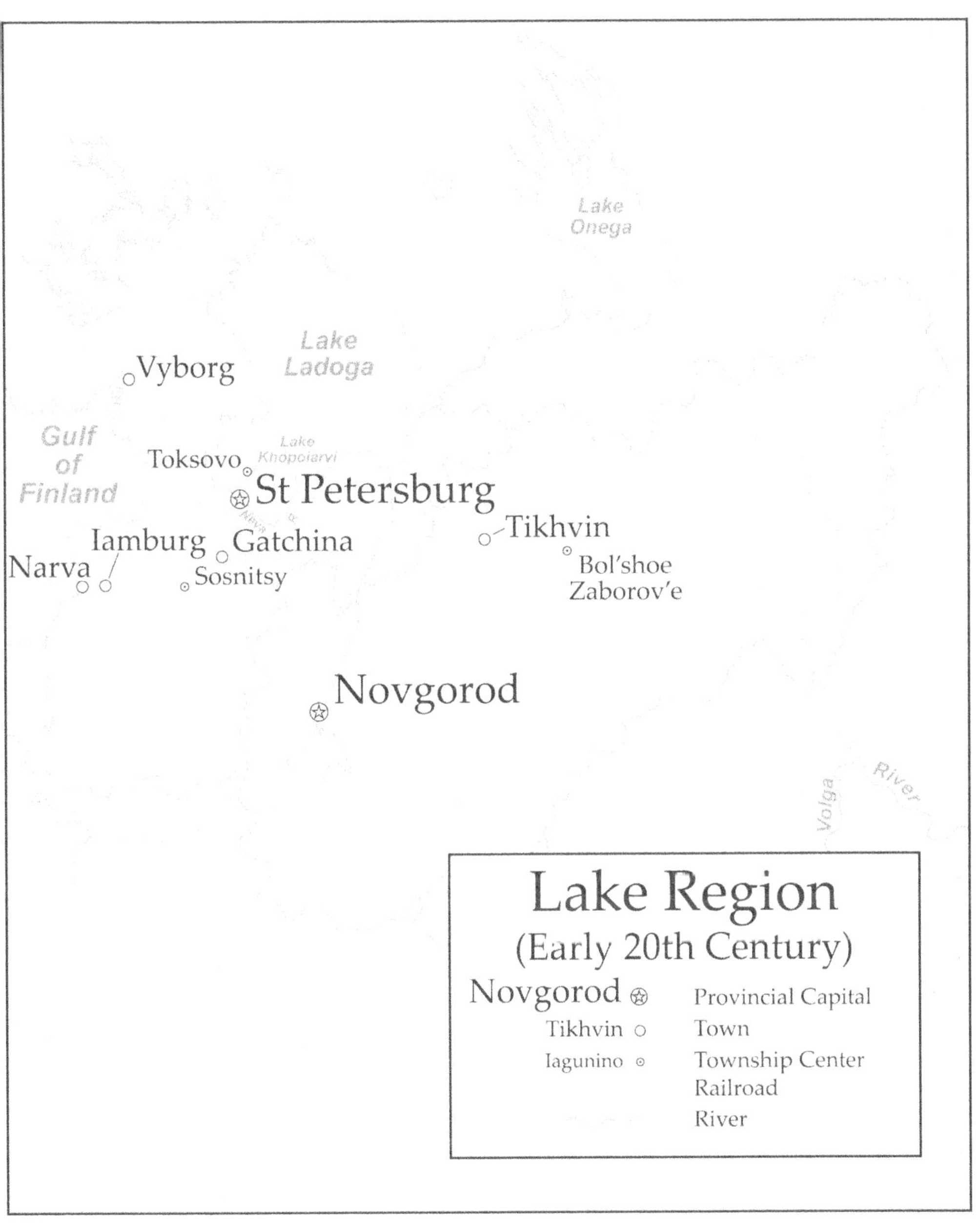

Lake Region, Early Twentieth Century

The Peasant Question and the Law

THE PROBLEM WITH PEASANTS

Peasants are the long-term others of Russian history. In the last decades of tsarist rule, radicals, reformers, and conservatives worried about the threat that the huge rural population posed to their disparate visions of a desirable polity. For Russia's elites, an empire overwhelmingly populated by people legally ascribed to peasant status did not mean that peasant life defined normality; social demography only underlined the magnitude of the peasant problem. In 1917 the system of legal estates was abolished by the Provisional Government, but the category "peasant" and its disabling associations did not disappear. Bolshevik authorities defined the proletariat by labor in factories not fields, and established social class as a determinant of political claims and rights. Peasants, acknowledged as allies in the revolution against autocracy, were demoted to a worrisome, unstable, potentially capitalistic element of the new polity. Inherited from the old regime, the notion of peasant backwardness became part and parcel of the outlook of Soviet leaders.[1]

A goal of the new government, as of the old, was civilizing rural Russia. From early Bolshevik crusades against superstition to Stalin's murderous assault on family farming, Soviet projects were directed against village institutions and their potential to obstruct the building of socialist society. During the seventy-four years of Soviet Communism, managers, professionals, industrial workers, and soldiers took part in multiple campaigns to educate and terrorize peasants into modern, compliant, and loyal Soviet citizens.[2] After the collapse of Soviet rule, fears about the retrograde values of rural people still structure the ways that a new era of reforms is imagined and carried out in Russia. Decades of treating peasants as second-class citizens may have made dystopian visions real: it could be argued that the disabling of rural society carried out since the 1920s has created in the Russian countryside the impoverished and downtrodden village of imperial and Soviet myth.[3]

Have peasants always been so "different" from other subjects and citizens of modern Russia? Or, to put this question another way, is it possible to view the daily-life practices of rural people before 1917 as "normal" phenomena, expressive of tensions as well as cohesions, of dynamism and conservatism, in Russian society? And can Russian peasants be regarded as participants in—rather than victims of or obstacles to—the development of legal governance? This is the major subject addressed in this book. I examine rural people in a particular intersection with the larger polity—the local courts where the vast majority of Russia's legal disputes were decided. I focus on the last years of the imperial regime, years that no one at the time knew as the last. I argue that legal proceedings were an accepted means of resolving conflicts in rural areas, that Russian peasants inhabited and shaped the legal culture of their country, and that the legal experience of the rural population constituted an unrecognized foundation for a law-based polity.

Legal proceedings in all societies are about settling conflicts, not about bringing out the best in litigants. In this respect Russian local courts were unexceptional. Rural people could be petty, vindictive, greedy, and demanding of the judicial system, as were litigants in other walks of life or other legal systems. The critical questions about legal culture concern the ways that disputes are resolved, not why people have disputes. What I explore in this book are the legal practices of rural people and the nature of the legal connection between rural dwellers and the state, not whether peasants were better or worse citizens than the rest of the empire's people. Russian peasants were ordinary in their usage of their courts.

RUSSIAN LAW AND RURAL INSTITUTIONS

Legal institutions were themselves an ordinary element of Russian governance, well before the period addressed in this book. Ancestors of twentieth-century Russian peasants had engaged state law for their own purposes for centuries, ever since the extension of political control by centralizing powers over agricultural products and agriculturalists living in the great forests and along the steppe borderlands of northeastern Europe. The Grand Princedom of Muscovy offered even its most modest subjects a system of litigation for resolving local and other disputes. As Nancy Kollmann argues, the provision of legal process for the defense of status-based honor served to integrate and control the widely dispersed population of Muscovy.[4] Imperial Russia inherited legal institutions and a practice of legal recourse by subjects from its Muscovite progenitor. Peasants, including the enserfed, made ample use of legal regulations to advance their interests and to defend themselves from encroachments on their rights.[5]

Although resort to legal process was a long-standing possibility for Russian peasants, the institutions, procedures, and regulations specific to rural justice in the early twentieth century were put in place by a series of reforms beginning in the 1830s. In pursuit of orderly administration, officials made major adjustments to the Russian legal system in the nineteenth century. These substantive transformations included compilation and publication of Russian statute law (1832), production of a criminal code (1845), reform of court procedure and creation of a professional bar (1864), introduction of local court systems for peasants (1839, 1861), revision of administrative and legal procedures in rural areas (1889), and abolition of corporal punishment (1863, 1904).[6]

These changes in the legal system were part of a gradual and profound redefinition of the linkages between central authorities and their peasant subjects. Before the dismantlement of the serf economy, the primary means of governing peasant society and the most effective apparatus of social control throughout the empire was patriarchal self-management at the village level.[7] The central administration relied on landlords and local agents to collect taxes, provide recruits, and muster labor services from serfs and other peasants, but to implement these demands as well as other tasks of regulation, the state had left peasants largely on their own. The manorial economy was managed for most practical purposes by peasant patriarchs, acting as intermediaries between peasant communities and their lords. State peasants—peasants who lived on land belonging to the state, the imperial family, or other imperial institutions—were expected to distribute taxation and other state-imposed burdens themselves.

Ending serfdom obliged the state to reconfigure social relations both in the countryside and in the polity as a whole. The elimination of serf-owning land lords as official intermediaries enhanced the already significant power of local people; as part of the emancipation, administrative and judicial institutions were put in place to redefine, contain, and coordinate peasant affairs. The differences in status between serfs and state peasants were erased.[8] After 1861 both former serfs and former state peasants were governed by the same regulations, compiled in a single legal code, *The Regulation on the Rural Estate.* Book 1 of this codification, *The General Regulation on Peasants,* defined the rights, obligations, and institutions of governance for the empire's peasants.[9]

The laws of post-emancipation Russia bound peasants to two collective bodies, both of which remained in place until the reorganizations following the 1917 revolutions. First, all peasants were members of a "rural society" (*sel'skoe obshchestvo*), which regulated use of common economic resources and performed many tasks of local governance. The basic principles that determined which villages and people belonged to which rural societies were shared economic resources and proximity. A rural society in post-emancipation Russia was usually a descendant from a peasant collective, also known as a commune (*mir*, or *obshchina*), that before 1861 had controlled cultivation of land in common either on a serf owner's estate or on state-controlled domains.[10] Being part of a rural society was not voluntary. Statute 47 of *The General Regulation on Peasants* required all peasants to be participants in a rural society for the regulation of their economic affairs.[11] The rural society was the lowest-level unit of peasant self-administration, and a most important one. The society's recorded resolutions were legal documents that established a legal record of land holdings, community membership, and other fundamental transactions. Representatives of a rural society were often legal spokesmen for their communities at other administrative and judicial institutions.[12]

Second, above the rural society with its economic responsibilities, *The General Regulation on Peasants* established the township (*volost'*) as the local authority over peasants' administrative and judicial affairs. Modeled on the church parish, a township combined several rural societies with their contiguous territories and peasant settlements. In theory, each township was to have authority over no fewer than three hundred and no more than two thousand male "souls," a taxation unit that counted all males in an area, thus roughly six hundred to four thousand people. In practice, townships varied in size; by the early twentieth century, more than half of all the townships were larger than the upper limit prescribed by law. The township administration was to be located within twelve versts (eight miles) from the most distant settlement of peasants subject to it.[13]

One duty of the township administration was the provision of justice. The framers of the emancipation were obliged to provide some kind of legal instance to emancipated peasants after their liberation from the authority of serf owners. *The General Regulation on Peasants* assigned township courts the task of adjudicating "quarrels and suits about property" and "misdemeanors" for the rural population.[14] In drawing up the new court's statutes, officials largely relied on a preceding legal initiative, directed at peasants who lived on state lands.[15] The result was the creation of a very localized court system, based on traditional principles of self-administration and central oversight, but with profound significance for the incorporation of peasants into the legal system and for the orderly, lawful regulation of rural affairs.

The township court—the lowest-level judicial forum accessible to peasants—is the setting for this examination of legal culture in rural Russia in the early twentieth century. Township courts were the most numerous of the empire's many different legal instances. They attracted an ever growing number of litigants from the 1860s until the outbreak of the First World War in 1914. Although members of other estates were subject to its jurisdiction after 1889, the township court was very much an institution run by and for peasants. Cases were heard and decided by three or four peasant judges, sitting in the presence of a scribe who recorded the proceedings. No lawyer or other advocate would be present at the court; litigants—usually peasants—presented their own cases. Testimony was oral, but documents and witnesses—again usually peasants—were summoned when appropriate to a suit or charge. The judges were instructed to decide cases "according to conscience, on the basis of the evidence contained in the case." Jurisdiction over petty crime was defined by a list of statutes. In civil cases, particularly cases involving peasant inheritance, the court was to be "guided by local customs."[16]

This book explores the ways that rural people used their legal opportunities and considers the significance of peasants' participation in the judicial system for local society and the imperial polity. I argue that the township courts provided a legal forum through which relationships of authority within families and villages were transformed gradually and peacefully, in case-by-case decisions. Although Russia's elites regarded peasants as backward, disorderly, and uncivilized, the records of township courts document men and women using the law to settle disputes over economic resources and social responsibility, and to combat the social damage of petty, but hurtful, criminality. Court proceedings reveal litigants' ideals as well as violations of them. A well-ordered peasant village was an aspiration that could be and was addressed, if not achieved, at Russia's township courts.

LEGAL CULTURE AS SOCIAL PRACTICE

I use the term *legal culture* to describe rural people's engagement with law at the township courts. This usage would not have been familiar to commentators on peasant affairs in early twentieth-century Russia, nor is it to be found in most studies of Russian peasants. Russian elites debated the merits and, from their perspective, mostly demerits of the township court system right up until the revolution against the autocracy in 1917.[17] Most observers considered peasants too primitive to understand "real" law and too uneducated to administer "real" justice. Some critics of the autocracy thought that by setting up a system of rural peasant courts outside the circuit court system introduced in 1864, the state itself had condemned the empire's peasants to wallow in their backwardness or, in the romanticizing variant of otherness, to linger in the authentic justice of their "customary law."[18] This construction of peasants' law as customary, and their courts as substandard, persisted throughout the imperial period and has dominated historical study of this era ever since.[19]

As powerful as the concept of a backward, homogeneous, custom-bound "peasantry" is the idea of Russia as a lawless polity.[20] This book accepts neither of these notions and examines the township courts as a legal system in which individuals, no more or less moral than any others, sought to resolve their differences and punish injustice through a process sanctioned and sustained by the Russian state. I ask readers to consider legal culture from a new perspective—as it was enacted in peasant courts—and to break with several tidy assumptions concerning law and its role in Russia.

Scholarship on law in imperial Russia has focused less on how it was used in litigation and more on legal theories. The most influential of these theoretical positions emerged from intellectual debates of the fin de siècle and revolutionary periods.[21] One long-lasting vision of the law in Russia, or what the law should have been there, derives from Russian liberalism. The learned and eloquent liberal jurists of the late imperial period, such as V. D. Nabokov, V. A. Maklakov, A. F. Koni, and I. V. Gessen, were active participants in pan-European legal scholarship and professional life.[22] Their referent for discussions of law was Western Europe, as they imagined it. A legal culture from this perspective required a single and uniform legal system for all citizens, an end to extra-judicial police and military tribunals, an active and free press, the jury system, protection of individual rights and civil liberties, a knowledgeable citizenry, rational codification of national law, regularity of judicial procedures, and independence of the judiciary. The absence of these conditions or violations of them in Russia both before and after 1917 constituted tragic setbacks for the prospects of a civilized polity, as defined by liberal reformers. Seeing imperial Russia as a law-based state did not suit their struggles.[23]

If liberal intellectuals of the late imperial period developed their notions of legality in a hostile dialectic with autocratic power and in accord with what they thought of as European law, other strong-minded intellectuals from the late imperial and early Soviet periods developed a different discourse about law in combat with a different opponent—the bourgeoisie. Lenin, Stuchka, Pashukanis, and others based their conceptions of "Marxist" or "Soviet" legality on a critique of bourgeois law and a rejection of the Russian liberals' position.[24] What liberals wanted—a European-style, law-based state—was thought by Marxist theorists to be dangerous and retrograde, and an obstacle to the construction of socialism. The history of law in Russia for almost a century focused on these two ideological positions—that of Russian liberalism and that of Russian Marxism, cast in seemingly eternal conflict with each other.[25] These ideas of law, however, were just that: ideas of what law might come to be in Russia, not investigations of current legal practice. The tight hold of political aspirations on scholarly discourse has only recently loosened, allowing study of law in a different mode, as it was engaged and shaped by its users in imperial Russia.[26]

Some controversies over law in Russia arise from adherence to unexamined terms. Three notions emerging from prerevolutionary debates shaped the question of legal culture in Russia and the conventional representation of township courts. These conceptions are, first, that a legal culture rests on citizens' knowledge of the written law; second, that a single, uniform national court system is essential to the construction of a citizenry; and, third, that state law, because of its "formality," stands in opposition to "authentic" peasant morality. I suggest, instead, that a legal culture rests on the citizenry's recognition of the legal system as a useful means of solving conflicts and punishing evil; that this recognition may be, and was in Russia, nurtured by a differentiated court system, including the township courts; and that there was no intrinsic opposition between the formality of legal process and its legitimacy for rural people.

My exploration of township court practice in subsequent chapters deals in detail with questions of peasants' knowledge and use of Russian statute law.

But a cautionary word about the criterion of written law is in order from the start. Knowledge of statutory law was the definition of legal competence for many Russian commentators on peasant legality, most of them contending that rural people were sadly lacking in this regard. This standard is a misleading measure of legal culture, in part because it was selectively applied, in part because it is inappropriate to the task.

Did peasants or non-peasants "know" the written law? Of course not, if we mean the mammoth opus of imperial legislation. Few people in imperial Russia, apart from legal experts, "knew" the texts of the huge numbers of statutes that could be applied to people's lives; even fewer could be said to have "understood" the various legal codes. Knowledge of the law in its literal enormity was not a capacity of the educated population, but it was nonetheless a demand that critics of rural courts placed on peasants. The exclusionary consequences of this brittle concept of the law highlight the importance of recasting the idea of legal culture. In this book, the definition of legal culture will be shifted away from expertise to process, away from knowing laws to accepting, employing, and respecting legal institutions. Rural people knew that the law could be used; they knew many of its protections and rules; the precise language of statutes was a matter for clerks and judges to engage.

Second, the notion that a single uniform judicial system was essential to the development of a legal culture should be questioned, rather than inherited, from past debates. From a numerical perspective, elite society's notion of which courts were ordinary and which were unusual was topsy-turvy. From the perspective of critics and jurists, the only courts worthy of the name were circuit courts, with their juries, created by the judicial reform of 1864. Township courts, however, were by far more numerous and used more often than higher-level instances. An estimate of the significance of township courts in the legal system is that these rural courts decided "80 percent of all cases from 80 percent of the population."[27] The township courts that processed the majority of cases coming from the majority of the population might have been considered the foundation for a unified system, rather than the circuit courts that served a minority of the subjects of the empire. But a demographic approach to legal experience did not occur to elites at the time. The prevailing discourse, which focused on a future Russia, took for granted the exceptionalism of the township courts and located "normal" law in the circuit courts instead.

In their devotion to the powerful ideal of a single justice for all, Russian liberals ignored other possible and extant ways of institutionalizing law. Even the democratic polities that liberals admired constituted different types of courts for different kinds of legal actions or for prosecution of different kinds of crimes. Elsewhere the existence of an array of courts—commercial, military, civil, misdemeanor, and criminal—was not an obstacle to legal culture. What may have loomed more ominously in reformers' minds was what scholars today would call the "legal pluralism" of the Russian Empire. Russian law accommodated many different types of local courts whose decisions in some cases could be made on customary or religious principles. The spectacle of courts empowering natives, Muslims, peasants, and other "others" as judges, as well as the belief that custom and law were antithetical, inspired contemporaries to regard township courts as substandard.[28]

A third article of received wisdom—the absolute dichotomy between custom and law—must be left at the doorstep if we wish to exit the world of Russia's elites and enter into the practiced legality of township courts. For Russian elites, this strict divide was axiomatic. Expertise was mustered to study state law and peasant custom in separate domains. Russian jurists regarded national law, ideally, as the product of reasoned governance extended over the entire population of a state. The nineteenth-century codifications as well as the 1864 court reform were revered as major landmarks on the long road to a fully legal polity.[29] Trained in continental civil law, Russian legal specialists understood law as a formal, state-generated system of written rules. This interpretation corresponded to the preoccupation with regulation, normality, and educational discipline described evocatively by Foucault and prominent in pan-European legal theory.[30]

Since custom and law were seen as different frames of reference, it was critical for those who wished to legalize the realm to find, catalog, and understand peasant tradition. The stock characters that define Russian peasants to this day in scholarly and popular imagination emerged between the emancipation and the end of the century—in the years between the mid-nineteenth-century public's idealization of "the peasantry" as the essence of their emerging nation and twentieth-century elites' unwillingness to let the puzzling "peasants" who surrounded them become ordinary individuals. Building on earlier ethnographies and reports, Russian statisticians continued in the early twentieth century to investigate the minutiae of "peasant" existence; their ways of understanding peasants were reproduced in both policy and theory.[31]

This intellectual and institutional context sustained the dichotomy of official law/peasant custom in elite discussions, despite several decades of litigation by peasants in the empire's local courts. A debate begun in the 1870s among specialists over whether and how "customary law" could be drawn into a national legal system raged well into the twentieth century,[32] although imperial legislation had long ago incorporated custom into rural jurisprudence. In an empire where on Sundays tens of thousands of peasants took actions at local courts, elite considerations of the law stayed in the stratosphere of theory. The practiced legal culture of Russian peasants remained invisible to political imaginations limited by formalistic definitions of law.

If there were strong incentives for Russia's modernizing elites to believe that peasants would have to be transformed before partaking of the exalted realm of law, it is not necessary for scholars today to perpetuate this view. We have both the sources and the concepts to embark on a more inclusive study of Russian peasants at their courts. First, the archival materials for studying peasant legal culture are abundant and accessible. Because documentation was a critical element in the legal practice of rural people, half a century of township court practice generated a massive written record. Books of registered complaints, case hearings, court decisions, and their fulfillments were filed away in imperial, Soviet, and Russian Federation archives. These dusty volumes, their notations produced on the spot by township clerks, open up the courtrooms of rural Russia to latter-day observers. All that is required is the willingness to read expressive handwriting and to engage the intertwined vocabularies of legal records and peasant litigants.

Second, extensive scholarship on law and society in other world areas enables a rethinking of what legality, legal culture, and legal consciousness can mean. Some schools of peasant studies still insist on the collective otherness of peasants, leaving them outsiders to the state. This enduring fashion for finding resistance everywhere in village life obscures the choices made by peasants—individually and collectively—in their relations to the state. If we are willing to forgo the romance of peasant resistance and reserve this powerful term for situations of intentional opposition to state policies,[33] legal theory provides alternatives to exclusionary and formalistic understandings of law and legal practices.

Four literatures in particular have been useful in my conceptualization of legal culture. The first of these approaches finds its home in anthropology and addresses law as processual and social rather than bound exclusively to state rules. The shift toward thinking about law as active in society rather than imposed on it has been taken in different directions over the last decades; its basic premise allows us to accommodate both state law and normative social practices as kinds of legality.[34] A second standpoint in legal studies is located at the crossroads of history and sociology. Legal culture from the perspective of historical sociology is seen both as a critical element driving social and political transformations and as a contingent product of particular historical circumstances.[35] A third literature focuses on legal culture in a society—the United States—that is firmly identified with rule of law. Working with sociological theories that connect action, discourse, and structure, scholars locate legality in the language and actions of ordinary people. In this analytic frame, practices, criticisms, and evasions of the law reinforce a culture of legality even for people who are only indirectly engaged with formal legal institutions.[36] Finally, the study of "legal pluralism," with its multi-disciplinary connections, can be helpful in understanding how legality works in imperial polities with multiple regimes of justice.[37]

Nowhere in this book do I use these theories to explain—by analogy or historical comparison—why peasant legal culture took the shape it did in Russia. My actors are rural people, not theories. Moreover, these actors were not people without history: like other inhabitants of the empire, Russian peasants lived in a specific institutional context, with their own experiences and memories. There is no reason to assume that they acted like peasants in faraway places and other eras, or like their grandparents who lived in different times. Comparisons with colonial situations or peasant culture as it is thought to exist elsewhere are not helpful if we begin with an assumption of likeness, rather than allowing the practices of historical subjects to shape our observations.[38] I cite interpretive literatures about the law for another purpose: they enable us to encompass rules, practices, and language in a single framework, to see ways that law inflects daily life, and to invoke the significance of these intersections for Russian society.

My concept of legal culture is historical, processual, and social. This study is attentive to a particular historical moment—the early twentieth century—seen from the perspective of a legal institution that had been in use for more than forty years. A processual perspective shifts our focus away from the static dichotomy of "custom" versus "law" and allows us to envision a legal culture in action and in transformation in rural Russia. If our understanding of the social admits the individuality of peasants and addresses their litigiousness, we grant peasants a role in Russia's legal history. Peasants could choose to go to court or not, in many cases, and through their choices of what to litigate and how to do so, they shaped the significance of the law. By looking at law in Russia's rural courts as a participatory process, we can see peasants as inhabiting and strengthening legal culture in their polity.[39]

The development of a confidence in the legal system as a primary means of regulation of mutual relations between people takes place over generations. Because legal culture happens at the intersection of legal institutions and their use by subjects, the state's practices can foster or set back belief in law. Nonetheless, people's faith in legal process is only indirectly related to the intentions of governors; state leaders may or may not have the construction of legal culture as an explicit goal. The state's institutions count—they can set the stage for engagement with law or undermine its possibilities—but they can have unanticipated consequences. The courts are largely what people make of them.

It is from this practice-based perspective that I address the experience of rural people at the township court, a jurisdiction that incorporated a large portion of the population into the empire's legal system. Users of township courts were not engaged, as were Russian elites, in an explicit struggle about the legality or arbitrariness of autocratic government—they were not contenders for state power—but they did participate in an unremarked process of interaction with state law. Peasants' legal activity in these courts should not be politicized as "for or against the state" or reduced to "resistance or accommodation"; instead, it may be regarded as one component in the uneven and incomplete reconstruction of the imperial polity in the early twentieth century.

PEASANTS AND THEIR RIGHTS

Like the idea of customary law, the construct of "a peasant world" has hobbled many of the most sympathetic investigations of rural Russian life. One goal of this study is to free the particularity of individuals' engagements with law from the burden of representing a whole peasantry that thinks alike. People who use courts, in most cases, are at odds with one another. My description of a legal culture in the countryside does not imply that peasants shared a single set of aspirations. A first step toward liberating peasants from "the peasant world" is to acknowledge the lineage and contingency of this idea. Recent scholarship is gradually working itself free from traditions of peasant studies set in motion by prerevolutionary historians, ethnographers, and other peasant experts.[40] The presence or absence of a critical stance toward Russian elites' interpretations of peasant life continues to divide scholarship on the peasantry in fundamental ways.[41] Yanni Kotsonis's study of the cooperative movement and Alessandro Stanziani's work on economic and statistical knowledge demand that we recognize the artifice of categories and methods used by Russian professionals, and examine their impact on latter-day imaginaries.[42]

The emancipation of peasant studies requires open-minded investigation of peasants rather than the peasantry. A few exemplary studies from this enormous field challenge the collectivizing traditions of earlier work and help us toward more democratic and individualized visions of rural life. Daniel Field's *Rebels in the Name of the Tsar* (1976) set one of the most interesting agendas for research, with his inquiry into how peasants thought about politics.[43] Cathy Frierson's 1987 article, "*Razdel:* The Peasant Family Divided," took issue with the framework of economic crisis and the trope of victimization that dominated much of peasant studies. Frierson addressed ethnographic sources as evidence of intellectuals' ideas about peasants, rather than as unmediated descriptions of life in the village.[44]

Three singular monographs from the mid-1980s opened up new views of peasants and their aspirations. Steven Hoch's *Serfdom and Social Control in Russia: Petrovskoe, a Village in Tambov,* Jeffrey Brooks's *When Russia Learned to Read: Literacy and Popular Literature, 1861–1917,* and Ben Eklof's *Russian Peasant Schools: Officialdom, Village Culture, and Popular Pedagogy, 1861–1914* made bold assaults on ideas of peasant community, backwardness, and collectivity. A major thesis of Hoch's book was that the serf economy depended on coercion exercised by peasants over peasants. The utter absence of such sacred cows as communal solidarity and cooperation, in favor of real cows and real serf-driving peasant patriarchs, set this book far apart from conventional visions of the countryside.[45] Brooks's remarkable study cut straight through traditional approaches to Russian peasants by asking what they read. This monograph assaulted the accepted notion of the peasantry as illiterate or nearly so and uncovered a new world of book-buying peasants who followed detectives and explorers into adventure and thrilled to romantic potboilers and tales of banditry.[46] Ben Eklof's study of peasant schools focused on contacts between teachers, parents, and pupils, and displayed the impressive extension of primary education accomplished in the half century after the emancipation of the serfs. If Brooks's peasants were reading books, it was because they had been taught in the schools Eklof described.[47]

Two aspects of these innovative studies illuminate my exploration of peasants' legal actions and ideas. First, each writer allowed peasants' agency in the construction of their lives. Hoch's patriarchs got their way, Brooks's readers chose their books, and Eklof's parents sent their children to school. What was important about peasants in these studies was not what was done to them but what they did themselves. Second, each of these books addressed the interactions between peasants and other people in imperial society. These intersections were not collisions between closed worlds or antagonistic classes, but rather areas in which peasant and non-peasant actors shared some space, room to maneuver, and the ability to engage each other. The harshest divide considered in these three works was that of master and serf. Hoch's study of this exploitative relationship nonetheless revealed linkages between two layers of patriarchy that were essential to the survival of both landlord and peasant economies.

Scholarship that both individualizes peasants and reveals their connections to others in the polity remains exceptional. For the most part, the burgeoning field of peasant studies is still cultivated in intellectuals' customary ways; it is difficult to go against the hegemonic notion of the village as a world apart—and like all other villages.[48] Part of the problem may be the category "peasant," which endures at least as tenaciously as peasants do. The field of peasant studies has its own journals, meetings, and imperatives. Should we perhaps discard the classification altogether?

The meaning of the label "peasant" is not easily pinned down, even by intellectuals who used the category in the imperial period.[49] Statisticians and other experts at that time were convinced that there was a "peasant economy," a "peasant family," a "peasantry," and they constructed their questionnaires and analyses accordingly.[50] The focus of many specialists in this period was on labor and production: two kinds of work—agriculture and handicraft (*kustar'*) production—were regarded as the authentic domain of peasants.[51] Describing peasants by their work accorded with the view that the real divisions in the empire were those of class, not legal estate. As an author of a survey of the empire's population insisted, the failure of Russian rulers to abolish the estate system put "contemporary Russian legislation . . . in a strange contradiction with the factual conditions of Russian life."[52]

What were those factual conditions? Experts seemed to think that working on the land and living in the countryside defined a common way of life, but this was a time when men and women of peasant status were flooding into cities, engaging in a variety of jobs and professions, attending institutes of higher education.[53] If peasants were defined occupationally, did they cease to be peasants once they took up nonagricultural labor or left their villages?

Despite the intelligentsia's antipathy to the estate system, one usage of the term *peasant* that made enormous difference to people's lives in Russia was precisely the legal one.[54] Estate (*soslovie*) in addition to religion, geographic locality, and nationality was the source of each person's legally defined rights and duties. The empire was based on the principle of subjects' "rightful obligation" to the state, with both rights and obligations assigned to people not directly as individuals but through their status as members of collective bodies.[55] Legal codes spelled out the rules for social life by addressing individuals through their collective status. Marriage, buying and selling, changing one's place of residence, bequeathing property were all regulated according to the estate, religious, ethnic, or regional status of individuals. It was by belonging to an estate, with its particular rules, or by being assigned rights that had earlier been assigned to members of another estate, that an individual gained the possibility of engaging legally in many of the most fundamental aspects of social life.

From 1861 until the spring of 1917 Russian peasants were governed by laws specific to people belonging to the "rural estate." These laws were contained in a "special appendix" added after the emancipation to the codified laws on estates. *The General Regulation on Peasants* contained the laws under which peasants could marry, adopt children or be adopted, acquire property, carry on trade, hold land, register themselves in other estates, be taxed and represented in social affairs, as well as listing their obligations to their families and institutions.[56] The first section of *The General Regulation on Peasants* described the "Rights of Peasants"; the last and critically important statute in this section declared:

> Peasants may not be deprived of the rights of the estate or limited in these rights otherwise than by a court or by a verdict of a society, confirmed according to the rule established in this Regulation.[57]

This statute underscores the importance of estate in defining an individual's rights in the imperial polity. To appreciate the significance of legal status in rural life, we must set aside the liberal criticism of the inequity of the estate system and ask instead how one attained rights at all in the Russian Empire. The estate system established in imperial law was the means to having legal status, to possessing rights, to being among the governed. No estate, no rights. But a right-less, status-less existence would hardly have occurred as a possibility to most peasants.[58] Instead, they took their estate-based rights for granted, as the ordinary way of things.

When peasants appeared at township courts, they were identified by their estate as well as by their names: "peasantman [*krest'ianin*] Ivan Semenovich," "peasantwoman [*krest'ianka*] Aleksandra Petrova." Merchants and nobles in their much rarer appearances at these courts were also registered by their estates. When peasants wrote petitions to local and higher authorities, or had such documents written for them, they also described themselves and their family members and neighbors with estate labels. "My husband, peasant of the Savvinskaia sloboda, Mikhail Ivanov Maliutin, has immovable property. . . ," begins a petition from his estranged wife, peasantwoman Feona Vasil'evna Maliutina.[59] The interlacing of status, locality, and person at township courts and in other institutional settings was both formulaic and significant. Estate status legitimated individuals' claims for justice from the state and its authorities.

Having the same rights as other people in the same estate does not create common interests among members of the status group. For peasants, as for others, estate-based rights were held and exercised by individuals. Litigation at township courts clearly shows the conflicts among peasants, who went to court to resolve quarrels over obligations, disagreements over property, and questions of responsibility. At court, peasants show no affect for a collective status as peasants; nor were they concerned to challenge the regime of rights in which they lived. The way to change one's rights in the polity was to change one's estate. Individuals interested in improving the conditions of their lives could aspire to leave the peasant estate for one with less arduous duties. A goal of many a peasant was to become a member of the townspeople's estate, just as a goal of many a merchant was to move into the nobility.[60] The estate system extended a regime of categorized rights over the population, provided rules for those who tried to move from one status to another, but did not by itself produce loyalty or collectivity among members of the same estate.

Because status determined possibilities for and set limitations on individuals in their relations to the state and to others in the polity, peasants at the township courts were peasants in two ways—by estate and as individuals. It was their legal status as peasants that entitled them—but not them alone—to use the township courts for certain kinds of legal action. At the same time, they exercised these collectively defined rights as persons, as men and women, who might or might not be agriculturalists and who might or might not be closely connected to their village societies. The court was a realm where peasants appeared as individuals—as a plaintiff, a defendant, a witness, or a judge. This book tells a story of peasants and law, not "the peasants" and "the law."

SOURCES, MYTHS, AND METHODS

The township courts were not the only legal instance used by Russian peasants. Civil suits involving more than three hundred rubles and criminal actions more serious than misdemeanors had to be adjudicated or prosecuted at higher instances. For certain kinds of cases, peasants could turn to or be required to appear at circuit courts, where they also served dutifully as jurors.[61] Furthermore, like other people in the polity, peasants might decide to try to settle conflicts outside any legal instance. I chose to base this book on cases taken to township courts for a number of reasons. First, for peasants who resided in townships, the township court after 1889 was the required first-level instance for misdemeanor charges and small-scale civil cases. It is therefore at the township court that peasants' juridical initiative is most observable. Second, the township courts offer a peasant's-eye view of the law, because usually all participants and observers—judges, litigants, and clerks—belonged to the peasant estate. Third, the township courts heard more cases than any other instance; if Russia had a legal culture, it should have been present in these modest but busy courtrooms. Fourth, the records of this instance, while scattered, are voluminous and can be used to trace legal activism over a wide area of European Russia.

Although elite contemporaries as well as later scholars turned to the township courts for evidence of peasant difference,[62] a new approach to these institutions has emerged in recent years.[63] Cathy Frierson reopened scholarly consideration of this instance with her articles on the debate over the township court and its procedures.[64] Gareth Popkins has gone the furthest in documenting the activities of these courts over the whole period of their existence and in a large number of provinces, as well as studying appeals of township court decisions.[65] A major difference between these studies and other, mostly earlier publications is their focus on rural people's usage of the courts. Records from township courts conventionally had been treated as evidence for some aspect of collective "peasant" culture; now they are seen as sources for understanding how people in the countryside employed law.

In this book I look at the ordinary usages people made of the township courts. Study of ordinary and, for most plaintiffs, voluntary engagement with the legal system reverses a long-term trend of finding resistant, exotic, or otherwise aberrant behaviors in the countryside. Scholars since the 1960s have moved away from condescending terms such as "primitive" or "barbaric"; nonetheless a residue of the customary, the lurid, and the separate clings tenaciously to work on peasants' legal activities. Historians' fascination with *samosud* (literally, self-trial)—an abstraction created by Russian ethnographers and jurists to describe peasants' "own" punishments of crime outside the legal system[66]—is a case in point. Considered a symptom of peasant backwardness by contemporary Russian elites, *samosud* has been transformed a century later into evidence of village resistance and subalternity.[67] This focus on extra-legal punishment of witchcraft, adultery, and horse theft has served to exoticize "the peasant" rather than to normalize, and make visible, peasant legal practice.

A quest for ordinary usage of the courts also goes against the grain of microhistories that privilege the exceptional as particularly revelatory of social systems and their constraints.[68] I want to challenge the assumption that what is interesting for historians must be the esoteric. Peasants should be allowed to be ordinary litigants, and still merit our attention, despite a long history of making and keeping them different. As Erich Auerbach concluded in his great study of literary realism, the validation of random moments through which people experience ordinary events enables the "elementary things that our lives have in common [to] come to life."[69] Going to court was not a random event itself, but the evidence of the small problems of daily life that brought people to court, evidence captured in the record books of a great bureaucratic empire, does allow—if the reader permits—a democratic view of the all-too-human concerns that link Russian peasants with both their contemporaries and ourselves.

The township court was not a violent place in the early twentieth century. The decorum of judicial proceedings and the absence of corporal punishment also contradict what is thought to be known of Russian peasants. The disparity between stories of beatings and the record of arrests and fines may stem from uncritical usage of earlier scholarship and from lack of attention to how the laws on the township court changed after 1889 and again in 1904 and 1906. I provide just one example of the kinds of sources that inform and distort later work. Many scholars have relied on Prince V. V. Tenishev's *Jurisprudence in Rus-*

sian Peasant Life. This synoptic analysis of peasant legal practice was based on Tenishev's father's enormous survey project of the late 1890s. When the volume was published in 1907, corporal punishment at the township court had been abolished for three years. Nonetheless, chapter 8, "Punishments Applied by the Township Courts," devotes five pages out of eight to the subsection, "Punishment by the Lash." The other categories of punishment permitted to the township court were "reprimand in the presence of the court"—one paragraph; "fine in money"—one page; "arrest"—one page.[70]

Tenishev introduces his pages on the lash as follows: "Corporal punishment, as has already been indicated, was abolished on August 11, 1904. Nevertheless it is interesting to record the population's attitude toward it." He comments later in the text, "peasants never prefer the lash to a fine or to arrest," and then continues, "although there exists a story about how one of the punished acted with total composure toward the prospect of a beating."[71] Much of Tenishev's message is carried by this and other "althoughs," but let me tell it differently: although corporal punishment was abolished in 1904, although it was used rarely at the time of the Tenishev survey (1897–1900), and although the evidence suggests that peasants never preferred bodily punishment, nonetheless Russian elites found that incidents of peasants submitting to, even choosing, the lash were "interesting" and worthy of retelling. The report of a peasant who asks that his arrest be converted to a lashing—an anomalous event, in Tenishev's own words—constitutes the last paragraph of *Jurisprudence in Russian Peasant Life.* A last paragraph and a lasting impression.

It is not necessary to begin our work with these old templates of victimization, brutalization, and difference. If fines and jail terms—not shaming rituals or whippings—were the usual sentences of township courts, we can still find interest in these punishments, how they were applied and to whom. By working with court records instead of ethnographers' surveys, we can discover what was ordinary in peasant jurisprudence and let the exceptional be defined by litigants and judges.

Tenishev's study suggests another kind of caution: the need to be attentive to changes in the law on the township courts. Many studies of the township courts cite the initial 1861 legislation, or the revisions introduced in 1889, from Russia's legal codes. But in the early twentieth century the courts worked with rules that had been modified significantly since 1889. Updated regulations were made available to township clerks and district overseers in handbooks published specifically for their use.[72] In my examination of township court practice I refer to compilations of laws produced in the early twentieth century. Not only did users of the township courts change over fifty years; laws regulating the courts changed as well.[73]

A close reading of how rural people engaged township courts reveals a legal system at work as well as the values, practices, expectations, and social resources of individual users of the law. To reconstruct legal culture in rural, early twentieth-century Russia, I use two different methods. I illustrate legal process with a wide range of case narratives, based as directly as possible on official records produced at township courts. Wary of argument from isolated cases or from cases chosen for their attention to a particular issue, I situate these narratives in the larger context of court practice through statistical studies of cases brought to ten township courts in three provinces. The homely courtroom scenes presented in this study are based on my readings and analysis of more than nine hundred individual cases recorded in official record books by local clerks, as well as on my surveys of more than 4,500 case records from these courts.

For purposes of analysis, I compiled four separate databases, described more fully in the note on sources and appendixes. Most of the calculations concerning court practice—gender and estate of litigants, frequencies of kinds of cases, and so forth—are based on detailed information from 907 individual court cases or subsets of these. My descriptions of case processing and analyses of outcomes are based on sequential readings of all cases recorded at a particular court, usually over several months at a time.[74] A major concern was not to select for types of cases but to let the record speak for itself. For many of these 907 cases I was able to collect a full set of 115 variables, for others I had more partial information. Statistical calculations about probabilities are based on 48 variables contained in this set of case data. Unless otherwise noted, figures, tables, and percentages cited in the text are based on this case survey.[75]

To supplement my case data set, I constructed two other databases from more restricted information. One of these is based on the "subject" of cases. Here I surveyed the subjects and outcomes of 889 cases at three courts in 1908, 1914 (before the war), and 1916. In a third data set I surveyed numbers of cases heard at a particular time. This survey covered 2,746 cases, heard at five courts, from 1905 through 1916. All three of these databases were derived from records generated at township courts by township clerks. Finally, I compiled a database of characteristics for each of the settlements in the ten townships. Using published statistics and archival information, I was able to identify population figures, geographical information such as distances to the township court or to the nearest city and railroad station, and other specifics—the presence of schools, factories, police headquarters, and drinking establishments—for most of the 253 settlements in the 10 townships.[76]

In any study of this sort, questions about selection are in order. There is no such thing as a typical village, any more than a typical peasant. I was fortunate, particularly since I began this project at a time of restricted access to archival finding aids, to be able to locate materials for townships that differ from one another in some essential ways—the greater or lesser role of agricultural or manufacturing or forest industries, variation in distance from the railroad and to a large city, differences in the scale of commercial activity and in policing. By constituting three different kinds of surveys—by case content, case subject, and case date—my databases could serve as checks on one another. To my astonishment and delight, these comparisons consistently confirmed my initial calculations. Now and then a slight discrepancy in the text stems from the use of different surveys, but overall a clear picture of how peasants used their courts emerges from the numbers.[77]

This book is about difference as much as it is about sameness. What is important in many of the chapters is how courts varied—how they responded to specific circumstances. Readers interested in a fuller presentation of the statistical analyses and frequencies reported in this book are encouraged to consult and comment on materials on my website: http://www.nyu.edu/projects/burbank/. My combination of textual and quantitative methods allows an intensive look at how township courts worked as well as a statistically strong presentation of who went to court in the countryside and why and what they got from their initiatives.

LOCALITIES

Most of the cases I describe and analyze took place at ten township courts, seven in Moscow Province—to the north, east, south, and west of the empire's second largest city—two in St. Petersburg Province, and one in Novgorod Province.[78] I make no claim that these townships are representative of the empire. Imperial law provided an array of local instances to its various populations, who were empowered to use a variety of legal procedures and normative rules. My study is exclusively concerned with peasants at township courts of central and northern Russia. Each village and township in my study had its own particularities—its own activist litigators, its own responsible citizens, its own upholders of village order, its own miscreants—and it is not my intent to establish a template for a uniform peasant "legal consciousness." What my choice of venues reveals is law activated by peasants from a variety of situations, representative of the conditions in which peasants in early-twentieth-century Russia made their lives.

Each of these courts was available to people registered as residents of the "populated places, consisting of peasant settlements" of the township. A populated place of this type was usually a village—*derevnia* or *selo*[79]—or, less frequently, a settlement associated with a monastery, church, court domain, marketplace, dacha region, or private estate. For example, in 1912 the "peasant settlements" of Iaguninskii Township, near the town of Zvenigorod in Moscow Province, were 29 villages (24 *derevni* and 5 *sela*) with between 7 and 136 households each, 1 "little settlement" (*vyselok*) with 3 households, and 5 estates with 1 peasant household each. The Iaguninskii Township Court thus served people from quite different social settings—the several hundred people who lived in the populous Savvinskaia sloboda associated with the Savvo-Storozhevskii Monastery as well as the single family living in the apparently bug-ridden "Cockroach Estate [*Imenie Tarakanovo*]."[80]

The people who lived in these settlements supported themselves in a variety

Straw trunk making, Kobiakovo, Zvenigorod County, Moscow Province, 1910s. *Photograph from the collection of Mikhail Zolotarev.*

of ways. Inhabitants of townships on the outskirts of Moscow were engaged primarily in farming, since they could sell their vegetables on the big city market. Peasants living at a greater distance from Moscow were more likely to work in manufacturing or outputting trades, in addition to growing crops at home or laboring outside the village. In Novgorod Province the residents of Zaborovskii Township combined agriculture with forestry. The areas of St. Peterburg Province included in my research were regions of forest industries, self-provisioning agriculture, and temporary or long-term labor outside the village. The following brief sketches locate each of the ten townships and provide a glimpse of the occupations of their residents.

Iaguninskii Township, mentioned above, was a part of Zvenigorod County in Moscow Province, an area of agriculture, forest industries, and small-scale manufacturing. The township settlements lay along and north of the Moscow River, as it flowed in large loops eastward toward the small city of Zvenigorod about fifty kilometers west of Moscow. This township was known for its many cottage industries; peasants working in their homes and workshops produced, among other items, furniture, dishes, coffins, baskets, suitcases, copper goods, cardboard, clocks, musical instruments, and knitted goods, and were active in the smelting and metal working trades.[81]

The seat of the township administration was in the village of Iagunino, a settlement that had once belonged to the Savvo-Starozhevskii Monastery and later to the state's domain. In 1913 there were ninety-three households registered

Broom-making industry, Zvenigorod County, Moscow Province, 1910s.
Photograph from the collection of Mikhail Zolotarev.

in Iagunino, and probably between seven hundred and eight hundred inhabitants. Iagunino was home to a state liquor store and one of the two parish schools in the township. In addition to these church-administered schools, nine *zemstvo* schools[82] were scattered among the township's other settlements.[83] Iagunino was only a little more than four miles from Zvenigorod, the central city of the county.[84]

Sharapovskii Township was also part of Zvenigorod County. The township, located to the south of Iagunino and the Moscow River, was an area of large noble estates. Many peasants registered in the villages of the township were the descendants of serfs who had worked the lands of princely and more modest owners. Half a century after the end of serfdom, the region was still studded with estates associated with peasant villages of small to medium size, or with no villages at all. In 1908 the leading official of Zvenigorod County's noble society was Count Pavel Sergeevich Sheremet'ev.[85] The Golitsyns and Patrikeevs figured among the other prominent noble families with estates in Sharopovskii Township.[86]

The township administration was located at Sharapovo, six and a half miles from Zvenigorod and six miles from the nearest railroad station at Kubinka on the Moscow-Brest line. One of the larger settlements in the area, Sharapovo was the site of seventy-two peasant households in 1911. In addition to the township administration, the village housed the local constable, a *zemstvo* school,

Workers from V. Platov's factory in Sharapovo, Zvenigorod County, Moscow Province. *Photograph from the collection of Mikhail Zolotarev.*

three tea shops (an environment that inspired cases at the township court), and three clock making enterprises.[87] Cottage industries were common in villages of the township; in addition to clocks, Sharapovskii residents produced musical instruments, knitted goods, and wheels.[88]

Selinskii Township belonged to the county connected with the ancient city of Klin, fifty-five miles north of Zvenigorod, in the northwest region of Moscow Province.[89] In the countryside around Klin, as in much of Moscow Province, rural people engaged in industrial and agricultural work in their own villages as well as in other areas of the province and the empire. Residents of Klin County usually found employment not far from home.[90] Elite reformers concerned themselves with the promotion of what they saw as appropriate productive activities for the region: bee-keeping, market gardening and orchard cropping, the cultivation of fodder grasses, and household crafts (*kustar'*).[91] Many peasants in this area engaged in industrial production, as workers or owners or both. Before the abolition of serfdom, peasants owned almost all the cotton weaving mills in the district.[92] Klin's rural factories, located in the countryside and not necessarily along the railroad that connected Klin to Moscow, were a source of irritation to labor organizers in 1905. A Soviet-era account of the revolutionary year regretted the "backward" consciousness of Klin's factory

Workshop of V. Platov in Sharapovo, Zvenigorod County, Moscow Province.
Photograph from the collection of Mikhail Zolotarev.

population. How could one organize workers who responded to Social Democrats, "It's you people in Moscow who go around without pants, but I'm my own boss: if I want I go to the factory, if I want I go home"?[93] In this region, as elsewhere, peasants' occupations and their attitudes toward their work refused to fit the categories set forth by both agronomists and would-be organizers of the proletariat.

Selinskii Township was one of the more industrialized of the county. An iron foundry employing one hundred workers was located in the township on the outskirts of Klin; a more typical small-sized soap-making factory was located in the village of Vasil'evo with its twenty-four peasant households. Private estates and peasant villages were intermingled over the township landscape, a reminder that half a century earlier most peasants in this area had been serfs. The township administration was located in the village of Selinskoe, which was also the site of the local constable's quarters, a *zemstvo* school, a private estate, a mill, and three tea shops.[94]

Both Ignatevskii Township and Grebnevskii Township were part of Bogorodskii County, a region east of Moscow known from the eighteenth century for cloth production. Before the emancipation of 1861, this area was inhabited by both private and state peasants. A large part of the peasant population, both male and female, were engaged in commerce, small-scale production, and factory labor.[95] In the nineteenth century the county was one of the most in-

Clock making in Sharapovo, inside view of small clock-making workshop, Zvenigorod County, Moscow Province. *Photograph from the collection of Mikhail Zolotarev.*

dustrialized regions of Moscow Province and of Russia, and was recognized for its cloth and metal goods, and its ambitious merchant families, many of them Old Believers.[96] Other products of the region were peat, ceramics, and bricks. The factories and population of this productive region were linked directly to Moscow and other commercial centers by the Moscow Vladimir–Nizhnii Novgorod Railroad, built in the mid-nineteenth century.[97] The enterprising rural population of Bogorodskii County did not neglect agriculture; in 1908 the region led the rest of Moscow Province in the production of grain crops per area sown.[98] The demand for literacy was robust in this area of enterprise and trade; half of the boys aged eight to eleven were in school in the first decade of the twentieth century. In 1906–7, 27 percent of girls in the district were attending school.[99]

Ignatevskii Township lay along a small river just to the south of the bustling factory town of Pavlovskii posad, famous for its flowered shawls and brocades. Factories and outputting shops owned by a number of different families operated throughout the township. The smallest settlement in the township was the 2–household villagette of Elizavetino, located on the estate of a gentry family.[100] Six of the villages in the township encompassed more than 100 households, 19 were composed of between 50 and 100 households, and 12 had fewer than 50 households. The largest settled place in the township was the village

Icon painting by Old Believers, Bogorodskii County, Moscow Province, 1910s. *Photograph from the collection of Mikhail Zolotarev.*

called Gorodok—"little town." This settlement had its own railroad station, 177 households, a parish school, and a large factory with its own hospital. The village of Ignat'evo, with 125 households, was the location of the township court in addition to silk factories, a parish school, a firefighting unit, two tea shops, and a shop that distributed materials to small-scale producers. The railroad station at Pavlovskii posad was less than a mile and a half from Ignat'evo.[101] The rural people of Ignatevskii Township were active in both factories and fields. The troubles and possibilities generated by the productive economy of this region showed up at the court at Ignat'evo.

Grebnevskii Township, north and west of Ignat'evo and Pavlovskii posad, located along the river Kliazma and its sources, was also a region of energetic production and mixed opportunities. The court met at one of the larger villages of the township—Novaia—in the center of a silk processing area nicknamed the "Russian Lyon." The silk factory at Novaia was owned by a local peasant who had done very well for himself; Ivan Likhanov's factory employed fifty-two people directly, producing silk material and dresses. In 1900 Likhanov, now a member of a merchant guild, sponsored a full-scale renovation of an eighteenth-century stone church. The *zemstvo* had established a number of schools throughout the township. A *zemstvo* hospital and a "free popular library" were located in the village of Grebnevo, on one of the several private estates of the township. Like Ignatevskii Township, Grebnevskii Township was connected to Moscow and other big cities by railroad. The township court at Novaia was a little over five miles from the train station at Shchelkovo.[102]

Nagatinskii and Tsaritsynskii townships were located to the south of Moscow in a zone that, for hundreds of years, had supplied the city with food, particularly fruits and vegetables. In the nineteenth century this area was recognized for its apples and berries; by the early twentieth century the cultivation of cabbages, cucumbers, and potatoes was displacing fruit crops. Peasants produced, imported, processed, and sold vegetables and fruits at Moscow markets or, in some cases, contracted with institutions and factories in the city.[103] People familiar with Moscow today and with the ever-expanding high-rise apartment projects to the south of the city may have difficulty imagining that in the late imperial period, and well into the 1930s, this region was covered with fields and, to a lesser extent, forests.[104] The area was the site of many small villages and, increasingly in the 1900s, occasional dacha settlements. A few cottage industries were practiced in this district, among them wire making in Tsaritsynskii Township and knitting in both Tsaritsynskii and Nagatinskii townships.[105] Proximity to Moscow attracted many new people to these townships, and some of these resident, but not officially registered, people show up in the township courts.

Of these two agrarian townships, Nagatinskii was geographically closest to Moscow. Some of the villagers in the township lived only a little over a mile from the city border, while the farthest villages were less than nine miles from the urban limits. Most villages in the township lay close to stations on railroad lines leading into Moscow and offering vital links to the markets of the city. The township administration in the village of Nagatino was not particularly well placed in this respect, since it was four and a half miles from the closest railroad station. Nagatino was a well-established peasant settlement, with 123 peasant households in 1911. Apart from the township administration, the village center had few attributes—one *zemstvo* school and no church. The township was home to a few factories—a brick-making enterprise and several leatherworking institutions—but the main business of this region was agriculture—producing vegetables for the Moscow market and for home consumption.[106] Proximity to the big city meant that many migrants to Moscow settled, more or less, in Nagatinskii Township; some of these newcomers appeared at the township court.

Tsaritsyno, the site of the Tsaritsynskii township administration, had its own station on the Moscow-Kursk railroad line, ten miles southeast of the city. The area, a domain of the crown for centuries, was legendary in elite society for its unfinished palace, designed by the major Russian architect Bazhenov for Catherine the Great. The ruins of the neo-Gothic palace, said to have driven its designer to suicide when he observed its resemblance to a tomb crowned by candles, still looms in the midst of a delightfully mysterious park. The woods and the long meandering pond permit visitors today to imagine the landscape as it had been in the 1900s—the abandoned imperial domain with its public garden, surrounded by cultivated fields, peasant houses, and farm buildings clustered along a narrow road on the far side of the tracks from a settlement of dachas for vacationing Muscovites. The area near the station catered to both leisure and business interests; the village had five vegetable stalls, a beer tavern, a restaurant, and a *zemstvo* school. Tsaritsyno's population consisted of fifty-five peasant households in 1911; no permanent residents were registered in the nearby dacha area, which supported a summer theater.[107] In the early 1900s Tsaritsyno's economy was oriented to the Moscow market. The ten miles by railroad to the second capital city presented particular opportunities to rural farmers, and sometimes landed them in the township court.[108]

Far to the north of Moscow in the ancient Tikhvin County of Novgorod Province lay Zaborovskii Township.[109] The township administration of this extensive region of northern Russia was located in a village called Bol'shoe Zaborov'e (Of the Big Fence). Provincial statistics for 1910 recorded the population of Bol'shoe Zaborov'e as 323—168 males and 154 females—although this may have included a larger territory outside the village itself. The village had once been part of the crown's domain; before 1861 inhabitants of Bol'shoe Zaborov'e had been state peasants. They held their allotment land collectively until the fall of 1909, when they decided to transfer it to hereditary household tenure.[110] The major economic activities of this region concerned forestry; controversies over woodlots and forests appear in cases brought to the court at Bol'shoe Zaborov'e. Most peasants in this area, as elsewhere, still engaged in agriculture for at least part of the year, in addition to their other productive activities. A flour factory owned by Aldr Eliazarovich Garut was located in the village of Sorochino in the township.[111]

Like Zaborovskii Township in Novgorod Province, the two townships I studied in St. Petersburg Province were located in what was called the "lake district" of the empire. The climate of this region is even harsher than that of the central areas of European Russia and the soil is generally unfruitful, but the area was rich in both forests and water resources. The rivers of the region linked it to both the Baltic and Volga basins. By the period of this study, railroad transportation was extensively used as well. Despite the sparse settlement of the area, elementary schools existed in many villages. The number of children of both sexes attending schools was increasing rapidly in the early twentieth century.[112]

Toksovskii Township, in Shlissel'burgskii County of St. Petersburg Province, was located in the center of the landmass between the Gulf of Finland and Lake Ladoga, more than fifteen miles from the nearest railroad station on the line linking St. Petersburg and Vyborg. The area surrounding the township's administrative center at the village of Toksovo was considered to be of exceptional natural beauty. A geographic guidebook from 1900 notes that this region of ravines, lakes, islands, and deep forests was nicknamed "the Petersburg Switzerland."[113] The dense network of waterways and the forests were a major economic asset. Logging and charcoal, brick, and cement making were important local industries. There were eleven "one-class" schools in the township and a "two-class" school in Toksovo itself.[114]

Ethnographic types of Finns (Karelians) of Novgorod Province. *Drawing based on a photograph, and published in Rossiia. Polnoe geograficheskoe opisanie nashego otechestva, Vol. 3: Ozernaia oblast' (St. Petersburg: A. F. Devrien, 1900). Reproduced Courtesy of the Hoover Institution Library.*

As its name suggests, Toksovo was originally settled by Finns. Shlissel'burg County had a large Finnish population, although Russian statistics on this sensitive question are less than reliable.[115] All the settlements in Toksovskii Township had Finnish names. Toksovo was located on Lake Khopoiarvi and was the site of a Lutheran church. In the unabashedly ethnographic style typical of the late empire, the authors of the guidebook mentioned above remark, "In general, the Finnish tribes are hard-working, honest, some of them are not wanting in poetic capacities . . . and musicality, although their creativity is marked by some kind of gloomy monotony."[116] In 1914 the township leader had a Finnish family name, and the township clerk was Russian. The names of the litigants at the Toksovskii Township Court—many with Russian given names and patronymics and Finnish surnames—suggest the long-term mixing of Finns and Slavs in this area.[117]

Sosnitskii Township was part of Tsarskosel'skii County, to the south and west of St. Petersburg. The region was traversed by the railroad connecting the Baltic towns of Narva and Iamburg with Gatchina and St. Petersburg. This area, too, was rich in water and wood. Swamps covered a large part of the township, a place where most peasants made their living for at least part of the year in industries of various kinds. A survey from 1907 divided the peasant households of Sosnitskii Township into those occupied exclusively with fieldwork (3 percent), those occupied with both fieldwork and industry (83 percent), and those occupied exclusively with industry (14 percent).[118]

Residents of the twenty-eight settlements of Sosnitskii township who wanted to find employment outside their villages could take advantage of a long-term connection between the township and the capital city. Work away from one's place of residence had played a central role in peasant economies for well over a century in this and other areas of poor agricultural production.[119] Most villages in Sosnitskii Township were not close to the railroad, but the township nonetheless had the highest percentage in the county of nonagricultural laborers employed in St. Petersburg. Twenty-one percent of the Sosnitskii residents working in the capital were women, most hired as servants in private homes.[120]

As these brief descriptions suggest, the people whose court activities we will be visiting lived in quite different physical environments. The variety and in some cases multiplicity of their occupations as agriculturalists, forestry workers, handicraft producers, outputters, maids, tea shop owners, merchants, and laborers of other kinds reflect choices available to people in the rural areas of the north and central regions of Russia's forest heartland in the early twentieth century.[121] The inhabitants of the two townships nearest Moscow were more likely than others to be farmers—providing food to the nearby city—while people farther away, either in Moscow Province or in the north, most often combined fieldwork with other occupations.

Despite the distance—physical and occupational—separating them, people of these areas were connected to towns and villages of the empire by networks of railroads, waterways, roads, and paths as well as by webs of administration, economic exchange, and knowledge. Their individual cases heard at local courts constitute a participatory but not consciously collective engagement with legal governance. Provincial and local authorities, as officials of the imperial administration, created and preserved the records of this extensive employment of the law. To turn back to the records of the period, without the preset cast of characters provided by turn-of-the-century elites but with attention to what litigants did at township courts, makes possible the representation of rural people as individuals engaged with the institutions of their times, in a changing configuration of possibilities and not always intended outcomes for themselves and their polity.

A NEW START

In the first years of the twentieth century the Russian government embarked on a round of reforms that, when bound together in historical hindsight, appear to challenge the assumptions of the past forty years. The most conservative and restrictive legislation on peasant institutions was set aside or overturned in a series of efforts to transform the peasant economy.[122] The state's legal initiatives of 1903 through 1906 significantly revised the relations of individual peasants to village authorities and the state. This wave of legislation provided the institutional framework for radical transformations of authority, opportunity, and well-being, in villages, the countryside, and across the empire.

In 1903 the government abolished "collective responsibility"—the principle requiring all members of a rural society to be held responsible collectively for taxes and other debts and payments.[123] In 1904 corporal punishment was outlawed in the rural courts, a measure that eliminated a glaring disparity in legal penalties applicable to members of different estates.[124] Over the next two years the government enacted several fundamental reforms that had been under discussion well before the revolutionary crisis of 1905–1906. The administration canceled all arrears owed by former serfs and their descendants on land allocated to them as part of the emancipation settlement. A number of restrictions on peasants' rights to acquire or renounce land allotments were abolished. Individual peasants who wished to enroll in institutes of higher learning or in state service were no longer obliged to obtain the permission of communal authorities. Peasants acquired the same rights to obtain a passport as other citizens. These significant changes in peasants' legal rights and social possibilities were consolidated in a law on peasant civil rights, issued on 5 October 1906.[125] Shortly thereafter the state announced another fundamental intervention in peasant rights to property and land use with the first of the controversial "Stolypin reforms." The law of 9 November 1906 allowed individual peasant households to claim a title to their land allotments and to consolidate their plots into individually, rather than communally, held property.[126]

The law of 5 October 1906 directly addressed the issue of unequal rights for peasants; its purpose was "gradual equalization of peasants with the rest of the population." The new rules were to "complete" the work of Alexander II, the "tsar-emancipator," by implementing the goals set forth in the 1905 October Manifesto—the "principles of civil freedom and of equality of all Russian subjects before the law."[127] The 1906 law took an important step in this direction by according peasants who entered state service rights equivalent to those of the nobility, by ending obligatory social labor as a punishment or a substitute for fines at rural courts, and by restricting the definition of crimes used by township court judges to those enumerated in an all-estate misdemeanor code. With respect to other subjects with different estate status, peasants would no longer be subject to distinctive and humiliating punishments or legal obstacles to employment and education.

At the time of the emancipation, the social contract between imperial administrators and local elders had been reinforced, not challenged, by the decision to attach peasants and their labor to their local communities.[128] Almost half a century later the state seemed to reverse itself on mandated collective responsibility. Would another social contract replace the integument of patriarchy and guardianship, exercised by village elders and state authorities, that earlier had bound the polity together?

The new round of legislation retained one principle that might be seen as an obstacle to any profound transformation of the polity. The system of estates and of differential rights and duties assigned by estate status was left in place, even after the Revolution of 1905 and even after peasants had acquired many of the rights granted to people who belonged to other estates. In this fundamental respect, the realm of political action and imagination to which peasants of early-twentieth-century Russia could aspire and the social context in which they acted remained structured by imperial premises of particularity and difference. The peasants who were the objects of this series of reforms and who were no longer governed by the same laws or confined to the same practices as their ancestors were still, legally, peasants.[129]

Moreover, the emperor had not given up his own patriarchal authority. Reform emanated from an administration that continued to function on paternalistic principles, expressing the emperor's fatherly care and responsibility for his subjects. Russian officials drew up the regulations of 1903–1906 in accord with their self-assigned role as guardians of peasant welfare. The strong challenge to local patriarchs expressed in peasants' new rights to take up places of residence and occupation without obtaining the permission of communal authorities was followed by reforms that enhanced another level of patriarchy. Under the Stolypin revisions of peasant land tenure, the property of each peasant household that held land in hereditary tenure—not through the rural society—was to belong to the head of household, not to the household as a whole. The government was wagering not just on the strong, but on strong men—on millions of peasant patriarchs to whom the law granted individual control over formerly collective and family means of production.[130]

The new start for peasant society—a "second emancipation" according to some[131]—contained radically transformative projects within a traditional framework. Peasants were granted much greater range for individual activity, through familiar patriarchal means. To some scholars, the "contradiction" between individualism and paternalism of the imperial system may appear as yet another fatal tension in the extended death agony of the old regime.[132] But while intellectuals see contradictions in first principles as perilous, most societies live with and articulate contradictory impulses and are not, as a result, on the verge of collapse.[133] What is of interest in the conflicting bases of imperial legislation—or any legislation, for that matter—is what people make of it, in both the long and short term.

This is where the study of lower-level peasant courts can speak to the questions of human choice and organization that Russian history sets dramatically before its students. Imperial law after 1905 provided a core of rights to rural people and legalized their independence from village elders. But would these legal opportunities be translated into a different social order? The local courts of rural Russia provide a window into the dilemmas of power, patriarchy, and aspiration at their most ordinary yet significant level. State law provided an arena in which litigants and judges could express and resolve conflicts between neighbors, families, and villages. Who could more powerfully accomplish the slow transformation of values that turn into real social revolutions than the millions of rural people who decided questions of responsibility, civility, and obedience in their local courts?

The Bolshevik Revolution has cast such a long shadow over the preceding decade that it is difficult to see the small-scale choices made by ordinary people and appraise them in open-ended ways. The years 1905 to 1917 are conveniently labeled the "last years of the old regime," but people living then did not know them as the last, nor did they know that the empire would be abolished and that a new regime would make their society "old." Most of the transactions of their lives had little to do with revolutionary politics but were part of a longer, less dramatic transformation. Even if Russian peasants were later caught up in a devastating whirlwind of civil war and revolution, it is important to recover their practices of conflict resolution, their definitions of social justice, their more or less shared values, and their engagement with the imperial legal system. A glimpse into the rural courts allows us to see how rural people used their institutions after the state created new possibilities for reconfiguring power in the countryside. By their actions, rural people at township courts made Russia a law-based state in their lives, for their time.

A Litigious Person and Her Possibilities

Among appeals cases awaiting decisions by the Senate in the summer of 1917 was the complaint of Praskovia Aref'eva, an illiterate unmarried woman of peasant estate from a small village in Sosnitskii Township, in the lake region to the west of Petrograd. Praskovia Aref'eva was one of many peasants from this township who had connections in the capital, and might be regarded as typical of rural women who sought work outside the settlements where they were registered.[1] But Praskovia Aref'eva's legal venture was not commonplace: the attentive bureaucratic practices of Russian administration left her file replete with no fewer than fifteen official decisions made by lower instances of the judicial hierarchy, accompanied by petitions, requests for information, and administrative notes—the detritus of one individual's obstinate struggle to further her interests through the law. Praskovia Aref'eva's appeal, still wandering through the imperial legal system at the moment of its demise, allows us with our archival fluoroscopes to catch a glimpse of the workings of this complex organism. The case displays the intersection of the township courts with higher legal instances, and permits speculative exploration of the legal imaginary of peasant litigants.[2]

Praskovia Aref'eva's pursuit of justice was not without secrets and lies, including at least one self-serving citation of an erroneous or faked date. Over the course of nine years of legal actions, she remained true, however, to a single goal—the recovery of her inheritance, as she defined it. The first legal instance to which this "peasant spinster" took recourse was a township court.[3]

On 12 February 1908 Praskovia Aref'eva, forty-two years old, registered as a peasant of Lemozha Village,[4] pled her suit for inheritance at the Sosnitskii Township Court. She asked the court to grant her the property of her deceased father, Arefii Gordeev, property she claimed was in the hands of one Frol Grigor'ev. The basis of Praskovia Aref'eva's claim was that she and her brother, Ivan Aref'ev, were heirs to their father's property but that, after the death of her brother, this property had been used illegally by Frol Grigor'ev, a townsman who had been taken in by her brother's wife. She, Praskovia Aref'eva, was suing on her own behalf and that of her two nieces, the living children of her brother; she requested recognition as an heir to her father's property.[5]

This case might suggest a focus on class and gender—here we have, apparently, a male from the townspeople's estate appropriating the family property of a village woman and her orphaned nieces, a case where the prerogatives of status and sex are satisfyingly allied against the ideal subaltern—a peasant female, solicitous of the young and helpless, and illiterate to boot. But as various authorities in the land were to discover, things were not that simple. In 1908 Praskovia Aref'eva had taken it upon herself to disrupt a long-standing settlement of village affairs, a settlement produced by the villagers of Lemozha in response to a family crisis.

TWO DEATHS IN THE FAMILY

That crisis began in 1894 and is recorded in documents copied from the family register of the Lemozha rural society from 15 May 1895. Praskovia Aref'eva's father, Arefii Gordeev, a peasant and a resident of Lemozha, died at the age of sixty-six in 1894, leaving one son, Ivan Aref'ev, aged thirty-three, and one daughter aged twenty-eight, our Praskovia Aref'eva. This death would seem to present no special problems to rural society, since a man's possessions normally would be passed on to his children, but, shortly thereafter, Ivan Aref'ev, the son, died too. In 1894 Ivan Aref'ev left behind a family—his wife, Irina Vasil'evna, and two young children, Aleksandra, seven years old, and five-year-old Elena. Making matters worse, Elena Ivanova was, by every account, "insane." Irina Vasil'evna's answer to this difficult situation was to find a new man to head her household, in the person of Frol Grigor'ev, from the town of Iamburg.[6] They married on 19 April 1898.[7]

Why Frol Grigor'ev decided to settle in Lemozha is unknowable, but it seems that village authorities were more than content with his presence. Three years after Frol Grigor'ev's marriage to Irina Vasil'evna, they granted his request to enter their rural society. On 25 April 1901 the Lemozha Village Assembly made an official declaration to this effect. Thirty-two of the thirty-seven heads of households agreed to make Frol Grigor'ev a member of their society and to allot him the "two-soul household plot" he occupied and one-and-a-half souls' worth of field land in exchange for his agreement to fulfill all obligations attached to the land and to pay the rural society twenty rubles a year for five years. The heads of household described their decision as meeting the request of the Iamburg townsman Frol Grigor'ev who has been living in our society to accept him among the peasants of our society, having considered among ourselves and taking into account that Grigor'ev came into the home of a peasant widow of our society, who has orphans, two daughters, from her first husband, and Grigor'ev for three years brought up the children conscientiously and behaved soberly and correctly (one of the orphan daughters is an Idiot).[8]

Twenty-two men signed this decision themselves, and ten more signatures were appended at the request of illiterate participants in the assembly. Ivan Andreev, the village leader who had presided over the assembly, signed among the literate. The township authorities validated this decision based, according to the villagers' declaration, on statute law empowering village assemblies to incorporate new members.[9]

This was not the only action the village assembly took with regard to Ivan Aref'ev's land. In the same year, 1901, on 22 May, a month after the rural society's acceptance of Frol Grigor'ev into its ranks, the same Lemozha Village Assembly under the same leader transferred one soul's worth of Ivan Aref'eev and Irina Vasil'eva's field allotment to Mikhail Ivanov, another peasant of the same village, in "hereditary possession." This time twenty-six of the thirty-seven household heads "signed" the decision.[10]

These decisions were submitted to higher authorities for confirmation. The deal admitting Frol Grigor'ev into the Lemozha rural society was stamped with the seals of the Sosnitskii township administration. The township authorities later received a copy of a letter dated 18 November 1901 from the St. Petersburg revenue department noting, on the basis of the decisions of the Lemozha Village Assembly and a second report from the same year, that Frol Grigor'ev had been "reregistered" as a peasant of Lemozha Village with a land allotment and that he had been "excluded" from the townspeople of the town of Iamburg. The transfer of part of Ivan Aref'ev's and Irina Vasil'evna's land to Mikhail Ivanov was graced with the signatures of the township leader and the township clerk, and was stamped with the seal of the county administration. A note in pencil added at some later point observes that this transfer of property—described as being in "hereditary possession"—had not been confirmed by the land captain for the area.[11]

Through its pragmatic decisions, the village of Lemozha, represented by its heads of household, seemed to have resolved its responsibilities toward its orphans, widow, and tax collectors, and, as the reallocation of some of Ivan Aref'ev's land to another villager suggests, its collective politics, whatever they may have been. Frol Grigor'ev apparently paid the agreed-on sum to the rural society; Aleksandra, his older stepdaughter, grew up, married, and left the village around or before the age of twenty; and all might have been well with the villagers of Lemozha, with the former townsman Frol Grigor'ev, and even with poor Elena had not Praskovia Aref'eva reappeared on the scene in 1908 with her request to the Sosnitskii Township Court to be declared her father's heir.

A PERSISTENT LITIGATOR

Your memory is not failing if you do not remember Praskovia Aref'eva's name figuring in the series of decisions made by the Lemozha Village Assembly in 1901. She did not appear in any of the assembly's deliberations, and it is not clear that she was living in the village at the time of the assembly's actions. When her father died, Praskovia Aref'eva had been an unmarried adult woman, aged twenty-eight, and there is no evidence that she received land or property at that point; nor is there any indication that her welfare had been of any concern to the village. The transfer of family responsibilities and land allotments from father to son, from Arefii to Ivan Aref'ev, appeared to have taken place in 1894 without formalities, and the village heads of household took more complex decisions only after Ivan Aref'ev's premature death. At no time did Praskovia, Arefii's daughter, figure in their decision to hand off both responsibility and land to the new husband of Ivan Aref'ev's widow. Looking back on these proceedings with regard to lineage, we see that Arefii's property was transferred first into his son's possession, and later in part to the care of the husband of his deceased son's wife and in part out of the family altogether. After his son Ivan's death, Arefii had no remaining male descendants. We know from later documents that by 1914 Praskovia Aref'eva was living in Petrograd on Izmailovskii Prospect. Perhaps she had left the village much earlier and was therefore excluded from the family's property settlements; in any case, she made no recorded attempt to claim her father's property as her own at the time of her father's or her brother's death.

It was only in 1908 that Praskovia Aref'eva appeared at the Sosnitskii Township Court to make her claim to inherit her father's property. What might have driven her to take this step? It is possible to imagine some connection to the first of Stolypin's land reforms in 1906, but this seems unlikely. First, the legislation privileged heads of household and thus would have only consolidated Frol Grigor'ev's hold on the property. Second, although the definition of a household head was not gender-specific, the law appeared to make no place for women, as individuals, to claim family property (women could be holders of collectively owned family property).[12] Finally, no participants or authorities in this case ever cited the Stolypin legislation or any other legal initiative as a basis for Praskovia Aref'eva's late claim to be an heir.

What appears to have brought Praskovia Aref'eva to the township court in 1908 emerges only indirectly from documents associated with her later appeals, because the event was so familiar to the village of Lemozha that no one needed to refer to it. In 1907 Frol Grigor'ev's wife, Irina Vasil'evna, died,[13] leaving him the head of household with control over the Aref'ev property. The only direct descendants of Arefii Gordeev were female: Ivan Aref'eev's daughters, Aleksandra, who had married and left the village, and the insane Elena, now aged eighteen, in addition to our litigant, Praskovia Aref'eva. Is it a coincidence that, within the year of Irina Vasil'evna's death, Praskovia Aref'eva appeared at the Sosnitskii Township Court to claim her inheritance and associated both Aleksandra and Elena with her case as "plaintiffs"? Perhaps now that Ivan Aref'ev's wife, Irina Vasil'evna, was out of the way, the Aref'eev "family" could reclaim its property from a stranger. Neither of the nieces showed up at court, but Praskovia Aref'eva's claim could not have been more direct. She asked the court to "recognize her as the inheritor of her deceased father's property now in the use of . . . Frol Grigor'ev."[14]

Praskovia Aref'eva's demand took some time to sort out. She presented her claim on 12 February 1908, and the case was settled that same year on 26 April. At Praskovia Aref'eva's request, the township court called three witnesses to the hearing—two peasant men from Lemozha and one peasant, Aleksei Zakharov, from another village, Zapol'e. These men testified as follows: Mikhail Kargov of Lemozha confirmed that Arefii's property was indeed in the disposition of Frol Grigor'ev; Dmitri Andreev testified that he knew nothing of the matter; and Aleksei Zakharov, from Zapol'e, reiterated what Mikhail Kargov had said. Frol Grigor'ev lived up to his image of generous spirit. As the defendant, he "explained that the inheritors to all property remaining after the death of the wife of Ivan Aref'ev, Irina Vasil'eva, were the latter's two daughters but that they recognized their obligation to divide off part of the buildings for Praskovia Aref'eva as well." Responding to Praskovia Aref'eva's request and Frol Grigor'ev's statement, the Sosnitskii Township Court found Praskovia Aref'eva's suit "in part proven" and, "according to the voluntary agreement of the defendant," pronounced the following arrangement:

> To oblige peasant Frol Grigor'ev to divide off for Praskovia Aref'eva from all the structures one of the front cottages, one of either of the two cows, and the household plot under construction on the left side that is six sazhens wide and twenty sazhens long. The cottage allotted to Aref'eva may be pulled down.[15]

This fine example of a pragmatic family division, and of an allotment of a significant amount of property to a daughter fourteen years after her father's death, was certified by the president and three judges of the township court. Their signatures were verified by the same authorities who had confirmed the 1901 arrangements with Frol Grigor'ev, in their capacity as court officials. But Praskovia Aref'eva, it turned out, was not content with her share of the deal. As the Lemozha village leader and two witnesses reported later, she refused to take the property listed in the court's order.[16]

Instead, Praskovia Aref'eva began what would be a long series of legal actions to get what she regarded as her rightful inheritance. She first appealed the township court's decision to the next higher instance, the Tsarskosel'skii County Congress.[17] But this enterprise was unsuccessful. On 5 December 1909 the county congress turned her down and upheld the lower township court. Not yet confounded, a year and a half later, in one of her cleverer moves, Praskovia Aref'eva simply began another case at the same township level. On

21 April 1911 she went back to the Sosnitskii Township Court, this time asking that she and her niece, Elena, be made Arefii Gordeev's heirs.[18]

Praskovia Aref'eva had probably noted that the entire personnel of the Sosnitskii Township Court had changed from the time of her first case three years earlier. Not only were the three judges new—an unsurprising fact since judges were elected for three-year terms—but, most important for Praskovia Aref'eva, on the day her case was heard the regular township scribe, Nikolaev, was absent and a substitute was temporarily fulfilling his functions.[19] Praskovia Aref'eva managed somehow to avoid having Frol Grigor'ev appear in court, but the two witnesses made a less than convincing case for her rights. One, Vasilii Vasil'ev, a peasant from Zapol'e and possibly related to Irina Vasil'eva, testified that,

> the indicated inheritance from Arefii Gordeev had been given over by Praskovia Aref'eva to the use of the society, because Aref'eva was not able to pay the obligations on the land, but, for what period of time, he, Vasil'ev, did not know.

Vasil'ev added that Frol Grigor'ev, now a peasant registered in the village of Lemozha, had conducted his household affairs "normally." A second witness, Mikhail Andreev from Lemozha, testified against Praskovia Aref'eva's right to inherit. Despite this testimony, on 30 April 1911, only one week after Praskovia Aref'eva brought her case, the township court with its new judges, but not in the presence of the regular township clerk or the township leader, decided in favor of Praskovia Aref'eva and Elena.[20]

It appears that our litigious daughter had finally succeeded against her village by manipulating the township court in a manner at least partly hidden by the documents. However, enforcing this decision was another story. The township leader, doing his job of executing decisions of the court, noticed the inconsistencies of the two decisions. Citing Praskovia Aref'eva's refusal to take the property allocated to her by the 1908 decision and the "lack of clarity" of the 1911 decision which gave her "all" the property of the deceased, he declared himself unable to carry out both decisions and reported this to the land captain. The land captain, also performing his job of supervision, wrote back to the township court on 15 October 1911, requesting an explanation.

Even before this letter was received by the Sosnitskii Township Court, the village was putting its house in order. Undoubtedly villagers had gotten wind of Praskovia Aref'eva's suit at the township court. Fortunately they had another letter from the land captain—it had been conveniently lying around for almost a year—in which he reminded them that they needed to choose a guardian for Elena Ivanova, who had turned twenty by 1910. Accordingly the village assembly convened on 9 October 1911 to deal with several outstanding issues connected with the Gordeev family property.

The Lemozha Village Assembly in October 1911 convened twenty-eight of the now forty-three heads of household with a "right to a voice at the assembly." The first item of business was to reconfirm Mikhail Ivanov's land allotment, the one soul's worth of field land that had been allotted to him as part of the settlement of 1901. The assembly's decision of 22 May 1901 was cited as authoritative in this regard. This allocation had removed one part of Arefii Gordeev's property out of the inheritance. The assembly then cited the 1908 township court decision that had allotted part of the household plot to Praskovia Aref'eva, thus removing that, too, from the property in question. Then the assembly drew up an inventory with values assigned to all the remaining movable property that Frol Grigor'ev and his stepdaughter, Elena Ivanova, held in collective possession. Half this property was assigned to Elena Ivanova and half to Frol Grigor'ev. Finally, the assembly made Frol Grigor'ev the guardian of Elena Ivanova and her property, which amounted to assigning back to him half the property they formerly held jointly, both land and movables as evaluated in the inventory, minus the share that had been allocated to Praskovia Aref'eva in 1908.[21]

The terms of guardianship in the assembly's decision required Frol Grigor'ev not to waste Elena Ivanova's property and to report on it to the rural society each year. The quality of Frol Grigor'ev's past behavior figured prominently in the decision:

> Frol Grigor'ev has been managing this property for several years, supporting Elena Ivanova from her early years, and taking into consideration that Frol Grigor'ev during the whole time that he was supporting Elena Ivanova treated her very well, did not waste the property, and on the contrary increased it, [the assembly] resolves to appoint Frol Grigor'ev the guardian of the insane Elena Ivanova and her property.

Thus Frol Grigor'ev, former townsman, now a peasant, attentive manager, and good stepfather, attained legal control over the bulk of the land and movable property that had once been in the possession of his wife's first father-in-law.[22]

There was still the matter of Praskovia Aref'eva to sort out. At this juncture, the land captain's official inquiry reached the township in the form of a communication asking for a "resolution of the quandary concerning the execution" of the two contradictory decisions about Arefii Gordeev's property made by the Sosnitskii Township Court in 1908 and 1911. The Sosnitskii Township Court responded to the land captain's inquiry by reopening the case on 4 November 1911. The principals were called to appear at court, and a new hearing took place on 10 December 1911.

The township judges were the same who had made the April 1911 decision in Praskovia Aref'eva's favor, but this time her charm failed to hold or maybe even take hold. According to the court's record book, "Praskovia Aref'eva, who asked for the fulfillment of the decision of the township court of 30 April 1911, number 49, furthermore insulted the court." Frol Grigor'ev, for his part, "explained that he considered only the decision of 12 February 1908, number 22, as correct; he did not know of the decision of 30 April of this year; at present, he was assigned the guardianship over the insane Elena Ivanova, whom he had supported since childhood." As the record dryly notes, "the case was not settled by agreement."[23]

With no agreement to be had, a long decision was made by the judges, a decision that recalled the whole history of the case, from 1908 to the present. The case record notes that Praskovia Aref'eva had been "dissatisfied with the property assigned to her" and that the court personnel had changed when she brought her second case. The judges blamed Praskovia Aref'eva for their ignorance of the earlier decision: she did not bring it up in court, and, moreover, "the court had no information about [Praskovia Aref'eva's] niece, Elena Ivanova, who had been declared insane [and thus] did not have in mind that in her place there would have had to be a representative of the wardship." The new court, including the substitute court secretary, had been "drawn into a deception" and had made a second decision on the same case, a decision that illegally gave Elena Ivanova, an insane person, property that the rural society had already granted to Frol Grigor'ev. On these grounds the court declared its own 1911 decision "illegal," found the 1908 decision correct, and asked the land captain to have the county congress overturn the 1911 decision "as unlawful."[24]

Within the year, on 9 August 1912, the Tsarskosel'skii County Congress dutifully followed up this request and overturned the 30 April 1911 decision that had briefly legitimated Praskovia Aref'eva's claim. Earlier in 1912 the Sosnitskii Township Court, composed of the same judges who had first been deceived by Praskovia Aref'eva and then undone their error, granted a *razdel*—a division of family property—of Frol Grigor'ev and Elena Ivanova's estate, thus filling in a step that solidified the village assembly's arrangements for Frol Grigor'ev's guardianship. By the end of 1912, four years after Praskovia Aref'eva's first disruptive suit and eighteen years after Arefii Gordeev's death, his insane granddaughter was still alive and being cared for, and the bulk of the property Gordeev once had managed had been transferred into the responsible hands of people respected by his former neighbors in the village of Lemozha.

But Arefii Gordeev's daughter, Praskovia, was also still alive, residing in St. Petersburg, and she did not give up. On 4 May 1914 she sent a petition to the land captain in charge of the Sosnitskii Township Court; she received no reply. More than a year later she tried again, still at the level of the land captain. By this time Praskovia Aref'eva's notion of how to win had changed; her petition suggests that she had resorted to professional help. She still based her petition on her right to inherit from her father, and, in line with her earlier behavior, she cited only the favorable (to her) township court decision of 30 April 1911. She omitted entirely the two township court decisions that had gone against her. What she called into question were the earlier 1901 decisions that had taken Frol Grigor'ev into the rural society and allotted him her family's property. She questioned the society's right to distribute "someone else's property," to admit a townsman, and to receive a payment from him. She backed up this charge with citations to four legal statements: a Senate decree from 1877, a Senate decision from 1892, a Senate decree from 1876, and a statute from *The Regulation on Land Captains.*[25] Praskovia Aref'eva, still illiterate herself, had her petition signed by someone else, Fedosiia Lavretskaia.[26]

Who might Fedosiia Lavretskaia be—an employer, a crony, a feminist, a lawyer's assistant, or perhaps a crook? Many women from Sosnitskii Township took up employment as servants in St. Petersburg. Perhaps Lavretskaia was Praskovia's mistress in the city.[27] One thing is certain: the illiterate Praskovia Aref'eva did not dig up those decrees and laws herself. Someone was now helping her with her claim against the village of Lemozha.

No one replied to Praskovia Aref'eva's petition of 14 May 1914, but when the same petition arrived again in October 1915, the land captain, one P. N. Kuznetsov, felt that he had to look into the matter. Within two days he duly wrote to the Sosnitskii township administration asking for information. Nikolaev, the Sosnitskii township leader, still at his post after all these years, sluggishly provided his superior with copies of the village's decisions from 1901 to 1912, decisions received by Kuznetsov on 2 February 1916. Kuznetsov, apparently a conscientious fellow, was still not satisfied and wrote back asking for more information on 15 February 1916. By 12 April 1916 it appears that Kuznetsov felt he knew enough, for on that day he rejected Praskovia Aref'eva's appeal. The grounds were new ones for this case but most convenient: "The petition about overturning the resolution of 25 April 1901 was first initiated by her on 3 May 1914, that is, after the ten-year limit had expired."[28]

To give Praskovia Aref'eva the benefit of the doubt, it is true that she had initiated her case well before 1914. But the land captain was responding to her petition to him, in his capacity as a supervisor over the lower courts, and, in this sense, her appeal was indeed long out of date. He must have felt that he had found a convenient way to escape the complexities of interference in village quarrels. No matter, Praskovia Aref'eva was not to be instructed. On 10 May 1916 she appealed the land captain's decision to the Tsarskosel'skii County Congress, the same instance to which she had unsuccessfully appealed the 1908 division of family property.

The county congress's response shows that it took seriously a complaint against the land captain's decision, but, like the township court in 1911, the congress had taken the case under the influence of another of Praskovia Aref'eva's deceptions. Her complaint against the land captain was based not only on a statute of *The Regulation on Land Captains,* on two Senate decrees from the mid-1890s, on a statute from the court regulations, and on her observation that there were "legal heirs" but also on the "fact" that she had learned of the resolution of the Lemozha Village Assembly in 1906, not 1901. The county congress heard the case two times. After the first hearing on 21 June 1916 the congress sent off for more information from the "book of resolutions" of Lemozha for 1901 to 1906. In a fine demonstration of the uses of local record-keeping and the concern for documentary accuracy within the legal system, the congress uncovered the fact that the 1901 date had been miscopied as 1906 in some of the documents.

This "mistake" created a serious problem for Praskovia Aref'eva, who, on 7 July 1916, petitioned the county congress to allow her to call in two witnesses. We will never know the spells she might have spun over these "witnesses," for the county congress was already fed up. On 26 July 1916, at its second hearing of Praskovia Aref'eva's case, the congress issued a three-page opinion. Praskovia Aref'eva was summoned to attend the hearing of the case, at which all the materials sent on by the township leader were reviewed. The county congress, composed of a president, four members including the land captain involved in the case, and a secretary, based its decision on the procedural ground of "remoteness in time." The point was made that the decision of 1901 was more than ten years old when Praskovia Aref'eva first petitioned the land captain in 1914. The congress clearly wanted to drum this lesson home and get rid of Praskovia Aref'eva and her appeals, for it glossed its decision as follows: according to many decisions of the Senate, the congress noted, the land captain was not allowed to overturn a village assembly after ten years, "no matter what kind of property rights had been violated"; the land captain had correctly counted the years from 1901, and thus the assembly rejected both Praskovia Aref'eva's complaint against the land captain and her demand to call in more witnesses.[29]

There was still recourse to be had in imperial Russia. Praskovia Aref'eva took her case to the provincial appeals court, the Petrograd Provincial Board. Pyramiding her complaints, and conveniently avoiding the issue of "remoteness in time," she submitted a hectographed petition, dated 24 August 1916, appealing the decision of the county congress on the grounds that the resolution of 1901 was illegal. She argued that there were legal heirs (citing an 1897 statute to back this up) and that the land captain should have seen that the congress's action was illegal and therefore overturned the case.

This complaint may be giving readers a case of déjà vu, but by now Praskovia Aref'eva had found a few more strings to play on. The first was sympathy for the downtrodden. In Praskovia Aref'eva's or, more likely, someone else's words:

> Now I, an illiterate woman, must try to restore the broken law, and submit everywhere petitions about the demonstrated injustice, which was obvious to the land captain.

The second line of reasoning concerned the rationality and justice of the law. "Even if we agree with the deadline [of ten years]," Praskovia Aref'eva added:

> it can be obligatory only for those people who took part in that resolution or to whom its contents were known. Such an understanding of limitations exists in all legal and administrative practice, and one shall not accuse a person who totally does not know about the existence of such a resolution of missing a deadline.

If the resolution had been published "in the Senate or other advertisements, the ignorance of which is always to be held against interested parties," Praskovia Aref'eva added, she would not be appealing. Finally, Praskovia Aref'eva observed, playing to family values,

> now I have the right to declare that I was all the time living in Petrograd in the capacity of a servant, and decisively knew nothing about the fact that the property inherited from my father could be given by the rural society to an outsider, and I the biological [*rodnaia*] daughter was to be subjected to exile with my inherited plot and the structures that were presented to me graciously by that unrelated person. I learned of this resolution only in 1908, when my case about inheritance was considered in the township court and Grigor'ev based his objections on that resolution.

To this stunning, and duplicitous, concern for the imagined sensibilities of the provincial board, the ever vigilant Praskovia Aref'eva added another new interpretation of the law. She claimed that the village assembly's decision of 1901 (this time around she acknowledged the earlier date) was not in force until 1906, when Frol Grigor'ev would have made all the payments to the society. Therefore she could not have appealed until then. She observed that one could imagine a case in which the society would set ten or twelve years for such payments, and then "I wouldn't have had the right to appeal at all."[30]

The Petrograd Provincial Board was presided over by fancy people, such as the governor, Count M. N. Tolstoi; a representative of the regional procurator's office; the president of the provincial *zemstvo* administration; and four permanent members. These people may have had better things to do on 2 June 1917 but on that day, nine months after the receipt of Praskovia Aref'eva's petition, they heard the case. Once again, documents were summoned from lower instances and, along with Praskovia Aref'eva's petition, were examined in detail. The provincial appeals court unraveled the contradictions in Praskovia Aref'eva's petition, and their six-point verdict spoke directly to her claims. Point 1 made it clear that the deal between the rural society and Frol Grigor'ev was made in 1901 and that this date was the one to which the limitations rules applied.[31] The court tersely rejected Praskovia Aref'eva's claim of ignorance: "The testimony of the complainant to the effect that the indicated resolution became known to her only in 1908 does not deserve attention." Wrapping up its response to all the other arguments in the case, the court remarked that "the remaining conclusions adduced in the complaint by the petitioner do not serve as a basis for overturning the appealed decisions of the congress." Praskovia Aref'eva's appeal was to be left "without consequences," in the official formula.[32]

No such luck. Praskovia Aref'eva went on to the Senate, with a final complaint. Her "last" petition was dated 28 June 1917, and it was forwarded by the recently renamed acting Petrograd provincial commissar of the Provisional Government to the Senate on 26 July 1917. By now Praskovia Aref'eva's legal imagination had quite run away with her; the new petition brought in new "facts," new dates, and new arguments. The matter at issue was no longer a family division but "buildings on land," which she claimed could be reviewed by the Senate. Her father was adduced to have died on 12 April 1912—perhaps she thought this might give her sufficient time for future appeals! She now claimed that

Frol Grigor'ev had kept the 1901 resolution a secret until 1905; that she had learned of it in 1908; and that, despite all her efforts, she had not been able to obtain a copy of the resolution until 1914. (Why, then, had she brought her second township-level case in 1911?) She rejected the "formal" grounds on which the land captain had turned down the petition and insisted that the congress's resolution "completely illegally deprived a member of a peasant family of land." No limitations can apply to this decision, Praskovia Aref'eva insisted, for "such a lawless resolution can never come into legal force."[33]

Those are Praskovia Aref'eva's last words on archived paper, and one wonders what this woman, registered in the summer of 1917 at Smolnyi Alley near Bolshevik party headquarters, did with her troubles in the coming months and years. The legal system that had engaged her for so long would disappear. This case invites us to examine the nature of that system, with its procedures, hierarchy, and open-endedness, and to revisit the legal practices and imaginaries of Russian peasants in the early twentieth century.

PEASANT VERSUS PEASANTS

First, as these records demonstrate, there is no one peasant. This case pitted a woman of peasant estate, who was born into a village family and left it to work in the big city as a servant, against the male heads of households, also of peasant status, of Lemozha Village, with their collective interest in getting their taxes paid, taking care of orphans, and other less visible concerns. The diverse behaviors, values, and standpoints of the actors in this dispute undermine the perspective that homogenizes individuals of peasant estate into a unified social group. Second, the case does not permit an easy differentiation between city and country ways or city and country people. Praskovia Aref'eva had spent most of her adult life in the capital and had access to legal assistance, but she was illiterate. Two-thirds of her opponents, the patriarchal definers of village interests back in Lemozha, could sign their names by 1901. Frol Grigor'ev, against whom Praskovia Aref'eva brought her suit, came from the city but chose to join a rural society, attain a household, and work the land. This case, like others, exposes conflicts of interest and desire among individuals, individuals who were ascribed to a single estate status but who did not therefore share a collective purpose, a collective identity, or a collective way of being.

The case also reveals the ways that individuals sought the assistance of the law from within the regime of estates. The peasants from Lemozha—some more than others—used their estate-based rights to seek personal advantages, to validate collective property rights, to assign family responsibilities, and to address and respond to higher authorities. Being a person of peasant status gave individuals legal means to inherit, to enter into contracts, to regulate their family lives, and even to register in another estate.[34] Estate and other group categories played a vital role in making connections between individuals and the imperial state. However Russian elites and historians have defined "the peasantry" and for whatever purposes, a practical meaning of "peasant"—for peasants—was that of legal status. This official standing with its defined empowerments was what counted for peasants at the township courts.[35]

The right-granting aspect of the estate system remains invisible to many commentators. Liberal and radical elites of the late imperial period were deeply hostile to the estate system, which they regarded as an obstacle to their ultimate goals—equality under the law for liberals, a classless society for socialists. Echoing these political critiques and wishes, much of the historical literature on imperial Russia retains this normative stance and regards the retention of the estate system as an indicator of Russia's backwardness. Rather than engage with the ways that people living in such systems may have used them, scholars and others project a primordial democratic ethos onto Russian society and assume that the empire's people, including peasants, were waiting to be freed from the artificial shackles of estates into functionally defined classes or the citizenship of equal individuals or both. It is necessary to step out of this essentialist conception of universal, natural, and self-evident rights in order to understand the imperial legal framework as it existed and the various social imaginaries it nurtured.

One study that engages with both official and informal understandings of status is Elise Wirtschafter's *Social Identity in Imperial Russia.* Wirtschafter has emphasized the fluidity of social identification throughout the imperial period; in her view, the estate system was "sufficiently malleable" to permit individuals to make their lives in occupations and social relationships in ways that did not correspond to the vision of society embodied in administrative acts.[36] Some aspects of this malleability, however, were made possible and legal through the estate system. In the case described here, Frol Grigor'ev wanted to become a member of a particular village household and to farm a particular plot of land. To do so in 1906, he had to become a member of the local rural society, a status only the householders of the village could grant him. Although Praskovia Aref'eva tried, perhaps under the influence of citified counsel, to claim that the village had no right to admit an outsider into its ranks, she was in this claim, as in so many others, completely wrong. One duty assigned rural societies by *The General Regulation on the Peasants* was control of their membership. The Lemozha rural society was exercising an ordinary administrative function, legitimated by state law, when it admitted Frol Grigor'ev into its ranks.[37] Once a member of the rural society, Frol Grigor'ev was transferred out of the townspeople's estate and into his new estate. He "became" a peasant, endowed with a peasant's legalized duties and rights.

The General Regulation on Peasants was not a constitution for a class or a corporate group but a set of rules pertaining to each peasant. The law expressed an individual's relation to the state, a relationship defined by the person's own status, not by his or her "belonging" to a nationwide group of individuals of similar status. The form of the statutes in *The General Regulation* articulates the individuality of subjects of the law, as in this example:

> Peasants are granted the right to reregister themselves in other estates and societies, according to the rules expressed in this Regulation, in the Laws on Statuses and in the Rules on Industry.[38]

The statute law did not create a social collective with shared values, but it did constitute a great number of individuals with identical rights, who may or may not in particular circumstances have been inclined to see status as a unifying principle. Some people of noble rank in this period and earlier used the grounds of estate to demand that the government privilege them as a collectivity.[39] The leaders of the Peasant Party after 1905 engaged in an attempt to mobilize status in their search for votes. But even these efforts to construct nationwide collectivities attest to the absence of an already united nobility and an already united peasantry. If we want to examine collective practices of people of peasant status, we must look at a different level of life—at the local level, at small-scale groups and institutions, like the rural society, to which the law granted authority and agency and through which collective goals could be achieved.

Using the legal authority of the rural society, some of the individuals in this case were able to assert their interests against others: the male heads of household of Lemozha were effective in thwarting Praskovia Aref'eva's extreme (from their point of view) demands. Inside that mobilized society, individual villagers—Irina Vasil'evna, Frol Grigor'ev, the village leader, the never again mentioned head of household who took over part of Ivan Aref'ev's field land, and other men and women who interacted with these figures—took action and made choices for their own reasons. That the village assembly used a language of moral economy in its legitimation of Frol Grigor'ev does not prove that this was "the" peasant mentality. Frol Grigor'ev was welcomed into "our society"—but this meant the well-ordered society of Lemozha, not "the" peasantry or a community based on solidarity at all times.

Praskovia Aref'eva was also a "peasant," and her persistent demand for "her" property reveals the desires of individuals, hidden beneath our categories. The documents hint that she could not work the land to pay her taxes and also had no desire to cart off the building materials she was allotted. What drove a woman employed as a servant in Petersburg to try to reclaim what she called her "inheritance" many years after her father's death? Did she want to return to her roots, to sell the land, to have some clout with villagers who had neglected her, to spite Frol Grigor'ev, to avenge some harm Irina Vasil'evna, her sister-in-law, had done, to fulfill the aspirations of her employer or other city acquaintance for a dacha in the countryside? We cannot know.

We can nonetheless observe how the imperial legal system allowed this subaltern to speak in her self-interest and to put alternative notions of justice before the courts. As a peasant registered in the village of Lemozha, she had the right to bring an inheritance case to the local township court. Her right to inherit was acknowledged locally by Frol Grigor'ev and the township court in 1908, in keeping with the legally defined right of peasants to allocate inheritances according to local customs.[40] The rural society, meeting in its legally empowered assembly, would have awarded her part of her father's property, but she wanted more. Praskovia Aref'eva also had the right to complain about a miscarriage of justice to the land captain and to pursue her complaints about legal decisions all the way to the highest court in the land. Thus a litigious individual, with the rights of peasant status, could first engage the localized justice of the township court, and later, if dissatisfied with the decision of peasant judges, could appeal on up the long ladder of legal instances against a collective interest defined, legally, by her erstwhile peasant neighbors in the village.

CHEWING THE LEGAL CUD

If we can withstand the impulse to impose collectivizing identifications—as subalterns, as resisters, as communalists—on peasants,[41] can we still discern the outlines of a legal imaginary available to people of peasant status in early-twentieth-century Russia? Praskovia Aref'eva's misadventures with the law suggest some features of legal culture in the countryside. First, the people involved in this dispute did have a legal imaginary—a sense that they could reach to legal means to resolve disputes. Both Praskovia Aref'eva and her opponents in Lemozha used legal procedures to authorize claims and to assure possession of essential resources. The law was the ultimate authority over allocation of property within families and villages; no individual or group in this dispute claimed that there was a power higher than the law. The village householders made sure that critical decisions were registered by legal authorities placed over them, and later referred to these official documents to legitimate their assignments of resources. They did not at any point imply that a local informal resolution was more just than a legal one, or that it could stand on its own. Even Praskovia Aref'eva's desperate final appeal that a "lawless resolution can never come into legal force" is based on the recognition of the grandeur and power of the law.[42]

Second, all actors in this case understood the basic structure of the legal system, how to use it, and how to address its institutionalized hierarchies. There was no confusion about which level of the system was relevant to one's interests. The township leader, when blind-sided with Praskovia Aref'eva's victory in her second township court suit, took the matter immediately to the land captain, who was responsible for confirming township-level decisions. Praskovia Aref'eva may have miscalculated when she tried to get her way by making a second case at the township level, but she had already tried to appeal it one step up and had been turned down. It was a bold move but not an uninformed one. Her mistake was to assume that once she had achieved a favorable outcome through her manipulation of the township court, the court's decision would not be challenged by other legal authorities. She did not make this mistake again, and instead marched her case straight up the ladder of appeals until it was pulled out from under her by the revolution.

Once involved in legal process, these people of peasant status relied on several notions of justice and authority to make their claims. First, at the village level, there were the resolutions of the village assembly, whose jurisdiction over property allocation was based on imperial law, and whose decisions were legally registered by the township administration. The assembly's decisions were legitimated by a range of ethical arguments and an appeal to state law, expressing the interconnectedness of local power and state oversight on which Russian legality rested. In this case, the village assembly's award of Arefii Gordeev's property to Frol Grigor'ev and to another villager, as well as the assessment of Frol Grigor'ev's payments to the rural society, were based on several moral claims—those of family descent and marriage, stewardship, good behavior (sober and correct), tax paying, and local well-being.

Once the village assembly's decisions became part of an official record, the documents themselves constituted a source of legitimacy for village people and for the other legal agents they encountered. Russian law for peasant litigants was written law in a most material sense—signed, sealed, and delivered. A legalized resolution—with its date, its stamps and seals, its content—became a source of authority for all subsequent legal actions. Praskovia Aref'eva's contorted arguments about "knowledge of the law"—perhaps a creation of a Petrograd lawyer or legal aid practitioner[43]—fell on deaf ears when she tried them out. It was the existence of earlier agreements, and their dating, which constituted reliable evidence in the Russian courts. That this was part of the legal imaginary of the people of Lemozha and the Sosnitskii Township Court is clear from the respect accorded to prior contracts, the concern about conflicting decisions, and even the rush to create a paper trail for Frol Grigor'ev's guardianship over Elena Ivanova.

What other kinds of authorities apart from local moral reasoning, state oversight, and official documents exercised a pull on those who took their claims to court? Praskovia Aref'eva used several kinds of argumentation to promote her case. She claimed a right to inherit her father's property, a claim that was upheld by all levels of the judicial system according to the agreement reached at her first township suit. (Her appeals against that original property settlement were rejected.) At no point was she denied the property she had been assigned in 1908. The claims of *rod*—of birth and family—moderated by other moral and pragmatic ends, were recognized by the legal system and by rural litigants. The issue of a female inheriting her father's property was never raised, for peasants had the legally established right to regulate inheritance according to local practice. Praskovia Aref'eva had potentially a greater claim to an inheritance than females of other estates, whose inheritance rules concerning daughters were specific and confining.[44]

When Praskovia Aref'eva petitioned the superior courts, she added new arguments that she, or her adviser, thought might sway the authorities. Among these were challenges to the rural society's rights to admit a non-peasant into its ranks, to allocate an individual's property, and to receive payment for that property. These issues concerning status-defined rights, collectivism, and private property—all important issues in 1914, 1916, and 1917—were swept under the rug by the land captain and higher bodies, using the convenient legalism of time limits (*davnost'*). Praskovia Aref'eva's other moral claims of inverse class and gender entitlements ("I, an illiterate woman, must try to restore the broken law") as well as her not so subtle criticisms of flaws in the interpretation of the law by lower instances of justice, including the land captain, were also ignored by higher authorities. Although Praskovia Aref'eva's efforts failed, her attempt to manipulate the higher courts through political argument should also be seen as part of a legal imaginary. Praskovia Aref'eva thought she had a chance of finding common ground with legal authorities outside the township and even in St. Petersburg.

Most important for representing the legal imagination of people of peasant status are notions that Praskovia Aref'eva and the Lemozha rural society shared. Praskovia Aref'eva saw the legal system as the way to address injustice; her opponents did as well. As a singular, perhaps cantankerous, certainly rebellious personality, Praskovia Aref'eva imagined that the law would be on her side. The local patriarchy of Lemozha imagined it was on theirs. Both sides did the work required to attain justice as they saw it through the system. The system also did its work, regurgitating all the documents it had produced, ruminating, and deciding repeatedly in favor of the original accord between village reason and state registration but, it seems, accepting without limit the right of the petitioner to reopen the same case.

It was not an efficient system, but it had merits, some of them consequential for considerations of legal ideas in Russia. At the most basic level, the system as we see it in this instance offered opportunities to challenge village patriarchy, even if it enabled a defense of the status quo. At a time of vigorous transformation of Russian social life and work, the law expanded the discourse on social being, and did not close it off. Second, it enabled people to make or meet these challenges to earlier practice in respectful ways, ways that some may view as wasteful of time and brains and passion but that encouraged peaceful nonviolent behavior. The men of the village did not just take Praskovia Aref'eva's property; they assigned that property in a process that legitimated the agency of all claimants. Praskovia Aref'eva herself reached up to the highest authorities in the land with her appeals. Finally, the system took its time and thus drew people into long-term, slow-moving interactions with the state. As Nietzsche complained in 1887, "One skill is needed—lost today, unfortunately . . . the skill to ruminate, which cows possess, but modern man lacks."[45] One effect of this ruminating legal system may well have been to nurture the legal imaginary of Russian peasants.

A Day at Court

Determined litigants like Praskovia Aref'eva could seek justice from provincial and national authorities, but most cases brought by peasant plaintiffs began and ended at township courts. Using two kinds of sources—cases in my surveys and statistics kept by imperial authorities—this chapter considers due process at township courts, the kinds of people who could be found there, and the complaints and accusations they presented. Books kept by township clerks allow a reconstruction of a day at a township court, with its docket of civil and criminal hearings. Clerks' records reveal the outcomes of cases, the amounts of suits and fines, the lengths of jail terms, and the dispatch with which decisions were fulfilled. The final section of the chapter surveys the numbers of cases and kinds of matters that were decided at township courts. The different angles of vision offered by local and provincial records converge to illuminate basic elements of court practice in the early twentieth century. The courts offered rural society predictable and simple procedures, speedy processing of registered cases, and efficient fulfillment of decisions. The accessible, quick, and orderly justice of township courts may account for why their huge dockets grew steadily from 1905 until the outbreak of the war.

STARTING A CASE

A case at a township court usually began with a petition. A person living in the township who wished to take a claim before the township judges started by registering a complaint or request at the township administration. The law set no fees for this service, nor did I find any records of payments for the registration of cases.[1] Printed forms were provided for the petitioner. At the Zaborovskii Township Court in Novgorod Province, people used a conveniently arranged universal complaint form, one page in length, with blanks left for specifying information. The heading of the page identified the petitioner and the court:

> 191_ year, ___________ day
> Peasant____
> ____
> ____
> declared to the ______________________Court the following:

The rest of the page was divided into two vertical parts. Along the left-hand side of the page, in a narrow column, five topics were printed:

1. About whom is this complaint brought?
2. What is the complaint? (When and where did the misdemeanor take place, and to whom was harm or losses caused or what is the demand of the plaintiff?)
3. Witnesses.
4. Other evidence, presented by the petitioner.
5. What are the demands of the plaintiff?

The center and right side of the paper were left entirely blank, providing a generous space for filling in answers and information corresponding to the standardized questions. At the bottom of the page, again leaving ample room for large handwriting, was the printed rubric, "Signature of the person declaring the complaint."[2]

Variants on this kind of form were used at all township courts. At the court in Nagatino, not far from Moscow, the complaint form asked the following questions:

1. What constitutes the complaint?
2. Who is the defendant?
3. What evidence is there, and were there witnesses? Who [are they] and where do they live?[3]

These simple and succinct forms spoke directly to the would-be plaintiff in ordinary language. The rubrics highlighted the personal quality of the action, displaying the petitioner's initiative and direct connection to the law. Although after 1889 local people of other estates could bring cases to the township court, the petitioner was assumed to be a peasant and was supplied with this printed title. Petitioners filled in the blanks with their names and the settlements in which they were registered. This self-presentation according to estate, name, and place of registration was the usual way that peasants identified themselves in legal contexts; it signaled their status and rights in the imperial polity. The complaint form both permitted petitioners to provide their own accounts of whatever had inspired them to begin judicial proceedings and at the same time solicited the kind of information critical to a court settlement. Hearings at township courts focused on the topics printed on the document: the substance of complaints, the plaintiffs' requests, evidence, and the testimony of plaintiffs, witnesses, and defendants.

Once a complaint form was submitted, it was given a case number and entered into a registry book maintained by the township clerk. This book, the "on the table register,"[4] provided an account of all complaints brought to the township court for settlement, day by day and year after year. The township clerk entered each complaint or request by number and date, with a brief rendering of its content. Later, when the case had been decided, the clerk would fill in the date the case had been heard and its new number as entered in a separate book of court decisions. A routine case entry in the "on the table register" for a case recorded at the Zaborovskii Township Court[5] reads as follows:

No. in Order	Month and Day	Contents of the Complaint or Communication	When the Township Court Decision Followed
1	2 January	Concerning the suit of peasant of Borovitskii County, Stepanovskii Township, Novoloka Village, Ivan Egorov, against peasant of Bol'shoe Zaborov'e Village Vasilii Efimov Smirnov for 130 rubles of debt according to a bill of exchange	Decided 12 April 1905 No. 43

The next step toward resolution of a township case involved setting a court date and calling the plaintiff, the accused, and any witnesses to the hearing. Formal documentation and efficient communication were essential and routine aspects of this procedure. For each party and witness in a case, a summons was issued on a checkbook-size piece of paper, printed on both sides and made out in multiple copies using carbon paper. Court officials in Tikhvin County of Novgorod Province, where the Zaborovskii court was located, used forms printed in Tikhvin, the county's central town, for this purpose.[6] The duplicate summonses were perforated so that one copy could be returned as evidence of its delivery to the recipient. The receipt copy was imprinted with the following information:

Возвратить.

ПОВѢСТКА. По ... дѣлу № ...

Крестьян ...

... Волостной Судъ вызываетъ Васъ ...

19... г., въ ... час. утра, въ качествѣ ...

по дѣлу ...

(См. на обор.).

Предсѣдатель Суда ...

Скоропечатня Грейверъ, Тихвинъ.

190 г. ... дня. Первый экземпляръ повѣстки получилъ

крестьян ...

Front and verso of a summons sent out by the Zaborovskii Township Court, Novgorod Province, 4 March 1911, and signed for on 5 March 1911.

TO RETURN

On the [civil or criminal] case No.____

SUMMONS.

Peasant [of village, county, province, name]

[The name of court] Township Court summons You ____ [on day, month] ____ __190_ yr., at __ o'clock A.M., in the capacity of [witness, plaintiff, defendant] in the case of ____ [suit from whom, about what]

President of the Township Court ____ [signature]

On the back of this form was a printed communication: "190_ yr, ____ day. The first copy of this summons was received by Peasant ____," with two lines left for a name and place of settlement to be filled in. The recipient of a summons signed this copy of the form, which was returned to the court for its records.[7] In cases of illiteracy, someone else could sign for the recipient. Before a case was heard, the township clerk would put all the documents for each case together—petitions, declarations, certifications, prior court decisions, summonses, sometimes even the envelopes in which documents had been mailed—for the use of judges during the hearing.[8]

WHO GOES TO COURT?

Reception of a summons as a party or "side" in a case ordinarily obliged people under the jurisdiction of the township court to appear in person at the hearing at the time specified. *The General Regulation on Peasants* provided for some exceptions based on territory or status, and also gave the judges a measure of discretion concerning personal appearances. People who lived outside the township and further than fifteen versts (ten miles) away from the court's location could send another person to represent them—"from their relations, domestics, or fellow villagers, as long as the last have no other business at the court." The court could allow other people to send representatives to court if there were "important reasons preventing a personal appearance at the hearing." In a rule that reflected both status-based privilege and the possibility that privileged people might use the township courts, people who were not under the jurisdiction of the township court—such as members of the noble estate—could send substitutes to represent them as victims of misdemeanors or as plaintiffs, or they could submit their communications to the court in writing.[9] People called to court as witnesses were bound by similar regulations to appear in person or, in cases of distance or other "worthy" reasons, could be questioned by the police or administrators of another township and have their recorded testimony sent to the court where a case was being heard. People not under the jurisdiction of the township courts who were called as witnesses were "not obliged to appear personally" at court, but their testimony, if considered essential, could be requested from the land captain. In such cases he was to obtain a written deposition.[10]

As these differentiated regulations suggest, overlapping categories of territory and status defined the universe of the township court's authority. After 1889 the jurisdiction of the township was expanded beyond the peasant estate. *The General Regulation on the Peasants* stated that in areas under the supervision of land captains, "townspeople, traders, craftsmen, and artisans" who lived permanently in rural settlements were to be subject to the police, courts, and regulations established for "people of rural estate," while "preserving all the rights, personal and estate, that belong to them."[11] These estate-based distinctions meant that peasants, townspeople, craftsmen, and artisans registered in rural areas were obliged to use the township courts for certain kinds of cases, whereas nobles and clergy—the major estates omitted from the 1889 list—could use the township courts if they chose. A misdemeanor subject to adjudication at the township court committed by and against a person subordinated to township authority had to be judged first at this instance. If a misdemeanor had been directed against a member of the nobility, the offended party was allowed but not required to bring the case to the township court. Because of their estate privileges, nobles could absent themselves from hearings and decline to appear as witnesses before the peasant judges, and thus could avoid a face-to-face encounter with lower-status legal authorities. The other options for litigation open to these "people of other status" were to go directly to the land captain, the circuit courts, or, for some, the Justices of the Peace.[12]

In addition to estate and place of settlement, religion, ethnicity, or occupation could have jurisdictional implications for subjects of the empire. The regulations on the township courts were studded with special provisions for people of various religions and ethnicities, rules that reflected the shifting priorities and capabilities of the state. According to the 1906 extension to *The General Regulation on the Peasants,* civil cases between Jews who lived outside of cities in the western provinces were to be taken to township courts, but township court regulations were not to be applied to "natives" of Stavropol Province.[13] The overall significance of these and other jurisdictional prescripts was to make the township court the first instance for misdemeanors and small civil suits for most people living in the countryside of European Russia. In the early twentieth century the township court was the most proximate legal instance available to about 85 percent of the population.[14]

Although township courts were primarily used by people of peasant status to resolve conflicts or to clarify relationships with other peasants, people who belonged to other estates occasionally appeared in township cases. Members of the townspeople's estate appeared in small numbers in most township courts, more frequently as plaintiffs (5 percent of pre-1917 cases in my study) and much less often as defendants (3 percent of pre-1917 cases). A townsperson, who

Table 3.1. Estates of Plaintiffs and Defendants: Pre–1917 Cases, Civil and Criminal

Estate	*Plaintiffs*		*Defendants*	
	Frequency	Percent	Frequency	Percent
Nobles	3	0.4%	0	0 %
Clergy	1	0.1%	0	0 %
Townspeople	35	4.9%	21	3.1%
Peasants	540	75.8%	664	96.5%
Officials, No Estate	133	18.7%	3	0.4%
Total	712	100 %	688	100 %

Note: This table and all others for which no source is provided are based on case data from my survey of township courts. See "Note on Sources."

could be a local person who had worked his way into a higher status as a merchant, might go to court to collect debts from his former or present-day neighbors. For example, at the Ignatevskii Township Court in Moscow Province on 4 May 1906 a townsman named Pelevin registered three complaints against three peasant defendants. His suits for between four and five rubles were terminated at the hearing on 29 May, for neither he nor his presumed debtors showed up at court.[15] In addition to the occasional townsperson, officials, usually policemen, of various estates not identified in the record, could be plaintiffs in criminal cases. In my study policemen were more likely to participate at the Nagatinskii Township Court on the outskirts of Moscow than at other courts.[16]

Members of the noble estate were entitled to send cases involving other township residents to the township court, but few chose to do so. Before the abolition of the estate system in 1917, noble plaintiffs constituted less than half of 1 percent of all the plaintiffs at the township courts I surveyed. Of course, nobles were ordinarily a very small minority of residents in a township, although some might hold significant amounts of land.[17] No nobles appeared as defendants in any of the township courts whose case records I examined. Bringing a case against a noble would have violated the jurisdiction of the court, and was beyond the law and probably the imagination of lower-status litigants. Table 3.1 provides the estates for plaintiffs and defendants in pre-1917 cases in my survey.

The statistics of the imperial bureaucracy provide another window on the users of township courts. Yearly reports filed at the governor's office described two categories of plaintiffs—those under the jurisdiction of the township courts and others not in the jurisdiction of these instances. These reports also indicate the very modest use of the court by nobles, clergy, and others not subject to the township's authority. Of 42,308 civil suits registered in the Moscow Province township courts in 1910, for example, only 612, or 1 percent, were brought by "people not in the jurisdiction of the township court." People not in the court's jurisdiction brought a somewhat higher percentage of criminal

Table 3.2. Gender of Plaintiffs and Defendants: Civil and Criminal Cases before World War I

	Civil Cases		*Criminal Cases*		*All Cases*	
	Frequency	Percent	Frequency	Percent	Frequency	Percent
Plaintiffs:						
Female	13	15.3%	61	16.4%	74	16.2%
Male	72	84.7%	311	83.6%	383	83.8%
Defendants:						
Female	3	3.7%	44	11.8%	47	10.4%
Male	78	96.3%	329	88.2%	407	89.6%

cases—813 out of 25,930, or 3 percent. If we combine both kinds of cases, people not in the jurisdiction of the township court constituted 2 percent of plaintiffs at all township courts in Moscow Province in 1910.[18]

This leaves peasants, who constituted most plaintiffs, most defendants, and most witnesses at township courts. Peasants accounted for 94 percent of the defendants in civil cases and 96 percent of the accused in criminal cases in the pre-1917 cases I examined. People of peasant estate accounted for 97 percent of all plaintiffs in civil cases and 81 percent of the plaintiffs in criminal cases in this same period. Peasants were 98.5 percent of witnesses called in civil cases and 93 percent of witnesses in criminal cases. These figures under-represent peasants' presence in the township courts, for the non-peasant plaintiffs in criminal cases were usually policemen, whose estate status was not registered. Most of the policemen and other officials who filed cases for aggrieved parties or appeared as witnesses would have been originally ascribed to the peasant estate. Even if the law permitted, or under some circumstances required, people of other status groups to participate in township courts in various capacities, the vast majority of cases before the township courts involved people of peasant estate, and only people of peasant estate.

The laws on access and obligation to the township court made no reference to gender.[19] Russian peasant women had the same rights and duties toward the court as peasant men. Women were never elected as judges, nor were they ever township clerks. The language of the regulations on the courts might legally have permitted the rare woman who had been made a head of household to serve in these roles, but nothing in township records indicates that the selection of female judges was ever considered by jurists or villagers. Women did appear in township courts as plaintiffs, defendants, and, more rarely, witnesses. Before 1914 women comprised 16 percent of plaintiffs, 10 percent of defendants, and 2 percent of witnesses at the courts I studied. Table 3.2 shows the percentage of civil and criminal cases brought by men or women before the outbreak of the war. Usually, but not always, the people at a township court hearing would be men of peasant estate.

GETTING TO COURT

The interval between the registration of a complaint and the hearing of a case at a township court was not long, especially when the means of transportation and communication in the rural areas are taken into consideration. Summonses had to be delivered in person to recipients, and litigants had to get themselves to the township administration in time for their assigned hearings. Most travel between the township administration and the settlements under its jurisdiction took place on foot or using horses.

The regulations on rural administration prescribed a maximum distance of 12 versts (8 miles) from the most outlying settlement to the central point of the township. This distance could be extended if the region was so sparsely populated that fewer than six hundred people would reside in an area defined by this radius.[20] The courts I studied showed that these regulations had been quite rigorously observed when townships were delineated. The township administration was not always located at the physical center of each township, but the distance to the administrative center and thus the court was never more than 14 versts in townships located in the central regions of European Russia, and not more than 20 versts in the thinly populated Zaborovskii Township of Novgorod Province. The mean distance of villages from their township administrations for seven townships in Moscow Province was 5.7 versts; for courts in St. Petersburg Province, 6.9 versts; and for Zaborovskii Township in Novgorod Province, 8.2 versts.

These distances did not affect usage of township courts. Plaintiffs at courts I surveyed did not come exclusively from the settlements close to the township administration, but instead from settlements scattered throughout the township as well as from outside its borders. The mean distance that separated plaintiffs in my survey from their township court was 4 versts, or 2.6 miles; defendants charged in their townships lived at a mean distance of 3.8 miles from the court. Almost three-quarters of the plaintiffs who were registered within the townships I studied and just over three-quarters of defendants registered in townships where their cases were called lived within 5 versts of the court.[21] These distances were manageable on foot, although getting to court and back required a considerable expense of time and effort.

How long did it take for the township administration to organize and muster the appearance of all parties at a case? My survey shows that township administrations generally scheduled cases promptly after they were registered. For example, on 13 January 1909, in the dead of the northern winter in Novgorod Province, Anton Andreev Smetanin filed a suit at the Zaborovskii Township Court against his own brother in a dispute over inherited land. The hearing date was set for a little more than two months later at 9:00 A.M. on 21 March. Three summonses—one to Anton himself, one to his brother, Pavel, and one addressed to three witnesses, Fedor Vasiliev Khonin, Ivan Vasilev Sanin, and Mikhail Smetanin—were all delivered and signed for on 8 March 1909. The case was heard on schedule and was decided on 21 March.[22]

Smetanin was a litigious man who took himself or was taken to the Zaborovskii Township Court repeatedly.[23] His case against his brother was heard almost nine and a half weeks after it was filed. This interval was longer than usual for the Zaborovskii court. Two years later a widow asking this court for a share of her husband's property filed her request on 24 May 1907. Three summonses were sent out; of these, one was received as early as 29 May. The case was heard and decided on 17 June, three and a half weeks after its registration.[24] In January and February 1905 the mean time between filing a case and a hearing at this court in the northern lake district was eight and a half weeks. In May 1906, at the Ignatevskii Township Court in Moscow Province, with its easier communications network, the mean interval between registration and hearing was only five and a half weeks. Litigants at this court could anticipate that hearings would take place within a few weeks and rarely more than three months after the filing of a complaint.

Speedy processing of complaints meant that cases could be settled promptly at township courts. For all cases I surveyed, including those in wartime, the average time between registering a case and the court hearing was 8.8 weeks. Official statistics on Moscow Province confirm this record of efficiency. For the entire period from 1905 through 1914, between 90 and 94 percent of all cases registered at the province's 168 township courts were heard within the same calendar year in which they were filed. The compact territory of the township facilitated the work of the courts. Prompt scheduling of hearings, rapid and effective delivery of summonses, and the willingness of litigants to obey them, meant that justice at the township courts was swift.

A SUNDAY IN THE COURTROOM

There was no set day on which township courts were required to hear their cases. *The General Regulation on Peasants* specified that township courts were to meet at least twice a month, "principally on Sundays and other holidays." If necessary, courts could meet more frequently and on other days.[25] The designation of a holiday as a time for court sessions seems to correspond to the state's priorities: workdays were not disrupted by justice. Township authorities adhered to the principle, if not the letter, of these rules. Hearings at most courts I surveyed were held from twice to five times a month. The number of court days each month and their scheduling were adjusted to accommodate local needs.

In 1905 the Iaguninskii Township Court in Moscow Province met twice a month from January through April, three times in May, twice in June, four times in July, five times in August, three times in September and October, and twice in November and December.[26] For most of the year, this court held its sessions on weekdays, not on Sundays or holidays as recommended. An outsider might expect that the court would meet less frequently in the summer when the harvest was in full swing, but local circumstances called for a different approach. Long hot days and nights of work in the fields generated many cases at the court. Rather than postpone hearings until a calmer time, the Iaguninskii authorities scheduled extra sessions in July and August, and held their hearings in these months exclusively on Sundays and other major holidays.[27] Thus, in winter, when demands of labor and for justice were not as acute, the Iaguninskii court met on the occasional weekday; in summer, people took themselves to court on Sundays and other holidays to deal with numerous, apparently urgent suits at the cost of a precious day of rest.

The Iaguninskii court's schedule was not universal, but in all townships the frequency of court days and the number of cases heard at each session varied over the course of the year. At the Zaborovskii Township Court in Novgorod Province, where the population was less dependent on fieldwork and crops came in on a northerly cycle, people registered a large number of complaints in February. Each court's agenda responded to local priorities, and balanced the intersecting demands of law and labor in its own way. (See Charts 3.1 and 3.2 for the schedules of Ignatevskii Township Court in Moscow Province and the Zaborovskii Township Court in Novgorod Province in 1906.)

Township courts might meet on different days, but their procedures were similar. A day at court would begin in the morning, when people summoned to hearings would arrive at the township administration building. The judges and the clerk would be seated at a table in the room used by the court. The judges would be wearing official medallions as well as any personal awards they had earned; they would be dressed in their best clothes.[28] The table, covered with a cloth, would have an inkwell and a stamp for impressing the township seal on documents, as well as record books and legal codes used by the clerk. One of the three or four judges would be the president of the court, who declared the court open and asked the participants to observe silence. The president would then call parties in the first case to come forward.[29] No oaths were administered, and no references were made to religious authorities in the court record.

Each hearing followed a similar procedure. After the parties had been called into the room, the president would ask the plaintiff to present orally the reasons for the complaint or suit. The plaintiff would present his or her case, which would be written down by the clerk. After the plaintiff finished speaking, he or she would be asked to sign the casebook just below the recorded testimony. With these signatures participants vouched for the truth of their testimony and signaled their participation in the court's proceedings. If a participant was illiterate, the president would sign in his or her stead, and enter the word "illiterate" in the record. After the plaintiff had testified and signed, the president would ask the defendant to present a response to the suit or accusation. The defendant, like the plaintiff, testified orally and then signed the record of

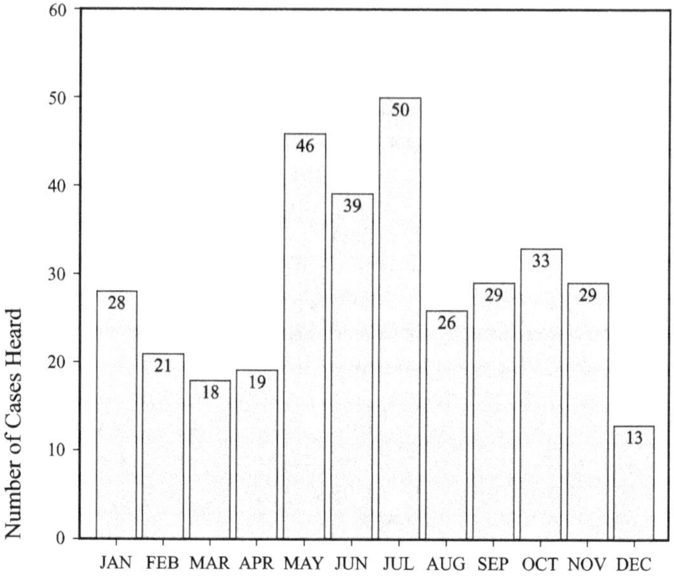

Chart 3.1. Cases Heard per Month, Ignatevskii Township Court, 1906. *Source: Date Survey.*

the statement. At this point, the judge would ask the parties if they could be reconciled. If reconciliation could be achieved, this would be written into the record book and the case would be closed. If the parties did not agree to reconcile, the judges proceeded to hear witnesses and to examine any other testimony. Witnesses, too, were asked to sign their testimony.[30]

Witnesses appeared in more than half the township court cases in my survey. At these courts one or more witnesses testified in 59 percent of cases heard before the war. In 27 percent of cases, one witness testified; in 32 percent of cases, two or more witnesses came to court. Occasionally as many as seven witnesses appeared in these prewar cases. People appeared as witnesses in various informal or official capacities.[31] At the Iaguninskii Township Court witnesses simply identified themselves as peasants in almost all cases, but occasionally a local policeman participated in court proceedings.

When all testimony had been heard, the judges made their decision. Observers noted that usually the judges went into a separate room to consult, and that often the clerk, legal codes in hand, went with them. The clerk would draw up a text of the judges' decision, providing a brief account of the reason for the outcome. The president would read the decision to the parties; immediately thereafter he would announce the procedures for appeal. The plaintiff and defendant, all the judges, and the clerk would then conclude the case by signing their names to the record book. In most cases litigants would indicate in the record book whether they were "satisfied" or "unsatisfied" with the decision.[32]

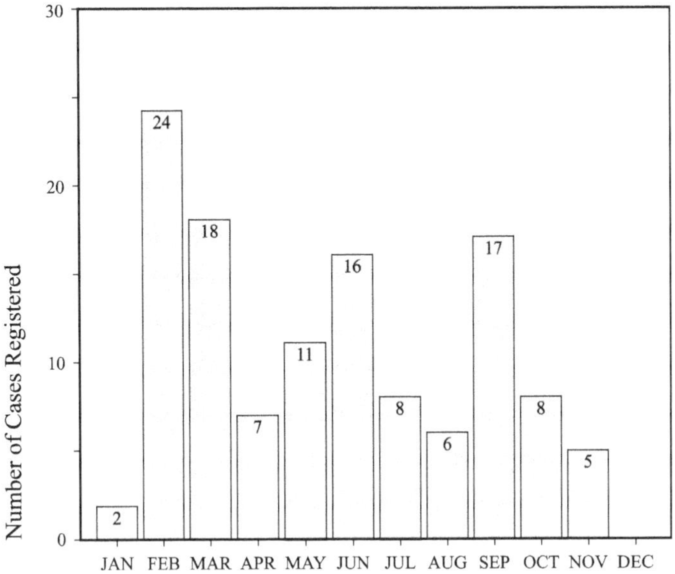

Chart 3.2. Cases Registered per Month, Zaborovskii Township Court, 1906. *Source: Date Survey.*

On one of those trouble-filled Sundays, 28 August 1905, President N. A. Kvardakov opened a session of the Iaguninskii Township Court west of the city of Zvenigorod in Moscow Province. Awaiting him, as well as the other judges, N. Pavlov and I. Novov, and the clerk, Adrian Terent'evich Akimov, was a docket of eight cases, two civil and six criminal. The week before, on Sunday 21 August, the judges had heard four civil cases and no criminal ones. Overall, in August 1905, sixteen civil cases and nine criminal cases were decided at Iagunino. This day, 28 August, had a large share of all the criminal cases heard that month.

The first of the two civil cases was a suit brought by a male peasant from the village of Toropenki—literally, "Little Hurry-Up"—against one of his neighbors for thirty rubles. The problem concerned a barn. The plaintiff had purchased this barn from the defendant for thirty rubles and had agreed at the time of the sale to allow the seller to store grain in the barn until his death. But later, the plaintiff claimed, the defendant had sold the barn to someone else. This elicited a long consideration of evidence by the court. In the end, the judges decided in favor of the plaintiff and awarded him thirty rubles.[33]

The second civil case of the day was brought by a man of noble status, Boris Varlamovich Karazin, who resided in the vicinity of the village of Anashkino. Karazin was one of the rare members of the nobility who exercised his right to bring a charge at the township court. He accused a peasant from the nearby village of Ust'e of allowing eight cows to trample grain on his fields. This charge of trampling (*potrava*) was one of the several kinds of conflicts over crops and land use that appeared frequently at township courts. After a long hearing, the judges awarded Karazin eight rubles for his losses.[34]

The first two criminal cases were brought by peasants against other peasants who had refused to pay family support to needy relatives. These cases were considered and recorded as "violations of family rights" under statute 143 of the misdemeanor code.[35] The judges condemned a man from the Spasskaia sloboda, six versts from Iagunino, to "harsh arrest" for fifteen days and to pay his father ten rubles each month over the course of a year for upkeep of the family. ("Harsh arrest" meant that he would be fed only bread and water.) In the second of these cases, Vasilii Artunov from Ust'e was confronted by fellow villagers for not having paid family support. Artunov confessed his guilt and was sentenced to seven days of "simple arrest" in the township jail. Despite the defendant's confession and punishment, the decision did not reconcile the parties. The judges informed the plaintiff that he could begin a civil suit against Artunov for damages.[36]

The next three cases heard on 28 August involved accusations of rowdiness and other kinds of uncivil behavior. These cases had been filed by the local policeman, Constable Malorossianov, who was quartered in a nearby settlement, the Savvinskaia sloboda. In response to a complaint from Trofim Afanasiev, a resident of Iagunino, the constable charged a group of peasant men, all registered in Iagunino itself, with violations of statute 38, which covered "arguments, fights, fisticuffs, or other sorts of rowdiness in a public place and violations of the civil peace." Mikhail Nikolaev, Fedor Baranov, Nikolai Fedotov, Fedor Ivanov, Emelian Ivanov, and Semyon Lukhin were accused by Afanasiev of making noise "around his house" late at night on 22 April. The judges decided that there was insufficient evidence of the violation, and the defendants were acquitted.[37]

The next two cases went somewhat better from the constable's perspective. He accused a peasant man living in the Savvinskaia sloboda of "making noise, swearing with improper words and generally carrying on shamelessly . . . without a shirt." Aggravating the seriousness of these disruptive behaviors was their context: at the time, a holiday, many people had been in the Savvinskaia sloboda. Testimony in this case convinced the judges that the charge under statute 43 was "fully proven." The misbehaver was sentenced to fifteen days of arrest.[38]

The final case brought by Constable Malorossianov concerned another resident of the Savvinskaia sloboda, peasant Mikhail Alekseev Lobzinov. The constable charged Lobzinov under statute 38 and testified that he had "in a highly unsober manner, made noise, sworn and generally disturbed the peace and quiet." When called on to tell his side of the story, Lobzinov declared that the charge was true and asked to have the punishment reduced. The judges were moved to grant his request. The opinion, recorded by Akimov, observed that the accusation was "fully attested to" but that the court would take into account Lobzinov's "sincere confession." The punishment was a "strong reprimand," delivered at the hearing. As with all other cases, this case concluded with instructions to both parties about how to appeal the decision, and with signatures, by all judges and both parties, of the official record. Lobzinov, apparently sober by then, signed his own name.[39]

The last case of the day involved a dispute over a fence. It was brought by two peasant men from the village of Ust'e. When called on to testify, Artamonov, the plaintiff, accused his fellow villager, Andrianov, of "*samoupravstvo*"—taking the law into one's own hands—when he broke down a fence Artamonov had constructed on his land. (On *samoupravstvo,* see chapter 5.) Andrianov, in turn, testified that it was true that Artamonov had put up a fence on his land, but with the permission of the "big *starshina*"—the head of the township administration—he, Andrianov, had taken it down. This failed to convince the judges, who convicted Andrianov under statute 142 of *samoupravstvo* and sentenced him to seven days' arrest.[40] This case concluded the docket at Iagunino for the day.

This day at the Iaguninskii Township Court provides a window on issues of importance to rural litigants throughout European Russia, but the docket should not be understood as typical of days at all township courts. It was the function of the court to deal with the particular—the particular interests, needs, and passions of individuals and the particular context in which they lived. The township courts of rural Russia, like other legal instances, applied established procedures to the resolution of a vast array of conflicts and aspirations. The state's straightforward rules structured court proceedings, enabled a flexible, open-ended setting for each trial, and empowered judges to make appropriate adjustments to the ways that cases were examined.

Sometimes it was necessary for the judges to visit a village in order to make a fair assessment of a case. This possibility was foreseen in the rules for the township courts, which stated that the court "examines cases not only at its permanent address but also away from it, going for this purpose, when circumstances require it, to the place where the case arose."[41] For example, in 1906, at the request of the village leader, the judges of the Iaguninskii Township Court went to the village of Rybushkino, "for the accomplishment of a local inspection . . . of the tearing down of a cellar-shop along the official lane, which belonged to the peasant Gordiono Merkalov Kurakin." During this hearing a map showing five plots of land and their measurements was drawn up and signed by all concerned users of these properties. The court's action in this case legitimated the revision of a local land agreement.[42]

This case, like others at Iagunino, exhibits the intersection of formal rules and pragmatism characteristic of local justice at township courts. N. A. Kvardakov and his fellow judges, still at their posts a year after our first visit to their court, could use their authority to facilitate a collective solution to a problem of rural renovation. Their resort to the location of the dispute was sanctioned by state regulations; their entering of a map into the official record guaranteed that a bargain among landowners would endure as a point of reference. In this case, as in the cases heard in August the year before, the Iaguninskii

Township Court exercised its state-granted powers in the cause of local harmony, civility, and welfare, with concern for questions of evidence and proof.

HOW A CASE ENDS

The announcement of a decision did not complete a case. First, there was some obligatory record-keeping to be done. The clerk had to write out his official account of the case, and each party was entitled to one free copy of the decision.[43] Once all documents were signed, the decision of the court, unless appealed, had to be fulfilled. Some decisions in civil cases required little follow-up—households were divided, land was transferred, orphans were handed over to their guardians, or, if a suit was judged "unproven," there were no payments or other transactions to enact. Acquitted defendants in criminal cases could simply go their ways once their cases had been recorded. But cases decided in favor of a plaintiff or an accuser usually involved some kind of payment or sanction, and it was up to the township authorities to see that the court's rulings were carried out.

Because township courts were empowered to decide civil conflicts involving sums of up to 300 rubles and cases about immovable property valued at 500 rubles or more, depending on the kind of land,[44] local officials might be required to collect quite large sums. In criminal decisions the array of "punishments" available to township judges included formal reprimands, fines from 25 kopeks to 30 rubles, and jail sentences of up to fifteen or, in special cases, thirty days. Corporal punishment was abolished in 1904 and was never mentioned in any of the thousands of cases I reviewed.[45] Fines were collected in cash, not in kind,[46] and were transferred to the township treasury of the court that decided the case.[47] Judges combined fines and arrests in a number of ways: a convicted person could be required to pay a fine or go to jail or both. Frequently judges set out the option of a fine or jail. Impoverished people sentenced to pay fines for misdemeanors were entitled by law to substitute jail sentences for their fines at the rate of one day of arrest per 2 rubles of fine.[48]

Judges worked precisely within these rules when sentencing people to arrest. The terms most commonly assigned in the criminal cases I studied were fifteen days (23 percent of all sentences), three days (17 percent), and five or seven days (14 percent each). Less than 3 percent of sentences were for more than fifteen days. When judges gave convicted people a choice of jail or a fine, they acted in the spirit of state regulations. At the courts I studied, 80 percent of sentences that spelled out alternative punishments designated days in jail equivalent to half the amount of the fine and up to the full amount. The most frequently assigned combinations of fines and days of arrest were a 10-ruble fine that could be fulfilled with 5 days of arrest, a 5-ruble fine that could be fulfilled with 3 days of arrest, and a 3-ruble fine that could be fulfilled with 2 days of arrest. Ten percent of criminal sentences defining alternative punishments offered a choice of 1 ruble or 1 day in jail.

As with jail sentences, fines and payments assessed by township judges fell entirely within limits set by court regulations. In the criminal cases I examined, fines varied from 50 kopeks to 16 rubles. Ninety percent of all fines were for 10 rubles or less. The most common fines were 10 rubles, 5 rubles, and 3 rubles, in that order. In contrast to fines, payments in civil cases were assessed at tremendously varying amounts, corresponding to the different kinds of suits brought to the courts. In the cases I examined, defendants in civil suits were ordered to make payments of as little as 1.5 or as much as 300 rubles—the limit set by the rules for the township court. Amounts of fines and payments generally reflected the modest resources of rural litigants. At the courts I studied, the majority of fines were for 20 rubles or less, and one-third of all payments ordered in civil suits were for sums of 10 rubles or smaller amounts.[49]

Decisions of township courts were to be put into effect "rapidly." Court rules gave township authorities some leeway in this task: "for particularly good reasons," arrests could be delayed for up to six months.[50] The courts overall adhered to the principle of prompt fulfillment of decisions; some cases were finished on the spot, but most were turned over to the township leader for completion. Because clerks were attentive about following up on decisions and entered the date when a sentence was completed in the court's records, it is possible to take a closer look at what due process meant for the convicted or the fined. Of the cases I surveyed, over 25 percent of jail sentences were completed within nine days of the hearing. Forty-five percent of all arrests had been fulfilled by the end of two months, and 70 percent by the end of three months. Ninety-four percent of recorded arrests were completed five months after the case. Thus, in almost all cases, sentences to confinement in the local jail were carried out well before the end of the six-month limit.

In my survey, violations of the six-month rule for arrests occurred only at the township court at Nagatino, just outside Moscow, where the defendants might have had an easy time disappearing into the city. Even so, all but one of these convicted people had fulfilled their sentences within seven and a quarter months. The only defendant in my study who managed to escape arrest for more than this interval was a twenty-two-year-old unmarried peasant woman, not registered in Nagatinskii Township, who was sentenced in absentia on 24 March 1914 to fifteen days of arrest for theft of a samovar and a pair of rubber boots. Even the unfortunate Anna Andreeva Sidorova was ultimately caught by the law: a year and a half later she fulfilled her sentence far away from Moscow at the city police station on the island of Kronshtadt in the Gulf of Finland near St. Petersburg. This conclusion of a case was noted in the record book by Mikhail Iakovlevich Belianchikov, the diligent clerk at Nagatino.[51]

The speed with which jail sentences were served suggests routine compliance with the law on the part of both convicted people and local authorities. Nineteenth-century observers noted that prisoners did not try to run away from the township jail, and there are no suggestions in the court records I read of any resistance to serving a sentence. The jail in rural areas was a simple room near the township administration. Those on "strict arrest" could expect to be fed only bread and water; others could have ordinary meals. Each day meant loss of work time and freedom, and separation from one's family, companions, and, in most cases, neighbors. It is difficult to know what this isolation from daily routine represented to a convicted person, but it is clear from court records that many a small-scale malefactor spent a few days in jail as a consequence of his or her behavior.[52]

If township authorities were speedy in getting people in and out of jail, they were slightly more lenient with the collection of fines and payments. Only 10 percent of fines and payments were collected within a month of the hearing date, whereas well over one-third of all jail terms had been fulfilled by this time. Some of these jail terms were served by people who, in accord with the terms of their sentences, had chosen to go to jail rather than to pay a fine; this practice reduced the number of fines township authorities had to collect. Although a lack of cash was probably at the heart of most civil suits, authorities still managed to collect most fines and payments rapidly. Within two months of the hearing date, half of all fines and payments had been collected in the cases I reviewed. Three-quarters had been collected within three months, and 90 percent within six months.

In a few cases in my records, losing parties made their payments more than a year after they had been assessed. One of these concerned the 8 rubles awarded nobleman Boris Varlomovich Karazin at the 28 August 1905 session of the Iaguninskii Township Court. This payment was not collected from the peasant defendant until 11 October 1906.[53] Another payment that was collected more than a year after the court decision also involved the Iaguninskii court; this payment was huge by township standards—100 rubles owed by one peasant to another according to a bill of exchange, outstanding since 1901. The Iaguninskii court ordered the debt paid in full on 30 May 1905 but did not collect this large sum until 28 September 1906.[54] The longest outstanding—and finally collected—payment I observed concerned a medium-sized debt of 8.5 rubles. This payment was assessed by the Iaguninskii Township Court on 14 August 1905, but the cash was not received by the plaintiff until 6 January 1907.[55] Authorities in other townships occasionally collected payments several months after a case was decided. At the Tsaritsynskii Township Court near Moscow on 29 January 1915 Ivan Andreevich Kuznetsov, from the village of Saburovo, was required to pay a debt of 1.5 rubles to Aleksei Alekseev Bumashkin from a neighboring village. This small sum was not collected until 12 December 1915, almost eleven months after the hearing.[56]

The different outcomes of these exceptional cases convey the quality of justice applied by township courts. Although township authorities acted expeditiously to fulfill decisions, they also exercised a degree of leniency, particularly with debtors in civil cases. Township officials did not apply the same flexibility to criminal cases. I found no records of fines collected more than four and a half months after a case was heard. Fines in criminal cases were collected more rapidly than payments in civil cases. Forty-eight percent of all fines in criminal cases were paid within a month of the trial, but only 10 percent of civil monetary judgments were collected by this time. The speedy collection of fines in criminal cases corresponded to the rapid pace at which jail sentences in criminal cases were fulfilled—45 percent of all sentences in unappealed criminal cases had been served within two months after the trial.

The discrepancy between fulfillments of civil and criminal decisions permits speculation about the motivations of local authorities. The pattern of generally prompt, occasionally slow, and ultimately successful payments in civil cases suggests that the law operated with a personal touch in rural areas. Law enforcers—the township leaders—could be counted on to collect legally recognized debts but were also capable of mercy or patience in the scheduling of payments.[57] The greater rapidity with which verdicts were fulfilled in criminal cases indicates that local authorities made distinctions among disruptive actions. The payment of legally defined debts was imperative, but in such cases delay could be important to accomplishing the goal.[58] Criminal acts, on the other hand, inspired prompt fulfillment of sentences. The flexibility of penalties in criminal cases, particularly the possibility of substituting a day in jail for each two rubles of fine, meant that most misdemeanors could be punished—this is the word used in the regulations, by courts, and by accusers—shortly after a court decision. Township officials may have been responding to higher authorities who were more concerned about crime than contracts between peasants,[59] but it seems more likely that local authorities themselves made distinctions between the different kinds of harm caused by civil or criminal violations.

Fulfilled in short order or delayed by a few weeks or months, what did these sentences and assessments mean to rural people? Court-assigned penalties can be compared to wages and prices in particular areas to suggest how fines or days in the local jail might affect an individual or a family.[60] In May 1908 the Ignatevskii Township Court, located in Bogorodskii County, Moscow Province, sentenced people in criminal cases to arrest for two days or to a fine of two rubles or to arrest for three days and to a fine of three rubles, in addition to ordering payments of eleven to fifty rubles in civil cases.[61] In this district at this time of year the average wage for a worker, on the employer's rations and without a horse, was fifty-six kopeks per day, as reported by Vasilii Andreevich Tunin, the court clerk.[62] If people convicted by the township court were paid at this average rate, a fine of two rubles in May 1908 would have cost an agricultural laborer, without a horse, just under four days in wages. Going to jail for two days would have entailed losing a little more than one ruble in wages. A fine of three rubles would have been the equivalent of about six days of work, and three days in jail would have meant only about one and a half rubles in lost wages to the imprisoned person.

These estimates offer insight into why culprits often chose jail, instead of a fine, but also into how local judges set fines and terms of arrest. If the judges had assessed jail sentences at the rate of one day of jail for a two-ruble fine, as in the exception allowed for insolvency, even more convicted people might have chosen jail, not paid township fines, and not suffered penalties financially equivalent to the value of the fine. The judges at the Ignatevskii court did not use the one-day, two-ruble ratio, and thus did not allow a convicted person to choose a reduced penalty. On the other hand, if these judges had been intent on maximizing fines, they would have had to set jail sentences that were at least double the fine. But this kind of calculation, which would have gone far beyond the formula for impoverished defendants, was never practiced. In my survey of cases, judges never set jail sentences higher than fines, except when the fine was less than one ruble.[63]

The ratio of days in jail to fines, as practiced at the Ignatevskii court, suggests the modulated pragmatism of township judges and, perhaps, acknowledges a loss beyond that of wages entailed by convicted people who went to jail. The basic formula for sentencing at this court was one ruble equals one day. A laborer who could receive average wages and was convicted of a small crime had a choice, for each ruble of fine, between working two days to pay his fine and losing these two days of wages or spending a day in jail and suffering the loss of only one day of work and wages—but also, we may surmise, an augmented affront to his dignity.

Another way of estimating the significance of a fine is to measure it against a major element in the family economy. In 1908, in Moscow Province, the average price for a peasant's horse was forty-two rubles in the winter or fifty-two rubles in the summer. A peasant's cow would sell for an average of forty-six rubles in the winter, or fifty-five rubles in the summer.[64] Fines of two or three rubles assigned in township courts in Moscow Province in 1908 thus represented roughly 4 or 5 percent of the summertime cost of a cow or a horse. The median fine for Moscow Province courts from 1905 to the outbreak of the war was five rubles—closer to 10 percent of the price of a horse or cow. This relationship of fines to prices provides a rough indication of the severity of penalties assigned by township courts. A five-ruble fine—the equivalent of ten days of work and a tenth of the price of a horse—was not a trivial sum for a peasant household. But such a penalty would not ordinarily destroy a family's economy forever.

HOW A CASE COULD LIVE BEYOND ITS TIME AND PLACE

Most cases at the township courts were not appealed, and this meant that, after fines and payments had been received or jail terms served, cases were over for the parties concerned.[65] But all cases had lives beyond these more or less rapid settlements, lives created by the records kept by township clerks. What clerks wrote down could be resurrected in future legal decisions, as in Praskovia Aref'eva's long suit. The record of a case could have a direct impact even many years later on property, power, and affect for inhabitants of a township and people connected with them. Once the court's record books had been submitted to the land captain for review, case documents became part of the network of printed and handwritten documents that bound people over many years into a society constituted in part through legalized memory. Archived records from township courts could have an even longer life, enabling historians and others to revisit the practiced legalism of an earlier time.

Keeping careful records was required by the regulations on the township court. These specified that an account of a hearing had to include the following vital information: the date ("year, month, day") when the decision was made; the names of the judges ("first and last names"); the estate status and names of all parties and witnesses; a "short account of the circumstances of the case on which the decision was based"; and the "essence" of the decision. For an appealed case, the clerk was required to note "all details necessary for the elucidation of the essence of the accusation or dispute and the decision."[66] These instructions are a testimony to lawmakers' concern for accuracy, individuality, and reason. Imperial regulations integrated township courts into a chain of legal authorities on terms that preserved the particularity of individuals, their claims, and their anticipated conflicts.

Books were essential to this ongoing and integrating practice of the law. Printed by private companies,[67] the volumes used by township clerks structured court procedures and organized information to be shared by litigants and authorities. The books on the table in the courtroom expressed a commitment to ongoing legal governance and accorded a degree of majesty to the law, its users, and its subjects. There was no standard record book for all township courts, either required or provided by the imperial government. Clerks and other local officials gave form to the law by configuring their court's record books and by taking down information in their own ways.

Official notions of legal process and the particularity of local practice were physically intertwined in the record of each case. In the books of the Tsaritsynskii Township Court in Moscow Province, four preprinted pages were allotted for every criminal decision. The text of a case began with a three-line title—

VERDICT
Of the Tsaritsynskii Township Court of Moscow District and Province
No. X

Then followed a grand but straightforward opening: "In 191_, on _____day, the *Tsaritsynskii Township Court of Moscow County* at its open session and composed of the President of the Court [*space for his name*], the Township Judges [*two lines for names*] in the presence of its clerk [*space for his name*] heard the criminal case concerning an accusation of . . ." Seven lines were left for the clerk to fill in a description of the case. Still on the first page of the record, several rubrics followed:

To the hearing of the case were called by summonses: The victim
[*two lines left blank for name(s)*]
The accused [*two lines for name(s)*]
Witnesses: For the side of the victim [*four and a half lines for names*]
For the side of the accused [*four lines for names*]

Did not appear at the hearing of the case [*three lines for names*]
It was resolved that the case would be [*space for "heard," "postponed," "ended"*]

The second page of each case record also had a title: "The Explanations of the Sides." More rubrics followed: "The Victim"—nine lines left blank; "The Accused in his defense testified"—15 blank lines. Then a third printed rubric: "Reconciliation was proposed to the sides, but this between them did not take place, the Court proceeded to the examination of the witnesses called to this case, about which witness . . ." Nine lines were left on this second page for witnesses' testimony. If reconciliation had been accepted, the case would have ended before witnesses were called. Very few criminal cases ended with reconciliation—less than 2 percent of the criminal cases I surveyed—and the case record anticipated continuation of the hearing.

Page three of a criminal record began with nine lines for further testimony by the witnesses. Part way down page three, a printed rubric announced the "Decision of the Court." The recorded decision began with the phrase, "Having considered the case at hand and listened to the explanations of the sides," followed by nine lines for the court to fill in its summary of the case. Another rubric followed the handwritten summary: "and therefore and under the 17th Statute of the Temporary Rules on the Township Court and on the basis of statute [*space for number*] of the Regulations for Punishments, Applicable by the Justices of the Peace, **SENTENCED**," followed by nine more lines for the sentence. The hearing record concluded with another printed rubric:

> This verdict was declared at the session of the court and explained with the right to appeal by an unsatisfied party within 30 days from the day of the declaration to the land captain of the 6th district of Moscow county, by the provision of a complaint in two copies to this Court.

Printed titles were provided to accompany the signatures of the "President of the Court" and the "Judges."

The case record was still not complete. Page four was entitled, "Page for notes on the fulfillment of this verdict." It was configured by four printed points of information:

1. When a copy of this verdict was given out [*two lines*]
2. When this verdict was appealed by an unsatisfied party and the proceedings of the Township Court about this presented to his Honor the Land Captain of the 6th district of Moscow County [*two lines*]
3. When the communication about the executing of this verdict was sent to the Township Leader [*two lines*]
4. When the verdict was carried out by the Township Leader

One final rubric for a signature was provided, this time for the township leader. The last printed heading on this four-page record was, appropriately, "Further Notes."[68]

Clerks used many variations on this format in their books.[69] The Nagatinskii Township Court added printed rubrics for the names and addresses of the accuser and accused at the end of the form, perhaps occasioned by the court's location near Moscow, where some litigants had street addresses.[70] The forms for recording civil cases were similar to this one for criminal cases, although the parties were called "plaintiff " and "defendant," rather than "accuser" or "victim" and "accused."[71] A civil case form might add a printed rubric concerning "written evidence" to the expected components of a case.[72] The statutes governing the court's powers to judge civil cases would be recorded for each case. A township administration might have forms preprinted for special purposes. The Tsaritsynskii Township clerk used a separate book to record cases that were ended before being heard by the court, with reasons provided for the official terminations.[73]

The record of a township court decision was never entirely formulaic. The clerk's account always made each case sensible as a whole narrative—with a charge or request, an exploration of the matter, a finding, a resolution, and an end to the case.[74] Record books usually provided two or four full pages for each hearing. If a case demanded more space than the printed pages offered, the clerk might squeeze an entry into the margin, extend the case a page or two, or provide for a continuation at another point in the book.[75] Clerks at the Iaguninskii and Ignatevskii courts in Moscow Province solved this problem by using a flexible design. All pages in their books for criminal and civil cases were lined to facilitate legible writing and headed with general rubrics—the case number, the "contents" of the decision or the verdict, and "when the decision was fulfilled." The account of the case, always accompanied by signatures of the court and litigants, could then be entered at whatever length the matter demanded. Most cases required two pages, but some took as little as half a page or as many as four pages to summarize.[76] Clerks adjusted record books to accommodate the scope of a case, rather than the other way around.

Variations in books used to record decisions display the personal attention of clerks to their tasks. At some courts, clerks kept separate record books for civil and criminal decisions. A "Book for Registering Decisions" was used for civil cases and a "Book for Registering Verdicts" for criminal ones, even though the judges in a township court often heard both kinds of cases in the same session.[77] In Novgorod Province the clerks at the Zaborovskii Township Court made record-keeping easier for themselves by keeping a single book for both civil and criminal cases. In 1905 this record book was called "Book No. 6 for the Registration of the Decisions of the Zaborovskii Township Court." In 1911 the same unified record book was entitled "Book for the Registration of the Decisions of the Zaborovskii Township Court of Civil and Criminal Cases in 1911."[78] The slight changes in the titles of these books suggest clerks' thoughtfulness about their duties. Occasionally a lapse or other problem in the supply of books meant that clerks had to improvise record-keeping procedures. At Iagunino in 1905 and 1906 the diligent clerk Adrian Terent'evich Akimov

№	СОДЕРЖАНІЕ РѢШЕНІЙ.	Когда исполнены рѣшенія.

Clerk's handwriting with flourishes, Iaguninskii Township Court, Moscow Province, 1905.

used a book prepared for civil cases to record criminal cases and at the same time kept a second "civil" case book for the real civil cases.[79] Two years later, in 1908, Akimov had to make other adjustments. That year he used a record book printed with rubrics for "orphans' courts" as his registry of complaints brought to the township court.[80] Perhaps the Iaguninskii administration had difficulties attaining the appropriate books on time, or perhaps the township was economizing on expenses.

Coordinating the different numbers assigned to complaints, hearings, and second hearings, and recording appeals, sentences fulfilled, and receipts for paid debts and fines, demanded careful attention to detail. Contrary to images of chaos and arbitrariness at the township court, the performance of clerks in this regard was exemplary. In every case in which I used a clerk's reference to a second record related to a case, such as an appeal or an earlier hearing, these entries had been accurately registered. This concern for getting the record right answered the state's demand for organized information, but it also had practical consequences for the administration of the township and for the well-being of people who lived in its settlements.

Keeping a record book was a formal, official activity, carried out with individualized skill and flair. Records were entered in ink. This necessitated some crossing out, when mistakes were made or when something in the hearing changed the clerk's initial entries. A clerk aspiring to elegance could embellish the legal record with elaborate flourishes or other decorative effects. The efforts taken to sustain record keeping even when the appropriately printed book was not at hand display the initiative and dedication of township officials. Local clerks, usually of peasant status, fulfilled the state's demand for bureaucratic accountability and at the same time wove a tissue of legal possibility for the future. Their routine professionalism transformed township hearings into official acts that could be accessed, reviewed, relied on, or challenged. The record books of township courts attached peasants' legal practice to the empire's wide web of law.

The magnificent documentary record created by rural officials stands in sharp contrast to charges of incompetence leveled against township courts. Clerks at all courts whose books I examined kept impeccable records, with only the occasional copying error or numbering mistake. The variety of record books and the inventive, functional usages of printed forms belie accusations of mindless formalism and impersonal bureaucracy. A township court record was a highly specific account of named and located individuals in confrontation with each other and with the personnel of the court, an account organized to give each litigant and witness room to speak. The preservation of testimony identified by its speaker was an ordinary but vital practice that sustained and produced a legal bond between imperial subjects. Litigants—accused, accusers, plaintiffs, and defendants—affirmed this connection when they put their signatures, or had the president of the court sign for them in their presence, on the records of their cases.[81]

LITIGATION BY POPULAR DEMAND

The township courts made due process—efficient, regulated, effective, and recorded justice—available to rural litigants, but were the courts responding to a demand for institutionalized legality? My argument that peasants perceived the township court system as a useful addition to and substitute for other official or informal rural institutions—village meetings, councils of elders, the village leader, gossip, collective violence—is based in part on the profusion of disputes brought to these courts in the late imperial period.[82] The records of the imperial administration demonstrate that peasants took their problems to the township courts in large and increasing numbers.

Peasants were not obliged to bring most cases to the township court. With the exception of criminal charges brought by local policemen, cases began because plaintiffs voluntarily filed complaints. Apart from townships located on the borders of the city of Moscow, police were involved in only a minority of criminal cases (see chapters 5 and 6). Most cases concerned matters of little interest to anyone outside a rural settlement: no official would bother to force suits about trampled grain or fences on township courts. Furthermore, nothing made it impossible for such issues to have been settled in the village by other institutions or by individuals on their own. Because the majority of civil and criminal cases brought to the township courts were initiated by peasants themselves, the numbers of cases at these courts are a powerful indicator of peasants' purposeful choice to use this legal instance.

Although statistics on numbers of cases heard at township courts were published yearly in official sources in early-twentieth-century Russia, the scale of activity in these courts was not analyzed or recognized as evidence of legal culture in the rural areas at this time.[83] Recent studies of the history of the township courts, however, display the widespread, enduring, and expanding resort to these courts by rural people. Cathy Frierson has identified a consistent pattern of increasing use of township courts from the 1870s to the turn of the century, based on statistics from several provinces.[84] The vitality of this instance in the early twentieth century is captured by records from Moscow Province in 1905, where township courts processed 47,761 cases in a single year (see Table 3.3).[85]

The 47,761 cases at Moscow Province township courts represent only the first layer of legal action taken by rural people in 1905. The Moscow Provincial Board, county congresses, land captains, and township courts constituted the ladder of judicial instances under the supervision of the Ministry of the Interior.[86] As Praskovia Aref'eva's case demonstrated, rural people could appeal township court decisions on up this hierarchy and beyond.[87] In Moscow Province in 1905, more than 60 percent of the criminal cases and more than 80 percent of the civil cases processed by the county congresses had originated in township courts, as had 42 percent of the criminal cases and 78 percent of the civil cases processed by the Moscow Provincial Board. Thus the township

Table 3.3. Number of Cases Processed in 1905 by Administrative-Judicial Institutions in Moscow Province

Legal Instance:	*Criminal Cases*	*Civil Cases*	*Administrative and Supply Cases*	*Total Cases*
Provincial Board	324 (1%)	789 (2%)	1,174 (10.4%)	2,287 (3%)
County Congresses	2,890 (9%)	5,022 (14%)	3,189 (28.3%)	11,101 (14%)
Land Captains	7,211 (22%)	3,833 (11%)	6,898 (61.2%)	17,942 (23%)
Township Courts	21,859 (68%)	25,902 (73%)	0 (0%)	47,761 (60%)
Total Cases	32,284(100%)	35,546 (100%)	11,261 (100%)	79,091 (100%)

Source: *OMG 1905*, pp. 81, 84, 92, 96, 100, 106, 112, 118, 125, 131.

courts of Moscow Province not only heard 60 percent of all cases processed in 1905 by the four administrative-judicial instances of Moscow Province, but they also produced the majority of cases heard on appeal at the three higher instances in this judicial hierarchy.[88]

The significance of appeals cases emanating from the township courts is open to multiple interpretations. Advocates of efficient governance interpret appeals as evidence of poorly functioning primary instances; other theorists may regard appeals as evidence of faith in the state's "higher" organs.[89] A more cautious point, but one significant to an exploration of legal culture, is that appeals display litigants' awareness of the available ladder of legal authorities. In his studies of appeals of civil decisions at township courts, Gareth Popkins observes that appeals in a number of provinces demonstrate "tenacious popular involvement" in judicial processes.[90] Litigants at township courts knew that if they were unsatisfied with decisions, there were higher legal authorities to which they could appeal. Both the large number of township court cases and the appeals generated by some of these cases testify to the extensive demand for legal action made by rural residents of Moscow Province at this time.

Another way of representing the attractiveness of township courts to rural people is to compare their usage with that of the other courts of imperial Russia. Public discourse of professionals at this time stressed the exceptionalism of township courts and the normality of other instances. Jurists regarded the circuit courts with their juries and lawyers as the embodiment of normal—by which they meant Western-style—law, and they abhorred both what they regarded as the irregular procedures of the township courts and the subordination of the township courts to the Ministry of the Interior rather than to the Ministry of Justice.[91] If one measures normality by numbers of cases processed and not by an abstract notion of "real law," a different picture emerges.

The relative usage of different kinds of courts can be assessed by comparing yearly statistical summaries produced by the Ministry of Justice and the governor's office in Moscow Province (see Table 3.4). As these compilations indicate, the township courts in Moscow Province received more than twice as many cases in a single year than the "normal" circuit courts. These statistics show the significant place of township courts in the legal system as a whole, and the im-

Table 3.4. Number of Civil and Criminal Cases Brought as First Instance: Circuit and Township Courts, Moscow Province, 1905

	Township Courts	*Circuit Courts*
Civil Cases	24,746	9,576
Criminal Cases	20,228	11,159
Total Cases	44,947	20,735

Source: *Sbornik statisticheskikh svedenii Ministerstva iustitsii*, vyp. 21, ch. 1: Svedeniia o lichnom sostave i o deiatel'nosti sudebnykh ustanovlenii evropeiskoi Rossii za 1905 (St. Petersburg: Senatskaia tipografiia, 1907), pp. 64, 84; *OMG 1905*, pp. 125, 131.

Table 3.5. Number of Courts of First Instance in Moscow Province, 1905

Type of Court	*Number of Courts*	*Percent of all Courts*
Township Courts	168	69.7%
Justices of the Peace	48	19.9%
Circuit Courts	14	5.8%
City Judges	11	4.6%
All First Instance Courts	241	100 %

Source: *Sbornik statisticheskikh svedenii Ministerstva iustitsii*, vyp. 21, ch. 1: Svedeniia o lichnom sostave i o deiatel'nosti sudebnykh ustanovlenii evropeiskoi Rossii za 1905 (St. Petersburg: Senatskaia tipografiia, 1907), pp. 18, 48; *OMG 1905*, pp. 122, 124.

portance of this instance as a locus for accumulation of legal experience, the shaping of a legal culture, and the connection of subjects to their polity.[92]

One reason for the vitality of township courts was their availability. Township courts were both nearby and numerous. The regulations establishing the township as an administrative unit of a very modest size guaranteed that a large number of township courts would be available and accessible to the rural population. Table 3.5 displays the number of first-instance courts of all types in Moscow Province in 1905, with the exception of the Moscow commercial court.[93] Constituting almost 70 percent of the courts available to inhabitants of Moscow Province, the township courts appear as the most "ordinary" of primary judicial instances.

The availability of the township courts to plaintiffs did not mean that court dockets were sparsely filled. Judges had some flexibility in the scheduling of hearings, but they still had large numbers of cases to decide each year. The average number of cases processed by a township court in Moscow Province in 1905 was 284.[94] The intensity of activity increased each year after 1905, rising to an average of 502 cases per court in 1913, and dropping off only after the outbreak of the war in 1914. The number of township courts in Moscow Province remained fixed at 168 during this period, while cases continued to pour in. In 1913 the 168 township courts of Moscow Province processed a total of 84,403 cases, an increase of 78 percent over the 47,761 cases processed

Table 3.6. Number of Cases Processed Yearly by Township Courts in Moscow Province, 1905–1914

Year	*Civil Cases*	*Criminal Cases*	*Total Cases*
1905	25,902	21,859	47,761
1906	26,778	24,425	51,203
1907	30,656	23,218	53,874
1908	36,238	24,221	60,459
1909	42,479	27,635	70,114
1910	44,552	25,930	70,482
1911	44,352	35,152	79,504
1912	47,121	35,470	82,591
1913	47,633	36,770	84,403
1914	46,676	27,331	74,007

Source: *OMG 1905–1914.*

in 1905. The relentlessly increasing numbers of civil cases, cases brought without any initiative by officials, demonstrates the robust demand for hearings at the township courts (see Table 3.6).

The enormous numbers of cases at the township courts, and an increase in these numbers over time, suggest, at a most basic level, that people brought cases to these courts with some anticipation of satisfaction and with some confidence in the usefulness of the endeavor. It is difficult to imagine that the more than 1 percent of the population of the region who in any given year brought cases to the township court did not respect the institution and its function.[95] It is more plausible to connect this outpouring of litigation with a widespread expectation by rural people that the township court could accomplish precisely what people in many settings hope for from the law—the resolution of conflicts and disputes in a nonviolent, regulated, and enduring fashion, authorized by the state and recognized as legitimate by the parties concerned.

WHY PEASANTS GO TO COURT: OFFICIALS' PERSPECTIVES

What kinds of problems did rural litigants seek to solve at township courts? Each year the imperial bureaucracy collected information on the numbers and kinds of cases submitted to the township courts. The categories and procedures established for clerks' annual reports reflect the priorities and concerns of officials in the Ministries of Interior and Justice, and offer an administrator's perspective on peasants' uses of the township courts. Imperial officials did not bother to understand the particulars of litigation or the origins of cases; their focus instead was on the scale of certain kinds of criminal activity and on the type of property settlements in the countryside.

Although civil cases outnumbered criminal ones at township courts, yearly reports on court activity always presented criminal cases first.[96] In official reports, criminal cases were grouped into eight broad categories, in this sequence: (1) misdemeanors against administrative order; (2) violations of decorum during church services; (3) violations of hunting and fishing regulations; (4) violations of passport regulations; (5) violations of regulations on construction and transportation; (6) personal insults; (7) theft, swindling, and fraud; and, finally, a catch-all category, (8) "all other kinds of misdemeanors." Each of these categories, with the exception of the last, corresponded to a section in the misdemeanor code used by the township court, the *Statutes on Punishments Applicable by the Justices of the Peace.*[97]

Local clerks' reports on numbers of cases in each of these official categories provide a rough indication of which kinds of petty crime were prosecuted in the township courts. According to records from 1910 from Moscow Province, the most common crime to come before township judges was a "personal insult." A total of 13,939 insult cases accounted for 54 percent of all criminal cases; insults were the most common "crime" adjudicated at township courts in all thirteen counties of the province. Across the province, the next most common criminal category in annual reports was "all other kinds of misdemeanors." These 8,098 miscellaneous actions constituted 31 percent of all criminal cases. "Thefts, swindling, and fraud"—a category of particular concern to the government[98]—came in a distant third, at 9 percent (2,373 cases). Each of the other categories listed in official reports was filled in with small numbers. One county in Moscow Province accounted for all but 2 of the 113 "violations of decorum during church services," a crime that had been officially abolished in 1906 but perhaps lingered in the visions of a few stalwart churchgoers in this area.[99] The most derisory number of criminal cases filed were those reported as "violations of hunting and fishing regulations." There were only 91 such prosecutions out of 25,930 criminal cases at the township courts of Moscow Province in 1910.[100]

Reports on civil cases also show incongruities between official categories and peasant litigation. Imperial authorities divided civil cases into seven reporting rubrics: (1) disputes over peasant allotment property held communally; (2) disputes over peasant allotment property held by single households; (3) "all kinds of disputes and suits" over immovable property; (4) "all kinds of disputes and suits . . . about all other kinds of disputes and suits"; (5) inheritance and family divisions of communally held possessions; (6) inheritance and family divisions of household-held possessions; and (7) inheritance and family divisions of non-allotment property. Civil cases indeed arrived in large numbers at the township courts, but the state's categories allow us to see little about their content. Taking 1910 and Moscow Province as an example once again, of 42,308 civil cases, 31,879, or 75 percent, were about "all kinds of disputes and suits . . . about all other kinds of disputes and suits." In other words, the state's residual category was the relevant rubric for three-quarters of the civil cases processed by township courts of Moscow Province. The next most populated rubrics were disputes over communally held peasant allotment property—4,667 cases, 11 percent of civil cases—and cases concerning inheritance and family divisions of communally held property—3,453 cases, 8 percent of civil cases.[101]

The state's categories were clearly not up to the task of describing in any detail why people went to court, but they neatly display the way officials imagined and measured the legal activism of rural people. Township clerks had to confront the discrepancies between state categories and township realities each year as they filled out reports on court activity. In 1910 Dmitrii Gerasimovich Vasil'ev, the diligent, long-serving clerk of Sharapovskii Township in Zvenigorod County of Moscow Province,[102] duly constructed a handwritten chart using the rubrics provided by higher judicial authorities. As in most years, he left blank or put insignificant numbers under many official categories. He made no entries for "a breach of decorum during church services," violations of the hunting and fishing regulations, violations of the passport regulations, violations of regulations on construction and transportation, disputes over allotments held as household property, disputes and suits over immoveable property, inheritance, and divisions of single-household property, or inheritance and division of non-allotment property. Out of 115 criminal cases, Vasil'ev recorded 11 misdemeanors against the administrative order and 9 cases of theft, swindling, and fraud. All but 5 of the 235 civil cases processed by the Sharapovskii court in 1910 were entered in two categories: 82 cases about communally held allotments and 128 "miscellaneous disputes and suits." Of the 115 criminal cases, 82 were registered as personal insults.[103]

The report of the Sharapovskii township court was not unusual. For Moscow Province as a whole in 1910, the most common kind of case processed at a township court (47 percent of all cases) fell into the category of "all other kinds of disputes and suits." The second most common kind of case in the province was a charge of insult—20 percent of all cases in the province, 24 percent at the Sharapovksii Township Court. Sharapovskii Township had a larger share of civil cases about communal property (24 percent) than had the courts of the province as a whole (7 percent), and Sharapovskii judges heard fewer "miscellaneous" criminal suits than other judges (3 percent as opposed to 12 percent in the province). The variations between Vasil'ev's report and the statistics on the entire province indicate that township courts were responding to the varying demands of their local clients (see Table 3.7).

Despite blind spots in officials' field of visions, provincial statistics suggest some preliminary conclusions about why peasants went to court. Global figures for the township courts in Moscow Province in 1910 show that the most common problem taken to these courts was a civil suit, described by point 2 of statute 125 of *The General Regulation on Peasants:*

> All kinds of disputes and suits between people under the jurisdiction of the Township Court, of a value of up to three hundred rubles, with the exception of suits over the right of ownership or right to possession of immovable property, based on enserfment or recruiting documents.[104]

What brought people to court most often was some kind of suit not about land, with a value of up to three hundred rubles. Second, personal insults, the number one cause of criminal cases, accounted for one-fifth of all cases at town-

Table 3.7. Numbers and Percentages of Decided Cases by Official Category, Moscow Province Township Courts and Sharapovskii Township Court, 1910

Category	*All Township Courts from Provincial Statistics*		*Sharapovskii Township Court from Clerk's Record*	
	Numbers	Percent	Numbers	Percent
Suits, "All Other Kinds" (Civil)	31,879	46.7%	128	36.7%
Personal Insults (Criminal)	13,929	20.4%	82	23.5%
"All Other Kinds of Misdemeanors" (Criminal)	8,098	11.9%	12	3.4%
Disputes over Communal Property (Civil)	4,467	6.5%	82	23.5%
Inheritance, Family Division, Communal Property (Civil)	3,453	5.1%	25	7.2%
Thefts, Swindling, and Fraud (Criminal)	2,373	3.5%	9	2.6%
Misdemeanors against the Administrative Order	676	1.0%	11	3.1%
Eight Remaining Official Categories	3,363	4.9%	0	0 %
Total Cases	68,238	100 %	349	100 %

Source: *OMG 1910*, pp. 114–117, 122–123; TsGIAgM, f. 846, op.1, d. 4, ll. 1–5.
Note: The total number of cases in Table 3.7 is lower than the total number of cases in Table 3.6, because Table 3.7 shows cases decided in 1910 while Table 3.6 shows all cases registered for processing in that year.

ship courts throughout the province in 1910. The state provided a category for this kind of crime, much prosecuted by people at the township courts. The third most common reason to go to court in 1910 was a criminal case involving "all other kinds of misdemeanors." These "other kinds" of petty crime that accounted for 12 percent of all cases in the province might have had implications for imperial governance, but the administration remained ignorant of their content. Fourth and fifth among officially categorized cases were disputes, inheritance, and family divisions concerning communally held property. The share of such cases (12 percent for these categories combined) at the township courts in Moscow Province displays the court as a site for legitimating control over the most important economic asset of rural people—their lands and homesteads. The state's category of theft, like that of insult, described with appropriate specificity a crime that came before the township courts. Although theft at 4 percent of all cases paled beside insults and "all other kinds of misdemeanors" as a criminal accusation at the township courts, it still was a matter of significance to rural people.

All these issues—suits over movable property, insults, miscellaneous misdemeanors, control over communal property, and theft—were more prominent at the province's township courts than misdemeanors against the administrative order. Challenges to governmental authority were of obvious interest to those who administered the countryside, either from a distance or within arm's reach of the governed. Three statutes of the *Statutes on Punishments Applicable by the Justices of the Peace* defined misdemeanors of this type that were to be prosecuted by township courts. Statute 31 dealt with insults directed against "policemen, . . . guards, employees of judicial and administrative institutions, . . . field or forest watchmen, while carrying out their duties." Statute 33 criminalized the damaging of official "insignia, signs, or advertisements . . . and public monuments . . . without the intention of showing lack of respect for the authorities." Statute 34 punished making public announcements without having obtained permission, where such was required.[105] More serious anti-government actions would have been prosecuted by other authorities and courts.

Eight of the state's categories—breaches of decorum in church, hunting and fishing violations, violations of the passport rules or of rules on construction and transportation, suits over property held by households rather than communes, disputes over reinstatement of violated immovable property, inheritance and family divisions of non-communal, non-allotment property—were very infrequently used by township litigants. These empty categories can have different meanings. Some kinds of property were uncommon in the countryside or not subject to regulation through the township courts. Some "crimes" may not have inspired local people to take action. There may have been many "violations of hunting and fishing regulations" in Moscow Province, but few such actions ended up in litigation at the courts. The township court was the place for resolution of more neighborly kinds of affairs, like disputes over inheritances, like insults, like a myriad of local headaches that could find redress before peasant judges.

The awkward fit between the rubrics provided for the scribe and the actual case record displays a disjuncture between what officials looked for and what peasants brought to trial. Official statistics nonetheless establish that peasants, provided with a legal institution outside but not far from their villages, used this opportunity extensively to solve conflicts they defined in their own ways. The generalizing reports on the township courts of Moscow Province provide a rough guide to the types of cases heard at township courts—suits, insults, other kinds of misdemeanors, control of land and family property, and finally theft. The increasing numbers of such cases heard at township courts display the attraction of legal process to peasants seeking justice in the Russian countryside. To see more clearly the content of their complaints and actions, we must turn to records kept by township clerks.

All Sorts of Suits and Disputes

CIVIL CASES AND RURAL SOCIETY

Moving from statistics produced by provincial administrators to on-the-table books used in township courts brings the content of rural litigation into closer focus. Clerks' handwritten accounts of cases display the topics of legal disputes as claimants described them to judges. Civil cases at township courts were about resources—money, commodities, labor, land, and other property. Suits over economic issues highlight the importance of law in the working lives of rural people. The resolution of civil suits (*grazhdanskie dela*) was a building block of civic life (*grazhdanstvennost'*) for rural communities. Township judges settled business disputes, enforced collection of debts, legitimated inheritance of property, and took resources out of the hands of the incompetent. The ability to use law effectively and rapidly for these purposes enhanced the economic and social possibilities of rural people. Township courts provided a venue for rural people to come to peaceful settlements of property disputes, even at a time when the state was making fundamental changes in rural land law. A close examination of cases peasants chose to present before legal authorities reveals what can be called a civil society in the countryside.[1]

Civil and criminal actions were not separated in life, and they coexisted in township court practice. The same judges often heard both civil and criminal cases in a single session, as on our day at the Iaguninskii court (see chapter 3). But court authorities did not blur the line between the two types of cases; the recognition that both losses and injuries caused to individuals were harmful to society was expressed by the provision of a legal way to address each kind of violation of the social order. Trampling of crops could give rise to a civil action for damages or to an accusation of criminal violation of rights or to both. Not paying family support was a criminal offense; it might also become a cause for an overburdened relative or other guardian to bring a civil case for damages to the township courts. Usually cases began under the appropriate rubric; occasionally judges advised litigants to begin a different kind of case.[2] The distinctions between civil and criminal cases were preserved scrupulously in case records, court decisions, and reports to higher authorities.

The jurisdiction of township courts in civil cases was set forth in *The General Regulation on Peasants*.[3] Point 1 of the empowering Statute 125 concerned "disputes and suits between peasants over immovable property forming part of a peasant allotment." Point 2 of this statute covered "all manner of disputes and suits between people subject to the township court up to the value of three hundred rubles, with the exception of suits concerning the right of ownership or rights of possession of immovable property based on acts of serfdom or recruitment." Point 3 concerned the same matters as point 2, if they were brought by people not under the authority of the township court against people under its authority. Point 4 singled out "matters concerning inheritance and [family] divisions among inheritors of peasant property" without limit of value if the property formed part of a peasant allotment, and up to five hundred rubles if the property was located in the township and was not part of a peasant allotment.[4]

These categories reflect the ways that state administrators conceived of economic conflicts in the countryside. The regulations described three kinds of property—peasants' agricultural allotments, movables, and family holdings—and anticipated four kinds of potential litigators—rural societies (who might dispute allotments between villages), individual peasants, people not subject to the township's authority, and peasant families. The statutes on court jurisdiction opened the way for peasants to settle disputes over several kinds of property in a legal forum.

Imperial law gave peasants access to legal process but did not require them to use it for civil matters. As in other times and places, most conflicts over property would end in agreements between parties, or by one side giving up, rather than by formal adjudication. Even in populations considered legally aware and active, only some injurious experiences turn into grievances; only some grievances are voiced as claims against offending parties; only some claims continue as disputes between opponents; and only some disputes are taken to formal litigation. Over the course of the twentieth century people in the United States resorted to civil litigation to resolve only a minority of their miscellaneous disputes. Estimates about legal action in other societies confirm the reasonable assumption that people ordinarily come to terms—or not—with each other without going to court. It is impossible under all but the most restricting circumstances to discover with any precision the proportion of potentially adjudicable situations that end as legal cases.[5] We must assume that, before turning to the township court, Russian peasants, like other people, often tried to settle claims by informal means, such as direct negotiations with the delinquent individual, family, or neighbors, or through the legal authority of the village society.

Set against the many means of dispute resolution available to rural people, the extensive usage of township courts for civil cases displays a robust demand for legal decisions on the part of Russian peasants. Their uses of township courts stemmed from a wide array of motivations, suggested in case records. Resentments, greed, violations of trust and duty, obliviousness to family obligations, as well as desires for fair treatment, loyalty, and forgiveness—all these might lie behind civil cases that ultimately made their way to township courts. Whatever the personal characteristics of Russian peasants who pursued their interests at township courts, their cases express familiarity with a world of business and property relations backed up by the law.

SUITS AT TOWNSHIP COURTS

According to provincial statistics, three-quarters of all civil cases—and almost half (47 percent) of all cases—heard in 1910 at township courts in Moscow Province were miscellaneous "disputes and suits" of up to three hundred rubles in value and not about land (see chapter 3). My survey of subjects of civil cases heard from 1905 through 1917 is consistent, though not identical, with statistics from Moscow Province. Case descriptions entered by township clerks in several areas produced six types of civil cases, categorized as they were registered by plaintiffs; of these, 78 percent were "suits" (see Table 4.1). Confirmations of inheritance arrangements and family divisions accounted for 17 percent of cases. The remainder of civil cases concerned family support, guardianships, or evictions of tenants.

The imbalance between suits and other kinds of cases does not mean that family settlements, such as inheritance and guardianship, were not issues of concern to rural litigants. Many an inheritance settlement or a guardianship could produce a suit at the township court, particularly during the war years. But these family property matters could be processed officially at other levels—by the village assembly, for example. The township court was not essential, even if it could be useful, for their execution.[6] What made the township courts particularly attractive to rural people, clerks' records suggest, was the possibility of settling "all manner of disputes and suits" in a legalized setting. Point 2 of Statute 125 of *The General Regulation on Peasants* opened up a floodgate: by the early twentieth century suits had become the major cause of litigation at the township courts.

What was the content of these multitudinous suits? At the most basic level, suits were about cash. People went to court to recover or receive a sum of money they believed was owed them. In most suits, plaintiffs requested a specific amount of money. In my survey of suits brought before the war, 73 percent of

Table 4.1. Subjects of Civil Cases, 1905–1917

Subject	*Frequency*	*Percent*
Suit	275	78.3%
Inheritance	46	13.1%
Family Division	15	4.3%
Eviction	7	2 %
Guardianship	5	1.4%
Other Civil Charge	3	0.9%
Total	351	100 %

plaintiffs designated a sum of money as the objective of their case. Occasionally plaintiffs sued for damages, the possession of an object, or a piece of land, without specifying a value.[7]

The sums of money requested by peasant plaintiffs were modest by elite standards but clearly meaningful to litigants. Almost half (48 percent) of prewar civil suits were for ten rubles or less. Another 23 percent were for between ten and twenty rubles. Amounts requested by peasant plaintiffs varied from two rubles, ten kopeks, to three hundred rubles—the maximum allowed under the court regulations. The median request in prewar suits in my survey was eleven rubles, thirty kopeks. Amounts sought by plaintiffs varied from court to court. Suits at the Iaguninskii court in Moscow Province were for smaller amounts than at other courts; plaintiffs in Zaborovskii Township in Novgorod Province filed a larger proportion of big suits. At no court I studied were more than half the suits filed for more than fifteen rubles. These figures suggest the persistent demand on the part of rural plaintiffs to settle cash obligations with people of modest means, as well as the precision with which plaintiffs kept their accounts. At the Ignatevskii Township Court, for example, there was no such thing as a whole ruble suit below the grand sum of eight rubles. Suits were filed for four rubles, twenty-six kopeks; four rubles, eighty-three kopeks; five rubles, thirty-two kopeks; and so on—amounts that recall the exigencies of this region of small-scale manufacturing, outputting, and commerce.

Money was thus a major issue at township courts; peasant litigators were clearly active in markets, and measured the value of possessions and commodities in rubles. But if money was the ordinary object of a suit, the controversies that led to suits at township courts were anything but uniform. From clerks' records, I identified twenty-three different causes of suits cited by peasants in their complaints or during hearings. Table 4.2 offers a glimpse of the ordinary actions—or inactions—that could push someone to begin a suit against a neighbor or other people at a township court.

The most common reason for a suit at the township courts I studied was a debt (20 percent of all suits). Controversies over land came next with 14 percent of cases, followed by unspecified suits (11 percent) and unspecified payments (10 percent). Other sources accounting for more than 5 percent of suits were "losses" designated in rubles, controversies over movable property, and

Table 4.2. Subjects of Suits, 1905–1917

Subject	*Frequency*	*Percent*
Debt	54	19.6%
Land Controversy	37	13.5%
Payment	28	10.2%
Losses, Money	20	7.3%
Possession Controversy (Not Land)	18	6.5%
Willful Harvesting	15	5.5%
Rent Controversy	13	4.7%
Sale Controversy	10	3.6%
Trampling by Animals (*Potrava*)	9	3.3%
Damaging Property	8	2.9%
Expenses	4	1.5%
Family Support (*Posobie*)	4	1.5%
Document(s)	3	1.1%
Usage Controversy (Land, Meadow)	4	1.5%
Fence Controversy	3	1.1%
Trespass (Animals)	3	1.1%
Work Controversy	3	1.1%
Eviction	2	0.7%
Family Division (*Razdel*)	2	0.7%
Live in House (Right to)	2	0.7%
Political Duties	2	0.7%
Taxes, Unpaid, etc.	1	0.4%
Wastefulness (*Motovstvo*)	1	0.4%
Suit (Unspecified Subject)	29	10.5%
Total	275	100 %

harvest violations. The sources of contention, described by litigants as the causes of their suits, can be aggregated to reveal the major areas of legal action. Business transactions—debts, payments, work controversies, expenditures, losses, and sales—accounted for 43 percent of all cited causes of civil suits from 1905 through 1917. Land was involved in 27 percent of these civil suits, in different ways. Fourteen percent of civil suits were occasioned, in the clerks' records, by a controversy over who in fact possessed a piece of land. Ten percent of civil suits began because of actions that took place *on* peasants' land—initiatives such as cutting grass, taking down a fence, or trampling grass on someone else's property. Peasants' suits over resources and possessions at the township courts displayed their active participation in a world of legally enforceable and enforced market relations.

Table 4.3 permits a closer look at the object-filled world of rural business. A profusion of items—crops, such as rye or oats or hay, bills of exchange, contracts, horses, cows, geese, sheep, outbuildings, logs, window frames, food, items of clothing—were named by plaintiffs as sources of the debts, losses, and possession controversies that occasioned suits. A sum of money was the most frequently named object in a suit (22 percent of cases). Eight percent of plaintiffs sued over *tovar*—a commodity, such as a piece of cloth or a clock, produced

Table 4.3. Objects Mentioned in Prewar Suits

Objects	*Frequency*	*Percent*
Money	17	22.4%
Land	8	10.5%
Tovar (Commodity, unspecified)	6	7.9%
Grass	5	6.6%
Rye	4	5.3%
Veksel (Bill of Exchange)	3	3.9%
Horses	3	3.9%
Barn, Shed	2	2.6%
Cow, Calves	2	2.6%
Fence	2	2.6%
Hay	2	2.6%
House	2	2.6%
Payment	2	2.6%
One Case Each:		
Bull, Clothing, Contract, Field, Food, Frame, Geese, Grain and Bread, Immovable Property, Logs, Meadows, Meals Provided at Work, Oats, Property (Whole Estate), Sheep, Travel Expenses, Yard, Woods	18	23.4%
Totals:	76	100 %

or exchanged; 9 percent of suits concerned grass cut allegedly in error on someone else's land. Money or products constituted the majority of objects named in civil suits. Land—mentioned as such or as a field, a meadow, and so on—was named in 16 percent of these suits. Creditors in debt cases mostly cited money only, although plaintiffs in these cases also sometimes mentioned commodities, meals provided to a worker (*kharchi*), hay, bills of exchange, and, in one case, two bulls.

Most civil cases at township courts were suits; most suits were for cash; and most suits were caused by conflicts over how people exploited resources—land, cash, and commodities. Peasants used township courts to protect their possessions and economic resources from abuses by other people. What was at stake for litigants in their civil suits were the ordinary and important conditions of legalized exchange relations—pay for labor or for products or services, fulfillment of contractual obligations, and enforcement of rights to resources. For these purposes—the crux of most civil suits in most times and places—the township court was a popular resort.

WORK, COMMODITIES, THE MEANS OF PRODUCTION, AND PAY

Township courts offered a way to resolve conflicts over labor and its rewards. Litigation could reveal contention among members of a work group, as in the following case heard at the Iaguninskii Township Court on 21 August 1905—a week before our day in court in chapter 3. Three men from the village of Iagunino—Gavrilla Osorkin, Gavrilla Zemliakov, and Matvei Erofeev—sued their neighbor, Stepan Ivanov Galkin, for two rubles, fifteen kopeks. The plaintiffs, all illiterate, charged Galkin with "clearing a wood lot without their knowledge" and sought from him the money he had been paid for his labor. Galkin testified that

> he together with the plaintiffs and other peasants had bought a section of state forest, that in response to a proposal by the forester, he and his family had cleared the wood lot and for this received three rubles, sixty kopeks. He was not willing to pay Osorkin, Zemliakov, and Erofeev anything, because they took no part in his clearing of the purchased wood lot. He asks to exact from the plaintiffs three rubles for his expenditures in clearing the wood lot.[8]

Galkin shakily signed his testimony. Confronted with this controversy, the court found that neither the plaintiffs' nor Galkin's suits were proven. The judges decided to stop the matter there—"to refuse Gavrilla Osorkin, Gavrilla Zemliakov, Matvei Erofeev as well as Stepan Galkin's countersuit." The decision was announced to all, along with the rules for appeal. The presiding judge, signing for the illiterate plaintiffs, noted that they were "unsatisfied." Galkin, perhaps content with the effect of his threat to sue in turn, signed in his wobbly handwriting once again.[9]

The response of the judges in this case illustrates the practical dispute resolution characteristic of township courts. In their decision, the judges responded not just to the complaint on the table but also and immediately to Galkin's demand for payment—his "countersuit." No time was wasted on a second case, presumably because the results would have been the same in any case. Galkin's neighbors registered their dissatisfaction with the verdict but did not appeal. Was it enough for them to make a stab at receiving some of Galkin's wages and, having lost, to have their claim of injustice officially recorded? This case displays the ability of the court to make quick pragmatic decisions in business disputes as well as its provision of a forum for official registration of disparate views.

The home industries widespread in the countryside created another source of work-related suits at township courts. The Iaguninskii Township Court, located in an area of textile fabrication, heard many disputes over supplies, materials, and food distributed to peasant producers through local stores.[10] In a single month, May 1905, these suits involved sums between 2.5 and 86 rubles, brought by people from both inside and outside the township. In one of these suits, a peasant from this township sued a peasant from another township who was in debt to the local store for 2.5 rubles of food. The accused peasant did not appear in court, although he had received his summons. The court supported the plaintiff and ordered the debt collected.[11] A Moscow guildsman[12] presented his case for 12.45 rubles for commodities "taken" from a shop, a debt, he claimed, that dated from 1902. The defendant, a peasant from the township, appeared in court and defended himself with a complicated explanation of the sales history of the materials in question. A peasant witness supported the accused. The judges turned down the Moscow guildsman's suit.[13] A local peasant sued a peasant from another village in the township over a long list of transactions at a local shop that had created a debt of 86.60 rubles. The accused did not appear in court. The judges ruled that the defendant was to pay the plaintiff 51.60 rubles.[14]

These suits over outputting and sales display important elements of township court practice. First, neither insiders nor outsiders to the township were privileged plaintiffs or defendants. The court did not give an advantage to Moscow merchants over local peasants or vice versa. Second, not showing up in court—on the part of the accused person—was almost a sure way to lose a suit. The township judges were authorized to rule *in absentia* if the defendant did not appear at the hearing, and such decisions were common. Third, almost all the principals in these cases were peasants, as were most outputters, storekeepers, and plaintiffs generally at township courts. Finally, note the specificity of the decisions and the willingness of the judges to adjust the amount of payment owed. These were resolutions made according to "conscience based on the evidence in the case," as decreed by the statutes on court procedure. Even when an accused person who did not show up in court was judged *in absentia,* the judges tried to figure out with precision the amount the losing party would be required to pay a creditor.

These cases were about work-related transactions, but occasionally the means of production were more directly involved. Earlier, in January 1905, a conflict over who owed whom for a Singer sewing machine reached the Iaguninskii court. The bill in question went back to 1891, and the sides would not be reconciled. The judges found that the machine belonged to the Singer Company and ended the case.[15]

Sometimes it was an animal that did the work, in the following case as a means of reproduction. In May 1905 the same Iaguninskii judges heard a suit brought by a male peasant from the village of Rybushkino against the rural society of Iagunino concerning two bulls. The bulls had been lent for fifty rubles to Iagunino for the obvious purposes, but then had been returned, fee unpaid, as "unsuitable." The plaintiff, aware of the problem, it appears, sued not for the full fifty rubles but for thirty-five instead. At court, he reduced his claim still further to ten rubles for his expenses and another ten rubles for feed for the bulls. Representatives from Iagunino's rural society came to the hearing and declared that they were willing to pay ten rubles for the expenses but nothing for the feed. The plaintiff apparently knew how far he could go, for he agreed to take ten rubles. All parties were satisfied with this resolution. The judges concluded that, "having heard the parties and taking into consideration the conciliating bargain between them," the village association should pay the plaintiff ten rubles.[16] In this case, the parties responded positively to the judge's routine proposal of reconciliation. Such "peaceful bargains" were ordinary—but not majority—outcomes of civil cases at township courts.

Selling cotton cloth in a village in Moscow Province, early twentieth century. *Photograph from the collection of Mikhail Zolotarev.*

The township court at Bol'shoe Zaborov'e (Big Fence) in Novgorod Province also considered cases about work-related conflicts. On 17 April 1911 the four judges, Aleksei Zubov, Iakov Semenov, Ivan Arkhipov, and Vasilii Osipov, and the clerk, Egor Zaozerskii, heard a case brought by Dorofei Khakhalev, a peasant living in Bol'shoe Zaborov'e but not registered there, against Vladimir Petrov from the village of Novosel'tsy, eleven miles from the court, and Ivan Chudin from Bol'shoe Zaborov'e. Khakhalev, a literate man, filed a suit for thirty-two rubles, twenty kopeks, for losses concerning commodities (*tovar*). He presented his case orally at court. Both Vladimir Petrov and Ivan Chudin appeared in court, along with three witnesses. The court required evidence for the precise amounts due Khakhalev and during the proceedings discovered that five peasant men owed their creditor small sums of money that did not add up to 32.50 rubles. Vladimir Petrov owed 5 rubles, Ivan Chudin owed 2.50 rubles, and three other men owed various small sums. The court ordered the five debtors to pay exactly what each owed for goods according to the evidence provided. Ivan Chudin paid his 2.50 rubles, but Fedor Mikhailov, who owed 5 rubles, decided to appeal the case. At this court, as in Iagunino, the judges were attentive to evidence and to each individual's share of responsibility.[17]

Women could also be involved in commodity cases. On 22 October 1911, the judges at the Zaborovskii Township Court heard a case brought by Aleksandra Kachalova of Bol'shoe Zaborov'e against eight peasant men from six different villages. She wanted payments for *tovar*. At the first hearing of the case, Kachalova's husband, Fedor Mikhailov, represented her in court with a written petition. When one of the key witnesses to these alleged violations did not appear, the case was postponed until 28 December. At the second hearing, Fedor Mikhailov again represented his wife. This was the same Fedor Mikhailov who had appealed the court's decision requiring him to pay Dorofei Khakhalov for *tovar* back in April of the same year. These court cases reveal the chains of indebtedness and exchange that linked people across this large township of forest and lakes.

Cases concerning commodities and payments for them could be found at all courts at most times.[18] One of the last cases resolved in 1917 by the Grebnevskii township court in the Bogorodskii County to the east of Moscow concerned a commodity received at a store. The judges heard the plaintiff and the defendant, both males, confirm that the defendant had been late in paying for his goods. The decision was that the sum—thirty rubles—had to be paid, in accord with the mutual agreement between the parties achieved at court.[19]

BUSINESS: DEALS, DEBTS, AND DOCUMENTS

In addition to controversies over work and commodities, township courts heard cases arising from conflicts over prices, bills of exchange, and outstanding debts. People might end up owing each other money in any number of ways, and the township courts were called on by sellers, buyers, and holders of IOUs both to enforce contracts and to settle up outstanding debts. The enforcement of sales of agreed-on commodities at agreed-on prices and the collection of contracted debts were achieved through civil suits at all courts I surveyed. A case from the agricultural zone south of Moscow where rural people were active in the marketing of vegetables and fruit to the city illustrates the centrality of contracts in peasants' civic sphere.

In November 1915 a peasant from the village of Shepilovo, Aleksei Alekseevich Bukashkin, brought Ivan Prokoforovich Kamochkin, a peasant from Blizhne-Beliaevo, a neighboring village, to the Tsaritsynskii Township Court for one of the miscellaneous suits that made up the bulk of this court's docket. This was a big suit: Bukashkin was asking Kamochkin to pay him sixty rubles for losses and seven rubles, twenty kopeks, for nonpayment, both claims involving a sale of cabbages. A suit over cabbage was not a trivial action in Tsaritsynskii Township. Over the previous decades, cabbage—fresh or pickled—had become one of the two major cash crops produced in the region. (The other was cucumbers, also fresh or pickled.) Farmers in the township grew and sold cabbage on a large scale, and some bought cabbage from outside the area and resold it, processed or not, in various Moscow markets. This case between peasants pitted a producer against a merchant, in a conflict with significance for many of their neighbors in the township.[20]

Peasant Bukashkin was a farmer, and peasant Kamochkin was—in function but not formal status—a merchant, or at least a merchant's son, who had contracted to purchase 1,000 poods (36,000 pounds) of cabbage from Bukashkin at forty kopeks a pood but, in the end, had hauled away only 125 poods and had not paid for 18 of them. At least that was how it looked to the claimant Bukashkin. But for Kamochkin, as his father insisted at the court, it was a question of quality. Yes, he testified, his son had agreed to purchase "fresh cabbage" at forty kopeks a pood, but then he had refused to take some of it "when it turned out to be of poor quality." He did not recognize any debt to Bukashkin.

Three witnesses appeared to testify in this case. One peasant from Shepilovo testified that Kamochkin had indeed contracted with Bukashkin to buy "all his cabbage without remainders at forty kopeks a pood"; that Kamochkin usually bought from other people, too; and that, although he needed 1,000 poods of cabbage, this time he bought only from Bukashkin. A second peasant from Shepilovo testified that he, too, knew about the purchase "without remainders" and that Kamochkin had also purchased from him at the same price but that, in the end, Kamochkin had also not come to take his cabbage for "an unknown reason." A carter-peasant from Tsaritsyno testified that he had hauled away 125 poods of cabbage from Bukashkin and that "between the buyer and Bukashkin a quarrel about everything took place."

According to the usual procedures, an attempt was made to reconcile the opponents. Kamochkin came up with an offer to pay the agreed-on price for 15 of the 18 disputed poods, but not the much more costly losses on the cabbage he had left behind. The plaintiff refused the proposal. The court's decision was the following: "The claim against Kamochkin is proven at the full proposed sum of sixty-seven rubles, twenty kopeks, because . . . Kamochkin . . . saw what kind of cabbage Bukashkin had, he was buying the 'poor quality' with the 'good quality.' The sale of cabbage is recognized as having taken place."[21]

In other words, a sale is a sale. This legitimation of market relations by a township court, similar to many other confirmations of contractual arrangements, displays the importance of this legal instance to the ongoing struggle for order in business matters. The peasant-farmers in this case might have competed with each other; both witnesses from Bukashkin's village suggested that Kamochkin was dealing with other local farmers as well. Instead, they supported their neighbor in his claim, even with the strong suggestion that his crop was not of the highest quality, against the peasant-merchant who might have bought their crops and who might buy them in the future. Enforcement of contractual relations, with their significance for planning and good order; protection against shady dealings with Bukashkins who sell substandard produce; a sophisticated idea of evidence and the ability to round it up; a show of village strength against a peasant-merchant—all these interpretations, and others, can be drawn from this example of local justice.[22]

A contractual agreement could be expressed in many ways, and it was best for plaintiffs at township courts to have some proof that a sale or other transaction had taken place and on what terms. Although witnesses could testify to an exchange, written documents were the preferred way to establish a claim at court (see chapter 6). Judges and clerks cited documentary evidence as the explanation for their decisions in 19 percent of all suits decided at the courts I surveyed, more frequently than they mentioned oral testimony (9 percent). Even if not cited as the basis for the judges' decisions, documentary evidence was entered into the clerk's case record in 37 percent of all civil suits heard from 1905 through 1917. Because the clerk was not obliged to enter such information into his books, this figure underestimates the impressive frequency with which documents, other than the initial complaint, were presented during township court litigation.[23]

In 1911 documents were recorded in all but one of the civil suits involving the contentious residents of Bol'shoe Zaborov'e in Novgorod Province. Litigants referred to the following kinds of written evidence: prior court records, inventories of property, petitions, and receipts. A receipt was critical to a suit brought by Ekaterina Danilova against her co-villager, Vasilii Ivanov. Ekaterina Danilova claimed that her neighbor owed her fourteen rubles. She was illiterate but presented a receipt to the judges. Her opponent did not come to court. The judges decided as follows:

> On 1 May 1911 the Township Court, having examined the case at hand, finds that the suit is proven by the receipt presented at the case from 1 October 1902, signed personally by the defendant, Vasilii Ivanov, and therefore in accord with Statutes 125, 133, 135, and 136 of *The General Regulation on Peasants* relating to the non-appearance of the defendant, has decided in his absence: to seek fourteen rubles from Vasilii Ivanov in payment of the debt in favor of Ekaterina Danilova.

Vasilii Ivanov paid this debt in full on 26 June 1911 and received a receipt for fourteen rubles from the township administration.[24]

This was not quite the end of Ekaterina's case, for Vasilii Ivanov shortly filed a suit against her. In his complaint, he demanded fifteen rubles, "for his travel to the city of St. Petersburg" and to a village. Presumably these journeys were related to his payment of his debt. The case was scheduled for a hearing on 11 July. Neither party showed up at court for this probably vengeful and probably hopeless case, and the matter was ended by the "non-appearance" of the two sides.[25]

Bills of exchange (*vekseli*) were not uncommon in rural areas in the early twentieth century, and they were good evidence to use in court. At the Iaguninskii court in May 1905, a peasant sued another over a bill of exchange from 1901 for one hundred rubles. The defendant refused reconciliation and said that he did not "want" to pay this debt. The court examined the bill of exchange, noted that it had been signed for the illiterate defendant by two townspeople, and told the defendant that he was obliged to pay. Pay he did, on 28 September the following year, in one of the longer intervals of debt collection at the township court, but not as long as the plaintiff had waited to bring his case.[26] In all the cases I examined where signed bills of exchange were presented, the judges honored the debts—of considerable amounts—certified by this kind of document.[27]

Meeting of the administration of the Pochinkovskii Credit Association, discussion of a loan, 1911. *Photograph from the collection of Mikhail Zolotarev.*

Documents were more likely to be produced in cases about debts than in civil cases generally. More than half the records of debt cases (52 percent) mentioned inventories, bills of exchange, court records, or other kinds of documents.[28] Whatever their evidence, debt cases were likely to be at least partially successful at township courts. Plaintiffs attained a verdict of "proven" or "proven in part," or amicable settlements, in 85.5 percent of the debt cases I surveyed, whereas plaintiffs succeeded, wholly or in part, in 54 percent of all civil cases. For peasant creditors, the township courts worked well.

CONTROVERSIES OVER USE OF RESOURCES

Disputes over the use of resources, usually land, were a frequent source of suits at township courts. The most common use violation to come before local judges was *potrava,* trampling of crops by animals. Trampling cases appeared at our August day in court at Iagunino; such cases could be found wherever the population was at least partly engaged in agriculture. Although most suits were for cash, in trampling cases peasants sometimes sued for objects—the damaged harvest—rather than for money.

The litigious residents of Bol'shoe Zaborov'e in Novgorod Province took these trampling cases to the Zaborovskii Township Court along with their other troubles. On 6 March 1911 Nikolai Mikhailov sought ten measures or fifty shocks of oats from his neighbors, Vasilii Chudin and Semyon and Dmitrii Fedorov because of trampling by their horses. Mikhailov presented a written petition to the court. All three defendants showed up in court—all illiterate, in contrast to Mikhailov—as well as three witnesses. Things did not go well for the plaintiff. At court Mikhailov admitted that he had not observed the rules on "protection of fields and meadows," and his suit was refused.[29]

Trampling and trespass were the bane of rural society; suits about these violations would arise in clusters between hostile parties. A month before Mikhailov's suit, Andrei Antonov, a townsman[30] residing in Zaborovskii Township, brought three cases against several peasants from the village of Kieva. The first case was for "trespass by twenty-six cows and seventy sheep and three horses on the straw and trespass by seventy sheep in the oats"; a second case was for two rubles, ten kopeks, for "grass cut on his land"; and a third was for "trespass by ten horses in the straw." This landowner, according to his claims, was plagued by local peasants who let their animals loose on harvested but not fully gleaned fields and who cut grass on his property. Later in the year, Antonov brought four more cases for trespass against the peasants of Kieva.[31]

Charges of trespass were by no means made exclusively by people of higher status against peasant locals. Just a few days before townsman Antonov filed his suits, we find a peasant suing a neighbor in his own village for "trespass of six cows, two horses, and fifteen sheep on uncut hay for value." The scale of the damages was different, but the problem was the same.[32] Whole villages, through actions taken by their rural societies, could be involved in trampling suits against each other. One of the many suits heard in the Iaguninskii Township Court in August 1905 began when the rural society of one village sued the rural society of another for fifty rubles. The cause was "trampling rye," and the suing village won its case.[33]

Another kind of land use controversy arose over "mistakes" in reaping the harvest. These were the kinds of problems that made it necessary for township courts to meet on those hot days in August, when people were otherwise occupied with cutting and storing grass and grain. At Iagunino, in August 1905, half the civil cases concerned trampling or other kinds of violations connected with the harvest. On 7 August the court heard a case brought by a peasant woman from the Sleskaia sloboda against her neighbor from the same village for "carried off hay." The plaintiff said that she had cut the hay, but the defendant had taken it away. In her suit the plaintiff calculated her losses at twenty-five kopeks for each pood of hay. Her case was supported by witnesses, and she won her full award of six rubles, twenty-five kopeks.[34] The next week, the court adjudicated two cases brought by men for "broken down grass" on their fields.[35] On 21 August the litany of cropping problems continued with three suits over rye.[36] In one of these, a male peasant from Iagunino claimed that his neighbor in the village, Ivan Erofeev Khrushchev, owed him five rubles for "leftover rye" relating to a conflict over fields in 1904. After a long hearing, he won the case at five rubles. Perhaps in this instance some neighborly peace was attained,

Haying, Moscow Province. *Photograph from the collection of Mikhail Zolotarev.*

for later a note was attached to the case. The plaintiff attested that he had received two rubles, and added in writing: "From Ivan Erofeev Khrushchev I will not demand any more money."[37]

These controversies over crops, trespass, and trampling concerned the correct use of land in rural areas. The question of ownership was not disputed; local parties could be expected to know who owned or controlled a piece of land. At issue was enforcement of people's right to crops, including stubble, grown on their land. This right was conditional on observance of practices that made clear who controlled a particular plot of land. If the rules on "protection of fields and meadows" were not followed, trampling could be a consequence, and even a landowner with high status might have to take his losses.

LAND: RENTS, SALES, AND TRANSFERS AT THE BIG FENCE VILLAGE

As the most fundamental resource of peasant households, land itself was the object of many controversies at the township courts. Land was rented, transferred, and sold in various ways by rural people, and conflicts over fulfillment of these transactions or their legitimacy produced some of the most complex cases heard by rural judges. Some of these decisions were made more difficult after the Stolypin regulations opened up the possibility of reconfiguring land holding in villages.[38]

The inhabitants of Bol'shoe Zaborov'e in Novgorod Province were involved quite regularly in civil cases about rental, use, and possession of land. In the fall of 1909 the villagers petitioned to transfer their allotment land from communal to household hereditary usage. At that time the village leader, Vasilii Amosov, had drawn up an "act" describing each resident's land. His list and the request to change to hereditary holdings were made at the height of demands for titles after the first Stolypin land reform in 1906.[39] Such requests would have been sent to the land captain, not to the township court, for ratification. Cases contesting or citing various aspects of this transition to household property—which the higher authorities may never have confirmed—provided grist for the mill of the township court at Bol'shoe Zaborov'e in the years to come, as did many other disputes over land and its use.[40]

Renting land in rural areas and among peasants was a common practice. "Violation of the conditions of a rental of land," like other claims related to contractual arrangements, was a charge that could be adjudicated by the township judges.[41] Sometimes rental cases were just about rental payments. In March 1911 the court heard the suit of Vasilii Ivanovich of Bol'shoe Zaborov'e against Viktor Fedorov of the neighboring village of Malaia Zaborov'e (Small Fence). Ivanovich wanted fifty-four rubles of "pay for the use" of a meadow. The literate plaintiff presented a petition at court to support his case. Fedorov, also literate, testified that he had "already paid" the plaintiff five rubles a year for the rent of the field. Six men showed up as witnesses, including Dmitri Khonin from Bol'shoe Zaborov'e. All these witnesses asked that the case be dropped and signed their testimony to this effect. The case was dismissed for lack of evidence.[42]

On the same day that the Zaborovskii court judges heard Vasilii Ivanovich's case, they also decided—at least for a while—a case brought by another resident of Bol'shoe Zaborov'e, Dmitrii Nikolaev Nikitin. This case concerning land use and possession suggests complications that could arise when the state offered villagers the possibility to turn collectively held land into hereditary household property. Dmitrii Nikolaev Nikitin's case was a suit against three brothers, Dmitrii, Efim, and Nikita Ivanovich Chudin, for two hundred rubles for "land sold . . . for use through the [rural] society for four years." Almost every element in this suit came into question—the responsibility of each of the Chudin brothers, the two hundred rubles, the notion of "land sold . . . for use," the sale through the rural society, and the four years. The case began with Nikitin's written petition—he was illiterate—on 1 March 1911 and lasted at least until September of that year.

At court on 7 March 1911 the plaintiff's claim was at first rejected by the defendant, Dmitrii Chudin. He testified that he did not accept the demand for two hundred rubles, because the "rules of sale of land had not been followed." There had been an agreement with Nikitin to pay "money in installments." Next, several witnesses testified about various aspects of this controversial "sale." Ivan

Nikolaev testified that Dmitrii Nikitin had indeed sold the land to Chudin for two hundred rubles, to be paid in four years, "in a business obligation which was supposed to be issued when the official decision was confirmed." Another witness, Aleksei Ivanov, testified that "in the township administration, Dmitri Nikitin was saying that he had sold the land and Dmitrii Chudin was saying that I bought it and they were saying that [it was] for two hundred rubles." The third witness was the township clerk, E. Zaozerskii, who testified that

> peasants Dmitrii Nikolaev Nikitin and Dmitrii Chudin came to the township administration concerning the sale of land from the first to the second, but I explained to them that I could not finalize it [literally, seal it, *ukrepit'sia*] and make a deed of purchase, but they both explained that they were not trying to escape expenses, then I wrote out the decision of the village meeting by which Dmitri Nikolaev Nikitin gave two *dush* [allotments] of his land to the society and the society transferred [it] to Dmitrii Chudin and his brothers Efim and Nikita Chudin. The peasant brothers named in the declaration were to take part in [paying?] money to Dmitrii Nikitin. For this transfer Dmitri Chudin was obliged to pay money to peasant Dmitrii Nikolaev Nikitin when the declaration would be confirmed by the land captain, about this matter they had to give a note for two hundred rubles over four years.[43]

This testimony probably came as no surprise to the litigants, and they decided to settle their deal over the land allotment peacefully and with a compromise. Dmitrii Chudin "promised" to pay Dmitrii Nikolaev Nikitin 189 rubles, 45 kopeks, over eight years, and Nikitin agreed to end the case. Dmitrii Nikitin, Aleksei Ivanov, and Dmitrii Chudin either signed or had a court official sign this arrangement for them.[44]

The clerk's testimony revealed with glaring clarity that a sale of land had taken place, despite his declared inability to confirm it or to provide a deed. The seller and the buyer of a piece of allotment land had convinced Zaozerskii to draw up a kind of land transfer that was legally binding at the time—a decision of the village assembly—and they had made arrangements for payment for this land over the next four years. Was this in anticipation of the land captain's expected legitimation of the village's request to transform its allotment property into household hereditary usage? Or was this an ordinary arrangement for peasants who recognized the value of allotment land and made the necessary arrangements according to a "binding business obligation" when they transferred land from one family to another? In any case, the court confirmed the compromise, and the clerk dutifully wrote down his own testimony as well as that of the litigants and witnesses. No attempt was made to cover up the circumstances of the "sale."

Unhappy rural families have their own—legal—ways of disrupting sensible arrangements. About three weeks after this compromise between Dmitrii Nikolaev Nikitin and Dmitrii Chudin, the two other Chudin brothers, Efim and Nikita, submitted a petition to the land captain in charge of their area. This petition, drawn up by someone with fancy handwriting, contested the settlement made by the township court. Dmitrii Chudin's brothers claimed that since

Dmitrii Nikolaev Nikitin had given his two *dush* of land to the village society two years ago, he had no claims on it. They had cultivated this land "without any obstacles or claims on Nikolaev [Nikitin]'s part," and they did not understand why suddenly he was asking for two hundred rubles. They found their brother's "amicable bargain" made at court on 7 March "immoral." The testimony at the hearing showed that there had been a "sale," but it was supposed to have happened four years ago and only if Nikitin had been able to give them a deed of purchase to the land. But he did not do this. He gave the land to the society instead, and therefore he had no right to ask them for payment. The two brothers requested "His Honor the Land Captain" to overturn the agreement made at the township court "without their consent."[45]

The Chudin brothers attached a copy of the declaration of the village assembly of Bol'shoe Zaborov'e from 12 April 1909 concerning Nikitin's land. This document, which had been copied out and attested to by the township clerk Zaozerskii, made a good case for Efim and Nikita. It described a meeting at which seventeen heads of household (a majority of the twenty-five officially registered at Bol'shoe Zaborov'e at the time) agreed to the transfer of two *dush* of Nikitin's land to the three Chudin brothers. The document provided reasons for this arrangement. Citing the statutes empowering the village assembly to transfer communal land, the declaration of 12 April 1909 was a response to the "oral request of our peasant from the same village Dmitrii Nikolaev Nikitin, who with regard to his not having any relatives, apart from himself, and having for himself sufficient land, . . . but not being able to work it enough to pay his taxes, and therefore declines the right to use part of his allotment land and to cut off from it two *dush* allotment and to transfer it to the use of the society." Furthermore, the meeting had decided to transfer this allotment to "our peasants of the same village Dmitrii, Efim, and Nikita Ivanov Chudin, as needy peasants with small parts of allotment land." This document, which followed the conventional formulas used by village assemblies, was signed by, or for, all the heads of household at the meeting, including Vasilii Amosov, the village leader, and Dmitrii Nikolaev [Nikitin] and Aleksei Ivanov. It was registered at the township administration by the township leader, S. Shlepakov, and the township clerk, Zaozerskii. There is one discrepancy in the copy of the document: The meeting was said to have been held on 12 April, but the last note on the document indicates that the "declaration" was entered into the records of the township administration on 8 April 1909 by the clerk Zaozerskii.[46] Could it be that Zaozerskii had indeed done exactly what he said in court—drawn up the "declaration" on 8 April and then submitted it to the village assembly a few days later on 12 April?

Two of the heads of household who signed this document in April 1909 were judges at the Bol'shoe Zaborov'e Township Court in 1911. One of them, Vasilii Osipov, heard the Nikitin-Chudin case in March 1911; the other, Andrei Zubov, was the president of the court but did not sit in judgment on this case. But even if Zubov had excused himself from the case for cause, he certainly knew its outcome: he signed the official copy of the court's proceedings later that month.

The recorded presence of the same people at both the court hearing in 1911 and the meeting of the village assembly in 1909, combined with the clear testimony given at the hearing, strongly suggest that Nikitin and Dmitrii Chudin had made a deal. Nikitin would cede his land—according to the accepted formula—and the Chudins would pay him over time for making sure that it went to them. The only official body empowered at that time to make transfers of allotment land was the village assembly. The clerk, Zaozerskii, knew this, and also knew that he had no authority to make a real sale, so he suggested the arrangement, which was duly backed up by the household heads of Bol'shoe Zaborov'e. Later, when Dmitrii Chudin was called to court to come through with his payments, both he and Nikitin were willing to reset the terms of the transaction and postpone the reduced payment for four more years. For all concerned, it was probably business as usual—except that two of the Chudin brothers later saw a way to have their land without the expected payment.

With land, a sale was not necessarily a sale, especially when higher authorities could be brought in. Eventually this case was heard by the members of the next higher instance, the county conference. There it was decided that the township court's confirmation of an "amicable settlement" was "incorrect," because "Chudin [Dmitrii] had not been delegated to settle this matter by the rest of the defendants." The congress decided to set aside the verdict of the township court and to send the case back to the same court for a new hearing.[47] The county congress—a body composed primarily of land captains—did not enter into the delicate issue of whether land could be bought and sold or whether the declaration of the village assembly had a fictive dimension. The overseers stuck to a more overt point of law: the deal was supposed to have been between Nikitin and all the Chudin brothers; Nikitin had brought a suit against them all; and all the brothers therefore had a right to represent themselves or be represented.[48] This judgment may have found little resonance in village opinion. Dmitrii Chudin was a man of some authority and wherewithal; even when his brothers attempted to overturn the township court's decision, they tried to postpone the hearing at the county congress because their brother Dmitrii was "absent earning money."[49]

How can we explain the unequivocal testimony at the township court about the sale, the discrepancies between the terms of the village assembly's "declaration"—a legally binding agreement—and the terms discussed by seller and buyer at the township administration, and the behavior of the parties in this case? First, many people from the village seemed to view the deal as justified. Dmitrii Chudin, the money earner in the Chudin family, was willing to extend his payments for the transferred land. The township clerk testified in court that he had written up the deal for the village assembly to ratify. It was only two years after the "sale" that the younger Chudin brothers protested their brother's extension of their obligation to pay Nikitin. One possible explanation of these phenomena is that sales were routinely carried out this way. It might have been an ordinary practice—and one facilitating economic life—to pay fees behind the facade of consensual transfers of land from one family to another in a village.

Another interpretation of this case could highlight the Stolypin land reforms and the disorder they inserted into village life. Before the imperial government's attempted reconfiguration of village property, land allotments would have been routinely adjusted by the village assembly. When someone like Nikitin, with no family, could not work the land sufficiently to pay his taxes and when people like the Chudin brothers were "needy," a village assembly would be called to reassign parts of the society's allotment land. But when the new land law of 1906 opened up the prospect of transferring land into hereditary household ownership—a prospect that this property-conscious village seemed to want to engage—a transfer of allotment land would represent much more than a reassignment of responsibilities and assets. By transferring his land before the village had converted its allotments into household property, Nikitin would have lost, possibly forever, an asset that under the new property arrangements would have been his to sell. Perhaps it was in response to this kind of calculation that so many people were willing to set terms for a sale of land that was supposed to be ratified with a "deed of purchase" by the land captain. The Chudins would get the land; Nikitin would have some revenue from his sale over the next four years; and taxes would be paid. The difficulty was that Nikitin and Chudin wanted to make this transfer at a point when property transfers were still administered by the village assembly. As the clerk told them, he was not able to draw up a title to the land. The practical solution at hand was to make a deal in the township administration, transfer the land through the society, and later, after the society's request to go over to household possession, the deed would be forthcoming from the land captain.

There was the rub: the transfer to household ownership of allotment land seems not to have taken place even two years after the village's petition. A state initiative designed to enhance responsibility of peasant landholders had encouraged villagers to enter into sales agreements but provided nothing to back them up. The best efforts of the court, the buyer, and the seller to get taxes paid, exchange land, and enforce contracts were frustrated by the laxity of higher authorities in carrying out their revision of land law. Some observers may criticize the new land rules for undermining routine, flexible, and legal arrangements for land transfers practiced by village and township instances. But even worse for the cause of order in the village was the limbo of uncertainty about how to transfer land legally. The Stolypin reforms, which were modified over several years, opened up a long, litigious interval of ambiguity, as people tried in more than one legal setting to attain official legitimation of their land transactions.

Attempts to change the terms of landholding and land rents could reach well back in time. A year after Dmitrii Nikolaev Nikitin's case against the Chudin brothers, another dispute involving land, rent, and possession, and another Chudin, was heard by the Zaborovskii judges. This case began with a petition from Nikita and Nikolai Arsent'ev Kutin against their co-villager Vasilii Chudin. The Kutin brothers asked the court to "declare the contract concluded by their sister about renting to him [Chudin] two *dush* of allotment land invalid and to take out of his use the land rented to him." Their petition of 15 April 1912 noted that their sister, Marfa Arsen'eva, had married and left for another township. As her only brothers, they wanted the land she had rented to Vasilii Chudin, but he refused to return it to them. Their sob story began:

> Our father left us all at the whim of fate as little children running off no one knows where, but our older brother at this time died . . . leaving us two little children and our sister Marfa Arsen'eva rented the land. . . . There was no guardianship established over us, and therefore . . . [Chudin] had no right to conclude such contracts, and . . . there needed to be an agreement of the rural society to rent land according to the [left blank] statute of the Gen. Reg. on Peas. of 1902.[50]

The participants in this case were called to the township court three times in the summer of 1912. The case was postponed twice, once because of illness, once because of "a misunderstanding." Before the final hearing, an important document was uncovered. This was the record of the contract between the Kutins' sister, Marfa Arsen'eva, and Vasilii Chudin. It had been drawn up at the Zaborovskii township administration on 31 March 1897 and copied out at the request of the Kutin brothers for a price of twenty-five kopeks. It was a superb contract that spelled out in detail a ten-ruble rent for the land. Chudin obliged himself to pay all taxes and dues shared with his fellow villagers and granted Marfa various rights, such as collecting firewood on the land. The contract also obliged Chudin—and this was the critical point for the case—to give the land back to Marfa's relatives if they wanted it.[51] When the case was called one last time for 9 September 1912 the plaintiffs did not show up, and the case was ended.[52] Perhaps the existence of the document gave the Kutin brothers all they needed to reach a settlement with Chudin, or perhaps they changed their minds about reclaiming the land.

This case underlines the crucial role of documentary evidence in township court decisions. An agreement between private parties was considered binding and figured in many verdicts. Problems arose when the agreement was made orally and with no witnesses; litigants realized this and tried to provide documents that would support their cases. Earlier court decisions, extracts from records of the village assembly, and transcriptions of oral contracts made at the township administration were ideal evidence that an agreement had been made. Such documents could be brought to bear on a recalcitrant defendant or, as in this case, could influence the plaintiffs to give up.

These suits over land at the Zaborovskii Township Court might have appeared arbitrary or incomprehensible to outsiders, but, at the township level, there was a logic to each case. Rents were paid or they weren't; land was transferred or it wasn't; contracts were fulfilled or not. The management of land was a critical matter in the Russian countryside long before the Stolypin reforms offered the prospect—enticing to some—of secure, hereditary possession. Individual peasants, their village assemblies, the township clerk, and the court were familiar with procedures that permitted transfers, rents, and the designation of specific use rights. That people manipulated these procedures to further their civil suits should be no surprise but rather a testimony to the ordinariness of rural people resorting to the courts.

FAMILY PROPERTY: INHERITANCE AND *RAZDEL*

In addition to settling conflicts over resources, the township courts were empowered to legitimate reallocation of family property after a death or when a family decided to divide into separate households. Russian law did not oblige peasants to bring inheritance cases to the township court. Since most movable property was held by households, it simply remained in the family after a death. Allotment land, as we have seen, could be reassigned by the village assembly. Nonetheless, many peasants did bring cases about inheritance to township courts, both as suits, like the one by the Kutin brothers for "their" family land, and as requests for official confirmation of uncontested transfers of property within a family.[53] In addition, members of families who wanted to separate into smaller households could ask township judges to examine the fairness of these divisions and to give them legal sanction.[54] By using courts to recognize new property arrangements as families changed over time, litigants enhanced order, security, and well-being in rural areas.

According to Statute 125 of *The General Regulation on Peasants,* the township courts were to examine civil cases concerning

> matters of inheritance and [family] divisions among inheritors of peasant property (a) without limitation of value, when the inherited property is part of a peasant allotment and the movable property belongs to that allotment; and (b) when the inherited property, located within the township, and not part of a peasant allotment, is not valued at more than five hundred rubles.[55]

To the dismay of some outside observers, the law did not provide rules for determining the fairness of inheritance claims or family divisions but simply instructed judges to make their decisions on the basis of "conscience" and "evidence" connected to the case. According to Statute 135: "In deciding suits and disputes among peasants, especially in cases about the division of peasant inheritance, the court is to be guided by local customs." If necessary for the settlement of such property issues, the court was to carry out a survey of the locale concerned.[56] These procedural rules for the township courts corresponded to the right accorded peasants to configure inheritance in local ways. Statute 13 of *The General Regulation on Peasants* stated this right succinctly: "In matters of inheritance of property, peasants are allowed to be governed by their local customs."[57]

Legalized resort to local custom was a building block of the imperial system. In accord with the empire's extension over territories inhabited by people with different religious affiliations and legal histories, imperial law subsumed various property regimes under its wide umbrella of legality.[58] In the early twentieth century some commentators and officials thought that these accommodations of legal difference presented obstacles to their goal of uniform governance. Jurists, however, generally did not treat "local customs" as antithetical to "law." Specialists on local regulations understood custom as a regime of adjudication, legalized by its incorporation into the statute law on property.[59]

The right to use local customs in inheritance cases gave peasants possibilities that were unavailable to people whose property arrangements were determined by the civil code. Township courts—and rural families—enjoyed flexibility in the allocation of land and movables; there were no laws obliging families to divide or pass on assets in any particular way. This freedom from fixed inheritance rules had important consequences for peasant women, who could inherit without restrictions at township court if families and judges so chose. Daughters' share of peasant land in a family with surviving sons was not limited to one-seventh of an estate, as in the civil code. As one notable expert on peasant practice enthused, "Customary law stands higher than Volume 10 [the civil code] with relation to the equality of the sexes in inheritance."[60]

Inheritance cases brought to township courts for official confirmation—not as suits—were only somewhat more than 1 percent of prewar civil cases at courts I surveyed but rose to more than 18 percent in the war years.[61] An uncontested case would be heard by the court at a single session; if not appealed within thirty days, the transfer of ownership would be complete. An inheritance case of this type would be registered by the clerk in the following fashion:

> A petition from Peasant Vasilii Iakovlev Shibashev of the Savvinskaia sloboda to confirm him and his brother Petr in the rights of inheritance to the property remaining after the death of his grandmother, Peasant woman Natalia Vasil'evna Shabasheva, of the Savvinskaia sloboda.[62]

In this case, heard on 12 May 1905 by the Iaguninskii Township Court, the plaintiff testified that his "blood relative" (*rodnaia*) grandmother had died in 1904, leaving him a house with a yard in the Savvinskaia sloboda. He asked to inherit this house with his brother and testified that they were the only heirs. The judges agreed, confirmed him in his rights to "property, both movable and immovable," and, as usual, announced the procedures for appeal.[63]

Many inheritance cases at township courts involved more complicated transactions and required witnesses to testify to the justice of the case. Witnesses testified far more frequently in inheritance cases than in suits or other township matters. In my survey of township hearings, witnesses appeared for court hearings in 77 percent of inheritance cases, in 38 percent of civil cases, and in 53 percent of all cases. A representative of the village society, a village official, or a township official testified in more than half of all the inheritance cases, both contested and routine. In 15 percent of inheritance cases, two or more witnesses appeared. Judges' respect for local knowledge and their attentiveness to evidence, as well as the law's concern for custom, were intertwined in this routine resort to testimony from people other than family members.

Petitions in inheritance cases sometimes combined appeals to both "custom" and the civil code. "Peasant widow Aleksandra Petrova" made the following request in a petition to the Zaborovskii Township Court in May 1907:

> In the beginning of January 1906 I married Peasant of the village of Bakharikha Pavel Fedotov. This my husband died in April 1907, having lived with me for a little over a year. His property was all undivided with his father and now is at the disposal of only his father, Peasant of the village of Bakharikha, Fedot Stepanov, who from this undivided property voluntarily gives me nothing and for my living and work in his family for fourteen months rewards me with nothing. I remain without means. Therefore I ask your honor the Zaborovskii Township Court to award me from my father-in-law . . . one-eighth of the household in kind or at least one-eighth of the value of the property remaining with him or 125 rubles. This one-eighth of the household I take as my inheritance because my father-in-law, the respondent, never divided the property with his son, my husband who died, and therefore can be considered belonging . . . to both of them by equal shares; for this man's half of the property I am the inheritor by the law for one-fourth, on the basis of the 1148 statute of the Civil Code.[64]

To her opening statement Aleksandra Petrovna appended a list of the entire property of the household. Each item was given a ruble equivalent. Household property, including two huts under one roof, three barns, two horses, three cows, eight sheep, and many tools, was set off from the husband's clothes—one fur overcoat, two jackets, two fur coats, two leather boots, two felt boots with rubber galoshes, two suits, two vests, three shirts, one fur hat, and one cap—as well as food. The total added up to one thousand rubles. A literate peasant signed Aleksandra Petrova's name for her.

Aleksandra Petrova's calculation of 125 rubles corresponded to exactly one-eighth the value of the household's movables. She must have had some worries about whether her request would succeed, for she added another paragraph after her first signature:

> And if the Township Court does not find it possible to allot me from this my father-in-law . . . that one-eighth part of all the property by inheritance, then I ask the Zaborovskii Township Court to allot me at least for living and work in the home of my husband and father-in-law a sum for the fourteen months of my living in that house.

Aleksandra's name was signed a second time after the addition; the petition was dated 21 May 1907. Then she must have had another thought about her case. She added another note, dated 23 May 1907, asking the court to call two men from Bakharikha to confirm the property held by the father-in-law.[65]

Aleksandra Petrova's case displays both the legal knowledge accessible to a peasant woman who married into a family of some substance and the discretionary powers provided to township judges through their authority to decide cases by local custom. Aleksandra's claim to one-eighth of the extended family's movable property was indeed supported by Statute 1148 of the civil code, which decrees that a "lawful wife" should inherit from her husband one-quarter of all movable property.[66] But there was at least one catch: Aleksandra's husband had held his property jointly with his father. Perhaps anticipating trouble on this score, Aleksandra made the unusual claim that the court should act as if her father-in-law and his son had divided into two separate nuclear families. There was potentially a second problem. Township judges were not bound by Statute 1148, because their instructions were to be guided by local custom in matters of peasant inheritance. Aleksandra's arguments, however, show how "custom" opened up legal options to peasant women. Nothing precluded the judges from accepting Aleksandra's plea for one-eighth of the family property, if they found that her claims rested on a local standard of fairness. This may have inspired Aleksandra to mention in her petition her months of uncompensated work in the extended household as well as her father-in-law's neglect. Unfortunately we do not know the outcome of this case, but it was given a speedy hearing. Aleksandra, her father-in-law, and her two witnesses were all summoned to a hearing at 8:00 A.M. on 17 June.[67]

Men could have their family troubles, too. In January 1909 Anton Andreev Smetanin brought an inheritance claim against his brother, Pavel Smetanin, to the Zaborovskii Township Court. The plaintiff, Anton Andreev, presented the court with a petition:

> After the death of my father Andrei Nikitin [Smetanin] there was left one *dusha* of allotment land in the use of my own brother Pavel Smetanin, who uses this land to the present. From this one *dusha* allotment from the use of Pavel Smetanin half, i.e., half of the allotment, should enter into my use, because after the death of my father the one *dusha* allotment taken from my father's share should be divided between me and my brother. I have asked my brother many times to cut off for me one half of the *dusha* allotment of this land, but he refused me.

The judges responded to Anton Andreev Smetanin's petition by calling to the court Anton, his brother, and three men whom Anton had designated as witnesses—Fedor Vasil'ev Khonin, Ivan Vasil'ev Sanin, and Mikhail Smetanin—to a court hearing.[68]

Anton Andreev Smetanin was well known to the Zaborovskii Township Court. In 1905 he had sued Fedor Pavlov Kachalov, who worked as a supervisor for a local landlord, for forty rubles connected with clearing a woodlot. In 1906 Anton Andreev filed two suits against a townsman, Grigorii Zimmer, once for twenty-one rubles concerning land and another time for fifteen rubles, seventy-five kopeks, involving forests. In 1907 Anton Andreev was in court several times: he brought at least five suits for debts that year and was sued at least twice by other people. This active litigator was almost certainly involved in some kind of outputting operation; in one case another peasant sued him for thirty rubles of losses for "commodities scattered on the street," and in another Fedor Pavlov Kachalov, whom Anton Andreev had sued in 1905, sued Anton Andreev in turn for fourteen rubles of losses for commodities received at the local store.[69] It was surely no surprise to the township court judges that the Smetanin brothers were at odds over the family's allotment land.

Land, household property, and animals were often at stake in inheritance cases, but savings and debts could be passed on as well. In 1915, when two women and two men from the village of Griaznoe Zamost'e (Dirty over the Bridge) petitioned the Zaborovskii court to be confirmed in their inheritance, they asked for a bank book in addition to land that had been in their mother's possession. The documents in this case included a death certificate, two copies of a village-level decision, and a description of the bank book and its contents—"the book of the Savings Bank, located at the Post and Telegraph Department of the village of Beloe in Novgorod Province book no. 1139 in the sum of 202 rubles 62 kopeks with %% [interest]."[70]

As part of this inheritance case, the family submitted two handwritten copies of an official declaration, through which one of the two sisters renounced her property rights in favor of her brothers:

> On 28 September 1915 I the undersigned peasant woman of Novgorod Province, Kirillovskii County, Volokoslavianskii Township, village of Bol'shoe Zakoz'e, Akulina Andreeva Ganicheva, living in the village of Beloe, Borovichskii County, L'zichskii Township, gave with this signature to my brothers, peasants of Tikhvin County, Zaborovskii Township, village of Griaznoe Zamost'e, Ivan and Andrei Andreevich Kolchin, that which remained after the death of my blood-relative mother, peasant of Tikhvin County, Zaborovskii Township, village of Griaznoe Zamost'e, Evdokiia Alekseeva Kolchina, of movable and immovable property and capital. I pledge not to enter into the right of inheritance and to renounce these forever in favor of my brothers Ivan and Andrei Kolchin; to this I sign peasant woman of Kirillovskii County, Volokoslavianskii Township, village of Bol'shoe Zakoz'e, Akulina Andreeva Ganicheva, and because of her illiteracy and at her personal wish, her . . . husband signed.[71]

The signature on this statement was witnessed by the township leader and stamped with the seal of the L'zichskii township administration.[72] Perhaps family relations were better in "Dirty Over the Bridge" than in "Big Fence" not far away, for this confirmation of inheritance and reallocation of family property at the request of a woman all took place in sixteen days. The case shows once again the effectiveness of certified documentation at township courts.

Monetary obligations, like other assets, could be inherited. On 29 January 1915 the Tsaritsynskii Township Court in Moscow Province heard a suit from a peasant widow against another peasant woman for 125 rubles according to a bill of exchange. The note had been signed over on 4 April 1912 to the plaintiff's husband, now deceased. Both women were illiterate. The respondent rejected the claim, but the plaintiff provided the court with the decision of another township court confirming her inheritance rights to her husband's property. The court declared that the case was proven, the obligation was now due to the widow, and the bill of exchange had to be honored.[73]

Inheritance cases at the township court helped rural people determine in orderly fashion the ways that property would move within a family when one of its members died. Another matter of great importance to rural families and one that produced a significant number of court cases was the definition of the household itself. Who was responsible for which property and for which dependents? Since the peasant household (*dvor*) was the payer of taxes and the holder of land allotments in most cases, it was of critical importance to know who was in and who was out of a household. Imperial law provided a formal way to change the composition of households through the process of family division (*razdel*). An extended family with more than one adult member, usually male, could be split apart into two or more new family units.

Observers in the last third of the nineteenth century generally regarded *razdel* as a negative phenomenon that turned the extended peasant household with its several adult workers and diversified labor potential into economically vulnerable nuclear families.[74] Sympathy for the plight of peasant daughters-in-law, however, could elicit a more positive response from elite commentators, as in the following comment from an 1899 political atlas:

> The economic harm of family divisions is unquestionable in individual cases, but it is significantly balanced out by the moral influence that divisions have on the individual side of the peasantry, increasing the significance of the person, freeing it from the family yoke and providing room for its development. In this sense, at a certain stage of development, divisions are not only an inescapable phenomenon but also indisputably progressive.[75]

The unwieldy image of an "individual side of the peasantry" progressing through family divisions made at the appropriate stage of development does little justice to the delicate balancing of collective and individual desires that shaped large and small families, before and after divisions, nor for the long history of *razdel* in the countryside.[76] Family divisions allowed rural families to adjust themselves not just to their economic situations, but to the desires, personalities, and capabilities of their members.[77]

As with inheritance settlements, the legal process of a family division usually took place at the village level. The rural assembly was empowered by *The General Regulation on Peasants* to decide and legitimate requests for *razdel.*[78] Cases about *razdel* could arise at the township level in connection with other matters, such as a suit, or in the context of an inheritance case where family composition had a bearing on legal responsibility. Occasionally family members appealed to township judges to obtain a division against the objections of a relative or to adjust an earlier separation of property. The Ignatevskii Township Court heard two such cases on 12 June 1906. In one, a man brought a suit against his father for "property according to *razdel.*" The court's decision was to allocate the son "five beehives or the value of twenty-five rubles and to divide the land by one *dusha* each." The father appealed this case to higher authorities. In a second case the same day, a brother sued his brothers for "an allotment of land according to *razdel* of one *dusha*." This suit was rejected by the judges.[79]

These and other cases of *razdel* at township courts display the legal system's enhancement of civility, productivity, and order in the countryside. In the ordinary way of things, a family division was a voluntary event, based on an agreement within the family and ratified by the village assembly. Cases brought to township courts presumably were ones where the family was itself at odds about division and its terms, and the village assembly was unable to make a decision satisfactory to the parties. Such destabilizing situations are easily imaginable in a small society where all family members would be well known to their neighbors. A township court decision might be seen as a desirable way to make a division of property that did not implicate directly the other families of the village. This was yet another matter in which the intermediary role of the township court—not identical with the patriarchal authority of any settlement but familiar to the bone with the social practices of the countryside—could use its authority to cut through the constricting ties of family and village life.

GUARDIANSHIP

The household was the basic building block of rural society, but peasant families could become dysfunctional. Orphaned children had no patriarchs to supervise their care and welfare; adults in charge of household resources could prove incapable of carrying out family and communal responsibilities. When a family unit failed, resources and authority could be moved into competent hands by establishing a legal guardianship (*opeka*). *The General Regulation on Peasants* charged village and township communities with the care of the "person and property" of orphaned peasant children. Local authorities were empowered to identify guardians and to supervise their actions in accord "with their local customs." Village authorities, township courts, and higher officials together formed a network of legal safeguards for the family property of unprotected and incompetent individuals.[80]

The village society was the first resort when children lost their fathers or both parents. Calamity could strike families rapidly, and the law made provisions for the quick reallocation of perishable possessions of minors. The village assembly was to decide such matters and record its decisions in a special book. The reallocation of other property, including allotment land, was also determined by the village assembly, but these more serious transfers had to be confirmed by higher authorities. If relatives of a minor observed anything in the community's actions that resulted in losses for the child, they could complain to the land captain.[81]

Formal assignment of a guardian was not the only means to ensure an orphan's welfare.[82] As Praskovia Aref'eva's case in chapter 2 revealed, villagers could arrange for the care of minors in a number of ways. Frol Grigor'ev had assumed responsibility for two minor girls—Praskovia's nieces—when he married their mother a few years after their father's untimely death. This informal assumption of responsibility for two orphans figured into the official decision of the Lemozha rural community to accept Grigor'ev into their society as a peasant.[83] In other situations, guardians were appointed formally by the village assembly. In the great web of patriarchal controls, the tsar was the guardian of the country's welfare, ordained by God, and these appointed supervisors the guardians of local orphans. A guardian's authority was not absolute, however, and his behavior could be challenged by relatives and other villagers. The township court entered into matters of guardianship as the adjudicator of disputes among peasants about guardians' behavior and about their disposal of the property of their wards.

In some guardianships sums of money were allocated for the care of the orphan; this money could become a source of contention and suits at township courts. The Tolmazov family from the village of Blizhne-Beliaeva appeared twice before the Tsaritsynskii Township Court in January 1915 after the death of a minor girl, Maria Tolmazova, aged thirteen. The girl's grandfather, Pavel Alekseevich Tolmazov, asked to receive three hundred rubles from the guardianship over Maria to compensate him for expenses spent on her funeral.[84] The judges granted Pavel's suit on the grounds that the claim was supported by documents—a death certificate and expense receipts—and recognized by the guardian. The amount paid to Pavel was limited to exactly the amount spent on the funeral, 293 rubles, 46 kopeks, according to the testimony at court.[85]

This was a huge sum, even allowing for wartime inflation. Moreover, Pavel Tolmazov returned to court two weeks later, asking for seventy-six rubles, ninety-nine kopeks, from the wardship. Again, the guardian, Maria's uncle, Petr Tolmazov, showed up in court to confirm this sum, a "debt" in his words. The judges again agreed, noting that the debt had been established by the testimony of the guardian.[86] Why was so much money being transferred after a ward's death? This case might cast doubt on the kind of justice meted out at the township court.

Responsible record-keeping clarified some of the ambiguities of Maria Tomazova's financial matters and opened up a window on the oversight of guardianship in villages and courts. Maria had been made a ward of her uncle on 15 March 1908 by a decision of the village assembly of Blizhne-Beliaevo. Representatives of sixty-three of the seventy-four households in the village attended the assembly. They signed a document, declaring that Ivan Pavlov Tolmazov had left behind a "minor daughter," six years old, and that "having taken counsel together, on the basis of the statutes of the Gen. Reg. we chose her relative and our co-villager, Petr Pavlov Tolmazov, as the guardian."[87] Maria was not an impoverished orphan. In her dossier was an inventory of her deceased father's property, all of which now belonged to her. She owned a house, several outbuildings, a barn, a yard, a stable, two carts, a wall clock, two samovars, two horses, a cow, plus miscellaneous items; altogether, in addition to the house, Maria's estate amounted to 1,620 rubles.[88]

A wardship did not end with the assignment of the guardian. Every year the village assembly had to attest formally to the quality of the guardian's care. These yearly decisions stated the exact amount of the ward's property at hand, recorded profit on and expenses against that property over the course of the year, and made a judgment about the quality of the guardian's behavior.[89] Year after year the village assembly of Blizhne-Beliaevo submitted an accounting for Maria's property, always signed by a large majority of the village household heads. By 1911 many of the inventoried items had been sold, and Maria's estate amounted to two bank accounts at the State Savings Bank and the Tsaritsynskii Credit Association.[90] These assets continued to grow over the next two years, as Tolmazov received income in excess of his wardship expenses and put it into the bank accounts. In 1913 the village's reports recorded the amounts Tolmazov spent on "nourishment, shoes and clothes, and other objects."[91] On 10 February 1914 the village assembly submitted a special decision to the district overseer. Petr Pavlovich Tolmazov had informed his neighbors that his ward was now thirteen years old, and that he wanted to use seventy-three rubles of her property to buy a sewing machine and put the rest into the savings bank. The meeting responded positively and unanimously to this request, and noted, "Moreover we add that the guardian Tolmazov is of good behavior and is a fully trustworthy man."[92]

On 9 December 1914, in the last report on Maria's assets before her death, the village meeting testified that her property consisted of 2,263 rubles, 8 kopeks, all at the savings bank.[93] In the eyes of his co-villagers and the township authorities, Petr Pavlov Tolmazov had been a good guardian. He had increased the value of Maria's estate by almost 80 percent in three years, and he had bought her a sewing machine. It is futile to speculate on what these actions meant for Maria Ivanovna Tolmazova's short life. Was she required to work herself to the bone as a seamstress for a relentlessly acquisitive uncle? Was she able to enjoy a good diet and pleasing clothing paid for by those annual and not small expenses for "nourishment, shoes and clothes"? Answers to such questions would reveal our imaginings of rural society, rather than how Maria lived. What we can observe is the close oversight over guardians required by the law and carried out by village and township authorities.[94]

Later, in February 1915, the Tsaritsynskii Township Court reviewed two cases concerning a different kind of guardianship—one established over an improvident adult. Through legal action at the township court, a spendthrift head of household could be prevented from ruining his family and running up taxation debts. If a guardianship was declared, the village leader would be responsible for sequestering a wastrel's movable property and overseeing the use of his agricultural allotment and farmstead.[95]

Guardianship was not a permanent status; people could regain their independence of action through good behavior. Semyon Grigor'ev Kormakov, who had been made a ward on 20 July 1913, came to the Tsaritsynskii court on 26 February 1915 to request "the removal from him of *opeka* for wastefulness." The judges at Tsaritsyno ruled in favor of his request, finding as follows:

> The request of Kormakov is [well] founded and deserved satisfaction since the society of peasants of the village of Saburovo has certified with a declaration presented to the court that he has corrected his behavior, does not squander his property, and on the contrary expands it.[96]

This formalization of independence worked its way through the legal system with relative rapidity once Kormakov had received his community's approval. The rural society of Saburovo recorded their decision on 25 January 1915; the township court removed the *opeka* at its session a month later; the decision was sent on to the Moscow county congress for approval on 19 March 1915; and the congress registered its confirmation of the township court's decision on 13 May 1915.[97]

The Tsaritsynskii Township Court decided another *opeka* case on the same day as Kormakov's. This request came jointly from the ward, Nikolai Ivanovich Volkov, and his village society. Volkov and two male representatives of the Khokhlovskoe society showed up in court and supported the request to "remove the *opeka*." Again the court found that the plaintiff had "improved his behavior," and the guardianship was ended. As in Kormakov's case, all the principals signed the court record; the documents were forwarded to the county congress on 19 March 1915; and the change in guardianship was confirmed by county authorities on 13 May 1915.[98]

Family members other than the spendthrift were directly affected both by irresponsible household management and by the establishment of guardianships. Relatives, particularly wives, could go to township courts to request the establishment of an *opeka* or its removal. On 3 March 1916 the four judges at the Iaguninskii court heard Tatiana Ivanova Shcherbakova's request to remove the guardianship "for wastefulness" that had been established over her husband in July 1912. Semyon Stepanovich Shcherbakov's movable property had been sequestered, and his land allotment and household garden had been put into distraint. Now, almost four years later, Semyon Stepanovich's wife returned to court with two witnesses from the village, Stepan Ivanov Galkin and Egor Baev, to request that the *opeka* be removed. The scribe Lanin recorded the following testimony:

> The petitioner Shcherbakova asks to have the guardianship for wastefulness removed from her husband, since at the present time he has reformed himself and carries on peasant economy independently. Illiterate.
>
> The witness Galkin declared that Shcherbakov at present behaves independently and fully economically. [signature]
>
> The witness Egor Baev declared the same as Galkin. [signature][99]

The Iaguninskii judges expressed their decision as follows:

> The township court having considered the circumstance of the present case finds that peasant of the village of Iagunino Semyon Stepanov Shcherbakov conducts a normal way of life and that the cause that gave rise to the establishment of the guardianship in 1912 has been removed, and therefore guided by the 11 st. of the law of 18 May 1911, decided to remove the guardianship

> from peasant Semyon Stepanov Shcherbakov of the village of Iagunino and free his property from sequestration and distraint.[100]

Guardianship cases illustrate the linkage between families, village societies, and township courts. Each case of *opeka* concerned particular individuals and households, but judges turned to village representatives for evidence of people's competence and behavior. In turn, villages and families used the courts to protect themselves against wayward members or to return reformed wards to responsible enterprise. *Opeka* and its removal were critical to order and productivity in the village; township courts provided the legitimation for these important transfers of power and resources.

Guardianship cases make explicit the qualities expected of members of rural society, as defined by peasants at their local courts. Responsible management of resources was essential for the survival and well-being of peasant households. The values promoted and sustained by township judges were not forgiveness or tolerance for poor behavior. The key words in *opeka* cases are "independence," "reform," and "economy." A man is assumed to be capable of self-correction; he can recover his innate competence as after an illness.[101] The behavior expected of a man who conducts "peasant economy" is productive: a proper head of a peasant household expands his property and does not waste it. Male and female members of households and village societies cited and measured productive activities to legitimate themselves and others as guardians, heads of household, or inheritors of property. Responsible economic activity—paying one's debts, honoring contracts, expanding the property of a household—defined a "normal way of life."[102]

PATRIARCHY, PROPERTY AND CIVIC LIFE

Guardianship cases, like other civil matters at township courts, show that patriarchy intersected with peasant legal practice in complex and intriguing ways. On the one hand, the basic premise of the township court structure—that peasant judges could represent the state and adjudicate disputes in a legal forum—was an adaptation of patriarchal authority. Judges were always males, of a mature age, chosen by assemblies of heads of households (also almost always male). This would seem to affirm the authority of elders, as practiced in villages for centuries. Moreover, civil litigation at township courts assisted tough and demanding peasant businessmen in the collection of fees, rents, and debts. Access to the law enabled people to carry on vendettas at a more elevated level than the village; strongmen could seek to enhance their power locally by getting the courts to back them up.

At the same time, township courts enabled gradual changes in the patriarchal order of the countryside.[103] The rules of evidence at court meant that a positive outcome for a local strongman was not a foregone conclusion. Deals between big men could be undone, if the documents revealed a contradiction that other people could exploit. The existence of a legal forum outside the village provided an opening for subordinate brothers (the Chudins), daughters-in-law, and relatives who had left for cities to challenge decisions made by village elders. Patriarchs could be sued by family members, neighbors, peasants from other villages, or business partners when a deal went wrong. At township courts, contentious, powerful women such as Ekaterina Danilova of Big Fence village could win against male competitors.

The appearance of women at township courts is not by itself evidence of social transformation. Peasants ordinarily engaged in pragmatic interpretations of patriarchal authority, adjusting property arrangements to the vagaries of biology and achievement. Brothers rather than fathers could be chosen as guardians (as in the Tolmazov family); women could be designated as de facto household heads. What was different about township court proceedings is that authoritative decisions were made not by people operating in their village environments but by judges selected to be township-wide officials. The law was mediated, in an exact sense of this word, by peasant judges who knew a great deal about rural life but whose power derived from their office and ultimately from the state. As for patriarchs in villages who appeared at court, they had to summon evidence and documentation as did everybody else.

Elite observers posed the question of patriarchy in rural life, while trying to contain it within their abstract categories. A description of peasant "custom" in Moscow Province at the end of the nineteenth century asserted,

> The old big Great Russian patriarchal family, with the unlimited power of the *bol'shak* [head of household] and the absorption of the interests of individual persons into the interests of the whole—of the family with the complete suppression of the individuality of its members, this family is gradually collapsing and splitting up into its natural components—small families, with a new, more or less independent character of its members.[104]

This observation, for all its questionable assumptions—that the traditional family suppressed individuality (at the very least the *bol'shak* had the chance to assert his personal preferences) and that the small family was "natural"—neatly registers the challenge that "the peasant family" presented to outsiders. For this intellectual observer, the shift away from patriarchal power meant that "contemporary peasant family life contain[ed] a mass of contradictions" and was characterized "by extreme inconsistency, vagueness, deprived of clear, typical characteristics, and only with difficulty submits to description."[105] At the heart of this intellectual struggle was a problem of perspective: elites insisted on seeing Russian peasants as a collective, rather than as individuals.

The essence of legal practice at the township courts was to ensure that individuals—not abstract collectivities—could come to socially acknowledged resolutions of their specific—not generalized—disputes. Civil litigation provides evidence of the ways that peasants chose to describe themselves as individuals. Although litigants identified themselves by status and place of registration, they registered their names in irregular and personalized ways. The different usages in township records—first name and patronymic or first name, patronymic, and family name—signal the changes in rural society ongoing at this time. The courts facilitated resolutions of the endless contradictions and inconsistencies that baffled intellectuals, without forcing rural people back into type.

If contentious litigation at township courts substantiated the worst fears of those who pined for authentic village collectivity, what did this escape from an assumed old order mean for the rural population? A look back at the kinds of civil cases brought to the township court and the kinds of people who brought them reveals some aspects of peasant families—not "the peasant family"—and their attempts at self-transformation.

Clerks' records show that the township courts provided a venue for challenging patriarchal authority case by case. Members of a single family did sue one another at court. Inheritance cases usually involved family members, their conflicts, or potential conflicts, as did family divisions. In my survey of civil cases from 1905 through 1917, relatives were parties in 28 percent of cases. These figures demonstrate a significant use of the courts to resolve property disputes internal to families. The sex and family relations of parties in civil cases reveal ways that authority was being reconfigured in the rural areas. Mothers and daughters-in-law occasionally brought suits for property against their relatives in the years before the war (see chapter 7), but most prewar civil suits involving family members were brought by men. Defendants in family civil suits were almost always males, presumably because they controlled most assets. But which male was in charge of family property was precisely the issue for many civil cases. The plaintiffs in prewar family suits I surveyed were sons, brothers, and fathers-in-law, not fathers. It was generally younger men who used the courts to seek property from elders. Not a single case record in my survey includes the term "*bol'shak.*" This epithet for the strongman of the peasant family retained its ethnographic interest to elites but was not used by peasants at court in the early twentieth century.

Individual litigants, of course, were after property, not patriarchy. The steady growth of civil litigation at the township courts reveals the active and ordinary participation of peasant men and women in a market economy.[106] Peasants, contrary to elite opinion, did not have to be introduced to unfamiliar principles fundamental to capitalist relations. The basic rules of the market were accepted without question. Litigants disagreed on whether items had been paid for or on the amount still due on outstanding bills, but no one disputed the basic terms of exchanges of commodities for money or of money for commodities. Every item in a peasant household could be assigned a price: this was an operation familiar to all families when they faced the inevitable reallocations of property after deaths or the voluntary reassignments of property during family divisions. Buying on credit at the outputting counter, renting land from neighbors, putting money in a savings account with interest—these were all not only possible but ordinary transactions in "peasant economy."

The township courts were critical to this orderly and everyday market activity in several ways. For one thing, the courts—with their elected peasant judges—

provided a forum for the public and participatory legitimation of market relations. Peasant judges and litigants alike affirmed the binding ties of contracts, enhancing predictability and trust among economic partners. In addition, the very forum of the courts—replete with record books, links to the imperial administration, and ritualized process—gave small claims significance beyond their local context. "Miscellaneous suits and disputes" were worthy of the state's attention, even if the state's representatives were men with beards and wizened skin. (The sheepskin jacket would have been left at home on such occasions, except in intellectuals' imaginations.) In this sense, the empire provided a powerful tool for peaceful social transformation: a legal instance accessible to the most humble to resolve the most basic, if small in sum, conflicts. Moreover, the indisputably—however maligned—democratic nature of judicial process at these courts created a space for shared definitions of responsibility. The state provided the procedures to deprive a wastrel of control over family resources, but peasant judges themselves made the decisions that removed such individuals from engagement in the market or allowed a reformed profligate back in. A critical element of the construction of market relations in the countryside was the legal possibility of extracting incompetent actors from them.

Civil cases from Bol'shoe Zaborov'e in Novgorod Province offer a glimpse at the intensity of legal actions in a single village. According to a village declaration of 1909, the heads of household officially entitled to vote at the village assembly of Bol'shoe Zaborov'e numbered twenty-five. An official statistical source for Novgorod Province listed the number of households as twenty-one and the population as 169 males and 154 females in 1910, including both adults and children. In civil cases from in 1905, 1907, 1908, 1909, 1911, and 1912 concerning Zaborovskii Township, I encountered the names of forty individuals from Bol'shoe Zaborov'e who either appeared as litigants or were called as witnesses. This number does not include two men who served as judges at the court. These forty names included people with twenty different last names, some of whom may have been related to one another. If we take these twenty last names as representing people from twenty different households, we could conclude that people from at least 80 percent of the households of Bol'shoe Zaborov'e (twenty-five households were cited in the village document) showed up at court in an eight-year period.[107] A conservative estimate, based on the official population statistics, would be that forty individuals represented 25 percent of the adult population of the village.[108] (These estimates are not inconsistent.) Even these approximations underestimate the level of participation at the court, for the forty names on which these calculations are based derive from my survey of civil cases. Still more people were involved in unrecorded civil matters in this period, not to mention criminal cases at this court. These rough figures nonetheless give a sense of the integration of the court into the business and family operations of a small village twenty-two miles from the nearest railroad station and seventy-nine miles away from the district city of Tikhvin in a sparsely populated region of the north.[109]

The choice to use a township court was a choice for legal order. As specialists on law in other settings have shown, it is impossible to relate numbers of court cases to external causes such as "social change" or "economic transformation," and it is misleading to interpret litigiousness as a sign of social or institutional dysfunction.[110] I make a more modest argument in this book. Russian peasants, through their activism in the township courts as litigants and judges, made law a powerful presence in their lives and, in so doing, enhanced civic life in the countryside.

Part of this civic life was a high regard for documentation. People did not have to be literate, in the modern sense, to participate in a legal culture based on written record. Illiterate rural people could rapidly obtain the paperwork essential to their legal affairs. If important to a case, the records of contracts or legal decisions could be copied out for submission at a hearing. The only legal fees recorded in civil cases were those for copying and certifying prior legal decisions, and these fees were modest.[111] To be effective at court, documents had to bear the signs of legitimized truth: witnesses, signatures, official forms, and seals established the validity of a contract or a trust. No oaths were administered at court hearings, where the signature of a participant was the formal way that testimony was "sworn." The clerk's notation of "illit." beside the name of someone who could not sign a name attested to the importance of writing and guaranteed the connection between individual and words.

Through the system of township courts, the state enabled rural people to use law in personal, orderly ways and enhanced the possibilities for good government in the countryside. But state actions could also provoke disorder. The Stolypin regulations of 1906 constituted a major disruption of the legal way that allotment land had been assigned and transferred in the past. Whether the reform would have changed rural society for the better is not the question here. What is relevant to legal culture is how a projected change in ownership rules affected a highly property-conscious society. Everybody in a village knew which allotment was held by whom before 1906, but when every parcel suddenly became an alienable asset, the rules of the land game changed. Still, people used familiar ways of dealing with the new situation—contracts, rents, village assembly formulas, and, finally, court suits, when the expected property deeds did not emerge.

It is hardly surprising that members of the legally aware rural population responded aggressively to the state's enormous revision of land law. The eighteen statutes added to *The General Regulation on Peasants* by the 1906 and 1910 Stolypin rules profoundly reconfigured peasants' property rights.[112] New laws "on the right of peasants to attach and detach parcels of communal land" were an invitation to revise property arrangements, and they inspired many a suit at township courts. Contestations over allotment land between peasants who sought to expand or defend their new property rights recall the long-term conflicts between noble neighbors over their lands and borders, the stuff of literary and anti-legalist satire.[113] Twentieth-century peasant litigants could take their claims and counter-claims, and their search for new or old order in the village, to peasant judges at the township court, where both local knowledge and state power could figure in the resolution of contentions over land, its price, and use.

The settlement of Stolypin-era cases was an arena in which the township courts could do their best but still be trumped later by the state's own tinkering with its disruptive revision of peasant property law.[114] The courts' regular business—the enforcement of contracts, the settlement of work disputes, the protection of rights to crops and other aspects of land tenure, and the legal transmission of family property—continued to be critical to the productivity and well-being of rural people who lived through this state-initiated transformation of landholding. That peasants chose to use township courts to resolve such problems is a testimony to their search for order, predictability, and good management of their resources, even during a property-rights revolution from above.

Small Crime and Punishment

STATUTE LAW AND RURAL LEGAL PROCESS

Township courts provided swift, accessible, and public responses to small crimes in local areas. Peasant judges were empowered to render verdicts on eighty-four misdemeanors defined by statute law and to sentence convicted defendants to modest fines and short terms of arrest. The courts operated strictly in accord with their legal mandate, confining their attention to actions criminalized by statute law and placed in their jurisdiction. Self-declared victims of petty crime could register cases directly with the township clerk or ask the local police to bring charges. In some areas police took an active role in the maintenance of civil order and the defense of public health. As in civil cases, court procedures offered both accusers and defendants a chance to represent themselves, call witnesses, declare their opinions of the verdict, and appeal decisions to higher authorities. Judges adjusted sentences to the gravity of offenses; punishments expressed carefully measured responses to violations of respect, social peace, and ownership. By using township courts to enforce personal dignity, public welfare, and property rights, litigants shared in the legal regulation of behavior and helped to shape standards of conduct for their society.

The number of criminal cases heard by township courts grew steadily in the early twentieth century. In Moscow Province criminal cases registered annually expanded from 21,859 in 1905 to 27,333 in 1913, an increase of 25 percent. After a spike of cases in 1906, plaintiffs registered more cases each year

Table 5.1. Estate of Plaintiffs in Criminal Cases Not Brought by Officials

Estate	*Plaintiffs*	
	Frequency	Percent
Peasants	342	92.9%
Townspeople	23	6.3%
Nobles	1	0.3%
Clergy	1	0.3%
No Estate Recorded	1	0.3%
Total	366	100 %

from 1907 until the outbreak of the war.[1] At courts near the city of Moscow misdemeanor charges increased at a faster rate than civil cases, a phenomenon that did not occur in more remote areas of the province. Criminal cases were processed rapidly at township courts, much more rapidly than at circuit courts. From 1905 through 1908 township courts of Moscow Province resolved between 80 and 85 percent of all criminal cases on their dockets within the same calendar year, whereas the province's circuit courts in this period resolved only 42 to 53 percent of their criminal cases annually (see chapter 6). Rural residents who brought criminal charges to a township court could expect a prompt judgment.

Not every criminal charge against any person could be brought to a township court. Township courts could adjudicate only a specific set of misdemeanors, committed on the territory of the township by people under the jurisdiction of the township court. More serious crimes—regardless of the estate status of accused perpetrators—were processed by other legal instances. The people subject to prosecution for misdemeanors at township courts were the same as those who were obliged to appear in civil cases—all permanent residents in the countryside, other than people of the noble and clerical estates.[2] Nobles and members of the clergy could choose to bring charges at township courts or go to other instances outside the locale where misdemeanors committed against them took place.[3]

In practice, most plaintiffs and almost all defendants in criminal cases at the township level were peasants. In my case survey peasants were the accusers in 93 percent of criminal cases brought directly by plaintiffs, without mediation by police or other officials (see Table 5.1). The rest of the plaintiffs who brought their own cases were usually townspeople, in addition to the very occasional noble or member of the clergy. The defendants in criminal cases were overwhelmingly of peasant estate—in over 98 percent of the cases in my survey (see Table 5.2). The few exceptions again were ordinarily townspeople.

Civil cases at township courts began with a petition submitted by a plaintiff, but a criminal case could be brought by either an aggrieved party or an official. In a wide-ranging clause, the regulations for the township court allowed the

Table 5.2. Estate of Defendants in Criminal Cases, Including Cases Brought by Officials

Estate	*Defendants*	
	Frequency	Percent
Peasants	534	97.1%
Townspeople	11	2.0%
Nobles	0	0 %
Clergy	0	0 %
Official, No Estate Recorded	1	0.2%
No Estate Recorded	4	0.7%
Total	550	100 %

initiation of criminal cases by "an order from the land captain, or by communications of the police, village and other authorities."[4] This statute both empowered officials to initiate criminal prosecutions and also offered rural people the opportunity to make charges indirectly. Peasants could register complaints with the local police, who would communicate charges to the township court. The level of official involvement in criminal cases varied enormously from court to court (See Table 5.3). In my survey, official communications initiated 9 percent of criminal cases at the Ignatevskii and Zaborovskii courts and 16 percent at the Iaguninskii Township Court. At the Nagatinskii Township Court near Moscow, official reports—usually from the police—initiated just over half the criminal cases.

Official participation in criminal cases was usually limited to communications from local constables asking the court to try a case. Policemen ordinarily did not attend the court hearings. Because policemen were themselves likely to be of peasant origin, even the rare appearance of a constable would have little effect on the estates of people in the courtroom.[5] My survey of criminal cases from 1905 to 1917 revealed a solidly peasant contingent of plaintiffs confronting an overwhelmingly peasant ensemble of defendants.

What were the misdemeanors eligible for prosecution at the township courts? Imperial law provided a clear response to this question. *The General Regulation on Peasants* listed eighty-four statutes, by number, and one misdemeanor, in words, to describe the jurisdiction of township courts in criminal matters.[6] The numbered statutes referred to the misdemeanors listed in the *Statutes on Punishments Applicable by the Justices of the Peace.* This comprehensive code, produced in the 1860s, defined crimes and punishments for Justices of the Peace, a legal instance eliminated in rural areas in 1889.[7] The third edition of the *Statutes on Punishments* was issued with the criminal code in 1885; published versions were updated with new legislation, as well as legal opinions and decisions made by the senate in its capacity as supreme appeals instance.[8] The single violation described in words, rather than by number, in *The General Regulation on Peasants* concerned illegal hunting and sale of game; it repeated and summarized the provisions of Statutes 56 and 57 of the *Statutes on Punishments.*[9]

Table 5.3. Officials as Plaintiffs in Criminal Cases in Seven Township Courts

Court	*Plaintiff's Status*				*Total*
	Officials		All Others		
	Percent	Frequency	Percent	Frequency	
Nagatinskii Township Court	50.9%	108	49.1%	104	212
Iaguninskii Township Court	16.1%	5	83.9%	26	31
Selinskii Township Court	15.4%	2	84.6%	11	13
Tsaritsynskii Township Court	13.9%	20	86.1%	124	144
Toksovskii Township Court	11.3%	12	88.7%	94	106
Zaborovskii Township Court	9.1%	1	90.9%	10	11
Ignatevskii Township Court	8.8%	3	91.2%	31	34
Total Cases		151		400	551
Average Percent of Cases Initiated by Officials or Others	27.4%		72.6%		100%

The law on peasant civil rights issued on 5 October 1906 specifically outlawed prosecutions by township courts for any misdemeanor not listed in the misdemeanor code.[10]

Because township courts followed statute law on misdemeanors used by other instances, it was not the case—as some observers believed—that crime was defined differently for township courts and rural people. What was distinctive for rural justice was the regime of punishments that could be applied by rural legal authorities and the kind of court in which cases were decided. Punishments at the township courts were established according to *The General Regulation on Peasants* rather than the *Statutes on Punishments Applicable by the Justices of the Peace.* In place of sanctions specified for each statutory misdemeanor, township courts used a single set of punishments for all criminal cases. Township judges could sentence convicted people to a reprimand in the presence of the court, a fine ranging from twenty-five kopeks to thirty rubles, or arrest of up to fifteen and, in exceptional cases, thirty days, under either simple or harsh circumstances. Harsh arrest meant being fed only bread and water.[11] For some misdemeanors, the upper limits on terms of arrest and fines at township courts were much lower than those indicated in the *Statutes on Punishments.* Jurisdiction had important implications for procedural justice as well. If a person under the authority of a township administration was accused of one of the misdemeanors assigned to township courts, the case had to be tried by the township court in the area of the purported crime. Rural people accused of these misdemeanors thus enjoyed—or suffered—justice rendered by their peers. Their judges would be peasants from their township, not noble Justices of the Peace or all-estate juries in the circuit courts.

The eighty-four statutes defining crimes punishable by township courts covered a multitude of activities that the state deemed violations of public life. In Appendix 2 these misdemeanors are listed by statute number, each with its description and the number of pages of related commentary published in a 1912

Table 5.4. Categories of Misdemeanors Described in the *Statutes on Punishments Applicable by the Justices of the Peace* (*SP*) and Usable by Township Courts

Type of Violation	*Chapter in SP*	*Statute Nos.*	*No. of Pages in SP*	*No. of Statutes in SP*	*No. of Statutes Usable by Township Courts*
Against Administrative Order	2	29–34	48	6	4
Against Decorum, Order, and Peace	3	35–51	40	17	12
Against Public Improvement	4	52–57	19	6	4
Of the Regulation on Passports	5	58–64	8	7	1
Of the Regulation on Construction and Means of Communication	6	65–87	31	23	6
Of the Rules on Caution with Fire	7	88–98	6	11	8
Of the Regulation on Post and Telegraph	8	99–101	2	3	0
Against Public Health	9	102–116	25	15	3
Against Personal Safety	10	117–129	9	13	12
Insults to Honor, Threats, and Violence	11	130–142	82	13	12
Against Family Rights	12	143–144	2	2	1
Against Others' Property	13	145–181	184	37	17

Source: *UN*, p. 576; *OPK*, st. 127. Since three of the eighty-four statutes assigned to the township courts are sections of other statutes, the total number of the statutes listed here is fewer than eighty-four.

edition of the *Statutes on Punishments.* Commentaries in the *Statutes on Punishments* derived from appeals decisions; they offer a rough guide to controversies at higher courts over the interpretation of statutes. The statutes in the first chapter of the *Statutes on Punishments* addressed procedural issues; all remaining statutes were grouped according to the type of criminal activity to be punished (see Table 5.4). The chapter headings of the *Statutes on Punishments* allow us to enter the legal imaginary of officials through their definitions of minor crime punishable at township courts.

The largest component of statute law in the *Statutes on Punishments*—chapters 3 through 10—concerned public welfare. Just over one hundred statutes addressed violations of order, authority, tranquility, communications and transport, health, and safety. Half of these statutes were available for prosecution at township courts. Violations of administrative order included charges of disobedience or insult to officials as well as "damage to official signs, insignia, advertisements, without intent of showing disrespect to authority." Public order was to be protected against many kinds of unruly conduct, including quarrels, fights, and inebriation in public if—an important if—it threatened "safety, peace, or decorum." Also deemed violations of social space were the "public presentation or distribution of clearly corrupting devices and images" as well as "shameless acts . . . in a public place." The misdemeanor code contained a large number of rules designed to preserve health and safety. People could be prosecuted at township courts for damaging bridges, contaminating water supplies, "breaking the rules on caution with fire," "not taking established measures to prevent danger from domestic animals," and a multitude of other careless or malicious actions.[12]

A second kind of minor criminality defined in the *Statutes on Punishments* was the violation of individual dignity, expressed in the thirteen statutes of chapter 11, on "insults to honor, threats, and violence." All twelve of the nonprocedural statutes of this part of the misdemeanor code were applicable by township courts: oral, written, and physical insults to other people were criminal offenses. Slander as a misdemeanor generated twenty pages of commentary in the 1912 edition of the *Statutes on Punishments*. Both the offender's relationship to the insulted party and the question of whether the insulted person had "given grounds for the insult" figured in the statutes.[13]

A third category of statute law concerned property rights. The omnibus chapter 13, "On Misdemeanors against Another's Property," contained thirty-seven statutes, seventeen of which were applicable by township courts. In addition to outright theft, the law criminalized such actions as "on someone else's land willfully . . . harvesting fruits or vegetables, picking berries or mushrooms, damaging trees in gardens, or pulling up garden flowers." Falsification of weights or measures and purchases of stolen goods were among the many property violations that could be punished at township courts.[14]

A final kind of misdemeanor listed in the *Statutes on Punishments* concerned violations of family rights: one statute criminalized nonpayment of support to indigent parents and was applicable at township courts, and a second, not usable by township judges, criminalized irresponsibility toward infants and other dependents.

Contrary to the widespread view that township court personnel were ignorant of statute law, rural courts made generous and accurate use of statutes applicable by township judges. Among cases where I recorded statute numbers, the court cited an applicable statute in over 94 percent of criminal charges and in over 98 percent of criminal decisions.[15] Occasionally an inappropriate statute cited in a charge would be corrected to a more fitting one in the court's final decision. At the township court in Tsaritsyno in March 1916 the police constable's protocol charged two peasants with statute 36—"violation of decorum during church services"—in addition to the familiar statute 42, "dangerously drunk in public." By the end of the hearing, during which both defendants confessed their guilt, the charges were changed to the correct statutes, in this case 42 and 38—"unruly conduct in public places." Statute 36 had been abolished in 1906.[16]

Not all statutes applicable by township courts were used by rural judges. Fifty-two of the eighty-four statutes listed in *The General Regulation on Peasants* were never used in charges or decisions at the courts I studied. These unused statutes, like the underused categories of civil law reported in official statistics (see chapter 3), appear to have been irrelevant to rural life. Statute 34—"making a public announcement without permission when required by law, without other unlawful goals"—was never charged by township authorities. Statutes concerning begging, illegal lotteries, building without a permit, nonmaintenance of sidewalks, damaging roads, smoking tobacco in forbidden areas, selling unsafe edibles, keeping forbidden weapons, not securing flowerpots in windows, not setting up warning signs around construction sites, wells, and cesspools testify to the regulatory zeal of Russian authorities but were not deployed by rural people at their courts. Some statutes that did reflect country values were nonetheless infrequently cited as criminal charges by township courts. Statutes 147—"walking or driving or riding across another's meadows or fields before the harvest of crops or grasses on them"—and 148—"driving cattle through another's meadows and fields, pasturing cattle on another's land or in another's woods"—show that state regulators did not ignore one of the most common property violations in the countryside. But rural litigants often were content with bringing civil suits against their neighbors for trampling crops; only a few bothered to treat the act of herding or pasturing cattle on another's property as a crime worthy of punishment for its own sake.[17]

One statute with direct relevance to rural life was conspicuously absent from criminal charges and decisions at the township courts. This was statute 57—"fishing or hunting at a forbidden time in unallowed places, by illegal means, or without observing the prescribed rules." This kind of violation was the same sore point mentioned in the single misdemeanor listed without a statute number as a particular charge of the township courts in *The General Regulation on Peasants*.[18] The state's attempt to confine hunting to certain times and places appears to have had no resonance at all with rural people. Violations of hunting and fishing regulations were never prosecuted by township courts in any of the areas I studied.[19]

Differences in perspective between rural inhabitants and state lawgivers should not be assumed or exaggerated.[20] Many of the statutes provided for township judges were used repeatedly by villagers and rural authorities. The statute cited most frequently in criminal charges and decisions was statute 38, "quarrels, fights, fistfights, or other kinds of unruly conduct in public places." Disturbing public peace as described in this statute accounted for a quarter of all decisions recorded with statute numbers in the courts I studied. Another commonly cited statute, accounting for more than one-fifth of decisions, was statute 55, "nonobservance of the rules on cleanliness and order in the street, and for letting animals roam on streets where this is not allowed." In my survey of verdicts, judges applied four of the seventeen statutes on property rights available to them. Perhaps more surprisingly, judges used seven of the sixteen statutes on crimes against public order and improvement described in chapters 3 and 4 of the *Statutes on Punishments*. The category of misdemeanor for which judges used the largest proportion of applicable statutes (nine out of twelve) was "Insults to Honor, Threats, and Violence." Confronted with offenses against individual dignity, rural judges fine-tuned their verdicts according to options provided by the misdemeanor code.

The translation of local grievances into misdemeanors described in *The Statutes on Punishments* was part of the ordinary process of making state law work for rural people. In criminal litigation, more than in civil actions, township courts were constrained by official definitions of right and wrong behaviors. Court personnel were impressively familiar with the law codes made available to them. Not once did I discover that the wrong statute had been cited in a verdict. An occasional slipup in a number or a charge according to an out-of-date statute would be corrected or thrown out by the court.[21] All criminal cases at courts I studied concerned actions that corresponded to a statute law, whether or not a statute was recorded by the township clerk as part of the accusation. In this most important sense of procedural justice, the township courts fulfilled the goal of the 1906 law abolishing prosecutions at township courts for misdemeanors not listed in the *Statutes on Punishments.*

Juxtaposing charges—rather than verdicts—recorded by township clerks with applicable statute law reveals the intersection of state rules and rural litigation in a somewhat different light. Court records allow us to view rural misdemeanors as plaintiffs described their cases, rather than according to statutes under which decisions were made. The printed rubrics of the registers used by the Tsaritsynskii Township Court for criminal cases provided ample room to record the nature of accusations; each case record began with the following words:

> 191_, ____ day, the Tsaritsynskii Township Court of Moscow District at its open session composed of the President of the court ____________, the Township Judges [two lines to fill in] in the presence of the clerk ____________ decided the criminal case of an accusation of [seven lines to fill in].[22]

The content of these seven lines, as well as other spaces between printed rubrics, provides the clerk's-eye view of local petty crime and controversies over it.

Court clerks recorded an impressive array of criminal accusations. Table 5.5 displays a list of charges registered either in words or by statute number, and provides the percentage of each kind of case in the whole survey of criminal cases registered from 1905 to 1917. The most frequent criminal charge at township courts was "insult in words." Charges for verbal insults (covered by Statutes 130 through 132) accounted for 21 percent of all cases. Various kinds of theft charges (under Statutes 169 and 172) accounted for 17 percent of misdemeanor cases; two public welfare issues—disturbing the peace (Statute 38) and violation of sanitation rules (Statutes 55 and 56)—were the subject of another 17 percent of all criminal accusations.

Like the statutes of the misdemeanor code, criminal charges registered at township courts can be grouped in three broad categories—cases about personal dignity, cases about public welfare, and cases about property rights. In my survey the most common kind of accusation to come before the township judges was a suit about personal dignity (56 percent of all cases). The next most common kind of accusation concerned public welfare (24 percent of all cases), and 20 percent of all accusations concerned property violations. There was considerable variation from court to court in the types of criminal charges put forward. In all but one of the courts I studied, dignity cases constituted the majority

Table 5.5. Types of Criminal Cases in Township Courts, 1905–1917

Type of Criminal Accusation	*Frequency*	*Percent*
Personal Dignity Charges:		
Insult, Word(s)	117	21.4%
Beating	63	11.5%
Samoupravstvo (Unlawful Assertion of a Right)	36	6.6%
Insult, Deed(s)	33	6.0%
Insult, Unspecified	22	4.0%
Slander	14	2.6%
Threat	11	2.0%
Insult to Authority	5	0.9%
Insult, Word(s) and Deed(s)	4	0.7%
Total Personal Dignity Charges:	305	55.7%
Public Welfare Charges:		
Misbehavior in Public, Unruly Conduct (St. 38)	48	8.8%
Dirt, Garbage, Sewage Violations	45	8.2%
Drunkenness	7	1.3%
Careless Driving of Horses (St. 123)	6	1.1%
Carelessness with Fire	6	1.1%
Cruelty to Animals	5	0.9%
Noise	3	0.5%
Illegal Commerce (Includes Illegal Sale of Alcohol)	2	0.4%
Disobedience to Authority	2	0.4%
Domestic Animal Attacks, Lack of Control	2	0.4%
Gambling	1	0.2%
Burying Animal in Illegal Place	1	0.2%
Non-Fulfillment of Public Duty	1	0.2%
Total Public Welfare Charges	129	23.7%
Property Rights Charges		
Theft	89	16.2%
Deceit, Fraud, Swindling	5	0.9%
Theft, Secondary Charge: Attempt, Aid, Harboring Stolen Goods	5	0.9%
Not Reporting Found Object	2	0.4%
Family Support	2	0.4%
Damaging Property	2	0.4%
Extortion	1	0.2%
Possession Controversy (Not Land)	1	0.2%
Suit	1	0.2%
Work Controversy	1	0.2%
Total Property Rights Charges	109	20.2%
Other Criminal Charge	2	0.4%
Total	545	100 %

of misdemeanors heard. Personal dignity cases accounted for 71 percent of criminal cases at the Iaguninskii court, for 73 percent of criminal cases at the Zaborovskii court in Novgorod Province, and for 85 percent of cases at the Ignatevskii court. Nearer Moscow at the Tsaritsynskii court, dignity cases were 59 percent of the criminal docket. In only one area, Nagatinskii Township, located very close to the Moscow city limits, did another kind of case predominate; here public welfare, expressed in a variety of charges, was the subject of 42 percent of cases. Across all courts, the proportion of accusations about property crime varied significantly: 7 percent at Iaguninskii Township, 9 percent at Zaborovskii and Ignatevskii courts, 13 percent at Tsaritsynskii court, and a high mark of 29 percent in Nagatinskii Township. A general pattern observable from these different courts is that charges of petty property crime were much more frequent at courts in close proximity to Moscow.

The variability in kinds of violations processed in different townships displays the adaptability of statute law to local needs through the system of township courts. Judges, clerks, and accusers used the misdemeanor code flexibly to prosecute petty crime as it was described by accusers in their localities. Statute laws defending public order, personal dignity, and property rights were activated by township litigants in their own ways. There was no obligation for rural courts to use all aspects of the statute law; some statutes were ignored by township courts. Some unused statutes described violations irrelevant to rural life—the nonmaintenance of sidewalks, for example. Other statutes applicable by township courts describe matters that could have been prosecuted in rural areas but were not. These unused statutes—such as the rules on hunting—define areas in which official and rural morality did not overlap.

Table 5.6 represents the proportion of statute law devoted to three categories of violations—against public order, personal dignity, and property rights—in the *Statutes on Punishments,* in the statutes available to township courts, and in the case records of the courts I studied. This comparison is a rough indicator of the attention that various kinds of crime drew from different quarters. A single statute might suffice to define a criminal action that was deemed particularly serious by officials or litigants or both. Moreover, the proportion of cases of each type varied considerably from court to court. The different divisions between kinds of violation nonetheless reveal the broad outlines of three legal imaginaries.

The writers of the misdemeanor code were particularly concerned to define a multitude of violations of public welfare (66 percent of statutes); next in number in the *Statutes on Punishments* were statutes on property rights (24 percent of statute law); and finally came the 10 percent of statutes concerning personal dignity. When officials decided which statutes township courts could use, they provided judges with a different mix of statutes—almost half (48 percent) concerned public welfare, 31 percent addressed personal dignity, and 21 percent addressed property crime. The typology of criminal accusations processed at township courts was somewhat different: more than half were personal dignity cases, followed by public welfare charges, and finally property violations.

Table 5.6. Types of Misdemeanors as Percentages of Statute Law Available to Justices of the Peace, Percentages of Statutes Available for Use at Township Courts, and Percentages of Criminal Cases Processed at Township Courts

Type of Violation	*Misdemeanor Statutes Available to Justices of the Peace (%)*	*Misdemeanor Statutes Usable by Township Courts (%)*	*Misdemeanor Cases at Township Courts from Case Data (%)*
Public Welfare	65.8%	48%	24.8%
Property Rights	24.1%	21%	19.4%
Personal Dignity	9.8%	31%	55.8%
Total	100 %	100%	100 %

Source: *UN, OPK,* st. 127, case data.

This excursion into categories of statute law and case records displays the effective and adaptable interaction of code and legal process at township courts. Statute law was not an alien imposition on rural society; it was a set of rules engaged at local courts. The misdemeanor code defined an array of violations that could be accessed by judges and clerks in their responses to charges made by rural people against wayward neighbors. There was an overlap between the perspectives of law writers about what kind of actions should be criminalized and the charges processed at township courts. If we imagine statute law and process at township courts as two lenses on minor crime, their intersection—the overlay of one lens upon the other—defines a shared vision of danger to the common good and of ways to combat it. The non-overlapping areas of concern comprise the available but unused statutes—such as the laws on hunting violations—that fell outside the moral frame of township litigators. In matters of personal dignity, however, both judges and accusers at township courts were vigorous users of statute law.

IN DEFENSE OF HONOR

The most common personal dignity case at township courts concerned an insult. Chapter 11 of the *Statutes on Punishments* defined twelve kinds of "insults to honor, threats, and violence."[23] The only statute in this section of the misdemeanor code that was not applicable by township courts was a procedural one. Statute 138 precluded punishing people found guilty of insulting behavior in cases where the insulted person had inflicted an "equal or more serious" insult on the accuser or if the insulted person took action under another legal regime.[24] The omission of this statute from those usable by township courts meant that in rural cases "mutual insulting" could be addressed and punished, if judges chose to do so. A discriminating attitude toward causality and responsibility turned out to be a hallmark of legal process at township courts.

On 28 June 1916 Tatiana Filippova Ignat'eva, a peasant woman registered in the village of Lutsino,[25] appeared before the Iaguninskii Township Court as a plaintiff in a small crime case. The accused, a male peasant from the same village, Prokhor Ivanov Dvorianinov, and a witness, Pavel Koletskov, also of Lutsino, were present at the hearing. The scribe, Lapin, recorded Tatiana Filippova's testimony before the three judges as follows: "in the month of May, Dvorianinov without any reason beat her, hitting her several times with his hand. She asked to have him punished for this." Tatiana Filippova could not sign her testimony; the presiding judge, Makarov, signed for her in the record book. The testimony of Prokhor Ivanov was then recorded: "The defendant Dvorianinov did not acknowledge his guilt, explaining that he had taken a stick out of Ignat'eva's hands, and she had called for help." The presiding judge signed for this testimony as well.[26] The witness, Pavel Koletskov, testified that "during a quarrel with Ignat'eva over chickens, Dvorianinov hit her several times with his hand." Koletsov, too, was illiterate. Following procedures, the parties were asked if they could be reconciled. The record dryly notes, "Reconciliation did not follow." The judges issued their decision as follows:

> The township court having heard the present case, having listened to the evidence of the witness Koletskov, found the charge against Dvorianinov proven, and accordingly under statutes 127.3 and 134 of the *Gen[eral] Reg[ulation on Peasants]* and statute 134 of the *S[tatutes on] Pun[ishments Applicable by the Justices of the Peace]* decided: to sentence peasant of the village Lutsino Prokhor Ivanov Dvorianinov for insult of Tatiana Filippova Ignat'eva to arrest for fifteen days.

The case concluded as usual with procedures that publicized and formalized the verdict. The decision was read aloud to both parties, as was the right to appeal the decision within thirty days, along with the procedures for such a complaint.[27] The judges and the scribe put their signatures on the case, with their titles stamped beside their names.[28] Prokhor Ivanov did not appeal the decision, but he also did not go to jail. On 17 July, just before the time for his appeal expired, he died.[29] His death was noted on the case record. On 20 August, two months after the case had been heard, the township scribe recorded that the case was closed.[30]

The conduct of Tatiana Filippova's insult case, as recorded by the clerk, was unexceptional in almost every respect. The calling of witnesses was both routine and important to criminal verdicts. As with other cases, testimony was signed by either the speaker or a court official, and all parties were informed of the decision, and the right and procedure for appeal. Fifteen days of arrest was, however, a severe sentence. The other convictions in criminal cases at the Iaguninskii Township Court in the first six months of 1916 resulted in a reprimand or arrests of two or seven days.[31] The factors that influenced the judges so strongly in Tatiana Filippova's favor are absent from this record. An argument about chickens appears not to have been considered a provocation to violence, and Prokhor Ivanov's assertion that he had taken a stick away from the plaintiff was not mentioned further. What is clear is the court's interpretation of this complaint of unprovoked violence as a type of insult. Tatiana Filippova had accused Prokhor Ivanov of a beating (*poboi*); but the verdict, issued under statute 134 of the *Statutes on Punishments,* referred to an "insult" to the plaintiff.[32] Was this personalization of violent behavior an example of arbitrary or retrograde values of peasant judges?

The application of statute 134 was not accidental or peculiar to peasant ideas of justice. The judges' use of the charge of insult reached back to a long legal tradition in Russia, one that applied to other, non-peasant estates. Laws regulating compensation for verbal and physical affronts to honor were included in Russia's legal codes from Muscovite times into the imperial period. The state's defense of the honor of its subjects has been interpreted as a fundamental aspect of Muscovite governance, providing a bond between each individual and the state order that assured his or her rights.[33] In early-twentieth-century Russia this bond was embodied in statutes concerning "insults to honor, threats, and violence."[34]

The primary rubrics for "insults to honor" in the *Statutes on Punishments* were "insults in words or writing," "insult in words or writing, with forethought or in a public place or among many people . . . or of a woman," "foul language against an employer and members of his family . . . or brazen disobedience to an employer . . . or overseer," "insult in words or writing of a direct relative from a preceding generation," "a provoked insult in deed against a non-relative," "an unprovoked insult in deed," "an insult in deed, with forethought, or in a public place or among many people, or of a person, not a relative, but who deserved particular respect, or of a woman," and "slander in words or writing." Qualifying for punishment as "threats and violence" were still other antisocial actions: "threat of violent harm, without mercenary or other criminal goal," "threat in words to kill someone or setting a fire, without mercenary or other criminal goal," "threat in writing to kill someone or set a fire," and "misuse of assumed rights [*samoupravstvo*] or use of force, but without severe beating, wounds, or mutilation."[35]

Each of these misdemeanors had a well-established place in the courts of late imperial Russia, including circuit courts and Justices of the Peace, as well as township instances. The *Statutes on Punishments* were filled with commentaries and citations of judicial opinions and appellate decisions that could help judges make decisions about such matters as the "difference between insult and slander."[36] Official descriptions of insults were important for rural people, because they defined the appropriate jurisdiction for prosecuting various injurious acts.[37] The graver versions of such offenses, such as "a threat . . . *with* a mercenary or criminal goal" or "the use of force . . . *with* severe beating, wounds, or mutilation," would require the intervention of the police and be decided by other, superior courts.[38]

In Tatiana Filippova's case at the Iaguninskii court, one might imagine that Prokhor Ivanov's actions would be considered "use of force," covered under Statute 142 in the section of chapter 11 on "threats and violence," rather than prosecuted as an "insult." This kind of legal dilemma had presented itself before, and the *Statutes on Punishments* provided helpful commentary on the "difference between force and insult in deed." The distinction hinged partly on the aggressor's intent and partly on the consequences of his—or her—actions. Several opinions from the 1860s and 1870s, consolidated in the following commentary, described behaviors that were considered violence without insult:

> Beating and in general violent actions of all kinds, not having the quality of serious beatings, wounds, or mutilations, and accomplished without the goal of insulting or showing disdain for the individual, but out of arbitrary vengefulness, are actionable under Statute 142, and not 134 or 135, because although offense in deed is accomplished usually by means of force, it is obvious that when such action expresses not primarily the intent to insult or express disdain, but arbitrary vengefulness, then the punishment must be defined by the major action.[39]

In other words, violence that was arbitrary and vengeful, but not directed against the victim's dignity, was not to be prosecuted as an insult.

The majority of later commentaries, however, emphasized the connection between violence and insult. A decision of 1883 observes the following:

> Since the carrying out of a beating always lowers the dignity of a man and includes an expression of contempt for his person, and therefore contains all real signs of insult, consequently those guilty of perpetrating light beatings must, depending on the circumstances of the case and on their relationship to the victim, be submitted to one of the exactions defined for insult in deed in general.[40]

Other citations from this decision hammered home the point. One ruling observed: "The carrying out of a beating based on a feeling of hostility to the victim, or on a desire to take vengeance on him or cause him pain, does not remove the significance of this encroachment on his person as an insult to his honor." The connection of violence to insult was generalized still further in another commentary: "The carrying out of light beatings, according to the system of our legislation, must always be considered as insult in action."[41]

The judges' use of Statute 134, "insult in deed, without any cause on the part of the victim," in Tatiana Filippova's case accorded neatly with the reasoning of other judges and other courts. Prokhor Ivanov's behavior was not interpreted as arbitrary vengefulness but as an intentional insult to Tatiana Filippova. Tatiana Filippova's testimony provided the court with the formula for deciding among the three different statutes concerning "insult in deed." She had indicated that Prokhor Ivanov had beaten her "without any reason," a charge that corresponded to Statute 134, and not 133—"with grounds on the part of the insulted"—or Statute 135 that criminalized "intentional" public insults to people of higher status.[42]

For the township judges, the choice of statute had no necessary bearing on the severity of punishment. Arrest of fifteen days was the maximum sentence the township could assign.[43] In the *Statutes on Punishments* designed originally for other courts, arrest of fifteen days was the minimum sentence for all the insult-in-deed statutes; this sentence was attached to Statute 133, "insult . . . with grounds." The maximum sentence in the *Statutes on Punishments* was three months in jail; it applied to Statute 135, presumably because violations of status were of particular concern to law writers. Statute 134 ("without any reason"), if it had been applied by a Justice of the Peace, could have produced a sentence of up to one month.[44] These differences between the sentencing possibilities of different jurisdictions point to the meticulous quality of township court process. The rural judges chose their statute in correspondence with their notion of the misdemeanor and independently applied to the insulter the maximum of punishments available to them. To this court, the crime was about unprovoked violent insult. Prokhor Ivanov's beating of Tatiana Filippova was an insult, and a serious one, for which the judges applied their harshest sanction.

This decision signals the strong interaction of official rules and peasant jurisprudence. Insult, honor, and personal dignity were concepts written into law for all estates in imperial Russia. They were mobilized in rural courts by judges and scribes who followed national legal codes. To see insult cases as "customary" or otherwise exoteric to the formal law is to ignore the defense of dignity in the legal system as a whole, in its codes, cassation courts, and professional discourse. To regard peasant concern for insult as quaint or primitive is not only to displace actual twentieth-century people into a past they may not have had but also to miss an opportunity to see rural society in action, exercising its disciplining, protective, and creative possibilities.[45] In the village of Lutsino, a settlement of seventy-six households and some six hundred people in 1913,[46] people would know that Tatiana Filippova had successfully defended her right not to be beaten.

Words were taken seriously in imperial Russia—not just by state censors but by the law and rural litigants.[47] The *Statutes on Punishments* provided lengthy descriptions of what constituted a verbal insult. "General conceptions of insults," a topic in the explanatory commentaries to Statute 130 on "offenses in words or writing," begins with the following definition, taken from an 1872 ruling:

> To swear, in the accepted conception, means either to use abusive and reviling words or to laugh at brazenly and sarcastically, and, in both cases, with the intent to dishonor, shame, or humiliate the person being insulted in either way.[48]

A second definition, which could have served as a covering principle for most insult cases at the township courts, put succinctly the notion of verbal insult:

> Insult in words should be understood as the enunciation of words that contain swearing or expressions, comparisons, and hints that are clearly insulting to honor and pronounced with the goal of humiliating and insulting the dignity of the person to whom they are addressed.[49]

These general guidelines were elaborated in several more citations from court cases. The *Statutes on Punishments* gave considerable attention to how differences in social rank between offenders and the offended might give rise to perceptions of insult and whether certain references to rank could be considered legal violations.[50] Accurate interpretation by both parties concerned and by the court was of the essence, as in the following case note: "Therefore the expression, 'You are worse than any townswoman [*meshchanka*],' can become insulting, if, in the opinion of the court, it was said to disparage the honor of the offended, when, for example, to the word *meshchanka* is added the word *any*."[51] Another court decision noted that "the word *merchant* [*torgovets*], taken by itself, does not contain anything insulting, but in conjunction with words that express a scornful attitude of the speaker to the person to whom such a title is applied, it can acquire an insulting character."[52] A verbal insult might also result from offensive uses of the familiar pronoun *ty* (you, *tu, du,* etc.), when the formal *Vy* (you, *vous, Sie,* etc.) would have been appropriate. Calling anyone *ty,* if the court recognizes that "this word was used with an intent to insult," was punishable under Statute 130.[53]

Insult in writing was the equivalent of oral insult and was covered by the same statutes in the *Statutes on Punishments.*[54] As with oral insults, the context of a written offense was critically important. A "master" who wrote in the passport of his servant woman a "certification of a quality of hers, the ascription of which is considered an insult," could be punished for his action. Similarly expression in a letter of doubts about the "possible existence of the marital tie between two known individuals and the designation of their relations as a civil marriage" was "insult in writing." Even an "insulting reference to an institution, for example, . . . a hotel, in which indecent conduct is allowed, can be regarded as an insult to the owner of the institution."[55] Of the ten "examples of personal insults" provided in Taganstev's 1912 edition of the *Statutes on Punishments,* half referred only somewhat indirectly to violations of propriety between men and women. It was an offense "to follow a woman on the street and ask a policeman more than once to take her into custody with no reason other than to find out her identity, when in fact her identity is well known to the guilty party." More directly, one commentary read: "a proposal by a man to a woman to enter into sexual relations with him must be considered a personal insult."[56]

In township courts, insults to sexual honor required little decoding. A case record from a hearing at the Tsaritsynskii Township Court, in the countryside southeast of Moscow, went directly to the point: "On the 13th of January of this year [1917], peasantwoman of the village Marino, Pelagea Riabinina, brought a complaint against a woman of the same village, Vasilisa Riabinina, [claiming] that the latter always insulted her, but that on the 1st of January Vasilisa called her a whore and also slandered her as if she had cohabited with her lodger . . . and as if she had gotten pregnant and poisoned the children, as a result of which she asks to have her brought to justice." This court heard two witnesses confirm that Vasilisa had called Pelagea a whore, and so on, and the result was a ten-ruble fine or ten days of arrest for this "verbal insult."[57]

Township clerks did not have to record each sexual affront literally, for the abstraction "improper words" was familiar to all people at court. This charge was the subject of the next hearing after Tatiana Filippova's successful case at

Iagunino on 28 June 1916. The hostile parties were two women from the village of Pokrovskoe, a settlement seven miles from the township administration.[58] Aleksandra Alekseeva's charge against her co-villager Varvara Nikiforova Ivanova was that "in April Ivanova had insulted her with various improper words." For this, she requested that Varvara Nikiforova be "punished."[59] Varvara Nikiforova Ivanova's testimony was recorded as follows:

> The accused Ivanova recognized her guilt, explaining that she had insulted Alekseeva because she had seen her in sexual relations with her [own], the accused's, husband.

A witness, also a woman from Pokrovskoe, was present at court, but the judges decided not to hear her testimony. A note of explanation was entered into the record: "The witness Kuznetsova, in view of a personal tie to the accused Ivanova, was not questioned." The two sides, as one might expect, refused to reconcile.[60] The judges determined that the accusation was "proven by personal confession" and sentenced Varvara Nikiforova to seven days of arrest for "insult in words" to Aleksandra Nikolaeva. Their decision cited Statute 130, "insult in words or writing." All the participants signed the record book; later, other authorities noted that the "decision was completely fulfilled."[61]

This case invites speculation about what was gained—or lost—by the parties to the suit. If the testimony of these women is taken at face value, Aleksandra Alekseeva had sex with Varvara Nikiforova's husband; Varvara Nikiforova caught them in the act and called Aleksandra Alekseeva a whore. For this insult in words, Aleksandra brought Varvara to court. Varvara, having testified in court about the immoral behavior of Aleksandra, went to jail for seven days. Aleksandra, it seems, could sleep with the husband of another woman, reject her censure, and even have her arrested for pronouncing "improper words." To be called a whore was an insult, regardless of one's sexual behavior. Insult cases were not about discovering whether a person had merited—or de-merited?—a demeaning description but about the social disruption of name-calling itself.

One may be tempted to regard this focus on the word-in-itself as a rural remnant of an outmoded legal order. Muscovite courts did not try to prove whether an insult corresponded to the truth about a person's character but only whether insulting words had been pronounced.[62] But this kind of thinking about personal honor was part and parcel of late nineteenth- and early-twentieth-century Russian law and social practice as well. An opinion written by a well-known legal specialist in 1870 and cited in the *Statutes on Punishments* observes, "Calling anyone a 'liar' definitively constitutes an insult."[63] Whether a person had lied or not was immaterial to prosecution under Statute 130. In the Moscow Bar Association in the early twentieth century, lawyers were disciplined for insulting characterizations of their peers, regardless of the accuracy of incautious charges.[64] Peasants were not alone in their efforts to have improper words punished; their use of township courts to defend themselves against insults accorded with the legal codes and legal discourse of Russian professionals.

Varvara Nikiforova's confession makes sense within a system that accorded real, punishable offense to insults. She wanted, apparently, to stick by her words and for her words to stick. Perhaps she could gain some satisfaction by having her insult recognized by the court, by not retracting or denying it, and even by going to jail for a few days to make her point. The judgment in this case did not prove that Aleksandra Alekseeva was not a whore. On the contrary, Varvara's testimony in this matter was given an official hearing, entered into the legal record, and probably became a subject of discussion in the village of Pokrovskoe.

Although it would be hubris—alas, all too ordinary—to explicate such cases with confidence, it is clear that insulting another person was not a trivial matter in rural Russia. In defense of dignity, peasants availed themselves of their legal possibilities in huge numbers, calling insulters to "legal responsibility" without the assistance of police or other official prosecutors. Litigants made sacrifices to get to court; judges and scribes devoted a considerable amount of their judicial service to insult cases. At the Sharopovskii Township Court, south of Iagunino in Zvenigorod County, of the 115 criminal cases brought to court in 1910, 82 (71 percent) concerned charges of some kind of personal insult.[65] No case record indicates that anyone in the township courtroom thought an insult was a joke. Expense of community time, careful application of statute law, observed procedural formalities—these all suggest that insults were grave affronts requiring legal response. The state lent a bit of its majesty to a person who could punish others for an insult.

The significance of name-calling to rural people is revealed more clearly in cases where verbal insult and physical violence were both involved, as in the following hearing at the Iaguninskii Township Court. On 7 March 1906 the Iaguninskii judges heard an accusation of "insult through words" brought by Grigorii Dmitriev Pil'shchikov, a peasant from a different township, against Stepan Ivanovich Rodin, a peasant from Savvinskaia sloboda. Located six miles from the court, Savvinskaia sloboda was an ancient settlement, originally attached to a monastery built in the fourteenth century. In 1906 this village was the most populous settlement in the township, the site of annual commercial fairs, a *zemstvo* school, and the quarters of the local constable.[66] Its commercial establishments and activities gave rise to many cases at the township court, including Grigorii Dmitriev's.

On the day Grigorii Dmitriev's case was heard, N. A. Kvardakov, the president of the Iaguninskii court, was absent. N. Sedov, another experienced judge, presided in his place. This change was probably related to the contents of this case. According to the court record book, the accuser, Grigorii Dmitriev Pil'shchikov, declared that

> on the 22nd of February in Kvardakov's tea shop in Savvinskaia sloboda, Rodin called him a convict and other names and hit him in the chest without any reason from his [Pil'shchikov's] side. He asks that he [Rodin] be brought to responsibility.[67]

Pil'shchikov signed his name neatly in the book, and then Rodin stepped up to tell his side of the story. The scribe recorded the following:

> The accused, peasant of village Savvinskaia sloboda Stepan Ivanov Rodin, declared that on the 22nd of February of this year he entered Kvardakov's tea shop where Pil'shchikov was. Then, addressing himself to Pil'shchikov, he asked why the latter had killed his [Rodin's] cat. Pil'shchikov, for this declaration, called him [Rodin] a convict. After that, he really did hit Pil'shchikov in the chest, because the latter had called him a convict. He does not consider himself guilty of insulting Pil'shchikov. Illiterate.[68]

The presiding judge, Sedov, signed Rodin's testimony. A witness, Ivan Egorov Privalov, also from Savvinskaia sloboda, appeared for the hearing. He testified that,

> on the 22nd of February of this year in Kvardakov's tea shop Pil'shchikov and Rodin exchanged insulting words. After Pil'shchikov called Rodin a shit, the latter hit Pil'shchikov in the chest.[69]

Privalov was literate and signed his testimony. In accord with the usual procedures, the judges proposed reconciliation to the two men, which they refused.

Privalov's testimony proved critical to the resolution of the case. The judges recorded their opinion as follows:

> The township court having examined this case and taking into consideration that as evident from the testimony of the witness Privalov there was mutual insulting between Pil'shchikov and Rodin, Rodin hit Pil'shchikov in the chest because Pil'shchikov had called him a shit, and therefore passes the following verdict: peasant of the village Savvinskaia sloboda Stepan Rodin is found not guilty and is acquitted by the court.

The judges and the scribe signed this case. The illiterate defendant had the presiding judge sign his response as "satisfied." Pil'shchikov, whose accusation had failed, concluded the case by signing that he was also "satisfied."[70]

The reasoning provided for this verdict displays a relationship between verbal insults and physical violence. Being called a "shit" justified hitting the insulter in the chest. Killing someone's cat, or pugnaciously inquiring about it, earned no comment from the judges and did not appear in their considerations. What counted was the unquestionable insult carried by such epithets as "[you] shit," uttered in the tea shop. "Convict"—meaning someone who had been jailed as a result of a conviction—was cited by both parties as a criminal insult, but it had apparently been used reciprocally and did not figure in the verdict. Whatever words the parties exchanged after that first equivalence were canceled out by "mutuality." The court was seeking to establish that the misdemeanor "insult in words" had taken place, but when it was proven, to the judges' satisfaction, that the accuser himself had uttered the major insult that led to physical violence and a further exchange of insults, they exonerated the defendant. The gravity of this "insult in words" could be measured in blows to the chest.[71]

This case also illustrates the court's concern for impartiality and its adherence to the rules for court procedure. The regulations for township courts stated that "a township judge has no right to take part in the decision of a case that involves him or members of his family."[72] Pil'shchikov's case originated in "Kvardakov's tea shop," presumably owned by a relative of N. A. Kvardakov, the president of the court in 1905 and 1906.[73] Just as a "personal connection" to the accused had disqualified a witness in Aleksandra Alekseeva's case for "improper words," in this hearing of an insult charge involving a relative's commercial establishment, the presiding judge temporarily left the bench.

Family members could use the township court to redress violence perpetrated within a household or between married people. The township court at Nagatino heard a number of cases of what we would call domestic violence. On 24 June 1913 Irina Vasilevna Rodina, a peasant registered in Sadovaia sloboda, appeared at court to support her accusation of her husband, Timofei Petrov Rodin for beating her. Irina Vasilevna testified that "outside the building of the township administration, her husband, Timofei Rodin, had beaten her and [she] asked to punish him." Timofei Petrov did not appear at court, but in accord with the regulations on absenteeism, the trial continued without him.[74] Two male witnesses testified as follows:

> Nikolai Nikolaev Molochkov, son of a court footman [an official rank], explained that he was sitting in the building of the township administration and heard the cries of the Rodins, and Timofei Rodin was swearing at his wife. [signature]
>
> Aleksandr Malinov, peasant of Zvenigorodskii County, Pavlovskii Township, Pavlovskoe Village, testified that he saw Timofei Rodin hit his wife once on the head. [N]ear the township administration he shouted. [signature][75]

The judges, F. I. Lapin, N. A. Pozdniakov, I. S. Chebyshev, and A. E. Grobov, cited Aleksandr Malinov's testimony—not the fancier man's account—as proof of the accusation and sentenced Timofei Rodin in absentia to seven days of "simple arrest."[76]

Nowhere in this record is marriage mentioned as having a bearing on the case. The judges' verdict and their acceptance of the case correspond to the commentaries in the *Statutes on Punishments* concerning insults in deed. A decision from 1871 observed that "since light beatings are considered personal insults, and since the law has not established punishments for insults between spouses, complaints of this type cannot be accepted by the court for examination, . . . but if the insult between spouses takes the form of violence, even without heavy beatings, wounds, or mutilations, then such action can be the subject of a complaint of one spouse against another."[77] The judges at Nagatino treated Irina Vasilevna's accusation seriously and convicted Rodin under Statute 134, the harsher of two statutes for insult in deed applicable when the offensive act was accomplished "without any cause from the side of the offended." The sentence, seven days in jail, was delivered officially to Rodin on 30 June, and he did not contest it. Rodin served his term in jail in early August.[78]

One week after this case was decided the Nagatinskii Township Court heard another complaint from a wife against her husband. In this case Avdotiia Vasil'eva Bogatyreva, from Kolomenskoe, charged her husband, Gerasim Vasil'ev Bogatyrev, with "insult in deed," committed on 16 May. At the hearing Avdotiia Vasil'eva supported her accusation and "asked to have her husband punished." Gerasim Vasil'evich "explained that he really had hit his wife with a rake; he recognized his guilt." There were no witnesses, but it appears that the judges were familiar with the defendant. Their finding reads,

> The charge is proven by the personal confession of the accused, but also taking into consideration that Gerasim Bogatyrev conducts a drunken way of life and demands money for alcohol from his wife and strikes her often . . . [the court sentences] Gerasim Bogatyrev to simple arrest for fifteen days.[79]

This lengthy sentence for domestic violence suggests the court's active and knowledgeable role in enhancing social welfare in its immediate community. Kolomenskoe was the site of two taverns and a shop that sold alcohol, too much temptation for the likes of Bogatyrev.[80] The judges did not interpret his confession as grounds to reduce his punishment; instead, they threw the book at him and made judgments about his character part of the official record. This conviction took force and was communicated to the township leader on 12 August 1913, but Bogatyrev did not go to jail until the end of January the next year. He completed his full fifteen days on 11 February. Perhaps this less than competent member of the community had been given a chance to improve his household economy in the busy summer months.[81] Both the decision and the fulfillment of this case displayed the pragmatic, informed justice characteristic of township courts.

Many insults were violent deeds, and most accusations of violence brought to township courts were determined to be insults. Threats also involved violence through a pledge to use it in the future. Insults, threats, and violence were grouped as related misdemeanors in chapter 11 of the *Statutes on Punishments*. When litigants brought accusations of "threat" to township courts, judges had to decide not only whether a threat had been uttered but also if the words in question constituted an insult or a threat in accord with the distinctions articulated by the misdemeanor statutes.[82] Township judges were attentive to the degree of danger and the kind of violation of personal rights contained in a menacing word or words.

Three out of the six criminal cases heard at the Tsaritsyno Township Court in July 1916 concerned threats. On 21 July Grigorii Tikhonovich Alekseev, a peasant living in the village of Borisovo, charged his co-villagers, Grigorii Alekseevich Golov and Golov's son, Anton Grigor'evich Golov, with threat. The case seemed to concern a real breach of local peace. Alekseev cited his neighbors for their threats to beat him and pull down the chimney from his cottage. He also charged that they had (in fact) "made noise in the house." All parties, all literate, showed up in court. The Golov men pleaded not guilty. In their cause, the village leader of Borisovo, Sergei Fedorovich Subbotin, came to court as a witness. His testimony was decisive, and the case was dismissed as unproven.[83] Efrosina Dmitreva Vashchanina, from the village of Blizhne-Beliaevo, also brought a case involving threat on 21 July. She accused her relatives, Fedor and Evdokiia Vashchanin, of "slander and threat," citing their threat to beat her and their use of "improper words." This case, brought by a literate woman against her illiterate relatives, also failed; the sole witness claimed not to know anything about it.[84]

A week later, on 28 July 1916, the three judges at Tsaritsyno, I. E. Timofeev, A. M. Kiselev, and O. N. Kamochkin, and the attentive clerk S. A. Chekaldin heard yet another charge of threat. This was brought by Feodosiia Ivanovna Krepkova, a peasant woman from Shaidrovo, against her neighbor in this village, Fedor Ivanovich Gubintsev. Gubinstev's alleged threat was that he would kill her chicken. Krepkova was illiterate; she showed up in court to present her case. Gubintsev, a literate peasant, also came to court and admitted that he had threatened to kill the chicken, which had entered his garden. Two female witnesses testified in the case. One noted that she had not heard the threat, but that "after this, the neighbor's chicken indeed croaked." The judges determined that, on the basis of his testimony, Gubinstev was guilty; they sentenced him to a four-ruble fine or two days in jail. The verdict was issued under Statute 135, "insult in deed with forethought." On 14 October, some two and a half months later, Gubintsev paid his fine at the township administration.[85]

Threats usually happened in a context that could evoke improper words or the prospect of violent deeds actionable as insults. In 1916 the Tsaritsynskii township court considered several cases involving charges of both "insult in words" and "threat." The judges issued their verdicts in these cases under the insult section of chapter 11–Statute 130, "insult oral or written"; Statute 135, "insult in deed with forethought"; and Statute 136, "slander"—depending on the kind of threat that had been uttered.[86] Threatening to beat someone up and pull down his chimney, and threatening to kill a neighbor's chicken, were indeed threats, but they also constituted insulting behavior. This kind of threat entailed a double insult: the articulation of the threat was insulting in itself, and what was said meant that the perpetrator was preparing to act violently against another person or against that person's property. If such threats were proven to have been uttered, defendants received verdicts issued under the harshest of the insult statutes—"insult in deed with forethought."

Very occasionally a court decided to consider a threat just a threat, deserving of punishment but not at the level of insult. On 17 June 1913 the judges at the township court at Nagatino heard a case brought by Petr Ivanov Monakhov-Novoselov, a peasant from the village of Gravornovo, against his co-villager, Sergei Aleksandr Shchuchkin, for "threats." At the hearing Monakhov-Novoselov said that "Shchuchkin threatened to roll him in the fields." Shchuchkin denied that he had inflicted a threat on Novoselov. A witness from Gravornovo, Ivan Alekseev Ershov, testified that

> Novoselov and Shchuchkin were quarreling, and Shchuchkin said to Novoselov that for those things you should be rolled in the fields.

The judges found these words objectionable and undesirable but not as offensive as some of the other terms they encountered in insult cases earlier that year. In March, for example, the Nagatinskii court had found the word *zhulik* (scoundrel) an "insult in words" and convicted the offender—a policeman!—to a six-ruble fine or three days of arrest.[87] In Monakhov-Novoselov's case, the judges chose to convict the defendant for a threat, not an insult. They issued their verdict under Statute 139, "threat to use force against someone, unmotivated by a mercenary or other criminal goal," and restricted themselves to the quite unusual punishment of a reprimand. Their opinion suggested that they recognized the sexual innuendo of Shchuchkin's "threat":

> Shchuchkin for his inappropriate threat addressed to Novoselov deserves a reprimand, so that in the future he will not repeat such ambiguous words.

The reprimand was accomplished on the spot, and the three judges signed their names as having "done the reprimand."[88]

The decision in this case shows that township judges could make a distinction between a sexualized taunt and an insult to dignity. To call someone a cheat was a significant insult and merited a significant fine, whereas to say that someone deserved getting "rolled in the hay" was "inappropriate." It wasn't clear that Shchuchkin was threatening to "roll" Novoselev himself. Still, the reprimand underlined the fact that certain words were dangerous and to be avoided. Shchuchkin's phrase might be considered an example of an "idle threat"—bad words without any intention of carrying through with them. The decision in the case was a rare example of a verdict that treated threatening words as words, not as insults.

Sometimes rural judges confronted violence that was just violence and not an insult or a threat. Chapter 11 of the *Statutes on Punishments* included a single statute penalizing low-level violent acts as such. Statute 142, "for *samoupravstvo* and equally for the use of force, but without heavy beating or wounds or mutilation," could be used by rural judges to respond to charges of assault. From the viewpoints of rural plaintiffs, many violent acts merited bringing a case against an offender to the township courts. In 18 percent of the criminal cases I surveyed, plaintiffs brought charges of *poboi* (beating) or *samoupravstvo,* punishable under Statute 142. The context in which violent acts occurred was critical to the decisions judges made when faced with charges of beating. Some violence cases were prosecuted as violations of the peace and punished under statutes concerned with public order and drunkenness. Most beating charges, however, were brought by individuals who accused other individuals of hitting them. In each case, judges made judgments about the nature of the violation, and considered whether it constituted an insult, a threat, or a use of force, or another kind of violation.

On 7 August 1905 Semyon Ivanov Baev, a peasant from the village of Iagunino, brought a charge of "delivering a beating" against his co-villager, Timofei Evstigneev Gordeev. Baev claimed that, on 19 July, Gordeev had "hit him four times on the head, and asked that he [Gordeev] be brought to responsibility." Gordeev, the accused, testified that on 19 July, "during a card game, Baev gave it to him with his hand, and in his turn he hit Baev on the neck once." Because Gordeev was illiterate, the presiding judge, Kvardakov, signed for him. A witness, Denisov, elaborated as follows, "Baev awkwardly knocked Gordeev in the face with his palm, and [Gordeev] after that hit Baev on the neck four times." Kvardakov also signed for this witness. Another witness, Ivan Zemliakov, supported the first witness's testimony and signed his name. The parties refused reconciliation. The judgment of the court read:

> The township court having examined the case at hand and taking into consideration that the accusation of Gordeev for having beaten Baev was fully established by the witnessed testimony of Denisov and Zemliakov and therefore on the basis of Statute 127 of *The General Regulation* and Statute 133 of the *Statutes on Punishments* condemned the peasant from Iagunino village Timofei Gordeev for beating Baev and imposed simple arrest at the township administration for three days.[89]

As this case shows, distinctions could be made between an intentional insult and a scuffle that got out of hand. The judges had before them witnesses who noted that Baev had "awkwardly" hit Gordeev with his palm; this kind of blow during a card game did not appear to qualify as sufficiently aggressive to legitimate four blows to the head (or neck). No words had been exchanged, or at least none were cited and recorded at court. The judges chose to convict Gordeev of "beating," and in their sentence cited the mildest of the insult statutes—"inflicting insult in deed, to a person . . . who himself gave grounds for the insult." No one claimed that an insult had occurred, and nothing seemed to point to a willfully degrading act. The judges were acting in accord with the view, expressed in the misdemeanor code, that any violence against a person was an insult. But by delivering their verdict under Statute 133, they acknowledged that this beating had been a response to violence and thus did not warrant punishment as intentional or unprovoked use of force.

Baev's case did not end with this ruling. After the court hearing, the plaintiff seems to have had second thoughts about sending his partner to jail. Nine days after the verdict, a note was entered in the record book: "1905, August, the 16th day, I ask that this decision not be carried out because of reconciliation. Peasant of Iagunino village, Semyon Ivanov Baev." The court appears to have supported this request, for no other action was recorded by the vigilant clerk Akimov.[90]

The court process in this case reveals the constraints on violence that, at least after the fact, were demanded by rural people. Four blows to the head were to be punished by three days in jail. (It is tempting to think that one day was cancelled out by Baev's "awkward" swipe at Gordeev.) The reconciliation, as recorded in this case, also gives a sense of the close intersection between rural people and their courts. The procedures for township courts specified that punishments could be cancelled if reconciliation was officially established.[91]

Baev, even having won his case, was able to effect a reconciliation after the verdict had been rendered and thus to prevent his neighbor from suffering arrest. Rural people's efforts to make a legal reconciliation even after a case had been decided is yet another sign of their participatory engagement with the law.

Judges were frequently called on to sort out responsibility for what appeared to be reciprocal beatings; often a charge of violence would bring a nasty web of harmful words and deeds before the court. Although verbal insults were serious, they did not justify any kind of violent reprisal, as the following case of beating suggests. On 18 March 1913 the court at Nagatino in the agricultural region not far from Moscow heard an accusation of "delivering a beating" brought by Fedor Egorov Gorokhov from Kolomenskoe against his co-villager, Maksim Stepanov Shliakov. At court, Gorokhov testified that,

> on the 10th of February in Sormanov's tavern, Shliakov interfered with his conversation with Burov. He, the victim [Gorokhov], objected to Shliakov, saying you shouldn't talk, about you they say that you froze yourself in the steam, is this true or not? Then Shliakov grabbed him by the beard and hit him a few times in the face, leaving him bloody and swollen.

Called to respond, Shliakov testified that,

> Gorokhov in Sormanov's tavern cursed him with all kinds of words and made various sharp remarks; he, Shliakov, lost his patience and hit Gorokhov two times in the face. He recognizes his guilt.

After this testimony and confession, three other men, all peasants from Kolomenskoe, appeared as witnesses. All of them told the same story: Gorokhov had "cursed" Shiakov or "said improper words," or "cursed with improper words," and after this Shliakov had hit Gorokhov twice in the face. Confronted with this testimony, the judges found that,

> Gorokhov himself, being drunk, compelled Maksim Shliakov to insult him in deed, [and] therefore Maksim Shliakov is judged culpable under circumstances reducing his guilt.

Shliakov was punished under Statute 134, inflicting insult in deed, without any grounds from the side of the offended person, to a fine of six rubles, but his sentence was reduced to a four-ruble fine or two days of arrest. (The court cited the amnesty of 13 February 1913 as grounds to reduce the fine by one-third.) This fine was paid on 3 August 1913.[92]

Once again the township judges interpreted an act of violence—two severe blows to the face—in the context of an exchange of insults. Shliakov was not let off because he had been provoked by Gorokhov's improper words; he was given a reduced sentence because those words had been uttered. The judges recognized that Gorokhov had provoked Shliakov's response, but they also held Shliakov responsible for his violent act in response to a drunk. This did not appear to have been a spat among equals, and the defendant's confession that he had lost patience and hit the plaintiff did not excuse his acts. A drunk's attempt at malicious *réplique* did not justify an insulting and, in this case, physical assault.

THE LAW IN THE WRONG HANDS

Although charges of violence were usually treated as personal insults, township judges sometimes condemned the use of force as a usurpation of legal rights. Statute 142 criminalized *samoupravstvo* and "the use of violence, but without heavy beating, or wounds or mutilation."[93] The essence of convictions for *samoupravstvo* was to punish people who had taken the law into their own hands.

Samoupravstvo means literally "self-rule." The term contains the root *prav[o]* meaning "right" and, not coincidentally, "law," but in a negative sense—taking a right or law unto one's self. The usual translation of the term is "arbitrariness," but only certain kinds of arbitrary actions counted as *samoupravstvo*. The *Statutes on Punishments* devoted twenty-nine pages of commentary to defining this misdemeanor. Under the rubric, "General conception of *samoupravstvo*," the following conditions were cited:

> For a legal understanding of criminal *samoupravstvo*, the following is necessary: 1) that the actions of the person accused of *samoupravstvo* were directed toward the establishment or accomplishment of his real or supposed by him to be [real] rights . . . ; 2) that these actions were willful, i.e., undertaken against the established authorities or in violation of legal order . . . ; 3) that they were connected with the violation of the rights of another person, who in fact possessed or enjoyed these rights . . . ; and 4) that they were accomplished with force against the possessor of rights or people substituting for him, or without violence, but in their presence and clearly against their express will.[94]

At township courts the kinds of rights in question usually concerned things—money, movable property, grain—and the legal control of them. *Samoupravstvo* was not the same as theft; in a case of theft, there was no conflict over who had rights to the property. Russian law recognized that there would be disputes over legal control of property; *samoupravstvo* could be charged when someone—wrongly in the plaintiff's view—claimed a right that another possessed. "The existence of the real or proposed rights of the accused" was a "condition of *samoupravstvo*," declared the *Statutes on Punishments:*

> The action of an accused party, consisting of having taken from the victimized person a purse of money, and having taken from it some money, which according to his [the accused's] explanation, was owed to him by the mother and father of the victim, and having returned the purse itself with the remaining money, constitutes not theft, but *samoupravstvo*, because these actions consist of the taking of property not with the goal of seizure, but of establishing rights that the accused claimed for himself.[95]

The rules on *samoupravstvo* recognized that individuals could have different notions of their rights and insisted that legal authorities were the only ones

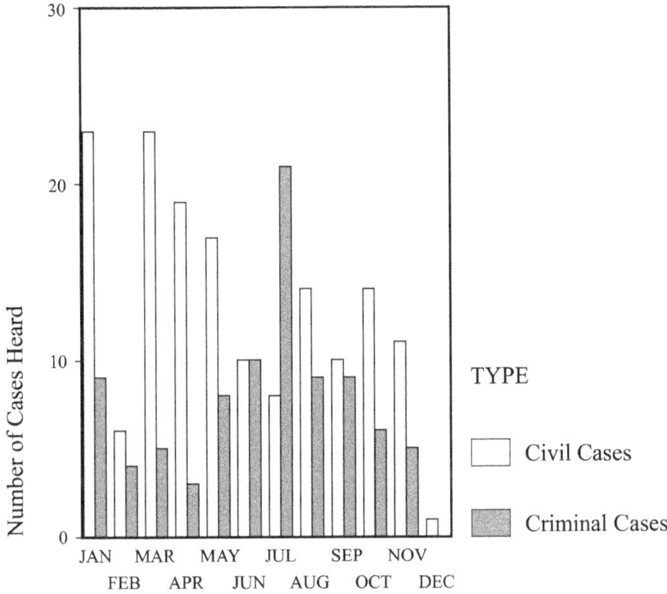

Chart 5.1. Number of Cases Heard by Month, Ignatevskii Township Court, 1916. *Source: Data Survey.*

who could resolve conflicting claims. This point was made repeatedly in the commentaries to Statute 142, as in the following decision: "Willful retention of another's money or other movable property must be recognized as *samoupravstvo,* if the guilty party really had the right, or had a basis to believe that he had the right, to receive this money, but, instead of exacting it through the established means, kept it back willfully."[96] Rightful possession was to be determined by the courts, and not by individuals acting on their own. The inclusion of *samoupravstvo* and the lengthy commentaries on it in the *Statutes on Punishments* draw attention to the efforts of authorities to enforce the rule of law in the empire. Litigation at township courts, where *samoupravstvo* was a not infrequent charge, shows that rural people were aware of the law's authority and were willing to use it against people who claimed rights illegally.

One of the cases at our day in court at Iagunino involved a charge of *samoupravstvo* and a claim about legal rights. In response to the accusation of having broken down a fence on someone else's property, the defendant claimed that the township leader had given him permission for his action. The court did not find his claim to have acted with "established authority" convincing, and he was sentenced to seven days arrest.[97] In addition to fences, crops were frequently the objects of *samoupravstvo* charges.[98] In rural areas *samoupravstvo* cases broke out when people were sowing or harvesting. At the Ignatevskii court, as elsewhere, civil cases usually outnumbered criminal ones, but in July 1916 this court heard more than twice as many criminal cases as civil ones:

plaintiffs registered ten charges of *samoupravtsvo* and five charges of "driving cattle through another's meadows and fields," in addition to the usual array of civil cases and two charges of insult and three of beating (see Chart 5.1).[99]

Charges of *samoupravstvo* usually arose among co-villagers, and sometimes between brothers. The accusation was linked to a context where rights were known, and an assertion of control over property could be seen by one side or another as an unauthorized claim.[100] *Samoupravstvo* charges were not confined to peasants. In a case at the Ignatevskii Township Court in 1906, a peasant accused a townsperson of *samoupravstvo,* involving his losses of eight rubles for a window frame.[101] No one forced peasants to bring this type of charge to the township court; most *samoupravstvo* case were brought directly by plaintiffs without the assistance of the police.[102]

An accusation of *samoupravstvo* did not mean that a defendant had in fact usurped the authority of the law. What was an arbitrary seizure of property in the eyes of an accuser could have been a legal act. For this reason, village authorities and other witnesses were often important to the outcome of a case.[103] At the courts I studied, *samoupravstvo* cases resulted in convictions in 25 percent of cases, a lower conviction rate than that for criminal cases in general (51 percent) and for personal dignity cases (39 percent). This lower conviction rate may reflect the respect for legally defined rights implicit in the charge of *samoupravstvo.* When an aggrieved party decided to charge a neighbor who seized contested property with *samoupravstvo* rather than with theft, the accuser acknowledged that rights were in dispute at the same time as he or she demanded a legal resolution of this conflict.

It was Russian lawmakers, not peasants, who grouped insults, threats, violence, and *samoupravstvo* together in the *Rules of Punishments.*[104] The ways these statutes were activated at township courts suggest connections between personal honor and rights in rural life, as well as judicial distinctions made by peasant judges. When plaintiffs brought charges of insult, "beating," and "*samoupravstvo,*" township judges issued rulings under statutes most appropriate to each case. Physical violence was usually punished as some kind of insult; *samoupravstvo* decisions usually involved property. Insulting words and violent deeds were crimes against individuals' right to dignity; *samoupravstvo* was an offense against a legal order that protected both economic and social rights.

Do charges of rights violations heard at the township courts mean that rural people were particularly law-abiding or law-violating? One might interpret the multitude of cases concerning insults, beating, and *samoupravstvo* to mean that the inhabitants of Russian villages demanded obedience to the law or, alternatively, that they were inveterate violators of established rules. Plaintiffs and defendants could be seen as having different perspectives on this question. Plaintiffs accused their neighbors of having committed misdemeanors; are their accusations evidence of rural demands for law-abiding behavior? Defendants were charged, in large numbers, with having committed illegal actions; are these charges evidence of massive disregard for the law?

No categorical conclusions concerning respect for or rejection of the empire's laws can be drawn from records of township courts. For one thing, there is no reason to force all of rural society to share a single set of values—the error of collectivization. For another, court records cannot reveal the kind of affect the law evoked in everyday life. In all likelihood, rural people in late imperial Russia, like their compatriots and other people in other places, did not think about the law most of the time. Nonetheless, they knew the law could be invoked to punish certain offenses. Neither plaintiffs nor defendants rejected the definitions of misdemeanors produced by the state. The law was there to be used by people who felt they had been victimized by others, and to set right, through punishment, breaches of individual and collective rights. Law-abiders, lawbreakers, both, or neither, rural people were law users—active seekers of legal redress and participants in the legal resolution of perceived injustice.

THE RURAL PUBLIC SPHERE

A significant proportion of criminal cases at township courts concerned public welfare. Attention to these issues varied from court to court; in my survey as a whole, public welfare was the subject of 24 percent of criminal cases. The accusations in these cases concerned harm caused not directly to individuals but to the social and physical environment in which they lived. The *Statutes on Punishments* provided township judges with a long list of violations of public order; judges used certain of these statutes liberally in their decisions. Public welfare issues brought to township courts included violations of "decorum, order and peace," as well as "public improvement," "personal safety," "administrative order," and "caution with fire." At most courts I studied, violations of "decorum, order, and peace" predominated.[105] In clerks' records, two charges accounted for most of these breaches of the peace. These not unrelated violations were unruly conduct and public drunkenness.

The most used statute among the twelve "unruly conduct" charges available to township judges was Statute 38, applicable to "quarrels, fights, fistfights, or other kind of unruly conduct in public places and generally for disturbances of the social peace."[106] The abuse of alcohol, a major concern of Russian social activists,[107] was the subject of five statutes and lengthy commentaries in the *Statutes on Punishments.* At some township courts charges were brought under Statute 42: "for appearing in a public place in a state of manifest intoxication, threatening safety, peace, or decorum." Although alcohol was a common element of disturbance cases, it was a violation of the public sphere, rather than simple overindulgence in drink, that was most consistently punished by township court authorities.

Members of the rural public took less initiative and probably less interest in prosecuting disorderly behavior and public intoxication than in defending violations of their personal rights. Whereas the vast majority of cases involving personal dignity were brought by individuals, police were more frequently than not the accusers in cases concerning the public good. At the Iaguninskii court, police were unassisted plaintiffs in 57 percent of all public well-being cases, as opposed to 5 percent of personal dignity cases. At the active Nagatinskii Township Court police brought 79 percent of public welfare cases, although they were the plaintiffs in only 5 percent of personal dignity cases. When the charge concerned some kind of unruly conduct, police were plaintiffs in 80 percent of the Nagatinskii cases and in almost all such cases at the other smaller courts. The zeal of the police in matters of rural public welfare should not, however, be exaggerated. With the exception of the Tsaritsyno court near Moscow, where a constable would often come to court to testify in a disorderly conduct case, police usually did not appear at hearings of their charges. In cases where a police report had been filed but no authority appeared at court, the testimony of victims and witnesses, if there were any, and in particular that of the defendant, was the primary evidence used to convict or acquit on the registered charge.

Intoxication as such was not a subject of enthusiastic surveillance on the part of either policemen or the rural public. Even the busy Nagatinskii Township Court, which decided 212 criminal cases in 1913, heard only 2 cases brought by the police concerning drunkenness, and both these cases involved other charges as well.[108] Of more concern to at least some citizens in the countryside was the unruly and hurtful behavior that was frequently associated with inebriation. Drinking bouts could result in personal insults—verbal, physical, or both; these would be prosecuted as violations of personal dignity. Alcoholism as a way of life was condemned by township judges, as we have seen in the case of domestic violence in the Bogatyrev family of Kolomenskoe, heard by the Nagatinskii judges in 1913.[109] But if township courts treated the consequences of intemperance seriously, they only infrequently convicted a person for being drunk in public, without having (yet) caused anyone any harm.[110] The important part of Statute 42 for rural judges appeared to be conduct "threatening safety, peace, and decorum." In none of the cases I read was a defendant convicted for inebriation alone and not in connection with some other kind of bad behavior.[111]

It is nonetheless clear from court records that public intoxication was not an unusual event, for men at any rate. (No woman was ever charged with being drunk, or consequences thereof, in any case I read.) Taverns and tea shops were the context in which many a case of breach of the peace, as well as violations of personal dignity, occurred.[112] Testimony and decisions in unruly conduct cases suggest that defendants rarely disputed charges of intoxication and were usually convicted on the basis of their confessions.[113] The most common sentence in cases concerning inebriation was a five ruble fine or three days in jail. Sometimes defendants would plead for a reduced sentence, as in the case of disturbing the peace heard at our day in court at the Iaguninskii Township Court in Moscow Province. In that case the court rejected the charge under Statute 42 of public drunkenness and instead sentenced the defendant under Statute 38 for unruly conduct in a public place.[114] This verdict accords with the emphasis put on public disorder, rather than public drinking, at township courts.

A village holiday, Bogorodskii County, Moscow Province, 1910s.
Photograph from the collection of Mikhail Zolotarev.

Occasionally township judges used their most severe sentence—fifteen days in jail—for disturbances of the peace. The following cases heard at Nagatino in 1913 illustrate the problems strong drink could cause. On 21 March judges F. I. Lapin, N. A. Pozdniakov, and A. E. Grobov heard a case initiated by a report from the local police. Constable Gubochkin's declaration charged Ivan Nikolaev Uzlov under Statute 38 with unruly conduct. The constable did not appear at court, but the township leader testified in support of the charge. Uzlov, who was already in custody, "explained that he had been drunk and with his shoulder he had pushed the watchman Avdoshin." Ivan Alekseev Avdoshin, also a peasant from Nagatino, testified in more detail:

> Uzlov had hit him once in the ear at Pavlov's tavern and because of this they stepped out of the tavern and Uzlov ran away. He, Avdoshin, took custody of him on the 26th of February in the evening when he went out on duty.

The court convicted Uzlov on the basis of Avdoshin's testimony, commenting that "Uzlov had been caught in the act on the street and that, in addition, Uzlov was well known to the court for his incidents of disgraceful behavior." Uzlov appealed his fifteen-day sentence, which was ultimately upheld.[115]

Two months later, on 20 May, the same judges joined by a fourth member of the court, I. S. Chebyshev, heard a similar case. The police declaration charged Egor Pavlov Repin, a peasant from the village of Novinka, under both Statute 38 (unruly conduct) and Statute 42 (intoxication). Again, no one from the police appeared in court. The defendant's words were recorded as follows: "Repin recognized himself as guilty of wild conduct in Molochkov's tea shop. He was very drunk." The judges declared the charge proven by "personal confession" and sentenced Repin to "simple arrest" for fifteen days. This sentence was fulfilled one month later.[116]

Case records are rich in descriptions of behaviors considered violations of the public sphere: wild conduct, disgraceful behavior, making noise, disturbing the peace, and swearing appeared in charges, confessions, and decisions at township courts. On 3 March 1916, at the Tsaritsynskii court, five of the eight criminal cases concerned transgressions of public order; each was communicated to the court by the police. (The other three cases concerned various kinds of insult and "beating" charges brought by individuals.) These public disorder cases involved peasant men, singly or in pairs, from various villages in the township. The attentive local constable showed up at court for the hearings; in two cases, the village leader appeared as well. Testimony in court, including that of the defendants, confirmed the following actions: "swearing and insulting," "intoxication and wild conduct," "strongly drunk," "drunk and disturbed the tranquility and peace," and "drunk and made noise." Every one of the defendants, with the exception of one who had been drafted into the military, appeared at court and confessed to his behavior. All were convicted, with the exception of the drafted man, whose case was delayed. Their sentences ranged from three-ruble fines or two days in jail to ten-ruble fines or 5 days in jail. In one of these cases, the police constable cited two peasant men from the village of Orekhovo under Statute 38 with "playing an accordion and tambourine" at the tea shop owned by Matvei Iakov Lapchin, who was also cited for having allowed this activity. All defendants showed up in court and testified in support of the charges against them. All received sentences of three-ruble fines or two days in jail.[117]

What meaning did these violations of public order hold for rural people? That police alone—and not victims—brought most charges of "noise-making" in my survey suggests that noise by itself was not of much concern to peasants. Local constables were probably well acquainted with tea shops and taverns as locations for both noise and other more problematic behaviors; the arrests of accordion and tambourine players could have their roots in other kinds of problems. There is little to suggest that people generally thought their public sphere should be free from accordions. A rare case in which a "victim," not just a policeman, brought a case concerning noise and intoxication to court provides perspective on attitudes toward public well-being expressed in misdemeanor cases.

On 7 August 1905 the judges at the Iaguninskii Township Court heard a case against Semyon Surov. The police report cited Surov under Statute 42 for public intoxication. No policeman attended the hearing. The victim, a certain Emelianov, showed up in court with witnesses to support his charge that Surov on May 1 was "drunk on the street," that he "made noise" and "hit" him. Surov defended himself, in a way, as follows:

> He declared that in fact on May 1st he had been very drunk, but he didn't make noise in the street. Whether he hit Emelianov or not, he does not remember.

The judges found the charges of "destroying tranquility and peace" fully proven and sentenced Surov under Statute 42 to a six-ruble fine or arrest for three days. When the sentence was read out, Surov—the convicted man—wrote that he was "satisfied."[118]

Several strands of social discipline were united in this case. The victim had been affronted by Surov's blow and filed charges with the police about disturbance of the peace. Ordinarily an unprovoked act of violence like this one would be interpreted by all parties as an insult. But both the victim's testimony and the defendant's confession of intoxication suggested that Surov had been incapable of committing a personal insult. He recalled that he had been "very drunk"; he denied making noise on the street; and he could not remember whether he had directed a blow against the plaintiff. Insults—in word and deed—had to be inflicted consciously. Emelianov could still punish Surov by reporting his disorderly conduct to the police. The police filed their citation under the statute penalizing public intoxication, which seemed to fit the actions described by all parties.

It is possible that Emelianov received some satisfaction from the court's decision. It showed that he had been assaulted by a drunk, not by a thinking person; therefore his dignity had not been besmirched. But why was Surov satisfied as well? Surov's confession and his acceptance of his guilt fit the pattern of many drinking and public disturbance cases. People living in Russian villages did not seem to be alarmed by drinking itself, but they prosecuted other violations that occurred as a consequence of intoxication. Defendants were almost always willing to confess that they had been drunk in criminal cases, even though the meaning of their testimony—unsurprisingly under the circumstances—was not always clear. Being drunk meant that one had not been capable of inflicting an insult and perhaps less at fault for other kinds of violations, such as noise and swearing. Judges took confessions seriously in their verdicts: "Personal repentance" or "personal acknowledgment" was cited as grounds for verdicts in almost every drinking case in my survey.[119]

To be "very drunk" was an explanation that everyone understood. Like other people in other parts of Russian society, rural men participated, regularly it seems, in the routine of getting drunk. At the same time, peasants accused of various disorderly or harmful acts accomplished under the influence did not shirk responsibility for their violations. They confessed; they paid their fines; they went to jail. The officially recorded acknowledgment that one had been "strongly drunk" constituted a recognition of the realities and obligations of social life.

In addition to disorderly conduct, violations of propriety were sometimes prosecuted at township courts. "Shameless acts in a public place"—usually accompanied by the more frequent accusations of noise, wild behavior, and swearing—were punishable under Statute 43. At our day in court at Iagunino, the constable who supervised the unruly Savvinskaia sloboda accused a defendant of "generally committ[ing] excesses . . . without his shirt."[120] Gambling occasionally was prosecuted under Statute 41 on "unpermitted amusements" or under Statute 46, which criminalized "games of chance . . . not in a gaming house."[121] At Tsaritsyno, in 1916, Maksim Ivanovich Butuzov was charged by the police with "allowing games for money in his tea shop" and convicted, after conclusive testimony by a witness, to a five-ruble fine or three days in jail.[122] Such charges concerning gambling and tavern-keeping were very rare at township courts.

Township courts occasionally prosecuted challenges to public authorities. Disobedience to officials carrying out their duties was criminalized by Statute 30, a very infrequent charge.[123] Insults to policemen or other authorities were punishable under Statute 31, a statute used at the Nagatinskii court near Moscow but nowhere else in my survey of cases. The local constable in this area—the Simonovskii District—served under the authority of the Moscow city police. He sent many cases to the Nagatinskii court and was active in the defense of his rights as an official.[124] In 1913 he brought four charges of insulting authorities, sometimes in conjunction with other citations, to the judges at Nagatino. The court convicted all defendants to arrest of fifteen days, although some of these terms were reduced to nine days by the amnesty declared in connection with the Romanovs' tricentennial. In these cases, as well as another charge of insult to authority brought by a Justice of the Peace, the defendants were not registered residents of the township.[125]

Nagatinskii Township, with its growing and unruly population, may have been the site of particularly contentious relations with policemen. At Tsaritsyno, not far away but where most defendants were residents of the township,[126] insults to authority could be interpreted as just insults. In March 1916 the Tsaritsyno judges heard a case brought by the leader of the village of Marino, Fedor Andrev Artomonov, against his co-villager, Vasilii Mikhail Chekhanov. The illiterate village headman claimed that Chekhanov had insulted him in words, calling him a "scoundrel" among other things. There were no witnesses, but the defendant—a literate peasant—pleaded guilty. At court, the parties reconciled and the case was ended.[127]

Occasional insults to policemen or village authorities that landed defendants in the dock at township courts do not add up to a culture of resistance to the state. Defendants usually pleaded guilty to such charges and served whatever sentence was determined by the judges. Higher authorities took no particular interest in these cases, apart from collecting statistics on their numbers. Allowing peasant judges to decide cases involving insults to policemen granted local society a degree of control and surveillance over the officials who were authorized to make misdemeanor charges and to record them for other citizens. It is impossible to conclude from testimony in township cases that local people favored or opposed police discipline. What we can see is that, in the relatively few cases involving insults to authorities, officials took the initiative to bring charges; defendants and witnesses showed up in court; and the verdict usually went in favor of the police.

DIRT AND OTHER DANGERS

In some areas policemen, township courts, and disgruntled members of the rural public together engaged in legal actions to protect public health. The misdemeanor code was prolific on this subject: 71 of the 153 violations in the *Statutes on Punishments* concerned public health and safety, and 33 of these were applicable by township judges.[128] Township courts generally made only limited use of statutes on public improvement, construction and communication, fire, post and telegraph, health, and safety; most courts in my survey heard no cases at all directly concerning public health. At Nagatino and Tsaritsyno, however, a considerable number of such cases did arise, primarily under two statutes concerning "public improvement." This improvement concerned one thing—the control of garbage, sewage, and animal waste in villages in close proximity to Moscow.

Court records show that it was "outsiders"—peasants not legally registered in a village of a township—who appeared to be the main source of trouble. Charges concerning sewage and dirt, of course, were registered against people who resided locally, but in 69 percent of all such cases the defendant was not registered as an inhabitant (and taxpayer) in the township.[129] At Nagatino, in 1913, where an even higher percentage of defendants were nonresidents, such cases usually began with a police citation under Statute 55: "Non-observance of the rules on cleanliness and order in the street, including allowing animals where they are not allowed."[130] Armed with Statute 55, courts carried on a battle against filth of many kinds.

On 13 May 1913 the Nagatino judges considered a case filed under Statute 55 against a peasant woman, Maria Vlas'evna Filippova, registered in another county of Moscow Province. A complaint had been registered with the police on 28 March; as usual in these cases, no one from the police appeared at court. The accused woman testified that "in the spring at the time of melting snow water flowed into her courtyard from the fields and streets and it really was dirty in the courtyard." Called as a witness, a local watchman, Fedor Sofranov, declared that "the courtyard of the establishment belonging to Truzhanov and rented to Filippova was dirty; in the courtyard were human defecations and spillover from the outhouse." Safranov's testimony was decisive for the court, and Filippova was sentenced to a ten-ruble fine or five days of arrest. She paid the fine on 2 August.[131]

Dubrovka, where Filippova lived, was surrounded by fields, but it was also practically on the Moscow city limits and three kilometers from a railroad link to the city. Many peasants from other areas settled in these Moscow borderlands, and they were far more likely than people registered in the villages of Nagatino Township to be charged with health violations. Dubrovka had two registered taverns for its 120 households.[132] Taverns and tea shops could also be a source of dirt.

Two weeks later, on 27 May, the judges at Nagatino heard another charge of violation of Statute 55, again initiated by a report from the police. The accused, Petr Ivanov Chelnokov, was a tavern keeper in the township and a peasant registered in another county of Moscow Province. No one from the police came to the hearing, held a little over a month after the registration of the complaint, and the defendant himself was absent from the courtroom.[133] The case against Chelnokov amounted to the testimony of Gavril Filippov Danilov, an official watchman for the Simonovskii District. Danilov testified that,

> around the tavern it was dirty and Chelnokov's janitor in front of them poured out a bucket of tea leaves and refuse from Chelnokov's tavern . . . onto the street.

The judges found the charge proven according to Danilov's testimony and convicted Chelnokov of "dirtying the square around his property with tea leaves and . . . refuse that Chelnokov allowed his servants to pour out of his establishment" and sentenced him to a three-ruble fine or three days of arrest. Chelnokov unsuccessfully appealed this verdict to the land captain and ultimately paid his fine on 12 September.[134]

Watchmen were well informed about the state of courtyards and streets, and they testified in the majority of cases about public health heard at Nagatino. These lower-level officials did not always support complaints, but they often provided the decisive evidence concerning garbage, dirt, and worse. Judges understood the difficulties and fine points of maintaining order in the village. When the active constable of the Simonovskii District issued a citation on 1 May 1913 against Emilian Evdokimov Ermolov under Statute 55, the accused managed to prove in court that he had behaved responsibly. Ermolov, a property owner from outside the township, explained that on 26 April "the cleaning of the courtyard was going on and the courtyard really was dirty but that on 27 April all was put into order." A watchman, Semyon Ivanov, testified that "at the inspection Ermolov's courtyard was not especially dirty, but that there were a few piles of manure and that, in one place, slops had been poured out." The judges decided that the police charge was not proven because, according to the clerk's record,

> when the report was filed they were cleaning the manure bins and the cesspit and because of this there was disorder in the courtyard, as there usually is during cleaning up, but on the 27th of April, that is, a day later, Ermolov had put his property in order.[135]

Not all homeowners were as conscientious about cleaning up their courtyards as Emilian Ermolov. The very next case heard on 10 June 1913 at Nagatino concerned another peasant from outside the township. The constable's report, filed 28 April, accused Fedor Ivanov Khrushchev of violating Statute 55. The police, as usual, did not appear, and the defendant testified that "his courtyard was clean." Two witnesses appeared. A janitor, Karl Mikhailov, testified that "there was manure in the courtyard, which two or three days later Khrushchev took away." A watchman, Makar Alekseev Alekseev, observed that "in the courtyard there was manure raked into piles, and this still was in the courtyard in a frozen form." This case developed further and the judges' verdict was based on the following finding:

> The evidence of witnesses and the personal acknowledgment of the accused, given at the time of the composition of the police protocol, establishes that Khrushchev's property was in a dirty condition: there was manure, mixed up with animal guts, being used to feed dogs by the renter of the woodpile.

Khrushchev was sentenced to a five-ruble fine or three days in jail. He paid his fine to the township leader on 22 August.[136]

These cases about courtyards had been filed during the spring thaw and floods that made life difficult—and dirty—throughout most of central and northern Russia.[137] At Nagatino, in 1913, 57 percent of the year's health and safety cases were heard in April and May alone. Of the thirty public health cases heard by the Nagatino judges in April, May, and June, all but three were charges of violations of Statute 55. In the winter, when most filth was naturally "in a frozen form," violations of rules on public health were usually filed under Statute 56—"discarding dead livestock, garbage, or sewage in a place not designated for it."

In January 1913 the police brought seven such cases to the Nagatinskii court, all against peasants who were not registered in the township, all of whom were convicted to sentences of fine or arrest. No cases concerning filth were heard from July through December at Nagatino, when other problems were apparently more pressing.

The seasonality of public health cases at Nagatino opens a window onto local policing in rural areas. The police were not engaging in arbitrary repression. There was, after all, something that needed regulation: nobody wanted animal guts spilling into their courtyards during the spring thaw. Local policemen fostered order—physical order—in rural areas by responding to complaints that arose—like water and mud in the spring—with regularity according to the time of the year.

Although the police filed a far greater proportion of public health citations than charges of personal insults, it would be a mistake to see these issues as belonging to separate disciplinary spheres. Individuals could have brought public well-being charges themselves but instead they exercised their right to file a complaint with the police. In public health cases, where the issues were sewage, dumping animal carcasses, and the like, township inhabitants probably had their reasons for wanting the police to initiate cases. Hauling neighbors into court for insult may have given some satisfaction, but how was one to act effectively when garbage was the issue? It might be difficult for a local resident, whether registered in the township or not, to challenge the slovenly ways of peasants who were wealthy enough to own taverns or tea shops. The police could be useful in these matters, and so they were. As Table 5.7 shows, police were likely to be plaintiffs in cases that concerned nonresidents or health or both.

Outsiders and others who violated health and safety regulations paid for their poor conduct; their fines went to local treasuries. In Nagatino Township, in 1913, the price of not cleaning up one's courtyard varied from 1 to 16 rubles; 57 percent of fines in health cases were 5 or 10 rubles. Altogether in this year the Nagatino judges issued sentences amounting to 290 rubles, to be collected in the cause of public sanitation in their township. Because outsiders disproportionately paid these fines, in this respect at least they were drawn into the maintenance and definition of public life in rural areas. Were migrants dirtier than longtime residents? Did they care less about their rented houses or their taverns? Were they more difficult for locals to confront? One thing is sure: the sewage flowed in the springtime, and the police filed suits to punish people for not cleaning it up.

The township courts considered a few other dangers to public well-being. Occasionally a "caution with fire" violation came before a township court. Most cases concerning fire—such as arson—were serious crimes and would be heard in other venues,[138] but township courts were charged with enforcing fire prevention. Statute 88 of the *Statutes on Punishments* concerned the proper construction of stoves and chimneys; Statute 89 applied to cleaning chimneys; and Statute 91 addressed the need to have fire-extinguishing materials in settled

Table 5.7. Police as Plaintiff and Defendant's Residence: Criminal Cases concerning Health and Safety

Type of Criminal Case	*Residency of Defendant*	*Police Not a Plaintiff*	*Police a Plaintiff*	*Total*
Criminal Cases Not concerned with Health Issues	Defendant Township Resident	237 86.5%	37 13.5%	274 100%
	Defendant Not a Township Resident	33 35.1%	61 64.9%	94 100%
	Total	270 73.4%	98 26.6%	368 100%
Criminal Cases concerned with Health Issues	Defendant Township Resident	1 9.1%	10 90.9%	11 100%
	Defendant Not a Township Resident	7 26.9%	19 73.1%	26 100%
	Total	8 21.6%	29 78.4%	37 100%

areas.[139] At Tsaritsyno a peasant from outside the township was sentenced in 1916 for carelessness with fire in a bathhouse in the village of Saburovo. Three witnesses showed up to testify about his poor repair of the bathhouse stove. The result was a conviction under Statutes 88 and 89 and a fine of five rubles or three days of arrest.[140] Similar cases charging carelessness with fire were heard at Zaborovskii and Nagatinskii township courts.[141]

Another public space violation concerned animals and their control. Statute law about the correct supervision of animals could be found in chapter 10—"Personal Safety"—of the *Statutes on Punishments*. Even the remote Zaborovskii court in Novgorod Province could hear the occasional case of "careless driving." In February 1905 a peasant charged a peasant from a different village in this township with "careless driving of his horse" in an incident that involved damages to a sled.[142] Most cases in my survey involving animals were heard back at Nagatino. In 1913 two charges under Statute 121—"not taking established measures to prevent dangers from domestic animals"—were filed by police for victims of attacks by dogs. In both cases the victim appeared in court with witnesses to back up the charges, and the dog owners, not registered residents of the township, were assessed fines. One dog owner had to pay both a ten-ruble fine to the township and twenty-five rubles to the victim.[143]

At Nagatino the police also brought cases about animals under Statute 43.1—"for causing domestic animals needless suffering." This violation of "decorum, order, and peace" criminalized inadequate care of animals—allowing horses to suffer hunger and thirst, not shoveling manure from their stables, not letting them out into the air.[144] When police charged four men under Statute 43.1 at Nagatino in January and February 1913 the defendants, most of them not registered in the township, did not appear at their hearings. In all likelihood they were not feeding their horses adequately, for instead of paying fines—as did owners who had not cleaned up their courtyards—these defendants all served jail sentences. In one case at Nagatino of "causing animals to suffer" a written inquest was drawn up and introduced as evidence. In another, two city policemen came to the hearing as witnesses.[145] At all the courts I studied, cases about care of animals arose in the dead of winter, were brought by the police alone, and resulted in convictions with sentences of fines of three to ten rubles, or the usual arrest equivalents. Although there were no immediate human victims—as in the dog-bite cases—police took action against people who failed to care for horses by registering complaints, making reports, conducting inquests, finding culprits, and compelling them to serve their sentences.

THEFT

At Nagatino what police filed most protocols about was theft. Accusations of theft or other property violations accounted for 29 percent of criminal hearings at Nagatinskii Township Court in the years I surveyed, an exceptionally high proportion of this kind of crime. Nagatinskii Township's many newcomers and its proximity to Moscow may account for this high rate of petty theft. As noted above, at most courts theft and related crimes "against another's property" constituted a much smaller proportion of criminal cases, ranging from 7 percent in Iaguninskii Township to 13 percent in Tsaritsynskii Township.

These statistics display the relative place of theft among types of criminal cases heard at township courts but cannot represent theft as a proportion of criminal activity in the rural areas. As with other serious crimes, thefts of a certain gravity would be prosecuted at other instances. Township courts could hear only misdemeanors listed in seventeen statutes of chapter 13 of the *Statutes on Punishments.* The violation most often cited at township courts was Statute 169: "theft of an object worth no more than five hundred rubles, when a case of theft or swindling for the first or second time." Less frequently courts heard violations under Statute 172 on attempted theft and harboring stolen goods. Very occasionally local authorities filed charges of falsification during exchanges and sales (Statute 173), swindling (Statute 174), and not reporting a found object or money (Statute 179). For most purposes "theft" and "Statute 169" were equivalent accusations at township courts.[146]

The cases of theft brought to the Ignatevskii Township Court in Bogorodskii County—an Old Believer area—were few, but each was considered carefully. In May 1906 the police registered two charges under Statute 169. These were the only property crime complaints in a month when forty-eight cases, of which twenty-six were criminal charges, had been registered by the clerk. In one case of theft, heard a month after its registration, a peasant was convicted and given a severe sentence—"three weeks of strict arrest." This sentence, which exceeded the usual fifteen-day limit, accorded with special provisions in the *Statutes on Punishments.* "In especially important cases of theft, swindling and appropriation of another's property," the courts could convict people to thirty-ruble fines or thirty days of arrest.[147] The only other accusation of theft at Ignat'evo that month, filed under Statute 169, was deemed by the judges to be beyond their competence and sent on to the land captain.[148]

Most thefts, even at courts that examined few of them, were about minor although disruptive and hurtful crimes. Ten years later at Ignat'evo, on 5 May 1916, Ignatii Vikent'evich Lobanovskii filed an accusation of theft against two peasant men from the village of Ivanisovo, for stealing two ducks. When the case was heard on 31 May, neither the plaintiff nor the defendants appeared in court. The nonappearance of both sides ended the case.[149] At Iagunino, in Zvenigorod County, in May 1916, the judges heard Evdokiia Stepanova Efimova, a peasant woman from the village of Sharapovo, charge Vasilii Timofeev Glazunov, a fourteen-year-old peasant from the same village, with stealing three rubles, seventy-five kopeks, and some postcards. The police filed the report that opened the case, and five witnesses, including one twelve-year-old boy, came to court to testify. Most of the witnesses defended young Vasilii, and he was acquitted.[150]

Theft cases at township courts concerned ordinary commodities and ordinary possessions of ordinary people. Case hearings reveal objects thieves found worth stealing or, from the plaintiffs' side, objects worth going to court about. These items included on occasion a prized and practical possession such as a watch or a samovar, but usually more homely objects were at stake. Towels, saddles, rugs, linens, harnesses, boots, blankets, alcohol, hens, ducks, potatoes, plates, and boards were the stuff of accused theft at township courts. And money, too: 19 percent of theft cases I examined were about cash. The most common item to steal was clothing (31 percent of all theft cases), followed by tools and equipment (17 percent). Other popular items were household goods: linens, pots and pans, and crockery accounted for 12 percent of objects mentioned in theft cases. Food was a rare target, although barnyard animals (7 percent) might be counted in this category. From this motley array of stolen (or, at any rate, missing) property, one can reconstruct the world of objects belonging to or coveted by peasant dwellers in the townships. Clothes made a difference in this society, as did money. Households used plates and samovars. People did not go to court (or jail) for basic foods, like bread or flour, but a chicken was an attractive target. The many thefts of tools, harnesses, boards, and equipment reveal the laboring life, legal or not, of peasants at this time.

Almost all cases about theft at township courts were brought by peasants against peasants. In one case at the Zaborovskii court in 1905, a townsperson, the owner of a mill, brought an accusation of theft against a peasant; at Nagatino, in 1913, a townsperson and a peasant from outside the township were convicted together of theft in a case brought by a local peasant.[151] These cases involving townspeople were exceptional, and no one of any higher status was involved in a theft case at the courts I studied. The significant variation in theft cases was that they occurred more frequently at Nagatinskii and Tsaritsynskii townships than in outlying areas.

Variations in the proportion of theft cases show that the township court system responded flexibly to the particular needs of localities. As peasants took up residence near Moscow, with its markets and employment, they, perhaps even more than others, needed the services of the courts. Some of these new inhabitants in areas near big cities were the very troublemakers who caused problems addressed at township courts. But the township courts were not simply the protectors of longtime residents against unruly newcomers. The 25 percent of all theft accusations originating in complaints from people who were not legal residents of Nagatinskii Township show that newcomers, too, turned to the local court to prosecute others for stealing their property.

Theft cases heard at Nagatino in 1913 expose some of the tensions in this society of old residents, newcomers, merchants, renters, artisans, carters, farmers, and police. Although the township's fourteen villages and approximately nineteen hundred households harbored a good number of petty thieves, at least some of these bad characters were well known to the authorities. On 22 April the court heard a charge filed against Pavel Ivanov Petrukhin, a peasant from another township, for theft of "various things worth the sum of eighteen rubles, eighty kopeks," from two peasant men, Kiril Stepanov Gorelov from the village of Dubrovka and Dmitri Pavlov Umokhen, who lived at the perhaps appropriately named Khitrov (wily) market. Umokhen testified that "Petrukhin had stolen two blankets and two lace-up boots for the sum of seven rubles, fifty kopeks." Gorelov claimed that "Petrukhin had stolen leather boots costing five rubles from him." Petrukkhin testified that he had "stolen the blankets, lace-up boots, and leather boots from Umokhen and Gorelov and recognized his guilt." The verdict reads:

> the accusation is proven by the personal acknowledgment of the accused and, taking into consideration Petrukhin's previous conviction, the court pronounces him guilty of theft under circumstances augmenting his guilt.

This conviction resulted in the maximum sentence of thirty days of arrest as well as a payment of five rubles, fifty kopeks, to Umokhen and five rubles to Gorelov. The judges, attentive as usual to detail, adjusted the values of the declared losses. Petrukhin declared himself "satisfied" and served his sentence immediately, from 22 April to 21 May.[152]

Not all bad apples confessed. On 6 June, in this same year, the Nagatino judges heard a case against two peasant men from outside the township, Karl Tikhonov Emelianov and Stepan Kuz'min Sviridonov, charged under Statute 172 with "attempted theft" of meat. Both denied the charges, but a village supervisor testified that "he had seen at Saikin's [enterprise] Emelianov cut [off] the meat entrusted to him for transport and give it to an unknown who turned out to be Sviridonov." Based on this testimony, the judges convicted both defendants of "attempting to steal meat from Saikin" and sentenced them to thirty days each. Emilianov was already in custody. He declared himself "satisfied" with the verdict and served his sentence. But Sviridonov apparently got away, for neither his arrest nor any final disposition of the case was recorded by the clerk.[153]

Township judges made distinctions between theft and buying stolen goods. In a case heard on 17 June at Nagatino, Vasilii Fedorov Shamov, an outsider from another township, was accused of stealing part of a harness, causing losses of ten rubles to Ivan Mikhailov Tsybin. At court, Shamov testified that he had received this harness part from his workman, Ivan, who had bought it at the Horse Square from an unknown person for five rubles. Shamov's brother backed up his testimony. A second witness, a peasant from yet another township and an artisan, testified that, although he knew nothing about the theft, he recognized the item that he had made for Tsybin. The court found that, although the harness in question belonged to Tsybin, it had not been proven that Shamov had knowingly bought stolen goods. The decision was to acquit Shamov but to oblige him to return the harness part in question to its owner, Tsybin. As recorded by the clerk, Tsybin received his harness on 17 July.[154]

Women were defendants in 20 percent of the theft cases I surveyed. At Nagatino, women were charged with thefts of money, clothing, and many other items—needles, a frying pan, cooking pots, scissors, plates, women's boots, and other items.[155] Most, but not all, of these accused female thieves came from outside the township, another indication of the considerable in-migration that Nagatino enjoyed.[156] In one case a forty-seven-year-old woman resident at a tavern in the village of Dubrovka, accused of stealing three plates and forty-five kopeks, was acquitted. Not all women got off, though: in a theft charge heard in 1914 at Nagatino, a peasant woman (age twenty-two) from outside the township accused of stealing a samovar and a pair of women's rubber boots was sentenced to strict arrest of fifteen days.[157] Female peasants accused of theft were convicted at a lower rate than males but not in any statistically significant way. The gender-neutrality of decisions at township courts contrasts with elite society's sympathy for females as victims, rather than agents, of crime.[158] In theft, as in other kinds of cases, both peasant men and peasant women were held responsible for their actions.

Most of the females accused of being thieves at Nagatino were nonresidents, but their place of registration also did not affect verdicts. Nonresidents were not convicted at a significantly higher rate than residents. What appears to have been decisive in cases about theft is the individual case itself: the testimony of all parties and of witnesses; the personal qualities of the defendant, known for his or her bad qualities or not; the circumstances of the case; and the intentional or unintentional actions of the parties. Being brought to trial for theft did not mean that a conviction would result. In my case survey the conviction rate for theft was 41 percent. The filing of a police report and a citation under statute law were only the first steps in local justice. These initial procedures had little bearing on final decisions about responsibility and punishment. The trial itself—the decisions of peasant judges after a court hearing—determined whether a person would be convicted as a thief and sent to jail.

Table 5.8. Conviction Rates for Theft at Different Judicial Instances: 1912, 1913

Court	*Number Judged*	*Number Convicted*	*% Convicted*
All Circuit Courts and Appeals Instances (1912)	51,105	33,503	66%
All Justices of the Peace and Township Courts (1912)	209,791	64,159	31%
Nagatinskii Township Court (1913)	51	22	43%

Sources: *Rossiia 1913 god,* pp. 393–396 (figures for 1912); TsGIAgM, f. 10, op. 1, d. 91.

Of course, those with little property suffered most if a pair of boots or a blanket was stolen. The location and dynamic economy of Nagatinskii Township provided many a temptation to its inhabitants. At the same time the Nagatinskii Township Court, aided by police and local watchmen, managed to bring a good many petty criminals to justice and to get a few pairs of boots returned to their owners. Nagatino's 1913 conviction rate for accused thieves was 43 percent—a little higher than the average for my survey; higher than that of other misdemeanor instances of the empire (31 percent), as reported in the government's statistics for 1912; and lower than the rate of conviction for major thefts prosecuted at circuit courts and appeals instances (66 percent) (see Table 5.8). These global figures are susceptible to many interpretations, including accusations of laxness at the township courts. But it might also be reasonable to expect that defendants in petty theft cases would be more frequently acquitted than people accused of major thefts whose cases were prosecuted with the resources of circuit courts and appeals instances. Nagatino's higher conviction rate compared to that of the empire's other misdemeanor courts generally could be a sign that its judges, police, and many witnesses were effectively, yet carefully, responding to the demand of the population in this bustling area to punish theft.

That theft was considered an evil by users of township courts at this time and in these places is unquestionable. No defendant justified taking someone else's possessions; no witnesses or parties at court mentioned poverty or other excuses for theft. Many defendants in theft cases "recognized themselves as guilty"—in those words—and fewer appealed verdicts than in other kinds of criminal cases. Just as "convict" was an actionable insult, so was an accusation of being a thief. On 11 July 1913 three male residents of the village of Kolomenskoe appeared before the hard-working judges at Nagatino. Ivan Fedorov Forofonov had accused his co-villagers, Nikita Kuzmin Karasev and Ivan Ivanov Karasev, of "insult in words." At court Forofonov, an illiterate man, explained that "on the street in the village of Kolomenskoe, the Karasevs had insulted him, by saying he had stolen a cow." After denials by the defendants and testimony by witnesses, the Karasevs were convicted of "swearing on the street and insulting Forofonov with improper words."[159]

MISDEMEANORS AND SOCIAL VISION

Criminal cases reveal people's notions of justice—of legitimate and legally enforceable constraints upon behavior and speech. By bringing criminals to township courts, rural people enacted their ideals of a good society. What kind of social vision did these charges against thieves, insulters, and, to a lesser extent, noisemakers and sewage-dumpers express?

Forofonov's case is a reminder that personal dignity and property rights can be seen in the same moral frame. The separation of violations into civil and criminal, personal damages and social ones, is a strong feature of the legal imaginaries of jurists and intellectuals. Some elite observers regard the ability to make such distinctions as critical to a developed legal culture. But law is a used system—in legally active societies—and the formal distinctions that matter to legal specialists are not necessarily relevant to users of the law. Law users want things fixed; they want debts paid; they want cows back; they want a public space in which they are not called bad names and not hit with sticks. Through their demands for court decisions, plaintiffs called the state's authority into their lives; criminal cases reveal their expectations of the law.

First, rural people claimed for themselves, and from their fellow citizens, freedom from physical violence against their persons. If a member of society violated this condition, a victim was justified in demanding that the aggressor be "brought to legal responsibility." An unprovoked assault was to be punished as a criminal act, either as violence or as an insult in deed. Although it is possible to cite assault cases as evidence of violent behavior in the village—which certainly existed—court cases show that rural people in early-twentieth-century Russia expected willful violence to be punished, and punished by the courts. Township practice reveals that litigants distinguished between an unplanned scuffle and an intentionally demeaning assault. The court did not punish all violence; a violent response to an initial insult could be justified. Township decisions put an emphasis on the first strike—the breaking down of social restraint—and thereby demonstrated that self-control and social responsibility were to be expected in rural society.

Second, rural people claimed freedom from verbal insult. A person was not to be labeled a "convict," a "whore," or a "shit," or besmirched by any other "improper words." The price for a verbal assault on another's character was legalized punishment, even if this language had been provoked by improper—but not insulting—behavior. Words could be the equivalent of physical violence; as with physical assaults, a critical question was who had been the aggressor. Although mutual insults could cancel each other, initiating a confrontation with a verbal insult was potentially a criminal action. As with physical violence, instances of verbal assault could be redressed through the law. Only the court could officially define a particular name-calling as criminal and assign a punishment to the aggressor. The large numbers of insult cases at the township courts suggest the importance rural people attached to legal process as a defense of one's integrity.

Peasants who took their insulters to court, and could prove their claims or have them proven, could regard their personal integrity as having been defended by the law against the assaults of their maligners. But what of those parties to a case who declared their satisfaction with a verdict against themselves, or who confessed their aggressive acts or words at court, knowing that this admission would incur punishment? One might imagine that an intention in these confessions could be public shaming of the accuser, but this purpose would have been better served by moving quarrels out of tea shops and backyards and into village streets. An explanation more consistent with court records is the value set on the legal process itself. A "guilty" aggressor gained an intensification of the insult by its repetition at the court. An insult could be fortified by official registration; an insulter's willingness to be arrested could sustain a judgment of another's character.

Cases of defiant, self-incriminating declarations can be understood as yet another way of using courts to define ethical and unethical behavior. Insulters who incriminated themselves or declared themselves satisfied with their convictions were practicing not civil disobedience but what we might call uncivil obedience. The law set the terms for insults; insulters obeyed these rules; and they achieved their insults by being willing to suffer a legal punishment for them.

A third claim made by plaintiffs bringing criminal cases was that their possessions should not be misappropriated. Village society was not tolerant of thieves. Ordinarily people had no doubts about who owned which object or animal, and violations of the right to one's own property were both reported to police and prosecuted at the township courts. Even in Nagatinskii Township, items that had been stolen and sold to unwitting purchasers could be identified and returned to rightful owners. According to *The General Regulation on Peasants,* people of peasant status were entitled to "acquire as their property immovables and movables" and also to "alienate," "mortgage," and "distribute" these possessions in accord with legally defined procedures.[160] In civil cases residents of rural areas took full advantage of their right to manipulate their property and to engage in contractual arrangements. Criminal cases about theft and *samoupravstvo* complement peasants' exercise of civil rights with their demand for prosecution of people who violated ownership.

Violence, insults, theft—these were all unwelcome in the rural public sphere. A fourth claim, a right to tranquility in the physical sense of the term, is heard less insistently at township courts. How much did rural people care—or how many rural people cared—about noise, swearing, "wild conduct," and similar disturbances in taverns and on village streets? Police were not the only people to bring these cases to the courts, and there were usually witnesses to this kind of charge. Still, the evil in these cases seems to have been less about disturbance of the peace than about violence occurring in connection with loss of control. Inebriation was almost always a police charge, rather than a case brought directly by a civilian, but many drinking cases involved violent actions that were at the heart of why defendants found themselves in the dock.

Finally, there was dirt. Did it matter much? Dirt cases in my study occurred much more frequently in Nagatinskii Township than elsewhere, and it may be safe to say that in congested areas police and at least some citizens cooperated in a struggle against mud, manure, and other effluent that spoiled neighborly relations. To clean up one's own courtyard was a public duty in the crowded villages of Nagatinskii Township. Here again, individual and social obligation were integrated in a moral code articulated in statute law and activated at township courts. Homes were not castles in rural Russia, and they were definitely not people's "own" castles. The law, policemen, watchmen and neighbors could enforce "regular" spring cleaning upon any renter or owner of a house.

In all these matters—violence, insults, theft, a certain degree of peace and cleanliness—the law provided a means for shared regulation and reparation of public life. The misdemeanor code displayed the dreamworld of a well-ordered polity, a realm produced by debates, decisions, and controversies among rulers and administrators at the highest levels of the government. But peasants had their dreamworld, too. A place where no one was called a scoundrel, where no one stole boots and plates, where too much drinking did not lead to violence, where neighbors cleaned their courtyards. They could try to get there through the township courts.

Peasant Jurisprudence

Legal culture in Russian townships was built on revelatory and equitable court process, informed use of statute law, and the engaged participation of rural people. What happened in courtrooms mattered. Outcomes of cases did not depend on generalized characteristics of plaintiffs or defendants, on kinds of charges or claims, or on other conditions that did not involve the hearing. Township judges considered the particulars of each case; their decisions corresponded to testimony and evidence; their verdicts enforced standards of responsibility and respect. At a time when peasants were engaging in new kinds of work, moving to new areas, and choosing new ways to live, township courts responded rapidly to family conflicts, challenges to dignity, and petty crime. The courts' case-by-case address to moral issues raised by litigants made law an active element in a gradual but significant transformation of rural society.

Township judges and clerks worked within a regime of local representation and official regulation. Candidate judges were elected from each village in the township; from among these candidates, the land captain selected judges for a three-year term. Clerks were chosen by elected township officials. Both clerks and judges had to meet qualifications designed to ensure that they would be responsible and respected authorities. These selection procedures were augmented by an array of disciplinary procedures, enabling rural people to bring wayward authorities to justice for malfeasance. Like punishments, the rewards of judicial office—salaries, status-based privileges, and honors—depended on a network of regulatory and material practices connecting local society with the state.

CHOOSING A JUDGE

The people with most responsibility for deciding what justice at township courts could mean were judges. The flexibility of the courts' procedures—the ability to adjust charges to actions revealed in testimony, the right to respect local custom in family cases, the range of sentences—gave judges a wide field of discretionary authority. The absence of lawyers or other legal specialists from township courts meant that judges made their decisions without the benefits or pressures of professional advice. The appeal and effectiveness of law in the countryside derived in large part from the qualities of the men who sat in judgment on their peasant peers.

Elite observers thought they knew their peasant judges, but, as usual, they knew different things. Proponents of township courts found peasant judges to be fair arbiters, informed by village tradition; detractors observed only childish simpletons or venal drunkards.[1] Criticism of peasant judges was one motive for the reform of local administration in 1889. The office of land captain—to be occupied by a member of the nobility—was created to oversee the township court. This reform in turn proved controversial. To liberals, the land captain represented reaction: his intrusive supervision of rural affairs was thought to obstruct the desired evolution of backward peasants into citizens. Especially reprehensible from this perspective was the land captain's power to appoint township judges.[2] This apparently democratic critique revealed the usual elitism of Russian public opinion; it was assumed that peasants were helpless in the face of administrative superiors. Moreover, the common view that the land captain hand-picked the township judges, although technically correct, significantly misrepresented the process by which judges were chosen after 1889.

Contrary to received opinion, election of judges by rural constituencies was not abolished with the introduction of the land captaincy. According to the 1889 legislation and in practice, all peasant judges were elected. Every three years, each rural society in a township elected a single candidate judge. From among these candidates, the land captain chose township judges as well as alternates for three-year terms in office. The 1889 law envisioned that under ordinary circumstances all judges elected by village societies in a township would become either judges or substitute judges. In each township the list of judges elected by peasant societies was to contain at least eight people; among these, four were to be made permanent judges, and the rest their alternates. The land captain did not choose judges on his own; he simply prioritized the list of judges elected by peasant communities.[3]

An election and selection of this kind was carried out in Sharapovskii Township in the countryside south of Zvenigorod at the beginning of 1911. On 3

January 1911, when a new judicial term was about to begin, the land captain of the third district of Zvenigorod County, writing from his seat in Odintsovo, sent a mimeographed letter to the township administration in Sharapovo requesting a list of candidates for judgeships at the township court. He asked the township administration to indicate how long each candidate had already served as a judge and whether a candidate had been reelected for a new three-year term. This form letter also noted that, although there were no requirements for the position, the land captain wanted the township administrators to inform him of each candidate's qualifications and also if any candidate did not have the right to serve as a judge. A week later the land captain sent out another letter to Sharapovo, asking that all elected candidates be summoned to meet him at the township administration, where he would personally acquaint himself with these men.[4]

The right to serve as a judge to which the land captain referred was described in *The General Regulation on Peasants:*

> To the office of Township Judge are chosen peasant householders who have reached the age of thirty-five, enjoy the respect of their co-villagers, and [are], if possible, literate. Those who cannot be chosen [are] (1) persons convicted of theft, swindling, misappropriation or squandering of another's property and not acquitted with a court verdict, and likewise those who were condemned by a court to corporal punishment, imprisonment, or another form of severe punishment. . . , (2) the keepers of institutions for retail sale of drinks, and (3) people occupying another post in the township or village administration.[5]

These straightforward qualifications were designed to produce judges with authority and experience, without axes to grind or vodka to sell. Through the appointment of such men, Russian officialdom incorporated patriarchal authority, legitimated local community, and encouraged respect for the decisions of its courts. The regulation took account of a specific perceived evil—the sale of alcohol—and, by means of the prohibition on holding multiple offices, widened the distribution of official authority in rural areas.

Demid U'lich Platov, the township leader, and Gerasim Vasil'evich Vasil'ev, the township clerk in Sharapovo,[6] were well prepared for the land captain's request. They had at their disposal sixteen written decisions from the rural assemblies of the townships, each of which named a candidate judge. Every assembly had filled in a mimeographed form with an account of its selection of its candidate, and every form was signed by those present at the meeting, or in cases of illiteracy, by representatives. Each document was stamped and signed by the leader of the rural society, as well as by Platov and Vasil'ev, for the township administration. Vasil'ev had saved himself and others some effort by running off copies of a single handwritten declaration, with the usual formulas and convenient blank spaces, to record these local opinions. The clear hand of the clerk in mimeograph purple evokes the combination of pragmatism, personality, and adherence to form typical of local secretarial practice.

The top half of each declaration began:

> 191_ year ___ day we the undersigned of Moscow Province, Zvenigorod County, Sharapovskii Township, ________ rural society, peasant householders of the settlement _______ in number __ people out of the whole number "___" of those having a right by law to a voice at the assembly, being today together in the presence of our Village Leader ________ and having taken up the election of a candidate for the office of Township Judge at the expiration of the term of service of the previous candidate, and guided by the 114 st. of the *Gen. Reg.*, declare: to elect as candidate for the office of Township Judge, peasant of settlement ______________________________ and about this we have drawn up this declaration which we confirm with our signatures.[7]

These forms were filled in with the appropriate information, including the names of the leader and the candidate judge. The rest of the page and sometimes another was filled with signatures of those participating in the election.

Elections of candidate judges followed procedures familiar to peasants who routinely participated in local governance. Both general agreements and a "majority of votes" were acceptable ways for rural assemblies to make decisions, according to *The General Regulation on Peasants.* In consequential economic matters a majority of two-thirds was required; for other issues a simple one-vote majority was sufficient; and in the case of a tie the leader was to decide.[8] The mimeographed document provided to assemblies in Sharapovskii Township does not provide a space to express discordant views in the selection of a judge. Whatever their discussions of a judicial candidacy might have been, villagers are recorded as being of one mind. By affixing his signature to the document, or having the clerk record his name on it, each individual gave his personalized assent to the assembly's collective choice.

Participating in an election of a candidate judge was one way that rural households influenced the quality of law in their area. To elect a township judge, half the householders having a right to vote, in addition to the rural leader, had to be present.[9] Table 6.1 displays the level of participation in each electoral assembly for the 1911 elections of candidate judges in Sharapovskii Township. The rural societies of this township varied considerably in size. The smallest, Mashovskoe, had only 15 eligible householders, whereas Chasovinskoe had 124 members.[10] Attendance at these election meetings was not uniform. At the Tganskoe assembly, only half of those eligible from four small settlements voted, just enough to meet the minimum requirement for an election. The Chatsovskoe assembly rounded up 80 out of 82 householders from its single village. The average turnout for all assemblies in Sharapovskii Township was 70 percent of eligible voters.

The elections in Sharapovskii township in 1911 display the representative democracy that sustained the township courts. Seventy percent of eligible household heads in the township had put their names to the candidacies of men who could become township judges. Because the judges ultimately selected were all householders in these settlements, these men would be known by at least their co-villagers, if not by others in the township. Candidates did not have the right to refuse election unless they were over sixty years of age or had al-

Table 6.1. Householder Participation in Elections of Candidate Judges, Sharapovskii Township, Zvenigorod County, Moscow Province, Elections for 1911–1913 Term

Rural Society	*Number of Settlements*	*Total Number of Eligible Voters*	*Number of Voters Present and Signing the Election Form*	*Percent of Eligible Voters Electing Candidate Judge*
Chatsovskoe	1	82	80	97.6%
Iastrebskoe	1	15	14	93.3%
Tatarskoe	3	97	80	82.5%
Grishakovskoe	1	38	31	81.6%
Mashkovskoe	1	11	8	72.7%
Nikiforovskoe	2	70	50	71.4%
Riazanskoe	1	52	37	71.2%
Mikhailovskoe	2	99	67	67.7%
Volkovskoe	2	42	28	66.7%
Khotiazhevskoe	4	63	40	63.5%
Sharapovskoe	4	116	73	62.9%
Chasovinskoe	1	124	76	61.3%
Nikolskoe	1	103	63	61.2%
Anikovskoe	5	28	17	60.7%
Bogachevskoe	5	110	57	51.8%
Tganskoe	4	65	33	50.8%
Mean:	2.4	69.7	47.1	69.8%
Median:		67.5	45	67.2%

Source: TsIAM, f. 747, op. 1, d. 66.

ready completed a term of service or were suffering from a severe illness or, after 1906, were enrolled in an educational institution.[11] There is no indication in the Sharapovskii documents that anyone refused his election as a candidate. All candidates proposed to the land captain were over thirty-five, and all but two were literate. Three were already serving on the township court. The sixteen candidate judges were men of experience, well known to those who had chosen them, and personally approved by 51 to 98 percent of the householders in their settlements of residence.

How, then, would the land captain choose from the names presented to him? Much depended, of course, on the man who occupied the post. In this case, the land captain's letter of 3 January to the Sharapovskii township administration indicated the factors he would use in his selection. The township authorities used these categories when drawing up the list of candidates elected by the sixteen rural societies. Names were submitted to the land captain on a handwritten, rank-ordered list, arranged in six columns with the following headings: Rank Number; Name of the Settlement of the Candidate; Name, Patronymic, and Last Name of the Selected Candidate; Age; Literacy of the Candidate; and "Has He Served Earlier."[12] The ordering of this list both answered the land captain's questions and proved crucial to the selection of the judges.

At the top of the list was Nikolai Gavrilov, from Busharino, fifty-three years old, literate, and already serving as the president of the township court. Next in line were the two other candidates who were already judges and who, like Gavrilov, had been reelected by their communities for a second term. By these names in the last column, the clerk entered "elected to a second three years." One of the four serving judges apparently was not reelected; his name figured nowhere on the list. The other candidates were described as having been "elected for a first three-year term." The literacy of each candidate was recorded; the two illiterate candidates were ranked thirteenth and sixteenth on the list. The recorded ages of the candidates varied from thirty-nine to fifty-seven; their average age was forty-eight. Age did not affect the rank order of the list. No candidate was marked as lacking the right to serve.[13]

The land captain made his choices directly on the list. He underlined the names of the top four candidates in rank order, and chose them—at least preliminarily—as township judges for the next three years. He wrote "18 years" in the column "Has He Served Earlier" for Gavrilov, the president of the court, and noted that the other two reelected judges were chosen for a second term. In a subsequent letter to the township administration, written in February after his rendezvous with the candidate judges at the township administration, the land captain formally appointed these four men, as well as four alternate judges, who had been ranked five through eight on the township leader's list. The land captain thus chose all judges and their alternates exactly in the order of the list submitted to him by the township authorities.[14]

Because the township administration had placed all township judges who had been reelected by their communities (three out of four) at the top of the list, the main principle of selection the land captain appears to have used was experience at court combined with local approval. But what of judge number four, the only newly appointed judge on the list? Sergei Petrov Stepunin, aged forty-five, from the village of Chasovnia, literate, appears on the list of candidates without distinguishing features, although the township authorities must have known the significance of ranking him in fourth place, just after the reelected judges. The individual resolutions of the local assemblies suggest a possible motive for his selection. Stepunin was elected by the assembly of Chasovinskoe, the rural society with the largest population and the largest number—124—of eligible voters in the township.[15] Perhaps township authorities considered it important to put a representative of this large settlement, with its brickmaking factory,[16] on the court. Two of the judges continuing on the court came from larger rural societies—Semyon Ivanov Kazennov, from Mart'ianovo, one of four villages in the Sharapovskoe society of 116 householders, and Ivan Timofei Rukin, from Boroviki, one of two villages in Mikhailovskoe society of 99 householders. The long-serving president of the court came from a small community, with only 42 eligible householders.[17]

Although there is no way of knowing how township authorities devised their rankings, the selection procedures draw attention to how local knowledge inflected rural justice. Because the township was a small administrative unit, in both geographic size and population (see chapter 1), it is possible that township administrators were acquainted with the candidates for the court. Sharapovskii Township had a total population of 9,434 on 1 January 1910; of these inhabitants, 8,874 were members of the peasant estate, and 1,171 were heads of household.[18] The resolutions of rural assemblies meeting in 1911 to choose candidate judges recorded a total of 1,115 heads of household with a voice in the assembly.[19] It would be well within the capacity of township administrators who had to witness all resolutions of township assemblies to know the candidate judges and to exercise informed choices when they made their list for the land captain. Personal connections among men of authority, for better or for worse, may have influenced the selection of judges.

A preference for experienced candidates accorded with the patriarchal and paternalistic ethos that imbued laws, administration, and society generally.[20] Both rural people and state administrators shared an ethic of respect for knowledge gained over time. The land captain had asked that years of service be indicated; the township administration fulfilled his request; the experienced judges were selected for another term. This conservative approach corresponds to the pattern of judicial service at other townships. The persons of judges changed only slowly at township courts. Judges reelected by their communities were reinstated by higher authorities for successive terms. The state enhanced the practice of long-term service with a series of awards. Nikolai Gavrilov, the president of the Sharapovskii Township Court, had already received his silver "Stanislavskii" medal in 1910 for having served three three-year terms.[21] At the courts, rapid turnover and youth were not desirable qualities.

Representative democracy, obligatory participation, and procedural formalism were fundamental to the selection of judges. The land captain's power to appoint was constrained by local approval ensured by elections. Local communities could reject unsatisfactory judges by not reelecting them as candidates for office. Attendance at assemblies was voluntary, but if rural people wanted government to happen, they had to take part in its routines. No election of a candidate would have meant no judge, at least no judge from one's community. It seems unlikely that people would have thought about their choices in this negative fashion, because the election of township judges took place in the ordinary way of rural administrative practice: a meeting of the rural assembly, a choice made and recorded, one's signature put to paper or one's name recorded by a representative, the whole process represented in writing, signed and sealed by township officials, and forwarded to higher authorities. A local voice was both solicited and guaranteed.

The land captain had his assigned part on this ladder of responsibilities. He called for the list of candidates; then he, like the peasants of the area, was required to make a choice constrained by rules. An attentive land captain would know if there had been numerous appeals against a judge or any of the township authorities, but it is likely that these people would have been eliminated

Judges seated around a table, in front of the township administration building at Bun'kovo, Bogorodskii County, Moscow Province, 23 June 1906. *Photograph from the collection of Mikhail Zolotarev.*

from new candidacies by elections. If a township contained eight or fewer rural assemblies, the land captain had only to distinguish between judges and alternates on the list of candidates submitted to him. Otherwise, he faced the probably baffling task of choosing from a longer list of candidates, few of whom he had met (unless they were repeaters). No wonder a land captain might just take the top of the list, thereby enhancing the authority of his subordinates in the township administration.

In addition to making "choices" from the list of candidate judges, the land captain administered the oath of office, required of all township judges and alternate judges before they began service on the court.[22] After the elections in Sharapovskii Township, Viktor Vasil'evich Panov, the land captain, visited the township administration in person, met the candidate judges, and administered their oaths. Only after this ceremony did he officially confirm these judges for the three-year term.[23] While performing their duties, township judges wore a light bronze medallion, with the coat of arms of the province encircled by the inscription "Township Judge" on the front, and an image of the emperor with the dates of the emancipation decree and the 1889 court reform on the back.[24]

THE QUALITIES OF JUDGES

The selection of township judges combined the procedural with the personal. At several levels—election at rural assemblies, structuring of lists by township administrators, and legitimation by the land captain—knowledge of personal characteristics could affect the choice of men who would sit in judgment on their peers. This choice was always about particular individuals; it would be misleading to search for a "typical" peasant judge. A few qualities beyond the basic requirements for election would nonetheless be shared by most township judges in the early twentieth century.

First, township judges were male. This was not a requirement in *The Regulation on Peasants,* but a "head of household" who qualified for an official position would always be a man. Second, judges at township courts in the early twentieth century would usually be literate to some degree. Again, there was no absolute rule, but literacy was regarded as important for performance of judicial duties. I found no obvious signs of illiteracy among judges at township courts, where they frequently signed testimony for illiterate litigants. Third, judges were likely to be men of some economic substance. There were no property requirements for office, but the post required judges to spend at least two days a month at court—a considerable expenditure of time. P. I. Peretriakhin, a judge in Nagatino from 1914 to 1916, was probably the same man who paid the highest taxes in Kolomenskoe in 1913.[25] In their elections to the judiciary, rural people appear to have associated wealth with duty and responsibility. Fourth, as men aged thirty-five or older and probably with substantial resources, judges would be people with considerable experience in their society. Some judges were chosen from families whose members had served earlier in local administration. At the Tsaritsyno court Judge S. N. Klopov, who heard cases in 1916, was probably the son of N. Klopov, who had been the president of the court at Tsaritsyno in 1909 and 1910. Men with the same last name can be found holding offices over the years as judges and clerks in the same township court.[26]

It was thus men of some education, possessing local knowledge and experience, elected by other household heads in their communities, and endowed with material resources who were chosen to decide cases at township courts. The election of township judges brought tens of thousands of such men into government service and granted them extensive responsibility for the well-being of their localities. The quality of judges' performance of their duties was the most important element of township justice. The characteristics most critical to judges' decisions—their personal notions of justice, of authority, and of the good—are the least available for study. Did township judges take bribes? Did they peddle influence? Did they sell verdicts for vodka? None of these behaviors is visible in legal records, nor would we expect to find them recorded in this source. It is reasonable to assume that township judges were subject to pressures and asserted their powers in a variety of ways, as judges have done in other times and places. The extensive and voluntary usage of the township courts by rural people can serve as its own verdict on the qualities of their judges.

CLERKS AND THEIR RECORDS

The only other official always present at a court hearing, apart from the three or four judges, was the township clerk. Critics of township courts attacked judges for their lack of education and close—presumably corrupt—connections to their communities. Clerks have been criticized for just the opposite inadequacies—their superior education and hence distance from peasant values.[27] One argument of this book is that the notion of disconnected, authentic peasant culture is untenable. Peasants were not isolated from others—including clerks—in the early twentieth century; their various values did not derive from sixty years of monolithic post-emancipation collectivity. Peasant litigants and judges respected literacy and knowledge.[28] The clerk's ability to consult earlier legal documents and to produce and maintain records of new decisions was indispensable to the sustenance of legal culture over time. Paper, writing, and bookkeeping created a network of legal actions reaching back to past agreements and forward to future decisions.[29]

The clerk was a civil servant, hired by the township administration. There were some restrictions on who could fill this office. No one excluded from state service or condemned at court or on trial or under investigation or "in general known for corrupt or depraved behavior" could be chosen as a township clerk.[30] Like other township employees, the clerk received a salary ordinarily set by the township assembly and paid from the township treasury. The county congress had the right to revise the salary upward, if it found that the local authorities were not paying the clerk, or other township officials, a sufficient amount. The clerk was not entitled to vote in the township administration or in the court. Only elected officials—the leader of the whole township and the leaders of the individual rural societies and their assistants—bore legal responsibility for the welfare and duties of rural dwellers; at court, only judges who had been elected by one or another rural society could make legal decisions.[31]

The clerk's job, first and foremost, was to record administrative and judicial decisions in appropriate books and to carry out all township correspondence. Attention to instructions and accuracy were critical to his performance. In the words of *The General Regulation on Peasants,* the clerk was "obliged, faithfully and in order, to maintain the indicated books and with necessary precision set forth in papers and certificates, issued by the township leader, the township administration, the township court, and township assembly, that which has been ordered and decided by them." Forgery by a township clerk was to be punished at criminal court with the same severity as forgeries by other civil servants.[32]

Keeping the township's books required both knowledge and skill. The clerk had to be familiar with the rules of township governance and the statutes of

№	СОДЕРЖАНІЕ РѢШЕНІЙ.	Когда исполнены рѣшенія.
35.	1905 года Августа 28 дня Ягунинскій Волостной судъ въ составѣ председателя Кагуданова, судей Колосова и Иванова, при заступающемъ дѣлопроизводителя Волостного писаря Акимова, слушалъ уголовное дѣло по обвиненію кр. д. Устья Василіемъ Евтихіевичемъ Артамоновымъ односельца Василія Абрамова Андріанова въ самоуправствѣ. По вызову въ судъ стороны и свидѣтели явились. Обвинитель кр. д. Устья Василій Артамоновъ заявилъ, что въ маѣ мѣсяцѣ с. г. кр. Андріановъ сломалъ на его усадьбѣ, принадлежащую ему изгородь, вопреки его желанію. Просилъ привлечь Андріанова къ отвѣтственности по 142 ст. Уст. о Нак. Василій Артамоновъ Обвиняемый кр. д. Устья Василій Абрамовъ Андріановъ заявилъ, что дѣйствительно въ маѣ мѣсяцѣ с. г. кр. Артамоновъ на его усадьбѣ поставилъ изгородь, то онъ съ разрѣшенія бывшаго Старшины Алексѣева раздробилъ поставленную	1905 г. 28 августа настоящее дѣло прошу дѣло [illegible] производствомъ прекратить. Василій Артамоновъ

First and second pages of a case record, Iaguninskii Township Court, August 28, 1905, case no. 35. Record of fulfillment is on the right side of the first page.

№	СОДЕРЖАНІЕ РѢШЕНІЙ.

на его усадьбѣ изгородь Артемонова Васильевыми обругалъ
Свидѣтели кр. д. Устья Иванъ
Никифоровъ Черешковъ по-
казали, что дѣйствительно
въ тѣхъ числахъ с. г. кр. Ан-
дріановъ сломалъ изгородь
Артемонова. Неграмотный

Пред. Судья Н. [illegible]

Волостной Судъ разсмотрѣвъ
настоящее дѣло и принимая
во вниманіе, что виновность
Андріанова въ проступкѣ,
предусмотрѣнномъ 142 ст.
Уст. о Нак. вполнѣ подтвер-
ждается свидѣтельскими
показаніями Черешкова
и потому приговорилъ:
кр. д. Устья Гавріила Ад-
ріанова Андріанова под-
вергнуть аресту при Воло-
стномъ правленіи на
семь дней. Приговоръ может
быть обжалованъ въ 30 днев-
ный срокъ Земскому Начальнику
2 уч. Звенигородскаго уѣзда

Предсѣдатель Суда Н. [illegible]

Судьи
Неграмот. Акимовъ   И. Павловъ
И. Новов[illegible]

Объявлено Артамонов[illegible]

criminal and civil law. *The General Regulation on Peasants* and the *Statutes on Punishments* or excerpts from them were available in the courtroom, as in the picture of the judges at Bun'kovo. Clerks could use published handbooks and legal compilations to assist them in their tasks. Almanacs for township authorities were published annually in the early twentieth century. N. T. Volkov's *Juridical Calendar for Township and Civil Servants* provided lists of civil and criminal matters in the township court's purview, indicators of the jurisdiction of various courts over other legal matters, holidays, excerpts from law codes, and examples of forms, as well as blank pages for notes. This handy publication was sold in twenty-eight bookstores in twenty-five cities in 1904. Clerks and others interested in furthering their legal education could order other "books for self-teaching" from advertisements in Volkov's handbook and in similar publications.[33]

Clerks recorded testimony as it happened during court proceedings. They had to keep up with the pace of hearings, enabling litigants and witnesses to put their names to their words in the record book. The occasional crossing out of errors and other corrections in case records give a sense of the attentiveness and speed with which the clerk had to work. Some clerks came up with shortcuts. One strategy that saved paper and effort was to record at the end of the day in a single sequence all the cases that had been closed because plaintiffs did not show up for the hearing. Occasionally a clerk used a mimeographed form or a rubber stamp.[34] Copies of summonses were made with carbon paper at some courts.[35]

Like other low-level bureaucrats in the imperial administration, the clerk spent a good deal of his time writing. Record-keeping could be individualized through handwriting; clerks wrote neatly—usually—and with a sense of style. In almost all the records I examined the clerk's attention to detail was meticulous. In the single case where Chekaldin—the diligent clerk at the Tsaritsynskii Township Court—appeared to have lost his usual attention to detail, handwriting was the giveaway. Near the end of the lengthy docket of cases heard on 17 December 1915 Chekaldin's writing deteriorated badly, and a new record-keeper took over for the last four hearings.[36] But this negligence—a result of holiday celebrations, perhaps?—was the very infrequent exception and not at all the rule.

The clerk did not have a set term of office, unlike elected township officials who served on three-year, renewable terms. Occasionally a clerk might hold office for only a few months, but for the most part clerks were kept at their posts for several years. When necessary, courts employed substitute clerks for short periods. In more than half the courts I studied in Moscow Province in the years before the war, clerks remained in their positions for at least six years. Most of the others were in their posts for at least three years. The following employment record provides an example of the kinds of turnover that could take place in a township. Adrian Terent'evich Akimov, whose work we have followed at the Iaguninskii court, assumed his duties as the clerk in Iaguninskii Township on 10 July 1905 and remained at his post through 1911. In 1912

Vladimir Fedorovich Ryzhenkov replaced Akimov at Iagunino. The clerk's position was formally vacant at the beginning of 1914, although a temporary person kept the court's records for two months. Then in March 1914 the position was filled by Lanin, who served through 1916.[37]

After reading hundreds of case records and inspecting thousands, I find it impossible to slight the performance of Russia's township clerks. Formality, individuality, and responsibility adhere to township records. It was the clerk's conscientious work that allowed litigants, overseers, and, later, historians to trace the path of a case through the legal network. The clerk registered and processed complaints as people registered them; he was present at all court sessions to record each case; he forwarded court decisions to litigants and to village and higher authorities; as verdicts were carried out, he returned to his books to fill in information about the completion of a case. In most instances a single case would have several numbers: one number in the complaint book, another number as a case heard at the township court, and often still another number in a record book of court decisions and their fulfillment. The clerk's records gave life to court decisions and created the objects—official papers bound in books, preserved in folders—that were essential to a culture of resort to law.

RURAL OFFICIALS AND POLICE AT COURT

In most hearings at township courts the judges and the clerk were the only officials present in the courtroom with litigants. But in 23 percent of the cases in my survey, other authorities—policemen, village representatives, watchmen, village and township leaders—appeared at court. These local officials were usually called as witnesses to provide testimony for the judges' consideration.

The kind of official most likely to appear at a township court was a representative of a rural society. When a rural society itself was a party to a case, the village or villages concerned would send one or more representatives to present their claims. Representatives of rural societies were critical witnesses in inheritance and related civil cases. When inheritance claims were contested, village representatives could deliver the opinion of a village or other collective as to whose claim was in order. Most important, village representatives could testify to the existence or absence of heirs not party to a particular case. At the Nagatinskii Township Court, village representatives testified in every inheritance case heard at sessions held in January and early February 1916. In addition, village representatives appeared in almost half of the many suits and at one of the two controversies over land heard at this time. In each of these cases, the village representative provided evidence of the village society's position. The testimony of a village representative was cited as a reason for the judges' decision in 30 percent of all civil cases heard by the Nagatinskii court at this time of local turmoil.[38] In addition to delegates of rural societies, other local officials—village and township leaders, clerks, and watchmen—were occasionally called

Policemen and firemen with the provincial administration, in front of the Society Bank building, Pavlovskii posad, Moscow Province, 1910. *Photograph from the collection of Mikhail Zolotarev.*

as witnesses at township courts. In my survey overall, representatives or other rural officials testified in 15 percent of cases.

Policemen were less likely to be present at court cases; in my survey they appeared in 8 percent of cases. The presence of police at criminal hearings was not required; even when a case was opened by means of a charge recorded at the local constabulary policemen were unlikely to appear in court (see chapter 5). Police were never called on to testify in civil cases in my survey. At the remote Zaborovskii court in Novgorod Province, no policemen crossed the threshold of the township court, as far as I could determine. At the Iaguninskii Township Court near Zvenigorod in Moscow Province, where police filed charges in 16 percent of criminal cases, representatives of the police did not testify in court about these or other cases. At the Ignatevskii court, police occasionally (9 percent) made an appearance in criminal cases. Only in the townships very near Moscow did police participate in any significant number of court hearings. At Nagatino policemen appeared in 29 percent of criminal cases, and at Tsaritsyno in 27 percent of such cases.

When policemen were present at township hearings, their role was almost always that of witnesses called on to corroborate or refute charges in particular cases. But police were not immune from prosecution at township courts, and occasionally a policeman appeared at court as a defendant. On 18 March

1913 the Nagatinskii Township Court heard Nikolai Andreev Papushkin's case against a policeman, Andri Grigor'ev Semenov, for "insult in words and slander." This case had been sent to the township court at Nagatino by a Justice of the Peace in the city of Moscow. The defendant Semenov appeared at court, along with three other city policemen called as witnesses. The clerk recorded the following testimony:

> Papushkin testified that, in the policemen's quarters, Semenov called him a scoundrel.
>
> Semenov testified that in the quarters he did not call Papushkin a scoundrel, but [illeg., unprintable?].
>
> Policeman of the third . . . district, badge no. 3203 Dmitri Geraskin testified that Semenov called Papushkin a scoundrel.
>
> Badge no. 3204, third . . . district, policeman Gavril Krasnov testified to the same as Geraskin.
>
> Badge no. 3260 policeman Tikhon Senashov testified that between Papushkin and Semenov there was mutual swearing and they [illeg.] each other. Quarrels between them happened often.

Evidence provided by the first two witnesses was cited as the basis for Semenov's conviction for insulting Papushkin. He was sentenced to a ten-ruble fine, reduced to six rubles or three days in jail in accord with the imperial amnesty declared in 1913. Semenov paid his fine on 1 June 1913.[39] An insult uttered by a policeman was still an insult and a misdemeanor to be punished.

Apart from the occasional policemen and, more frequently, representatives of rural societies, no other officials or experts appeared at township courts. Under restricted circumstances parties could send representatives to court, but these were usually relatives, and in no circumstances were they to be paid.[40] At most township courts, and in most cases, litigants were on their own to make their cases or to defend themselves against claims and charges made against them. The absence of lawyers and of legally trained judges was a sore point for critics of rural justice, who complained that township courts suffered from a lack of legal expertise. This criticism ignored the legal knowledge and experience of judges, clerks, litigants, and witnesses themselves, who year in and year out demonstrated familiarity and competence with legal process at township courts.[41]

WOMEN, MEN, AND FAMILIES AT COURT

Relations within families and among them were a critical arena of litigation for rural people. In the early twentieth century peasants engaged the many opportunities opened by expansion of employment in factories and cities, enhancement of educational possibilities, creation of new networks of information, restructuring of access to land, and the second revolution of expanded individual rights. Choices made by individual men and women concerning employment, marriage, and property affected families across the countryside and produced many a case at township courts.[42] In the short term, and with immediate significance for litigants, township courts provided an official forum for settling disputes between family members. In the long run, the myriad decisions made at township courts by peasant judges permitted orderly and gradual shifts in authority and values in rural society.

Peasant families—happy or unhappy—were different in their own ways, particularly at court. No single pattern of family organization existed in any region of the empire at this time; the extended patriarchal family, considered the standard arrangement in Russia by contemporaries, had been eroded—if it had even existed—well before the early twentieth century.[43] Litigants at township courts did not refer explicitly to the authority of patriarchs, nor, as noted in chapter 4, did they ever use the word *bol'shak* (the big one). The absence of such testimony does not prove that patriarchal authority was dead, but it does suggest that family power could be discussed in other terms. Township courts were a site of litigation by all possible members of households: sons and fathers, daughters and mothers, in-laws, adopted children, and orphans figured in the accounts of court hearings. Case records allow a glimpse of the desires evoked and obstacles encountered by rural men and women in their relations with other individuals and with their families.

Both men and women brought cases to the township courts, and both men and women were called to court as defendants. Before the beginning of World War I men were plaintiffs in 84 percent of the cases in my study; women were plaintiffs in the remaining 16 percent. The distribution of plaintiffs by sex was somewhat different if criminal and civil cases are considered separately: women brought 15 percent of civil cases and 16 percent of criminal cases (see Table 3.2). As with other statistics concerning rural courts, these patterns were not the same for all regions. The lowest percentage of cases brought by women before the war in my survey was at the court at Iagunino in Zvenigorod County of Moscow Province. Here men were plaintiffs in 97 percent of all cases. The court with the highest proportion of female plaintiffs was Nagatino near Moscow, where women brought 24 percent of all cases.

If women were plaintiffs in a substantial portion of cases at township courts, they were less likely than men to be defendants. Overall, in the courts I studied, women were defendants in 15 percent of cases. The representation of women as defendants varied with the type of case, by court, and over time. Before World War I women were defendants in only 4 percent of civil cases and in 12 percent of criminal cases. The lesser role of women as both defendants and plaintiffs in civil cases before the war probably reflects the highly unequal control of property by men and women in peasant families at this time. Women were not excluded from authority over land and products, but they nonetheless controlled far less property—especially family property—than men. This would be a plausible explanation for their diminished visibility as plaintiffs and defendants in prewar civil cases.[44]

Did men and women confront each other as opposing "sides" at township courts, or were the courts an arena for same-sex struggles? Overall, my statistical survey showed a weak correlation between the sex of the plaintiff and the sex of the defendant. Females who took cases to the township courts were somewhat more likely to charge or sue other females than men. Many cases nonetheless involved women suing or bringing charges against men, and it would be misleading to represent rural female litigants as unlikely or unable to haul male adversaries before township judges (see chapter 7).

In my statistical exploration of court cases, I found little to distinguish male from female litigants with respect to the kinds of villages they came from, their involvement in particular kinds of cases, or in the success of their suits and charges at court. The single strong correlation distinguishing male and female litigants was that women at court—both as plaintiffs and defendants—were more likely to be illiterate than males at court in these capacities. This finding is consistent with contemporary and later studies of literacy and gender in Russia.[45] I found no significant difference in literacy between female plaintiffs and female defendants.

For both male and female litigants in my survey, there was a moderate correlation between the literacy of plaintiffs and the literacy of defendants. This means that literate plaintiffs were more likely to sue literate defendants than illiterate ones, and that in criminal cases illiterate people were more likely to bring charges against other illiterate people. A possible interpretation of these relationships, as of the predominance of same-sex cases, is that the township courts were a realm in which people ordinarily confronted peers as their antagonists. Disputes among unequals might be more easily—if not equitably—resolved informally. The courts enabled literate peasants to try to collect debts from other literate peasants and allowed illiterates to call other illiterates to court for insult.

The one kind of encounter at the township courts that went against the pattern of equivalent literacy (or illiteracy) for plaintiffs and defendants was litigation between family members. Before the beginning of the war, cases pitting family members against each other accounted for 9 percent of all cases at the courts I studied.[46] The most frequent kind of family case with identifiable parties was one brought by a brother against a brother. Brothers faced off against brothers in 35 percent of these prewar family cases. With fathers bringing 18 percent of cases, and mothers 18 percent, the older generation was just as active as sons. Less visible, but still present occasionally as plaintiffs, were sons, wives, and sisters.

Any kind of matter could cause these family controversies at township courts, but the literacy of sides in family cases provides a clue to their significance in rural life. First, it was only in family cases that a difference in literacy between plaintiffs and defendants was common, and, second, in family cases, unlike other ones, it was extremely rare that both parties were literate. Family disputes at township courts usually involved parties with a significant disparity—literates charged illiterates and illiterates charged literates. Two literate family members would be very unlikely adversaries at township courts. This pattern of litigation suggests that families used township courts to confront their difficulties at a time of social differentiation. Members of families with disparities in literacy could well be divided in their aspirations and ideas of entitlement. Illiterate families probably suffered and fought over their disadvantages. Literate families might better be able to regulate their differences without the help of local judges; their quarrels over more substantial assets might qualify for consideration at other judicial instances. To all rural families, township courts offered a way to settle disputes over authority, property, and responsibility, outside the family and outside the village, but some kinds of families—those with internal disparities or shared disadvantages—made more recourse to this legal forum than did others.

Occasionally litigants explicitly challenged patriarchal presumption, as in Irina Vasilevna Rodina's successful case against her husband for beating (see chapter 5). Such assertions of rights against unjust treatment by spouses or fathers do not mean that parties at court or judges saw themselves as combatants in a collective struggle over family authority. In Irina Vasilevna's case and others, what counted for judges was the case at hand and the individuals involved. But cases resolved one by one can make a difference over time. The township courts were both an immediate resource for problems faced by rural families and an agent in the gradual transformations of relations between men and women, fathers and sons, and sisters and brothers in rural areas.

Occasionally family members acted for family interests at township courts. The court could be used to defend minor members of one's family against abuse by others. In 1913 a peasant living in Nagatino but registered elsewhere brought an accusation of beating his nine-year-old daughter to the Nagatinskii court. The defendant, a local resident, was convicted according to the testimony of two witnesses and sentenced to a fine of ten rubles or five days in jail.[47] Another father brought a case in 1916 to the Tsaritsynskii court, accusing two women of "insult in words" of his daughter by their daughters.[48] In these cases parents took legal responsibility for the welfare and behavior of minor members of their families. Only rarely were adults represented in court by other adult family members. Usually both women and men spoke up for themselves. In all the cases I surveyed I found only one instance where a woman was represented by her husband at a township court, and this was the formidable Aleksandra Kachalova of Bol'shoe Zaborov'e, who had sued eight peasant men for their debts to her. Apparently she did not have time in her busy schedule to come to court and instead took advantage of her right to be represented by her husband (see chapter 4). That women were almost never represented by their husbands in court suggests strongly that township judges did not assign authority in family matters exclusively to males, patriarchs or otherwise. Both court process and decisions display the gender neutrality of township judges.

INSIDERS AND OUTSIDERS

The presence of nonresident litigants in township cases is another indicator of the courts' effective accommodation of dynamic social circumstances. In my survey, almost exactly one-third of all cases involved one or more nonresidents of the township in which the court was located. "Outsiders" of this kind were both plaintiffs and defendants. Legal residence in court records referred to the place where a person was registered and did not reflect a person's actual domicile. In Nagatinskii Township nonresident litigants often lived locally, in their own homes, in rented quarters, or with relatives. Particularly in areas near Moscow nonresidents might have been living in the township for some time. For these reasons, many nonresidents might better be described as "newcomers" to an area, whereas others—such as merchants from a nearby town—were indeed physically residing elsewhere.

The likelihood of nonresidents appearing in a case as one or both of the parties varied greatly from court to court, reflecting the variety of social circumstances in north and central Russia. At the Iaguninskii and Ignatevskii township courts in Moscow Province but not near the metropole, outsiders were parties in only 8 and 3 percent of cases, respectively. At the remote Zaborovskii court in Novgorod Province people not resident in the township were parties in 10 percent of cases. In places of large-scale in-migration, such as the two courts in my survey close to Moscow, cases much more frequently involved one nonresident or two. At the Tsaritsynskii court, outsiders were parties in 28 percent of cases, and at Nagatino, with its active police force and citizenry, two-thirds of all cases involved outsiders.

One might surmise that outsiders would have been defendants rather than plaintiffs at township courts: newcomers might be more unruly than old-time residents, and the close connection of judges to their localities would seem to discourage nonresidents from bringing charges. However, in my survey, defendants were only slightly more likely to be outsiders than were plaintiffs. For all courts and in all cases, "outsiders" constituted 26 percent of all defendants and 22 percent of plaintiffs. Township courts both facilitated the prosecution of newcomers for misbehavior and accommodated nonresidents' own charges and suits. At the Iaguninskii township court where only 8 percent of cases involved outsiders, there were more nonresident plaintiffs than defendants. Merchants registered in other areas were able to use this court to collect their debts from local producers. In both Tsaritsynskii and Nagatinskii townships, the percentage of outsider defendants was higher than that of outsider plaintiffs, but nonresidents still brought significant numbers of cases. At Tsaritsyno, outsiders constituted 19 percent of plaintiffs and 24 percent of defendants; at Nagatino, outsiders were 44 percent of plaintiffs and 54 percent of defendants. The close relationship between proportions of outsider plaintiffs and defendants in each location indicates that township courts effectively served a locality, with all its inhabitants—permanent or migratory.

Analysis of legal residence of pairs of opposing parties at township courts provides another perspective on the inclusiveness of township-level justice. In the most typical case both parties would be local residents, according to their official registration. A plaintiff from inside a township would be far more likely to bring another local resident to court than an outsider: 90 percent of defendants accused by local plaintiffs were registered in the township of the court. But a plaintiff from outside a township was only somewhat more likely to bring charges against another outsider rather than an insider. Outsider-outsider cases were most usual at the Nagatinskii court, where so many of the "nonresidents" were, in fact, newcomers. My survey does not support in any definitive way the notion of a generalized antagonism between "insiders" and "outsiders" or between new and old residents. Residents were not more likely to sue nonresidents for any particular kind of action or violation. Rather than seeking boundaries where they may not have existed, we can attribute the significant numbers of nonresidents at township courts to the responsiveness of the township court system to the local population's needs. Through the demands of their litigants, township courts were drawn into regulating social relations for a mobile peasant population.

RESOLUTIONS THAT ARE NOT DEFEATS

Township court decisions did not always result in a clear victory of one party over another. A clear-cut decision for or against the plaintiff's suit or a condemnation or acquittal of a criminal defendant were not the only options available to judges. Decisions of a more ambiguous and perhaps less conflict-burdened kind were made in 37 percent of cases in my survey. After judgments in favor of plaintiffs or defendants, the second most common kind of decision was to "end the case"—25 percent of all decisions. Less frequently judges made decisions related to procedural issues, such as postponing a hearing or referring a matter elsewhere. There were no clear winners and losers in some family cases; confirmations of inheritance or family divisions and settlements of guardianship issues accounted for 12 percent of decisions. In addition, contending parties could reconcile at township courts; their cases would end with an official recognition of a consensual agreement.

The most common reason for "ending a case" at township courts was the absence of one or both parties. In my survey, absence of parties was recorded by the clerk in 21 percent of township hearings. A civil case was more likely to be ended because of absence than a criminal one: at all courts and in all years absence was cited as an explanation for a decision in 23 percent of civil cases and in 18 percent of criminal cases. Only plaintiffs had the power to end a case through absence. Defendants were required to come to court, and if they did not appear at a hearing, they would be sentenced in absentia.[49] Clerks came up with various shortcuts to register plaintiffs' absences and their consequences at court. At Nagatino, to speed up record-keeping, the clerk used a special stamp with the formula "the plaintiff having publicly received the summonses did not appear at the court hearing and did not declare a reason to the court for this nonappearance" and another stamp that read "[decided] to end consideration of this case."[50]

There was great variability in the percentages of cases ended by absence at individual township courts. Although the clerk at Nagatino was prepared for absences, in all but 4 percent of cases parties appeared for their hearings at this busy court. In Grebnevskii, Iaguninskii, and Ignatevskii townships, plaintiffs were absent, and cases ended for this reason, in much higher percentages than at the Tsaritsynskii and Nagatinskii courts. Absences of parties as an explanation of ended cases ranged from a low of 4 percent at Nagatino to a high of 42 percent at the Zaborovskii court in Novogorod Province.[51] The significant number of cases ended because of absence of one or both parties invites us to consider why people might decide not to appear at a court hearing. Were these absences a sign that the township court was an undesirable place to settle a dispute?

Ending a case because the person who filed a complaint did not appear in court was an official and useful part of township legal practice. The rules for ending cases corresponded to the voluntary nature of most township litigation. Rural people themselves, and not authorities, initiated all civil and the majority of criminal cases, and these plaintiffs retained the possibility of settling their cases before they reached the court. After registering a case, a plaintiff could renegotiate a debt, drop an accusation against a neighbor, or reconsider a family matter. The initiation of a case might itself encourage adversaries to come to an agreement before the court hearing. Litigants were more likely to reach such out-of-court settlements in civil cases—mostly about money—than in criminal cases—mostly about reputation. The neighborhood one lived in could also make a difference. At Nagatinskii and Tsaritsynskii courts near Moscow, defendants were most likely to be nonresidents, at least officially, and parties were less likely to have lived near each other for a long time. People in areas of long-term residence, like Zaborovskii Township, were much more likely to be absent from their scheduled hearings. At the least, these plaintiffs spared themselves the more or less long journey to court; perhaps their pretrial settlements made some contribution to social harmony at home. Differences in rates of cases ended because of absence show once again the adaptability of township courts to different and changing social contexts (see Table 6.2).

If many cases ended because plaintiffs decided not to pursue their claims, a few disputes resulted in reconciliations at the court. At every case hearing, opposing parties were invited to reconcile, and their responses were entered by the clerk in each court record.[52] Consensual agreements made at a case hearing were rare. They accounted for only 2 percent of all case decisions in my survey, and were mentioned as reasons for "ending"—as opposed to deciding—cases in only 4 percent of such outcomes. Considered in conjunction with the frequent use of nonappearance to end cases, the small number of formal reconciliations at court suggests that people tried with some success to settle cases

Table 6.2. Residency and Absence as an Explanation of Closed Cases

Court	*Percent of Nonresident Defendants*	*Percent of Cases Ended by Absence*
Grebnevskii	0%	27.0%
Iaguninskii	1.4%	30.5%
Ignatevskii	2.7%	67.3%
Zaborovskii	4.9%	41.7%
Tsaritsynskii	24.0%	10.0%
Nagatinskii	53.9%	4.4%

out of court and proceeded with their hearings only for more intractable disputes. This process of selection corresponds to ways that people in other law-based societies exercise their legal opportunities.[53] Would-be litigants in rural areas used township courts with discrimination to resolve issues that could not be settled among neighbors and relatives.

The record of "ended cases" at the Tsaritsynskii Township Court for 1914 offers a local perspective on the many ways that hearings could be concluded without victors and losers, at least in the short run. Over the whole year, the clerk recorded 162 ended cases. In 86 of these cases, the plaintiff did not appear; in 55 cases, both sides did not appear. These cases were closed by the presumably intentional nonappearance of the person who initiated the case. The large number of absences was probably influenced by the outbreak of war in August. The clerk recorded the following reasons for ending the remaining cases: reconcilations (4 cases); missing documents (4 cases); a problem with a summons (3 cases); illness of the accused and a missing petition (1 case); the location of other relatives (1 case); incompetence of the accused (1 case); plaintiff calls off the case [explicitly, not just by not appearing] (1 case); "not adjudicable," in the case of a man suing his father for the right to live in the family's house (1 case); not adjudicable because of status rules (1 case); and, finally, the plaintiff had been drafted (1 case).[54] Litigants' initiatives, procedural concerns, practical obstacles, attentiveness to the personal circumstances of parties—all these were critical to deciding that a case could be heard—and potentially have a winner and a loser—at the township court.

THE REASONS OF JUDGES

How did judges make the decisions that were so important to persistent litigants and to legal culture in the countryside? Apart from the clerk's expertise and possibly copies of codes and handbooks, there were no sources of formal legal knowledge available to township judges. According to court regulations, judges were to decide cases "according to conscience, on the basis of the evidence in the case."[55] Close readings and statistical analysis of case records, although unable to reveal conscience, show that outcomes of cases depended very strongly on "evidence in the case." Three factors were critical to judges' decisions—the defendant's testimony, the testimony of witnesses, and documents.

A gross measure of judicial discrimination is the generalized outcome of cases. Courts that routinely satisfied all plaintiffs or turned all cases down might be looked on with suspicion: hearings would have no connection to results. Township courts in early-twentieth-century Russia were not rubber stamps: in my survey as a whole, plaintiffs at township courts were successful in 56 percent of cases. This success rate requires elaboration and disaggregation. In a civil case I defined success for a plaintiff as a decision that satisfied a claim, wholly or in part, by means of a judgment against a defendant or a "peaceful agreement" at court. In criminal cases plaintiffs—be they police or civilians or both—"succeeded" if the verdict included a conviction of the defendant on all or part of any charge or if parties came to reconciliation at the hearing. Plaintiffs' successes can be read as a kind of conviction rate, reflecting the percentage of cases in which the plaintiff attained some kind of satisfaction—the payment of a debt wholly or in part, a peaceful resolution of a conflict, a fine or an arrest of an accused person. In the 44 percent of cases in my survey where the plaintiff did not succeed, outcomes would include outright losses for the plaintiff—when a defendant was acquitted or a suit not upheld—or rejections of the case, decisions to postpone a hearing, or endings of the case because parties did not appear. The ratio of successful to failed outcomes suggests that plaintiffs found it worth their while to bring cases at township courts, but also shows that simply registering a case did not determine its outcome. One had to appear before the judges and make a case.

If we examine civil and criminal cases separately, we find some differences in the likelihood that a plaintiff would succeed. Judges did not uniformly decide in favor of plaintiffs or defendants in either kind of case: in civil cases plaintiffs succeeded 54 percent of the time; in criminal cases plaintiffs succeeded 60 percent of the time. As with other aspects of township litigation, there was considerable variation in the plaintiff's rate of success in different kinds of cases at different township courts. At the Iaguninskii court, for example, plaintiffs were much more likely to succeed in civil cases than in criminal ones. Decisions at this court satisfied plaintiffs in 72 percent of civil cases, but in only 39 percent of criminal cases. At the Ignatevskii court as well, plaintiffs won more frequently in civil cases than in criminal ones, but at this court the rate at which plaintiffs succeeded was much lower than elsewhere. Judges at Ignat'evo were more likely than those at other courts to rule in favor of defendants: plaintiffs won 43 percent of civil cases but only 12 percent of criminal ones. At Nagatino the judges were much more likely to rule in favor of plaintiffs overall, and plaintiffs were just about as likely to win a civil (74 percent succeeded) as a criminal case (72 percent succeeded). At the Tsaritsynskii court, like Nagatino not far from Moscow, judges were more likely to satisfy plaintiffs in civil cases than in criminal ones, but the conviction rate was significantly lower than at Nagatino. At the Tsaritsynskii Township Court plaintiffs succeeded in criminal cases 53 percent of the time, below the general average.

This variation from court to court displays the township court as an institution of judicial reasoning. Different judges ruled differently from locality to locality, in response to a multitude of all-too-human dilemmas, and in accord with principles of conscience they may not have articulated. Yet rule they did, often with very concrete explanations of their decisions. It would be presumptuous to claim to know the reasons for any particular verdict or the values that shaped decisions generally or the particular circumstances that surrounded each courtroom and may have affected judges' rulings. Corruption, pressure, and bribery—endemic in any "rule-of-law" state—were no doubt present in some measure at township courts. But even if, as elsewhere, litigants tried to influence judges' opinions with means at their disposal, judges ultimately had to pronounce decisions in the courtroom and register them officially with the imperial administration. To understand their verdicts at a rudimentary level we can both look at what they said their decisions depended on—this was given in the account of each case—and also search for patterns in decision making overall. In earlier chapters, we examined the procedures followed in civil and criminal cases, and the kinds of cases presented to township judges. In what follows I discuss elements of case hearings that appeared to have an influence, statistically, on decisions judges made.

The factor that worked most strongly to predict a decision for or against the plaintiff at township courts was the defendant's testimony. It may seem obvious or trivial that the testimony of the defendant would be critical to the outcome of the case: defendants who pleaded not guilty would be more likely to be let off, and those who pleaded guilty would ordinarily be convicted. In repressive legal systems, however, defendants' testimony might make no difference to an outcome. Or if compulsion was used to force confessions, most defendants could be expected to plead guilty. Neither of these happened at the township courts. There is no trace of any effort made to force defendants to confess at the township courts, and there is strong evidence that judges took defendants' formal recognition of their obligations and their misbehaviors seriously.

Defendants exercised choice in their testimony at township courts, choice that had a strong impact on the outcome of the case. In my survey defendants pleaded not guilty, justified their actions, or rejected the plaintiff's charge in 60 percent of cases, whereas they pleaded guilty, or agreed with all or part of the plaintiff's charge, in 39 percent of cases.[56] In criminal cases, as we have seen, accused people often pleaded guilty to charges of drunkenness or agreed that their courtyards had been dirty. In some insult cases the person brought to "legal responsibility" might testify that she or he had, in fact, addressed the plaintiff with improper words. These cases would result in convictions by township judges. In civil cases, too, defendants who recognized their debts to plaintiffs would be required to pay up. Judges also were attentive to defendants' not-guilty pleas, which clearly worked against plaintiffs' chances of success.

The second most influential factor in case outcomes was the testimony of witnesses. If witnesses were, collectively, for or against the plaintiff, this tended to decide the case. As we have seen in many cases, judges frequently cited witnesses' testimony in their verdicts. "Proven by the testimony of the witness" and "proven by the confession of the accused" figured often in recorded decisions. According to court regulations, most residents were obliged to appear at township trials if called to testify. This was another way in which the township court engaged local society in the law: resolutions of cases depended to a very high degree not only on the words of the concerned "sides" in a dispute but also on those of people who would know the "circumstances of the case" and who could testify at court about observed events.[57]

Documentary evidence was a third factor in outcomes of cases at township courts. Documents of some kind appeared in at least 62 percent of all cases, a figure that is more likely to underrepresent than to overrepresent their presence.[58] Documents could support or undermine plaintiffs' cases, and hence their direct impact on decisions is obvious only when they were cited in verdicts. But documents had a calculable impact on the outcome of the case when combined with other factors. The effect of the defendant's testimony on the success of the plaintiff's case was stronger if a document was involved. The oral testimony of witnesses (for or against the plaintiff's case) was also reinforced by the presence of a document. Plaintiffs who could both summon witnesses to support their cases and bring documents to court were more likely than others to win their cases. This finding accords with the attention to documentary evidence that we have seen in individual civil cases. It suggests judges' high regard for official paper and demonstrates that "evidence in the case"—in the form of defendants' admissions, witnesses' testimony, and documents—was the foundation of decision making at township courts.

Individual case records offer a finer focus on how township judges came to decisions. An example of the critical role of a defendant's testimony is provided by a case heard at Nagatino on 18 March 1913. Aleksei Ivanov Belov from the village of Borisovo in the neighboring township of Tsaritsyno was charged with theft of "boots, costing two rubles, belonging to Ivan Artamonov, from Smirnov's barn." At court the illiterate defendant denied the charges: "he did not steal the boots from Smirnov's barn and does not recognize his guilt." No one came to court to support the charges filed by the police. The judges found that the "accusation was not proven against Belov and was based only on the oral declaration of the accuser Smirnov." They acquitted the defendant.[59] The critical factor was not the defendant's word as such but whether there was sufficient proof of the accusation. Without evidence to support the charge, even if it had been filed by the police, the defendant's testimony was decisive for the case.

The nature of the accusation or the suit was sometimes in question at township courts. In addition to the interval after registering a case, the court hearing itself offered an opportunity for plaintiffs to change their minds about their charges and their goals. A father seeking support from his son and willing to take him to court to force the issue might reconsider as he contemplated the prospects for the familial economy. In one such case at the Iaguninskii Township Court in 1908 Vasilii Afanas'ev Mozhukin registered a suit against his son for food support. During the hearing, however, the elder Mozhukin explained that he "wanted to carry out a voluntary division of property with his son." Perhaps the younger Mozhukin had made it clear that he would not support his father unless the family and its property were formally divided. When Vasilii Mozhukin sought a legal division of the family property from the judges, his earlier case for food support, filed as a criminal accusation, was ended at his request.[60]

Township judges were generally attentive to the particular charges filed in cases and could adjust criminal complaints to accord with those listed in the *Statutes on Punishments*. On 7 March 1906 the Iaguninskii court reformulated a charge filed by the vigilant local constable Malorossianov. The accusation against Kalinin, a resident in Savvinskaia sloboda, that hotbed of disturbances, was "unruly conduct with the use of marketplace and insulting words" directed at a certain Berezin, who participated in the case as the "accuser-victim." Although constable Malorossianov had filed charges under Statute 43 "for shameless [acts] or acts connected with seduction of others in a public place," the judges convicted Kalinin under more appropriate statutes—Statute 38 on unruly conduct and Statute 42 on public drunkenness. The misdemeanor described by Statute 42—"appearing in a public place drunk to unconsciousness or in a disgracefully drunk condition"—gives the impression that "seduction" may have been beyond Kalinin's capacity at the time.[61]

When sentencing Kalinin—who appears to have been a real troublemaker—the judges also applied Statute 16, to be used in convictions for two or more criminal acts. This statute instructed courts to choose the sentence that was "harsher," because the "aggregate of actions is . . . considered a circumstance that increases guilt."[62] In addition to his four-ruble fine for Statute 38 violations and two days of arrest for the drunkenness charges, Kalinin was ordered to spend three more days in jail "for the aggregate of his actions."[63] Berezin, the offended man, declared his satisfaction with this outcome. Kalinin, apparently unrepentant, signed "unsatisfied," although he appears not to have appealed. The same judges who were able to take into account and reduce sentences for "heartfelt repentance" in other cases were apparently unimpressed by Kalinin's capacity for responsible behavior.[64] This decision illustrates the township judges' knowledge of the misdemeanor statutes and probably their acquaintance with local circumstances as well.

Attention to the kind of cases that plaintiffs wanted to bring as well as a concern to fit the charges to the behaviors of defendants were hallmarks of jurisprudence at the township courts. Judges and clerks were considerate of plaintiffs' changes of heart at hearings but were also discriminating in their use of statute law. The distinction between civil and criminal cases was routinely observed, as in the following hearing at Iagunino. On 7 August 1905 the Iaguninskii Township Court heard a case charged under the very infrequently used Statute 174—on swindling and falsification of various kinds. The police registered the accusation but did not appear at court. Nikita Grigorev Kandakov, a peasant from the village of Sergeevo, accused the defendant of extortion, but the judges rejected the criminal charge. The accused, in their view, was not engaging in extortion, and the plaintiff was advised to bring a civil case for a debt of ten rubles, which turned out to be the issue in this case.[65]

Some might consider this decision evidence of the judges' understanding of abstract legal categories, but the more important point is that township judges were adept at fitting the circumstances of particular cases to the legal procedures available to litigants. Both violations of civil contracts and petty crime are harmful to the social good, and the distinction between civil and criminal cases is not "natural" or identical in legal systems. When judges advised litigants to bring different kinds of cases, they put their knowledge to practical use and enhanced the significance of law in rural life.

The empowerment of peasant judges was perhaps the most essential and certainly the most controversial aspect of the township court system. Critics faulted judges' lack of legal training and bemoaned the absence of a jury at township courts. From the perspective of local litigants, however, the township court offered a kind of jury trial, where cases were decided collectively by people who had been elected by village societies. Analysis of court cases processed by these small juries of peasants' peers reveals values rural people might expect to find enforced at township courts.

First, peasant judges' justice meant adherence to the rules established for township courts. Inappropriate charges were thrown out; cases were not decided if plaintiffs dropped them; reconciliations were recorded; and charges were adjusted to fit behavior. Second, township courts were made available to all adults in a region who applied to bring a case. It is impossible to prove that no would-be plaintiff was ever turned away, but clerks' registers indicate that hearings were scheduled for all recorded complaints and requests. Third, and perhaps most impressive, judges did not favor certain kinds of plaintiffs in their decisions. Analysis of case outcomes shows that categorical differences between litigants did not determine judges' decisions. Women and men won or lost their cases in equal measure, as did insiders and outsiders to the township, literate and illiterate parties. Fourth, evidence and testimony were the most critical factors in the outcome of a case. Decisions at township courts were not predetermined by personal qualities, but by defendants' and witnesses' testimony, as well as documentary evidence.

Property cases display the actions of these small juries of peasant judges in matters critical to families, rural societies, and the imperial polity. In cases about allocation of property—usually involving inheritance or family divisions—township justice was founded on legally defined obligations, adequate documentation, and earned rights. The legal decisions of the past were to be supported. The township court was no place for judicial revisionism: prior agreements made at village meetings or at township courts were respected.[66] Documentation was critically important: a missing inventory could be grounds to dismiss or postpone a case. By giving procedurally correct decisions a decisive role in case outcomes, township courts enhanced a culture of legal precedent.

Another factor in inheritance and other property cases was the judges' respect for what we might call "just deserts." Rights to inherit had to be earned through work or participation in local family life, as in the following inheritance case from the Grebnevskii Township Court in Bogorodskii County of Moscow Province. On 26 June 1917 the judges of the township court, Lobanov, Teretin, and Il'in, with Rulev presiding, heard a request from Ivan Semenov Kirillov to be confirmed in the rights of inheritance to the property of his deceased brother. Ivan signed the following entry in the case record:

> Ivan Kirillov testified that he had left his family's home twenty-four years ago while his father was still alive and in the home remained his brother Vladimir, who lived in it until his death. Ivan Kirillov requests to confirm him in the rights of inheritance to the indicated house, barn, and land around the home, because he was a participant in the acquisition of this property.[67]

Ivan was opposed in this request by his sister-in-law, Anastasia Kirillova. Anastasia neatly signed the following testimony as "Anastasia Kirillova," although the clerk recorded her first name as "Nastasia":

> The wife of the deceased Vladimir Semenov Kirillov, Nastasia Ivanovna Kirillova, declared that after the death of the father of the Kirillov brothers, the structures were completely rebuilt by the Kirillovs' sister Evdokiia Semenova before her marriage and by Nastasia's mother and her husband, Vladimir, for which reason she, Nastasia, considers herself the full inheritor of the property left after the death of her husband.[68]

Anastasia/Nastasia refused the judge's proposal to end the case with reconciliation. Important to the resolution of this case was the testimony of an illiterate witness. Mikhail Ivanov Tret'iakov came to the trial and testified "that Ivan Semenov Kirillov did not participate in the funeral of his father and that after the death of the father the structures were rebuilt, in which process Ivan Kirillov took no part." The judges ruled: "The court decides to reject the suit, because Ivan Kirillov did not participate in the funeral of his father and in the rebuilding of the house that he [the father] left, and [he] left the home of his father already twenty-four years ago."[69]

The decision in this case disinherited a son in favor of a daughter-in-law—if inheritance rights are considered as having originated with the Kirillovs' father's death—or, if the home and surrounding property and structures belonged to Vladimir Kirillov, the judgment favored a wife over a brother. The judges did not bother to cite "local custom" in their decision; for them, the critical factor was that Kirillov had left home and not contributed to the homestead's construction after his father's death. Anastasia, a woman who had married into the family, remained the possessor of her husband's and her father-in-law's former property.

Local justice at township courts valued performance of family responsibilities—improving or at least sustaining a household's economy—and living in the family. Other aspects of this "just deserts"-style family justice could be negative: if one had already received significant resources from a family, one was unlikely to get more, even if in a direct line of descent. Confronting an acquisitive and rich woman in the Ul'ianov family of Bol'shoe Zaborov'e, the judges refused to give her an extra share of her father's property, saying that she had already received enough as a dowry.[70] Fairness—not a fixed idea about who should control family property—stood behind judges' decisions. In inheritance cases, as at township courts generally, gender made no apparent difference to the judges. In my readings of cases the sex of a litigant was never cited as a reason for a property settlement.

Judges' concern for "just deserts" was not oriented toward absolute equality, toward subverting the rich, or toward bringing everyone down or up to the same level. The courts took no punitive action against debt collectors and made no redistributions of property to equalize access to resources. If plaintiffs provided sufficient evidence—documents and witness testimony—then judges ordered defendants to pay their debts. Without such evidence, judges refused "unjust" claims to acquire more goods, and they turned back unsupported charges from debt collectors. Adjustments in property relations made at township courts were unique to the cases at hand and based on proof, not on some overarching principle of who should possess what and how much of it.

Limits on judges' power to redress injustice in access to productive resources were, in part, a consequence of the purview of the courts. Questions of large-scale land repartition or the status of landholdings were decided in other venues—village meetings, regional land committees, or the upper reaches of the imperial administration.[71] The township court was a place where, in the vast majority of cases, individual people brought individualized conflicts. But if local courts were not a place for making policy or addressing collective demands, they were the locus for decisions that slowly reshaped family and society in rural areas. In this sense, township judges were unwitting but thoughtful agents of peaceful, participatory change, from generation to generation, in villages across the empire.

THE REASONS OF PLAINTIFFS

The township courts would have had no significance for Russian life and legal culture if they had not been used by rural people. What made these courts attractive to people who wanted to collect a debt, settle an inheritance, or set right a violation of personal honor? The point here is not that rural people preferred the township courts to informal, personal, family, or village-level settlements: we must assume that most court cases, as elsewhere, resulted when people could not settle disputes themselves, within families, among neighbors, or at village assemblies, or when informal, village-level sanctions—as in the case of insults—were not satisfying to accusers. When other means failed, why did rural people bother to persist, to leave their villages, usually on a Sunday or another holiday,[72] and journey to a township court?

These decisions to go to court imply that Russian peasants regarded themselves as part of a larger polity. Avid litigation at township courts is inconsistent with images of a distinct peasant world, isolated from the state. Rural plaintiffs chose to seek legal decisions in the larger realm of officialdom and legal majesty. At the township courts, justice was sought not from village strongmen or through theatrical display but at the intersection of elected officials, state rules, and recorded process. If co-villagers wanted to maximize their neighbors' knowledge of their differences, they could have remained at home and simply carried on their quarrels in public; in extreme cases of harmful behavior, the village assembly was entitled by law to decide whether expulsion from the village was warranted.[73] Profuse use of township courts suggests that village-level alternatives were not satisfactory in many situations. For many rural people, the township court—a legal instance invested with the authority of the state—was a useful place to turn.

Court procedures offered permanence and security unattainable in informal settings. Formalities—signed testimony, the registration of the grounds for the judges' decision, the announcement of appeals procedures—were assiduously observed at township courts. Court protocols integrated litigants into legal process and, through repetition, invoked regularity and order. The enthusiasm with which rural people sought legal solutions to their conflicts suggests their respect for decisions recorded in thick books, signed by judges and litigants, and stamped with official seals.

Other venues in Russia offered the appealing qualities of official majesty and ceremony to peasant litigants, and peasants, in some cases, could have brought their legal matters to circuit or other courts. Some of the abundant usage of township courts may be attributed to peasants' choices among legal institutions. Rural plaintiffs may have preferred justice delivered by small juries of their peers—the peasant judges—to law enacted by cross-class juries and educated judges. The expense and complication of engaging lawyers to plead their cases, as well as distance, presented other obstacles to the usage of circuit courts. Another pragmatic consideration may have counted for would-be plaintiffs: the township courts were fast.

The township courts of Moscow Province worked much more efficiently than the Moscow circuit courts. Circuit courts decided between 42 and 53 percent of criminal cases registered each year between 1905 and 1908, whereas township courts decided, on the average, 80 to 84 percent of their criminal cases. The Moscow circuit courts performed better in civil than in criminal cases, but here, too, they were less efficient at resolving cases (88 to 90 percent) than the township courts of the province (94 to 96 percent).[74] Although circuit courts of Moscow Province heard many fewer cases than township courts,[75] each year they left a far greater proportion of their cases undecided than did the humble, busy, and efficient township courts.

Township courts were the place to go for rapid justice, although they were not uniformly speedy. Percentages of cases resolved within a single calendar year by courts in selected counties of Moscow Province display the challenges faced by authorities in different areas of the province. Because people could register cases in December, in the ordinary run of things most courts would have a few unresolved cases on their records for any calendar year. Some townships in Moscow Province were more successful than others at keeping up with their dockets. Zvenigorod County—the location of Iaguninskii and Sharapovskii courts—had a stellar record of case resolution. From 1905 through 1914 township courts in this area resolved, on average, 96 percent of cases by the end of the calendar year. Bogorodskii County, home to Ignatevskii and Grebnevskii courts, was not far behind, with an average of 92 percent of cases completed within a given year. The region that dragged down the efficiency of the province's courts was the county close to Moscow. At the courts within Moscow County, which included those at Nagatino and Tsaritsyno, an average of only 78 percent of cases was resolved each year. "Only" is a relative notion. Overall the annual resolution rate for all provincial township courts from 1905 through 1914 was 89 percent, a more than respectable showing for this lowest, and disparaged, judicial instance.

For processing civil cases, even township courts near the Moscow city borders were very efficient. Between 1905 and 1914, when the number of civil cases increased dramatically, township courts in Moscow County resolved 94 to 96 percent of civil cases annually, a rate similar to that of township courts in other counties. The problem slowing down township courts in Moscow County concerned criminal cases: only in Moscow County did significant numbers of criminal cases remain unresolved in most years. From 1905 through 1912 Moscow County's township courts resolved, on average, only 62 percent of criminal cases within the year they were registered. This lower resolution rate for criminal cases heard at township courts near the empire's second largest city stands out against the very efficient pace at which other township courts in the province dealt with their criminal caseloads.[76]

Township courts close to Moscow, as we have seen, were exceptional in a number of respects. First, this county was the only one in the province at which criminal cases outnumbered civil ones. Second, from 1905 to 1913, the numbers of registered criminal cases increased two and a half times in Moscow County, an explosion in misdemeanor cases that happened nowhere else in the province. Third, and perhaps relatedly, the police were much more present in this region than elsewhere. Police alone—without another registered plaintiff—brought a much higher percentage of criminal cases in the township courts at Tsaritsyno and Nagatino than at the other courts in my survey. At Nagatinskii Township police were the sole plaintiffs in 37 percent of the criminal cases I examined; at Tsaritsyno police acting on their own brought 32 percent of criminal cases. My survey considered cases heard by courts and thus, in most cases, resolved within a particular year. Other police-initiated cases may not have been heard promptly at Nagatino, Tsarytsino, or elsewhere in Moscow County, particularly because police were not zealous about showing up in court. Without an insistent victim, there may have been little impetus to bring witnesses or accused parties to "legal responsibility." Another possible explanation for the less than rapid resolution of criminal cases at township courts in Moscow County is the greater presence of people not legally registered in the townships. Although outsiders of this kind were often plaintiffs at township courts, it could be that migrants called to court as defendants had more resources than others to escape delivery of summonses and more opportunity to evade the law.

Despite these pressures, even courts in Moscow County made progress in catching up on residual cases before the outbreak of the war. The annual resolution rate in 1913 for criminal cases in this county was 83 percent, up from a low of 53 percent in 1910. For the province's township courts overall, and for the entire period from 1905 to 1914, 82 percent of criminal cases were resolved within the year they were registered. Interpretations of this impressively rapid performance for justice in the countryside should accommodate three facts: first, in every county most criminal cases were initiated by citizens, not by police; second, the majority of these criminal cases were about insults; and, third, sentences were fulfilled even more rapidly in criminal cases than payments ordered in civil ones. If a person wanted a quick and official defense of violated dignity, the township courts were a promising place to turn.

The steady increase in the numbers of civil and criminal cases in the years before the war might have been expected to overload the township court system. Provincial statistics on numbers and resolutions of cases that were new in a particular year compared to cases left over from earlier years show that only at township courts in Moscow County did vestigial cases count for a significant proportion of the caseload. In 1906 vestigial cases accounted for almost 20 percent of the cases waiting to be processed at township courts in Moscow County. For the other counties, vestigial cases were a much less significant proportion of yearly dockets: 9 percent in Bogorodskii County, 6 percent in Klinskii County, and 2 percent in Zvenigorodskii County. The percentage of registered cases decided within one calendar year at township courts in most counties of Moscow Province increased between 1905 and 1907, fell back more or less until 1912, and then began to rise again through 1914. The proportion of cases—both civil and criminal—decided within a year for all township courts in the province with the exception of those in Moscow County, ranged from 90 to 98 percent throughout the entire period—a very rapid rate of case processing. Even in Moscow County, where the total number of registered cases grew from 12,525 in 1905 to 27,814 in 1913, the percentage of cases resolved rose to 88 percent of the total by 1913. These figures demonstrate that, except in Moscow County, where a modest accumulation of cases from earlier years occurred from 1910 to 1913, township courts in Moscow Province kept up with the demand for litigation throughout a period of growth, movement, and change (see Chart 6.1).[77]

Another plausible reason for why rural plaintiffs turned in such high numbers to the township courts, and did so increasingly over time, was the town-

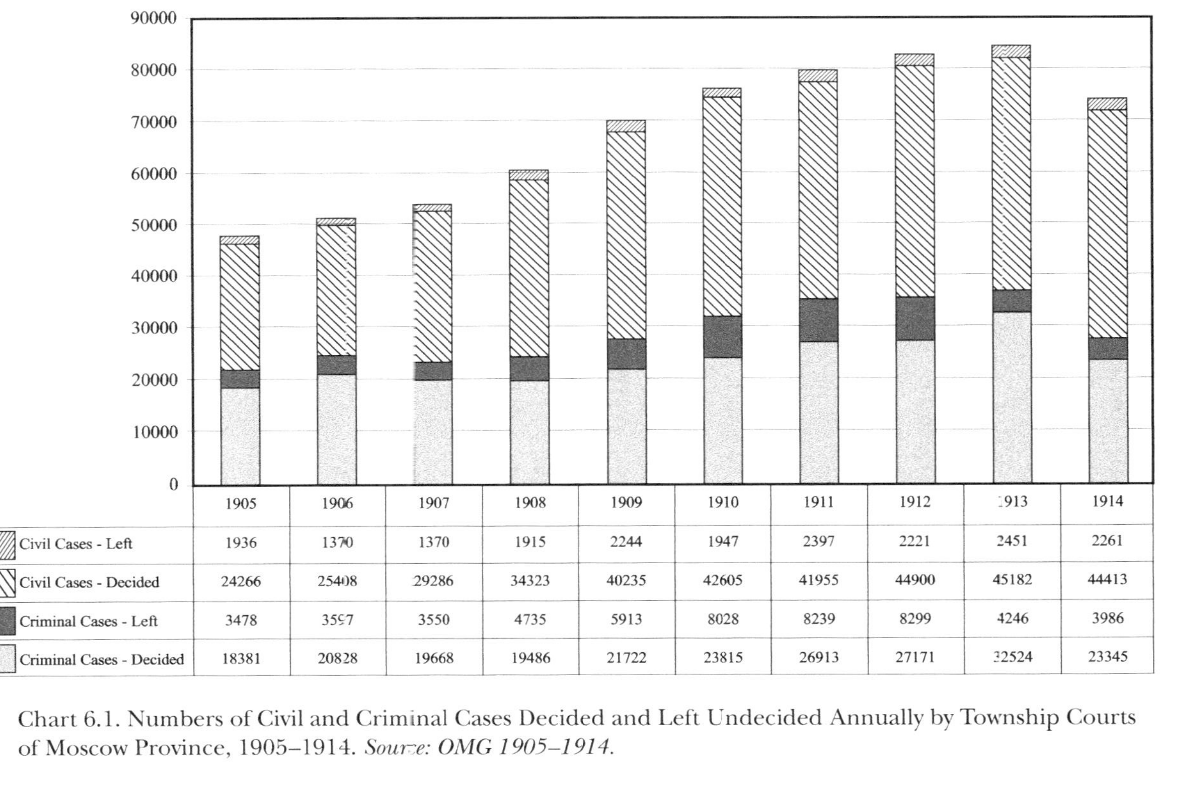

	1905	1906	1907	1908	1909	1910	1911	1912	1913	1914
Civil Cases - Left	1936	1370	1370	1915	2244	1947	2397	2221	2451	2261
Civil Cases - Decided	24266	25408	29286	34323	40235	42605	41955	44900	45182	44413
Criminal Cases - Left	3478	3597	3550	4735	5913	8028	8239	8299	4246	3986
Criminal Cases - Decided	18381	20828	19668	19486	21722	23815	26913	27171	32524	23345

Chart 6.1. Numbers of Civil and Criminal Cases Decided and Left Undecided Annually by Township Courts of Moscow Province, 1905–1914. *Source: OMG 1905–1914.*

ship administration's ability to ensure fulfillment of judgments (see chapter 3). When decisions were not appealed, the sentences and orders of township courts appear to have been carried out. Offenders showed up at township administrations to be arrested or to pay their fines.[78] Not fulfilling a court decision could result in a new trial and another sentence. In a rare case about nonpayment of a fine, Aleksei Kvardakov, the leader of Iaguninskii Township, brought a charge on 14 June 1916 against Semyon Shkunov, a peasant from the village of Shikhovo. The township leader testified that "he had called Shkunov to the [township] headquarters on the 30th of May to pay the sum of money imposed by a decision of the court, but having received the notice he did not obey the order of the leader [and] did not appear." The accused man came to the hearing and "explained that he did not appear [at the township administration] in accord with the command of the leader, because he was driving a horse to the city of Zvenigorod, and the horse fell sick." This excuse did not hold with the township judges, who declared Kvardakov's suit "proven" and ordered Shkunov to jail for two days. This time Shkunov obeyed: he fulfilled his sentence on 28 August 1916 and also paid the large amount—ninety-five rubles—that the court had leveled against him earlier.[79]

THE POLITICAL ECONOMY OF THE TOWNSHIP COURT

By exacting payments from recalcitrants like Shkunov, township judges served rural society, not themselves. There was only a very indirect connection between case outcomes and compensation of court personnel: fines assessed by judges in criminal cases augmented the township's funds for "local obligations."[80] These funds, controlled by township officials and assemblies, were used for local welfare, insurance programs, and administrative costs, including the salaries of clerks and judges.[81]

The primary source of revenue to pay "local obligations" was taxation. Township courts, like grain reserves, roads, water supplies, and fire-fighting equipment, depended on resources collected from the rural population. Each year village and township assemblies allocated local obligations among their constituent households, adjusting amounts to land allotments, capacity to pay, and village and township needs. Funds for local purposes were not an insignificant proportion of taxes paid by peasant households. In Iaguninskii Township local charges collected in 1904 were, on average, 23 percent of the amount collected for the state and the *zemstvo*.[82] Allocations for village expenses remained in the village society; funds for township expenses were delivered to the township leader by the village leader or by a tax collector.

Most rural people paid their taxes, including local ones, regularly. Payments made by household heads were entered with dates and amounts into township records. Communities or individuals in arrears were exceptional occurrences in the areas I studied.[83] Compensation of judges and clerks from township funds earmarked for collective obligations rounded out the circle of mutual responsibility that connected rural people with local public institutions. While elites debated the meaning of individual taxation in the polity, peasants routinely paid both assessments for local services and taxes to provincial and imperial administrations. In this material respect, rural people were already the responsible citizens that Russian elites dreamed of creating.[84]

Both compensation and discipline of judicial personnel were part of an interactive mechanism of local initiative and official oversight. The payment of court personnel from local funds was not voluntary: the law required township officials to use local resources to pay these salaries. Annual compensation for judges was set by the county congress of land captains; salaries were not to exceed one hundred rubles annually for the president of the court or sixty rubles for the other judges. The government provided judges with official recognition of their service—oaths taken before the land captain, badges, and medals—and exempted them, like other elected officials, from duties in kind for the duration of their terms.[85]

The General Regulation on Peasants provided procedures for complaints against judges and clerks. For any major crime, these officials were to be tried at an appropriate court. For petty violations, clerks could be fined by the township leader; a fine of any significance had to be authorized by the land captain. Peasants were authorized to take complaints about judges and village and township leaders to the land captain.[86] The citizenship regime of rural justice combined representation with control: peasants possessed rights to choose their township judges and officials, directly or indirectly, and to seek assistance from higher authorities in cases of malfeasance.

These procedures of local governance—with their interlacing of local responsibility and official oversight, and their concern for appropriate allocations of public funds—appeared nowhere in contemporary studies of township courts. Commentators instead purveyed images of rough justice, bought with buckets of vodka shared or unshared by corrupt judges and their clients.[87] Such portraits of disorderly, unregulated peasant courts are impossible to square with economic, judicial, and managerial practice in the townships. Casebooks from township courts, surely not a fiction of administrative imagination, show public justice in early twentieth-century rural Russia functioning with precision, speed, and regularity. Judges heard multiple cases at their busy Sunday sessions. The day at court was not long enough to permit drinking bashes after every case. There are no indications in record books that cases were decided by partying. It is time to give judges and clerks of Russia's township courts credit for their orderly routines, their fulfillment of elected and appointed offices, their provision of efficient legal services, and their role in governance—the governance of the countryside, paid for by country people on whom the imperial economy and polity depended.

Legal Recourse in a Time of Troubles

Were any times ordinary in late imperial Russia? For most of the twentieth century commentators considered 1905 to 1917 an era of acute crisis. The view that the imperial regime was heading inevitably and with good reasons for a fall was widely shared by scholars; historians differed more over the beginning of the end—proposed dates start with 1730—and the cause of death than about the prognosis of decline.[1] Since 1991 this consensus on impending doom brought on by contradictions, unresolvable tensions, and the like, has been eroded as intellectuals reassess imperial Russia in the shadow of the Soviet Union's own collapse. When reopening questions about long-term, short-term, structural, cultural, and other causes of the state's undeniable failure in 1917, it may be useful to make the same shift in perspective that has structured the argument of this book. What do records of township courts tell us about expectations and understandings of rural people who lived through these times?

For rural litigants at township courts, the period from 1905 to August 1914 was filled with opportunities as well as challenges. The Stolypin land reforms and the law of 5 October 1906 on peasants' rights opened paths to change but did not determine it. Settling disputes at court was one way to hasten or ride out shifts in household economies, to accommodate or combat new ambitions, to prevent or propel the occasional family disaster. Some people wanted changes; others wanted the old ways. The same individuals could use legal rules for different goals in different circumstances. Perhaps because the courtroom was a place for activists—at least where plaintiffs were concerned—it is difficult to find any sense of imminent social breakdown in case records. Legal resolutions were sought by people who thought the past was connected to the future in a predictable way. That is what cases and decisions were about: organizing the future according to expectations created in the present and rules produced in the past. From the perspective of township courtrooms, 1905 to the summer of 1914 was not a time of systemic crisis.

The war changed most of this. What happened after August 1914 was a catastrophe for rural people, a tragedy beyond imagination. The war with its endless casualties and seeming endlessness destroyed the society peasants had sustained. The horrifying losses of families and neighbors, the blasting of future plans, the rapid changes in economic prospects, and the government's shifting policies presented rural people with inescapable burdens, not of their own making.[2] Still, as in the past, peasants had to pay their taxes and feed themselves. They carried on. At times they used their courts.

WORLD WAR AT TOWNSHIP COURTS

The ongoing operations of township courts after August 1914 assisted peasants as they reorganized their work and resources in response to dreadful losses and new possibilities. Legal settlements were important for the wartime economy and for civilians in rural society. Case records display peasants' efforts to persevere in their various enterprises and to resolve ordinary and extraordinary problems through law. The regularity with which courts held sessions and decided cases in wartime testifies to the strength of rural governance and the success of legal structures established a half century earlier. The tendency to elect older men as authorities and the minimum age of thirty-five meant that mobilization had little effect on the cadre of judges. Peasant judges continued to be selected and to serve. Township clerks, who could be younger, might be subject to conscription; occasionally a clerk was replaced in the middle of a term.[3] In none of the townships I studied did court activity cease during the war years.

The most important function of a township court in wartime was simply doing what it had done all along: giving people legal opportunities to sue for losses, defend their dignity, transfer resources, and protect their property. Litigants initiated civil and criminal actions for the usual sorts of things throughout the war years. Occasionally a suit offers a glimpse of the war economy, as in the following case heard at the Iaguninskii Township Court on 24 May 1916.

On that day Lev Vasilev Kolchkov, a peasant man from the village of Lokotnia, brought a suit against Matvei Ivanov Vorlamov from Pokrovskoe, another village in the township, for sixty rubles. Vorlamov, a peasant and an enterprising outputter, had himself earlier filed several suits in attempts to collect small sums from people in his debt.[4] Kolchkov explained his case as follows:

> He had fulfilled Vorlamov's order for lathe work of 9,000 pins for grenades for the sum of 210 rubles. The defendant Vorlamov had paid him at various

> times 150 rubles but is not paying the remaining sum. He asks to exact 60 rubles from him.

Vorlamov testified in his defense, claiming that he had in fact paid for the products.[5] Four witnesses from Lokotnia were called by the plaintiff, and three showed up in court. A fourth, Vladimir Kolchkov, was not questioned because he was living elsewhere. The plaintiff asked the court to proceed in the absence of the testimony of this witness, presumably a relative of his. The following testimony was recorded:

> Witness Golovanov testified that Kolchkov worked for Vorlamov for what sum he did not know. Vorlamov paid Kolchkov money at various times and how much he paid he cannot testify to, but he supposes that Vorlamov did not pay Kolchkov all the money. [signature]
>
> Witness Kuzin testified that Kolchkov worked for Vorlamov, [and] in his presence Vorlamov paid ten rubles for the work. How much money he still owed, he, Kuzin, could not testify to. [signature]
>
> The witness Filimonov testified the same as Kuzin, adding that in his presence Vorlamov paid Kolchkov fifty rubles for the work on the pins and sent ten rubles to the wife of the plaintiff. [illiterate]

The judges made it plain in their decision that they did not find this testimony convincing evidence for the debt and ruled to reject the suit.[6]

Kolchkov's fellow villagers had given their neighbor little support in his case against an outputter from another village. The scrappy plaintiff exercised his right to appeal. He received his copy of the court's decision on 18 June 1916, within the allotted thirty-day period, and sent an appeal to the land captain. The land captain forwarded the case to the county congress, which decided on 12 August 1916 that Vorlamov had to pay Kolchkov his sixty rubles. It was then Vorlamov's turn to protest. The result of his appeal was a decision upholding the original judgment: the suit was rejected once again. The township court received word of this outcome on 25 November 1916.[7]

The nature of the outputter's order is the only aspect of this case that clearly distinguishes it from many prewar suits over work and pay. Both parties appealed, which was unusual but not necessarily related to the war. In general, the rate of appeals of township-level decisions rose slightly during the war years, from 14 percent to 18 percent of the cases in my survey. The higher instance in Kolchkov's case ultimately supported the township court, the usual result of appeals recorded by township clerks.[8] The court system functioned efficiently—six months from start to finish, with two appeals included. The settling of such suits in a timely fashion was vital to production—both civil and military—in the countryside. The stress of the war on institutions of governance figures prominently in many explanations of the imperial regime's collapse,[9] but it would be difficult to pin any blame on malfunction of township courts.

If the basic mechanism of the township court system continued working in wartime, there were nonetheless significant changes in what judges encountered when they performed their duties. One difference is the amount of

Kolchkov's suit: wartime inflation is apparent in the large sum he sought from Vorlamov. A suit for sixty rubles would have been well above the average for the prewar period, when suits of this amount or more accounted for only 10 percent of cases in my survey. Inflation increased both prices and amounts requested at the township courts. More than half the wartime suits were for more than thirty rubles, and 26 percent of plaintiffs asked for payments of sixty rubles or more. The courts continued to settle very small suits, but these came up much more rarely. Before the war began, suits for five rubles or less accounted for 23 percent of cases; in the war years, these small suits fell to 11 percent of cases. The median suit before the war was eleven rubles, thirty-one kopeks; during wartime this rose to thirty-five rubles, twenty-five kopeks. This increase in the amounts requested by plaintiffs displays the responsiveness of township courts to shifts in the economy and to rural society's ongoing need to settle conflicts over resources and work.

A transition to larger awards involved no real change in legal practice at township courts. But in other respects the docket judges faced was quite different from prewar times. Most obviously, the number of cases fell.[10] The steady expansion of cases registered at township courts came to a halt; the caseload of most courts declined significantly as soon as the war broke out (see Table 7.1). In 1914, at the township courts of Bogorodskii County, plaintiffs registered 89 percent of the number of 1913 cases. In the overworked township courts of Moscow County, registered cases dropped from 28,814 in 1913 to 20,635 in 1914. In some areas the drop in numbers of registered cases allowed the courts to improve on their already quite high efficiency rate. The township courts of Bogorodskii County decided 93 percent of all the cases registered in 1914, an improvement of 1 percent over the previous year. Over the course of the war the number of cases heard dropped back further. By 1916 the Ignatevskii Township Court was hearing far fewer cases (245) than it had heard in 1906 (351). The court in Iaguninskii Township heard 76 cases in 1905, 338 in 1914, and 187 in 1916.[11]

The decrease in numbers of cases at township courts was not the only difference judges and clerks witnessed as they went about their duties. The kinds of people who brought cases to township courts and the kinds of matters courts were called on to decide also shifted after August 1914.

The major change at township courts in wartime was that men were missing. Before the war men had been the large majority of plaintiffs and defendants at township courts. With mobilization, the proportion of men and women at the courts shifted dramatically. From 1905 to the outbreak of war, men initiated 87 percent of cases in my survey, excluding those brought by police alone. During the war years the percentage of cases brought by men fell to 57 percent. Similarly the portion of defendants who were male fell in wartime. Before the war 90 percent of defendants in contested cases at township courts had been men; in the war years, men's portion of defendants dropped to 75 percent. The gender of witnesses also changed. Before the war the first witness called to testify in the township courts I studied was a male in 98 percent of

Table 7.1. Cases Registered, Cases Unresolved, and Percentage of Cases Resolved at Township Courts in Four Counties and Average County of Moscow Province, 1913 and 1914

County	*1913 All Registered Cases*	*1914 All Registered Cases*	*All Reg. 1914 Cases as % of All Reg. 1913 Cases*	*1913 Unresolved Cases*	*1914 Unresolved Cases*	*Unresolved 1914 Cases as % of Unresolved 1913 Cases*	*Resolved Cases in 1913 (%)*	*Resolved Cases in 1914 (%)*
Moskovskii	28,814	20,635	72%	3415	3143	92%	88%	85%
Bogorodskii	11,307	10,103	89%	875	728	83%	92%	93%
Klinskii	5252	5406	103%	383	313	82%	93%	91%
Zvenigorodskii	5049	4526	87%	219	158	72%	96%	97%
Average County	6492	5692	88%	516	481	93%	92%	92%

Source: *OMG 1913–1914*.

cases. During the war males were called as first witnesses in 73 percent of cases. These changes in the gender composition of litigants and witnesses at township courts meant that the always male judges were now in nearly half their cases deciding complaints and suits brought by women plaintiffs. In one-fourth of their cases they would be confronting female defendants. In more than one-fourth of cases the first witness would be female. Seen through the lens of gender, the township courtroom was quite a different realm than it had been before the war.

These statistics point to the magnitude of the war's devastation in Russian villages. Township courts in Moscow Province were far from the front, but their inhabitants were connected to the war by mobilization, changes in their economic circumstances, and, above all, by the carnage that killed soldiers from the area. The drop in cases at township courts captures the deep and tragic inroad of international conflict into family and community ways of being. The impact of the war shows up as an absence: the absence from courts of people who might have brought concerns before the law. Their motivations, as for litigants generally, would have been base or noble or something in between. Malice, greed, offended sensibilities, ambition, searches for fair rewards, justice, or fresh starts—the ordinary struggles that could have become the stuff of litigation would not be lived or heard at court.

Another somber reflection of the war at township courts concerned survivors. When men were killed away from home, village families had to reorder their lives in new ways. Court records reveal the efforts made by families and villages to reallocate property and to legitimate the reconfiguration of their resources through a legal process. Although peasants brought more civil than criminal cases to the township courts in ordinary times (see chapter 3), during the war dockets at the township courts shifted even more toward civil cases. The Ignatevskii Township Court heard 156 civil cases and 89 criminal cases in 1916, a ratio of 1.8 to 1.[12] The increase in the proportion of civil litigation was driven in part by an explosion of inheritance cases at township courts. Before the war inheritance cases accounted for only a very small percentage of civil cases at the township courts I studied. After 1914 their numbers skyrocketed. In 1915 inheritance cases were 10 percent of civil cases at the courts I studied; in 1916 they rose to 24 percent. In 1917 inheritance was the subject of 22 percent of civil cases.

These grim figures were not distributed evenly across time and place; they represented losses specific to battles, military disasters, and to particular units of soldiers. To take a horrific example, the Iaguninskii Township Court reviewed 44 inheritance cases in 1916, out of a total of 207 civil cases. Of these cases, one-fourth—eleven cases—were brought in one month, August 1916, and all eleven of these August cases were brought by people from a single village. Ten women from Korinskoe, a village of only forty households, asked the township judges to confirm their rights to their husbands' properties at this time. In this grim fashion court records reveal the calamitous impact of the war upon this village.[13]

WOMEN AND POWER IN THE COUNTRYSIDE

The vital and sometimes primary role of women in family economies was recognized in many inheritance cases heard at township courts. Even if women did not initiate inheritance cases, their claims to family property could be legitimated by township judges. In the Kirillov family's inheritance case, described in chapter 6, the judges at the Grebnevskii Township Court disinherited a direct male descendant in favor of a daughter-in-law who had maintained her husband's home.[14] This decision from 1916 can be read as a kind of negative patriarchy: the judges expressly criticized the male heir's neglect of the family economy and of his father. This case may also reflect the personal qualities of the daughter-in-law, as well as the judges' application of the usual standard of fair reward for work and their attention to local needs in wartime.

During the war women began to initiate inheritance cases on their own. In the prewar period none of the few inheritance cases in my survey were brought by women. During the war years plaintiffs were female in 71 percent of inheritance cases at the courts I studied. Inheritance cases accounted for 43 percent of all civil cases brought by women at this time, whereas for male plaintiffs—although they, too, began more inheritance suits than in the past—such cases accounted for only 7 percent of all civil suits. The murderous impact of the war is visible in this abrupt change in the kind of cases brought by women at the township courts and in the much higher probability that an inheritance case at a township court would be brought by a women.[15]

Among the cases heard by Iaguninskii Township judges on 14 June 1916 were two inheritance claims brought by women from the village of Ust'e. Evdokiia Vasilieva Lukianova, with her daughter, Anna Stepanova Lukianova, asked to receive the land and property of Evdokia's husband. In a second claim, Praskovia Polikarpova Vinogradova requested the land allotment that had been assigned to her first husband, Aleksei Sergeev Artamonov. In both cases representatives of the Ust'e rural society appeared in court to testify for the plaintiffs. Not surprisingly, in the absence of any male heir, the Lukianov property was transferred on the spot to the deceased man's wife and daughter. But in the second case as well, the representative from the village society testified in favor of the petitioner, Praskovia Polikarpova Vinogradova. Aleksei Sergeev Artamonov's land allotment was also transferred immediately to a female claimant, his first wife. This decision to allocate property to a former wife may reveal village authorities' concern to find cultivators for communal property after the war had depleted the number of male heads of household.[16]

Even in the presence of surviving male relatives, widows could inherit allotment land and household property from their husbands. On the same day that the Iaguninskii judges settled inheritance cases for women from Ust'e, they also heard a contested case from Iagunino itself. Earlier in the year, on March 8, the court had heard a request for a family division from Vasilisa Kirilova Khrushcheva. Her husband had died, and she wanted to divide his property

Table 7.2. The Village Leader's Inventory before the Court's Changes, Iaguninskii Township Court, June 1916

Item	*Inventory Value in Rubles*	*Ruble Value Assigned to Vasilisa*	*Ruble Value Assigned to Efim*
House, 13 × 8 arshins(30.3' × 18.6')	125	0	125
Room	20	20	0
Courtyard (*dvor*)	30	30	0
Barn	15	15	0
Shed	7	7	0
Horse	43	0	43
Cow	60	60	0
1 Sheep, 2 Lambs	7	7	0
Cart with Wheels	20	0	20
Sleigh	7	7	0
Horse Harness	10	0	10
Watch	6	6	0
Samovar	5	5	0
Total Rubles	355	157	198
Land	*Total*	*To Vasilisa*	*To Efim*
Allotment Land	4 shares	2 shares	2 shares
Other Land	Not measured	½	½

Source: TsIAM, f. 749, op. 1, d. 38, ll. 24o–25o, 59–61.

with her brother-in-law, Efim Matveev Khrushchev. She claimed her rights as the wife of the deceased and the guardian of his children, Pavel and Aleksei Nikolaev Khrushchev. Efim Matveev agreed with his sister-in-law's request, and the court ordered a division of the family's property. One month later the court clerk recorded that this decision had been fulfilled. Efim Matveev had second thoughts, however; on June 14 he was back in court as a defendant in a new case brought by Vasilisa Kirilova. She testified that the property remained undivided and in the hands of her brother-in-law.

The total value of the Khrushchev family's moveable property was 355 rubles, in addition to four shares of land. Vasilisa Kirilova cited the court's decision on 8 March as evidence of her right to a division of this property and requested that it be carried out. Efim Matveev testified that he regarded the property as collective and did not want the division. He considered that a "division today would be burdensome" and that he could not afford it. The judges, who had access to an inventory of the property, asked the plaintiffs to increase the value of the animals to facilitate an equitable division. Both parties refused. In response, the judges, two of whom had heard the March case, took matters in hand. They changed the values of the inventory drawn up by the village leader to reflect higher values for the animals that were supposed to be allocated to Vasilisa Kirilova, thereby adding 41 rubles to her share of the moveable property and equalizing allocations between brother and sister-in-law. This technical adjustment favored Efim. As is apparent from the village leader's inventory before these changes (see Table 7.2), Efim was already getting the big-ticket items—the house, the horse, the harness, and the cart; Vasilisa's cow, sheep, and lambs were perhaps somewhat undervalued but hardly by 41 rubles.[17]

Even this effort to facilitate a settlement was not satisfactory to Efim. He appealed the court's decision to the land captain. The papers were sent forward by the township authorities on June 22, and the land captain forwarded the case to the county congress. Here the case was turned down. Efim appealed to the next instance, the Moscow Provincial Board. The board heard the case on 3 May 1917 and turned down Efim a third time. According to the township records, the division took place on 10 June 1917.[18]

This case displays both problems and possibilities faced by female householders in the war years. Vasilisa Kirilova managed to receive a large share of family property and succeeded in separating her household from that of her brother. While the township judges may have weighted the scales in favor of her brother-in-law, Vasilisa gained control over substantial economic resources—the barn, the shed, the productive animals—and some of the goods that established household status—the watch and samovar. The court record did not describe in detail the living arrangements that might have resulted from the Khrushchev family's division—one might think of Efim Matveev riding off on his horse, while Vasilisa Kirilova maintained the farm—but it is noteworthy that village authorities, the township court, the county congress, and the provincial board all supported this division of family property, putting about half of it in a woman's hands. The real obstacle to Vasilisa Kirilova's establishment of a separate household economy was not the legal system at any level but her brother-in-law's repeated attempts to prevent the division from taking place. Still, even Efim Matveev used legal means in his effort to hold onto the family's property. Both parties saw the courts as the way to resolve their quarrel.

A sad consequence of the war was conflict over personal belongings of soldiers killed away from home. On 24 May 1916 the Iaguninskii Township Court heard a case brought by Vasilii Efimov Martynov from the village of Ulitino against his daughter-in-law, Ekaterina Leonova Martynova. Vasilii Efimov testified that his son had been drafted and that Ekaterina Leonova had left home with his son's clothing. He listed his son's possessions with ruble values—a winter fur coat, 70 rubles; a summer coat, 10 rubles; a suit, 30 rubles; boots and galoshes, 10 rubles; a hat, 10 rubles, a coat with fur, 30 rubles; a fall jacket, 7 rubles; a pocket watch, 15 rubles—altogether, in his estimate, 182 rubles of clothing, which he wanted back.[19]

The daughter-in-law appeared in court and testified that she did not want to return the clothes; she had put them into storage at her husband's orders, where they remained. The illiterate Ekaterina Leonova continued: "At present she has learned that her husband was killed in the war, this was announced to her through the commander of the regiment." Two women and one man, all illiterate, from Ulitino came to the court to testify in this case. They all agreed that Ekaterina Leonova had taken her husband's clothing, but they added the following observation: "She lived with her husband for ten years, and is of good behavior." The court's ruling took this into account; the judges "found [that] Martynov's suit did not merit satisfaction" and rejected it. Martynov did not appeal the decision. A good wife could keep her late husband's impressive wardrobe from her father-in-law's clutches.[20]

These victories for female litigants at township courts reveal new powers in household matters that women gained in wartime. Court records also display the increased presence and authority of women in village affairs. The Tolmazov wardship case, considered in chapter 3, offers an individualized view of participants in village governance. The wardship records included yearly decisions made by heads of households in the village of Blizhne-Beliaevo in Tsaritsynskii Township. In 1908 the village numbered seventy-four households, and sixty-three heads of household signed, or had signed for them, the village's first official decision about Maria. All sixty-three voters were male. In December 1914, the year of the village's last report on the wardship, the village numbered ninety-nine households. In this year sixty-eight household heads—69 percent of the total—testified to the quality of the guardian's behavior. In the intervening years the number of households in the village had increased, and the percentage of household heads attending the supervisory assemblies declined, falling to 62 percent in 1913 (See Table 7.3.)

What was new in 1914 was not only the increased number of households but also that a few women were now voting members of the assembly. Four women, Agrafena Anarina, Ekaterina Anarina, Ekaterina Zhirkova, and Nastasia Koshelova, were listed as household heads and put their names on the assembly's decision. In the case of the Anarins, none of the male householders listed in 1908 were present in 1914, suggesting that these two women had taken over the affairs of this family. The Zhirkov family's membership had changed over this period, and there were two men listed by this name in addition to Ekaterina Zhirkova. Nastasia Kashelova was one of five people with this last name who testified in 1914; one male member of this family listed in 1908 was missing.[21]

The list of Blizhne-Beliaevo's householders gathered for an official meeting on 9 December 1914 shows that, contrary to earlier practice in this village, some women had become voting members of the rural assembly. It is impossible to know if these four women were temporary substitutes for men away at war—under way for almost four months—or elsewhere, or if some or all of these women had become officially recognized heads of household. That both men and women with the same last name were listed as household heads establishes that some women had not been absorbed into male-headed family units. The increase in the number of households, along with the presence of some women alongside men with the same last name, might be explained by the formation of new family units when men were killed, as happened with the Khrushchev family at Ust'e.[22]

Cases about inheritance, wardships, and family divisions in wartime reveal the network of law and village society encompassing and responding to new circumstances and new needs. Called on to legitimate or decide contested family matters, township courts were drawn into the transformation of women's

A peasant woman and her daughter, Pochinki, Moscow Province, 1900s.
Photograph from the collection of Mikhail Zolotarev.

Table 7.3. Attendance at Blizhne-Beliaevo Village Assemblies concerning Tolmazova Wardship, 1908–1914

Year	*No. of Households Having Voice*	*No. of Household Heads Attending Assembly*	*Percent of Households Represented*
1908	74	63	85%
1909	75	56	75%
1910	85	60	71%
1911	85	61	72%
1912	85	63	74%
1913	85	53	62%
1914	99	68	69%

Source: TsIAM, f. 378, op. 1, d. 387, ll. 1–17o.

roles. Judges' decisions at local courts, as well as the initiatives of male and female litigants, enabled rural communities, in case after case, to reallocate responsibility and authority to women during the war years. As household heads, these women could participate in the collective governance of rural society.

MEN AT COURT ON THE HOME FRONT

But what about men who stayed at home? The war meant a much reduced presence of men at township courts, but men were still more frequently found than women at case hearings. Men were plaintiffs in 59 percent of wartime civil cases and accusers in 80 percent of criminal cases, excluding those brought by police alone. They were still the majority of defendants—in 80 percent of civil cases and 65 percent of criminal ones. This last figure reveals a radical drop (from 88 percent) in men as criminal defendants after August 1914. Many men who might have been otherwise occupied were at war or dead.

Those who were not at the front already might end up there even before a judicial matter could be concluded at a township court. On 3 March 1916 the Tsaritsynskii Township Court heard a charge under Statute 42—public inebriation. A constable testified that Aleksandr Kondrat'ev Eremin, a peasant man from the village of Shepilovo, had been "deeply drunk." Eremin appeared in court and confessed his guilt, noting that he had been drinking eau de cologne. The judge convicted Eremin based on his testimony and sentenced him to a five ruble fine or three days in jail. The village leader was informed of the sentence but later communicated to the township clerk that "Eremin is drafted into the army." This note was entered into the case record on 1 August 1916.[23]

Apart from the mobilization of the convicted man, two other aspects of this case were connected to the war and its consequences at township courts. First, the temperance regulations seemed to have had little effect on males charged with drinking offenses. In my case survey, public inebriation accounted for a higher proportion of criminal charges against males after the outbreak of the war than before.[24] The prewar pattern of police participation in such cases and frequent confession by the defendants did not change in the war years. Observers from the *zemstvo* had been appalled by the amount of money that peasants in Moscow County spent on vodka before temperance rules were put into place; these observers believed that a new "sober village" was emerging as early as 1915.[25] This may have been wishful thinking about other people's vices, although court records do not say anything conclusive on this score. The police might have become more aggressive in pursuing drinking cases once the temperance rules went into effect, and the war might have driven more home-based men to drink whatever was at hand. But wartime rules clearly affected what men drank, as the testimony in this case suggests.[26]

A higher proportion of inebriation charges was one of several changes in the pattern of accusations against male defendants in the war years. The most usual charge in criminal cases involving male defendants was, as before, some kind of insult, but the percentage of such charges increased. Insults in word (20 percent of criminal charges against males), insults in deed (7 percent), and slander (7 percent) accounted for one-third of criminal cases against male defendants in the war years, up from 24 percent before the war. The kinds of insults also shifted: nonviolent verbal insults and slander were the subjects of 26 percent of all criminal cases against men in wartime, up from 14 percent of such cases before the war. This represents a significant increase from prewar years in the percentage of nonviolent insult cases against men. Two other kinds of criminal charges against male defendants were more frequent in the war years: s*amoupravstvo*—unwarranted exercise of an assumed right (see chapter 5)—accounted for 11 percent of surveyed cases against men in wartime, up from 4 percent before the war, and charges of beating rose from 9 percent to 15 percent of such cases.

Three kinds of criminal accusations against men dropped dramatically in my survey after August 1914. Charges of disorderly conduct, which had accounted for 15 percent of criminal cases against men in the prewar years, disappeared entirely after the war broke out. Another radical change was the percentage of charges concerning public sanitation. In the prewar years males had been charged with not cleaning courtyards, dumping garbage, and fouling water in 15 percent of criminal cases. Such charges against male defendants dropped off to 4 percent in the war years. Finally, thefts dropped significantly in the war years in proportion to other charges—from 22 percent to 9 percent of cases against men.

These shifts in charges involving male defendants accord with an overall change in the kinds of criminal cases heard in township courts after the war began, viewed through the categories of personal dignity, property rights, and public welfare (see chapter 5). Before the war personal dignity cases accounted for 38 percent of all criminal cases in my survey. In the war years this proportion grew to 74 percent. Corresponding to the drop in theft charges registered against male defendants after August 1914, criminal cases involving property rights of all kinds fell from 25 percent of criminal charges before the war to 9 percent during the war. Finally, public welfare cases, which would include sanitation charges as well as disorderly conduct, fell from 37 percent of criminal cases to 17 percent in the war years. A clear shift toward even greater use of township courts to defend personal dignity occurred after the war began.

A different contingent of men remained in the countryside, with legal concerns and violations that differed from those of rural men before the war. Many potential troublemakers were serving in the armed forces or were dead or incapacitated. The dramatic drop in accusations of theft and the disappearance of disorderly conduct charges during wartime suggests that the young men of rural Russia, like young men in other times and places, had been most at fault for petty property crime and for disturbances of the peace.[27] But if the countryside was calmer and property safer in wartime, there were still problems besetting villagers. Elder males left to manage families and to perform more labor than before would have their reasons to resort to alcohol and to indulge in other behaviors—violations of personal dignity, in most cases—that might bring them to justice at township courts.

GENDER, WAR, AND TOWNSHIP JUSTICE

The war increased the probability that a male defendant would be confronted by a female plaintiff at township courts. Before the war, male defendants in criminal cases ordinarily faced male plaintiffs. In only 10 percent of prewar criminal cases in my survey were men charged by women. During war years, women brought 24 percent of criminal cases against men (see Table 7.4). Perhaps women brought more cases because male family members who might have acted in their stead were away or killed at war. Perhaps women felt more entitled to bring charges than in the past. Perhaps men's actions had something to do with women's increased willingness to accuse them at court. A look at the kinds of cases that pitted women against men at township courts captures old and new tensions in rural society as well as litigants' demands for legal and peaceful resolutions of these problems.

Before the war the most frequent criminal charge brought by a woman against a man was the all too familiar "insult in words." These accounted for 44 percent of women's criminal cases against men in prewar years. During the war "insult in words" remained the most common female criminal charge against men, accounting for one-third of all such cases. Charges of "insult in deed" by women against men fell insignificantly in the war years, from 11 to 10 percent; charges of beating remained the same at 19 percent. *Samoupravstvo*—unwarranted exercise of a presumed right—remained a very infrequent accusation by women against men in war years, as did "threat." One new type of nonviolent dignity violation was charged in significant numbers by women against men at court after the war began: this was "slander."[28] Slander charges accounted for 14 percent of wartime criminal charges brought by women

Table 7.4. Sex of Plaintiffs and Defendants in Individual Cases: Prewar and Wartime Percentages and Number of Cases ( )

		Female Plaintiffs		*Male Plaintiffs*		
Type of Cases	Time Period	Male Defendant	Female Defendant	Male Defendant	Female Defendant	Total Cases
Civil	Prewar	15.0% (12)	1.2% (1)	81.2% (65)	2.5% (2)	100% (80)
	Wartime	27.8% (54)	7.7% (15)	54.6% (106)	9.8% (19)	100% (194)
Criminal	Prewar	10.1% (27)	3.4% (9)	78.4% (210)	8.2% (22)	100% (268)
	Wartime	24.3% (18)	24.3% (18)	40.5% (30)	10.8% (8)	100% (74)

against men. Altogether, personal dignity charges rose from 78 to 86 percent of female versus male criminal charges. Women continued to charge men with economic crime but at a lower rate that corresponded to the drop in economic charges overall. Theft accounted for 22 percent of their charges before the war; theft and other economic crimes were accusations in 14 percent of such cases during wartime. Thus in the war years women brought a higher percentage of dignity cases against men than they had in the past and a lower proportion of criminal charges concerning property rights. Neither before the war nor after did women charge men with public welfare cases. These statistics reveal several changes in rural society and legal practice.

First, women were more likely to charge men at court for verbal assaults on their dignity than in the past. The novel charge of slander itself accounted for a change in the share of verbal as opposed to violent affronts to dignity cited in cases brought by women against men. Before the war, verbal assaults on dignity accounted for 48 percent of all criminal charges that women brought against men, and charges concerning violence (insult in deed and beating) accounted for 30 percent of such cases. During the war verbal insults, including slander, rose to 57 percent of criminal charges by women against men, and charges of violent abuse remained almost the same at 29 percent. Does this shift mean that women were becoming more sensitive to verbal insults, more concerned to defend their reputations? Or might this mean that men, challenged but also inhibited by female authority, insulted women more frequently than in the past, thus goading more women to take them to court? Did the older men remaining in villages hesitate—to some degree—to insult their daughters-in-law with violence and use verbal abuse instead? The percentage of beating charges—charged by women against men—remained about the same in wartime as before.

Second, a shift toward increased female agency is visible in newly arising kinds of property and family cases at township courts in the war years. The subjects and numbers of civil cases brought by women against men changed after the war began. Before the war a civil case brought by a female against a male was always a suit, not a request for a family division or a confirmation of an inheritance. These prewar suits frequently involved debt collection by enterprising women active in outputting and other small rural industries. During the war women registered several kinds of civil cases against male defendants. As we might expect from the overall increase in inheritance cases, inheritance suits with a male defendant accounted for 15 percent of wartime civil cases brought by women. Family divisions, land, and economic issues each accounted for another 15 percent of such civil cases brought by women against men in wartime. Women asserted rights in economic matters concerning property damages, harvest controversies, possession disputes, and evictions, all subjects of their cases against men at township courts.

The criminal case dockets of individual township courts offer an overview of women's activism at law, exclusive of their role in inheritance and other civil suits. At the Iaguninskii Township Court, from January through June 1916, female plaintiffs charged male defendants with the following criminal offenses: insult in words (four cases), slander (two cases), insult in deed (one case), beating (one case), *samoupravstvo* (one case), and theft (one case).[29] Closer to Moscow, at the Tsaritsynskii Township Court, from January through August 1916, women brought the following criminal charges against men: beating (two cases), insult in words (two cases), slander (one case), beating (one case), theft (one case), and not reporting a found object (one case). Case records for both courts display the mix of personal dignity and property charges characteristic of female cases against men.[30]

Clerks' descriptions of the eight criminal cases brought by women against men at the township court at Tsaritsyno from January through August 1916 reveal more of the context and contents of these legal struggles. First, these eight cases brought by woman against male plaintiffs at Tsaritsyno accounted for more than one-fifth of all criminal cases heard between January and August 1916. The others were brought by men against men (fifteen cases), women against women (eight cases), or men against women (three cases).[31] Second, some of the women's accusations were brought against two defendants, one male and one female, and some were brought against two men. Third, it is only the gender of the parties that makes these eight cases similar; as usual, each case involved individuals in particular relationships and specific contexts.

The first criminal case heard in 1916 at Tsaritsyno was an accusation brought by a woman against a man. Avdotiia Nikolaeva Zamiatina, a peasant woman from the village of Borisovo, accused two male peasants, Ivan Alekseev Kisilev and Aleksandr Matveev Zharov, also of Borisovo, of stealing twelve chickens valued at thirty rubles. Both men—one literate, one not—appeared at court and pleaded not guilty. There were no witnesses. The judges decided that the accusation was unproven and acquitted the defendants. Avdotiia did not appear in court, but a record of the hearing was sent to her.[32] The second criminal case brought by a woman against a man at Tsaritsyno in 1916 was Anisa Irakhimova Peskova's action against her husband, Ivan Vasilev Peskov, heard on 3 March. Both parties were peasants from the village of Borisovo; both were illiterate. Anisa Irakhimova accused her husband of beating her. At court, Ivan Vasilev confessed his guilt. The parties then reconciled and the case was ended.[33]

On 21 April the judges heard another female charge against a man (and a woman). Ekaterina Khitrova, an illiterate peasant woman from outside the township, accused Pavel Nikitin Shatrov and Imaka Kozmineva Mochulova, both from the village of Shaidrova, under Statute 179—not reporting a found object. The defendants came to court and supported the charge. They testified that they had indeed "found" things on the road. The judges convicted them based on their "recognition" of their act at court and sentenced each of them to a fine of five rubles or three days in jail. Each of the convicted parties paid the fine; one on 25 April and one three days later.[34]

More than a month later, on 9 June, another female charge against a man and a woman was heard. This was one of the infrequent cases involving townspeople at court. Townswoman Maria Dmitr'eva Zhilokhova, from the city of Zvenigorod, charged two townspeople, Viacheslav Nikolaevich and Fekla Fedorova Nikolaeva, with "insult in words" and *samoupravstvo.* This charge appears to have been connected to a feud between Zhilokhova, Nikolaeva, and another woman; just prior to this case, the judges had heard an insult case brought by Nikolaeva against Zhilokhova. All parties in both these cases were at court. Both defendants were literate but the accuser was not. Viacheslav Nikolaevich testified that he was not guilty and asked the court to recognize the "bad faith" of the accuser. Nikolaeva also declared herself not guilty. A single witness appeared who said she knew nothing about the case. The judges did not allow testimony from a clearly partisan witness. Both defendants, literate townspeople and probably related, were acquitted.[35]

The next case heard on what must have been a day full of ill temper at Tsaritsyno was brought by Feodosiia Kirilova Bondarska, a peasant from another county, against a married couple, the Kochlinovs, both peasants from yet another county in the province. This case, too, was for insult in words, as well as threat. The plaintiff, illiterate, appeared in court to support her charge. The male defendant, Pavel Aleksandrovich Kochlinov, like the defendant in the preceding case, cast aspersions on the plaintiff, calling her accusation "unconscionable." The female defendant declared herself not guilty and then testified that it had all been the other way around—Bondarska had been the insulting party. Unfortunately for Liubov' Stepanova Kochlinova, a witness testified that she, Kochlinova, and not her husband, had called Feodosiia a "lawless woman" and "other improper words." The judges convicted Feodosiia and sentenced her to a two-ruble fine or one day in jail. Her husband was acquitted. The fine was paid on 1 August.[36]

In July 1916 the judges heard three more cases brought by women against men. On 7 July Praskoviia Potemkina, a peasant woman from Borisovo, accused a couple, the Strizhovs, of beating. All parties were illiterate. The defendants pleaded not guilty. Witnesses provided weak evidence. The result was an official reconciliation, and the case was ended. On 21 July Efrosina Dmitrevna

Vashchanina, a literate peasant woman from Blizhne-Beliaevo, charged a peasant couple of the same village with "slander and threat," accusing them of beating her and using the famous "improper words." Both defendants pleaded not guilty, and a witness testified in their favor. They were acquitted. The final criminal case brought by a women plaintiff against a male in this period has been discussed in chapter 5. This was Feodosiia Krepkova's case against her male neighbor in the village of Shaidrovo for threatening to kill her chicken. The defendant testified that he had indeed threatened to kill the chicken and was convicted.[37]

These female-initiated cases had little in common except the sex of the plaintiff. In one case of alleged beating, a woman brought her husband to court; in another, a woman brought an unrelated man. Both these cases resulted in reconciliation at court. In the single example of disputes between townspeople, the female plaintiff lost her insult case against a man and a woman. In another insult case, a peasant woman managed to convict another peasant women but not the defendant's male companion. One accusation of theft against two men was not supported, but in another case of "unreported found objects" a woman won her case against a man and a woman. The only outright victory—rather than reconciliation or loss—in the various insult, threat, and slander accusations made by women against men was that of Feodosiia Krepkova. Her opponent, Fedor Ivanov Gubintsev, confessed his "threat," was convicted, and paid his four-ruble fine.[38]

The contents, processing, and outcomes of these cross-gender cases were almost entirely routine for township courts. The judges—S. N. Klopov, I. E. Timofeev, A. M. Kiselev, and O. N. Kamochkin—appeared to have been guided by the same rules of evidence as in the past.[39] Defendant's testimony was crucial to outcomes. Men's guilty pleas resulted in convictions or reconciliations; all the men who pleaded not guilty were acquitted. As usual, acquittals were not based on the defendant's testimony alone; in no acquittal was there evidence to support the plaintiff's charge. In procedural terms, these wartime cases brought by women against men were resolved in accord with the ordinary legal practice of township courts.

Only one aspect of the decisions at Tsaritsyno stands out as exceptional: there were two reconciliations in cases involving beatings. These two cases—one brought by a woman against her husband and the other by a woman against a male neighbor—were the only cases in my survey where charges of beating ended with official reconciliations, registered in the courtroom. Most charges of beating resulted in convictions (53 percent) or acquittals (27 percent). Most of the remaining 20 percent of such cases were ended, which could mean that reconciliation or at least a decision to drop the case had been achieved outside the court. In my case survey it was only in wartime—and only in these two cases—that parties settled their differences in this kind of case in a formal way at court. Could it be that in the village of Borisovo, which numbered only fifty-three households in 1913 and probably had lost men to the war by 1916, people were more interested in making an official statement about resolving their disputes than in the past? Might women, now carrying so much of the economic burden in a small village, both want and be able to attain a formal reconciliation with the probably older men—husbands or others—whom they had charged with assault? One might imagine that at a time when each person's labor and income were even more critical to families than in the past, both parties recognized the value of the defendant's not spending time in jail or paying even what was now quite a small fine to the local treasury.

The records of all criminal cases heard at Tsaritsyno from January through August 1916 highlight the legal initiative of women at this time. Women brought 44 percent of these criminal cases—fifteen versus nineteen for men. This figure, however, does not adequately represent the relative use of the court by men and women. Ten of the male-initiated cases were cases brought by the police, without a named victim. All these police-initiated cases concerned public welfare—inebriation (the majority), dirt, and safety violations. Omitting these policemen's cases, women brought fifteen cases, whereas men—for themselves—brought only nine. In Tsaritsynskii Township in 1916, women were by far the more active of the sexes in bringing criminal cases on their own. The subjects of their cases were either personal dignity or property rights; it was left to the police (males, of course) to respond to violations of public welfare. No woman was identifiably the initiator of a case about male drinking. Probably more important matters—dignity and property—were on their minds.

Men shared these priorities, based on the content and outcomes of their cases. Like women, civilian men (not policemen) brought mostly dignity and a few property charges to the court at Tsaritsyno in 1916. As Table 7.5 shows, men had no more—and in fact less—success than women as plaintiffs in these criminal cases, particularly in their cases against women. Like women, male plaintiffs also reconciled with their defendants in two dignity cases. The only combination of plaintiff and defendant in which no reconciliations in dignity cases occurred was when both parties were female. Two women managed to reconcile, however, in a case where theft was charged.[40] In the single case of male-male reconciliation, discussed in chapter 5, the plaintiff was the village leader of Marino, Fedor Andrev Artomonov, an illiterate man. Artomonov accused a literate co-villager, Vasilii Mikhail Chkhanov, of "insult in words." These two men reconciled at court, after the defendant declared himself guilty.[41] Could this be another example of the search for social peace within a village during the hard times of the war?

More than half the criminal cases brought by men to the Tsaritsynskii court in these months involved family relationships, in various ways. In one male-male case, Ivan Andrianov Nemchinov, a peasant from the village of Bratskoe, charged Sergei Vasil'ev Kozlev of Borisovo for beating his (Nemchinov's) son; at the same time Nemchinov sued for losses. At court, in June 1916, Nemchinov claimed that Kozlev had "beaten his son and taken away a stand worth ten rubles." The defendant pleaded not guilty. Two witnesses appeared, however, and on the basis of their testimony the judges ruled that Kozlev was guilty of beating. The suit for losses was not proven. The convicted man was sentenced

Table 7.5. Sex of Parties, Types of Criminal Cases, and Outcomes at the Tsaritsynskii Township Court, January through August 1916

Sex of Plaintiff	*Sex of Defendant*	*No. of Dignity Cases*	*No. of Convicted Dignity Cases*	*No. of Reconciled Dignity Cases*	*No. of Property Cases*	*No. of Convicted Property Cases*	*No. of Reconciled Property Cases*	*Total No. of Cases*	*Success for Plaintiff (All Cases)*
Female	Male	6	1	2	2	1	0	8	4 (50%)
Female	Female	5	2	0	1	0	1	6	3 (50%)
Male	Male	4	1	1	1	0	0	5	2 (40%)
Male	Female	3	0	1	1	0	0	4	1 (25%)

Notes: If one of two defendants was convicted, this is counted as a conviction. Success of plaintiff is defined as a conviction or reconciliation. If two defendants are of different sexes, the sex reported is that of the defendant whose sex is not that of the plaintiff.

to pay a ten-ruble fine or to spend five days in jail. This was a harsh sentence for the times, but Kozlev paid his fine on 1 August.[42]

In two other cases brought by men to Tsaritsyno at this time family honor was at stake. On 26 May Fedor Fedorov Riabinin, a peasant from the village of Marino, sued two women from the same village, Tatiana Pazovkina and Praskovia Fedorova Chkhanova of "insulting his daughter in writing" in a letter written by their daughters. Riabinin brought the "naughty letter" to court. Riabinin was literate but not so the accused women. They nonetheless pleaded not guilty, testifying that their daughters had not written such a letter. The decision was based on an analysis of the handwriting in the letter. Because it did not match that of the daughters, the two women were acquitted.[43] In another family case, heard on 9 June, Matvei Fedorov Mandropov, from Borisovo, accused a female co-villager, Aleksandra Kutueva, of insulting his daughter "with improper words." Aleksandra, illiterate, pleaded not guilty, but the two parties reconciled at court.[44]

In these cases male peasants came to court to defend their minor children from insult by others—men or women. It is possible, but not provable, that the war had given new significance to these young people's persons in their fathers' eyes. The case of the letter evokes the ongoing transformation in literacy and its significance in daily life.[45] Because literacy was of critical importance to family economies and prestige, it is not surprising that a peasant man brought two illiterate women to court for their daughters' (purported) missive about his daughter. The reputations and activities of minor children—both sons and daughters—had always been important to peasant families, but perhaps fathers found it more imperative than before the war to defend their children's honor at court.

Lest we imagine that peasant men were becoming defenders of women's rights—the right not to be insulted—let us look at another man's insult case at Tsaritsyno. On 3 March 1916 Semyon Aleksandrovich Shtukaturov brought a case for insult in words against his own wife, Nadezhda Abramova Shtukaturova. At court Shtukaturov, illiterate, testified to a more critical problem: "he asked that his wife Shtukaturova would live with him and asked [the court] to re-domicile her in his household." Nadezhda Shtukaturova, also illiterate, testified in court that "she does not live with her husband because he insults her; living together with him is not going to happen." The judges, correctly and wisely it would seem, decided to dismiss this case as "not adjudicable," citing statutes on court jurisdiction.[46]

Family considerations also entered into cases women brought at Tsaritsyno. In Anisa Irakhimova Peskova's accusation of her husband, discussed above, the husband confessed his guilt for beating her and the parties reconciled. No reconciliation took place in two other family cases brought by women at this time. On 3 March 1916 Elena Ivanova Bulanova from Marino charged her daughter-in-law, Anna Bulanova, with insult in words and threat. The literate daughter-in-law pleaded not guilty at court. The Tsaritsyno judges did not hesitate to make a judgment on this confrontation, perhaps a common one, between an illiterate plaintiff and a literate defendant of the younger generation. They ruled that the case was "unproven" and acquitted the daughter-in-law.[47] The ordinary procedural considerations appear to be at work: the defendant's testimony was critical; there were no witnesses and no other evidence to support the charge. Without proof, the defendant was acquitted.

In a second case of intergenerational conflict between women in a single family, the judges ruled in favor of the mother-in-law. In this suit a daughter-in-law took the initiative. Maria Ivanovna Klimova, from the village of Saburovo, charged her mother-in-law, Aksiniia Kozminovna Klimova, with insult in words and not giving her bread. Both women in this family were illiterate, and both came to court. There were no witnesses. The testimony was recorded as follows:

> The victim, Maria Ivanovna Klimova, asked to bring her mother-in-law to legal responsibility because she offends her, doesn't give her bread, and, besides this, criticizes her householdery. . . .
>
> The accused . . . testified that she, as the oldest member of the household, carries it on independently, does not offend her daughter-in-law, there's sufficient bread to take at will, she does not recognize herself as guilty.

So much for that daughter-in-law. The judges ruled that Aksiniia's guilt was "not established," acquitted her, and refused the case.[48]

There was no single family paradigm, no clear generational victor, no winning gender at Tsaritsyno. But family disputes clearly mattered, and many of them did end up at court. At the township courts in my study the percentage of cases involving two or more contesting members of a family increased dramatically after the war began. Before the war cases within families comprised only 9 percent of cases; after the war began this share increased to 31 percent of all cases, both civil and criminal. This increase may be related to changes in both families and villages. The men remaining in the countryside, including family patriarchs and rural leaders, would be even more likely to be older and illiterate than in the past. Many women would be heading households; in some villages, as at Blizhne-Beliaevo, women might even have a few voices in rural societies. The loss of young men, the new power of women, and the vestigial nature of male authority in the countryside—all these demanded adjustments in family and village life. Whatever their particular challenges, rural people had the possibility of reaching beyond reconfigured families and village assemblies to the township courts. There, as we have seen in detail at Tsaritsyno, three or four male judges would listen to the circumstances of each case and come to decisions based on evidence.

LEGAL RESOLUTIONS AND LOCAL TRANSFORMATIONS

The township court system permitted rural litigants to find legal and peaceful solutions to the stresses of the war. Men and women could come before township judges to resolve their struggles over resources—land allotments, clothes, and labor—that were critical to the well-being of peasant families. The courts facilitated resolutions of personal conflicts, punished petty crime, and provided a flexible means to address new concerns as they arose. Both the kinds of cases heard and the ways they were resolved permit the identification of significant changes occurring in villages at this time.

The greater share of cases concerning evictions in court dockets opens a window on transiency in wartime Russia.[49] It had been possible to go to court before the war to expel someone legally from a house, but after the war began, eviction cases appeared in greater (although still small) numbers. At the Iaguninskii Township Court on 14 August 1916 Egor Vladimirov Lobanov appeared with a request to expel two women from his house in Iagunino. According to Egor Vladimirov, Ekaterina and Aleksandra Vishniakova were "gypsies of the merchants of Voskresenie" who had not paid their rent. He testified that

> he had let the Vishniakov gypsies live in his house on the basis of oral agreements at a payment of five rubles a month. The Vishniakovs had not paid this money for two months. He requests that they be evicted from the house.[50]

The judges Makarov, Shibalov, and Ramanov found the request justified and, in the absence of the defendants, ruled for eviction. A declaration to this effect was sent to the village leader in Iagunino on 26 August. The document was received on 1 September, and on 20 October the township leader testified that the decision had been carried out.[51]

A legal order to evict could be used to displace intruding outsiders, but such cases could also arise between villagers. The following cases from the Iaguninskii court presented judges with opportunities for creative dispute resolutions. On a single day in May 1916 this court heard four cases connected with complaints of Iakov Ivanov Korolev. In Lokotnia, a village of approximately 115 households,[52] Korolev had built a house for the Golovanov family. Korolev's cases stemmed from a dispute over how much Olga Tikhanova and Stepan Prokhorov Golovanov owed him for his work. Korolev tried to force the issue by living in the house and filing suits to evict the Golovanovs from it and to require them to pay him twenty-five rubles. The Golovanovs responded with a counter suit to evict Korolev. The judges considered each case separately and awarded Korolev ten rubles, not twenty-five, as a fair price for his work. In the end, Korolev was evicted from the house on 12 January 1916 on the basis of an earlier agreement made "peacefully" at court.[53]

With their decisions in May 1916 the Iaguninskii judges facilitated a new beginning, not just an end, to Korolev's prospects in Lokotnia. After his evictions, Korolev did not end up landless and homeless. On the day of his eviction case his suit against communal authorities in Lokotnia for an allotment of land and a homestead was also heard. This case was settled amicably between Korolev and the society's representatives: Korolev would have his allotment land. Rounding out the matter, the court clerk recorded subsequently that the Golovanovs paid Korolev the assigned ten rubles. Korolev was unsuccessful in his bid to evict the owners of a house he had built, and he was paid only what the court determined as a fair wage for his labor, but he successfully attained access to a basic economic resource—an allotment of plow-land.[54] This kind of resolution might not have been so easily produced before the war, when a full complement of young men would have been working in and outside villages.

An unqualified good—for most people, anyway—that came with the war was a drop in petty theft in the countryside. This book makes no argument about overall crime rates in rural areas, for township courts could address only misdemeanors.[55] However, the robust use of township courts suggests that numbers of misdemeanor cases corresponded in some fashion to occurrences of petty crime in the countryside. As Table 7.6 shows, criminal cases at township courts fell in Moscow Province even in 1914. Since the predominant type of criminal case prosecuted at township courts was, even more than before the war, about personal dignity, this drop in township caseloads reveals a reduction in economic crime.

This shift in the criminal case docket is clear in the records of individual township courts. At Tsaritsyno, of thirty-four criminal cases heard from January through August 1916, including cases brought by the police, only three were about economic issues. One of these was a charge of theft, another about not reporting a found object, and a third about not being paid for work. Of public welfare cases brought at this time, four concerned inebriation, two were about sanitation, and the rest (one case each) were violations of regulations on carelessness with fire, gambling, and noise. The remainder of criminal cases heard at Tsaritsyno in this period were the usual insults in word (ten cases), as well as beating, threat, *samoupravstvo,* slander, and other assaults on dignity. Thus 59 percent of criminal cases at this court were about people settling disputes over honor and respect. At the Iaguninskii Township Court, in 1916, the array of criminal cases was even more oriented toward dignity cases. At this

Table 7.6. Criminal Cases Registered, Undecided, and Decided, at Township Courts in Four Counties of Moscow Province, 1913–1914, with Average County and Totals for Moscow Province

County	*1913 Reg. Cases*	*1914 Reg. Cases*	*1914 as % of 1913*	*1913 Undecided Cases*	*1914 Undecided Cases*	*1914 Undecided as % of 1913 Undecided*	*% Decided in 1913*	*% Decided in 1914*
Moskovskii	16,764	10,287	61%	2,783	2,616	94%	83%	85%
Bogorodskii	4,642	3,582	77%	416	370	89%	91%	90%
Zvenigorodskii	1,862	1,583	85%	102	69	68%	95%	96%
Klinskii	1,503	1,549	103%	164	108	66%	89%	93%
Average County	2,828	2,102	74%	327	307	94%	88%	85%
Moscow Province	32,524	23,345	72%	4,246	3,986	94%	92%	92%

Source: *OMG 1913–1914.*

court the most common charge by far was "insult in words"—thirty-seven cases—followed by "insult in deed"—twenty-one cases. Of eighty criminal cases heard at Iagunino throughout the year, only three were not about dignity. These were one charge of engaging in illegal commerce, one of disobedience to authority, and one of theft.

The struggle for personal rights—the right not to be insulted or beaten or slandered—thus remained a central issue at township courts throughout the war. Most verbal insult cases were about the usual words. Commonplace insults, reported with some reticence in the court record, were about violations of ethics—accusations of sexual impropriety ("whore") or of deceit ("scoundrel") or of criminality ("convict"). But during the war new bad words began to appear in township court records, as in the following insult case heard by the Tsaritsynskii Township Court.

On 25 August 1916 two townswomen, Vera Aleksandrovna and Evgeniia Nikolaevna Mezhirova, both from the city of Voskresensk, brought a case against Maria Nikolaevna Sokolova, a peasant woman from another county, and a townswoman from Poldol'sk named Olga Nikolaevna Vainshtein. The charge was insult in words. At the same time, the judges, probably wisely, agreed to decide a reverse case, also for insult in words, brought by one of the defendants, the peasant woman Maria Sokolova, against Vera Mezhirova, the first plaintiff in the first case. The parties and six witnesses appeared in court. Vera Mezhirova, a literate woman, supported her case, testifying that the defendants had "sworn at and attacked" her. One of the accused, Olga Vainshtein, a literate townswoman who owned a dacha in the township,[56] testified in her defense that Mezhirova had insulted her. The second defendant, Maria Sokolova, of peasant status and illiterate, testified that Vera Mezhirova had called her a "depraved widow," an insult on which Maria based her countercharge of insult in words against Mezhirova. The six female witnesses—this case was indeed a public one—provided accounts of what had happened. Four of the witnesses supported Mezhirova's charge and told the court the content of the insult. Mezhirova had been called "*zhidovka* [yid-female]." Two witnesses said they had heard Mezhirova call Sokolova a "depraved widow," as defendant Sokolova had claimed. One witness said that Mezhirova had called Sokolova a "depraved widow" and that this had led to a "mutual quarrel."

These charges and countercharges produced one of the longest case records at Tsaritsyno for 1916. In the end, the judges decided that Mezhirova's case for insult was proven and that Sokolova's countercharge was not. They then proceeded to sentence both Vainshtein and Sokolova, but to different punishments. Maria Sokolova, the illiterate peasant woman who had filed the countersuit, was sentenced to fifteen days in jail. Olga Vainshtein, the defendant of townsperson status, was sentenced to five days in jail. Vera Mezhirova was "acquitted."[57] The sentence of Sokolova to fifteen days was the harshest allowed, exceptional in severity for this court and generally for township courts in the war years. Sokolova may have been an exceptionally nasty person; the willingness of so many witnesses, all peasant women, to show up in court to testify against her could be interpreted this way. But it is also conceivable that a particularly grave insult had been uttered. Sokolova had testified that Mezhirova had been the first to begin their insult session, an action that, like "mutual insulting," usually decreased the defendant's responsibility, if it did not end the case altogether. The sentence of Sokolova to fifteen days in jail under circumstances that ordinarily attenuated guilt indicates that the judges at Tsaritsyno, our old acquaintances S. N. Klopov, I. E. Timofeev, A. M. Kiselev, and O. N. Kamochkin, found "yid" a strong insult. They gave no explanation for the lesser sentence of arrest for five days meted out to Olga Vainshtein—a townsperson and probably Jewish herself—but she, too, was punished and not lightly.

This intriguing case shows, at a minimum, that it was possible in late imperial Russia to be sent to jail for uttering an anti-Semitic slur. The case was ordinary in procedural aspects—justice was pragmatic (the countersuit was dismissed), based in part on defendants' pleas (neither of them pleaded not guilty) and primarily on witnesses' testimony. What was new was the particular insult at the township court. In this case, as in others, township judges used familiar rules to address new violations of personal dignity that made their way into the countryside during the war.

Although judges followed the usual rules of evidence in producing their decisions, some aspects of township justice changed in ways that may have facilitated rural society's adjustment to the terrible stresses of the war. Courts in the counties in my survey were able to cut into their criminal case backlogs in 1914, leaving fewer cases unresolved than the year before (see Table 7.6). This meant that decisions, in most cases, could be had even faster than in the prewar years, an important contribution to the attraction of legal process. Second, while small crimes did not cease after August 1914, they were punished somewhat less severely than before the war. My survey of sentences at the township courts suggests that judges, overall, issued somewhat milder punishments in these years.

One might have thought that wartime inflation would have induced judges to punish misdemeanors with fines, rather than arrest, in order to fill up deficits in township funds. My survey revealed a shift in wartime away from sentences of arrest toward sentences in which the convicted person had the option of a fine or arrest. The most common sentence in the war years by far was "fine or arrest"—79 percent of convictions. Only 21 percent of sentences were to arrest alone. This is a shift from the prewar period when the most common sentence (57 percent) in misdemeanor cases was arrest, without the option of paying a fine. People convicted of small crimes in the war years were much less likely to be given a sentence of mandatory arrest and far more likely to be sentenced in a way that made it possible to pay a fine instead of going to jail.

It is highly unlikely that this shift toward optional fines was motivated by a mercenary attitude on the part of judges. The maximum fine remained 15 rubles throughout the war, making it impossible to collect sums that would compensate for inflation. Moreover, during the war, judges reduced both amounts of fines and terms of arrest. In my survey no convicted person was fined the maximum sum of 15 rubles in the war years. The mean fine in my survey fell from 6.49 rubles in the prewar years to 5.93 rubles during the war. Wartime inflation would have further reduced the significance of these smaller fines to convicted people and to local treasuries. Nonetheless, judges did not shift toward compulsory arrest as a disciplinary option but rather swung in the other direction—of making smaller fines an option for convicted people.

Judicial mercy in the matter of fines was matched by a reduction in the length of jail terms. The mean sentence in verdicts in my survey declined from 7.9 days before the war to 5.1 days during wartime. (The median fell from 6.46 days to 3.80 days.) People were sentenced to shorter prison terms, to lower fines, and more frequently received the option to pay rather than go to jail, than had been the case before 14 August 1914. This softening of penal sanctions did not affect payments in civil cases. Before the war half the successful civil suits in my survey were settled for 14 rubles or less; during the war half the civil suits decided in the plaintiff's favor involved awards of more than 22 rubles. The average award in a civil suit rose from 37.69 rubles to 46.27 rubles. As before the war, township judges respected distinctions between kinds of cases and kinds of damages. They ordered higher payments corresponding to inflated prices in civil suits, while reducing penalties, of all kinds, in criminal cases.

Litigants themselves took a role in the milder outcomes of township cases in wartime. The parties in my survey were more inclined to settle their disputes with a formal statement of reconciliation than in the prewar years. The percentage of cases, both civil and criminal, that ended with formal findings of "reconciliation" increased after 1914 from only 2 percent to 10 percent of the cases in my survey. Wartime cases discussed above provide examples of reconciliations after a female plaintiff charged a man with beating. It was not just women plaintiffs and male defendants who reconciled in the war years. In my survey I found reconciliations between male parties (50 percent of reconciliations at this time), between female plaintiffs and male defendants (31 percent), and a few reconciliations between female parties or a male plaintiff and a female defendant. Litigants were generally more likely to reconcile at court during the war than earlier, and reconciliation was more likely if the defendant was male, not female.

These shifts toward milder sanctions and toward reconciliation at township courts do not mean that villages were becoming kind and gentle places. After all, people were still dragging neighbors, husbands, wives, in-laws, and renters into court for many kinds of more or less reprehensible behaviors. And defendants, at least some of them, were still violating regulations, not paying their bills, trying not to relinquish family property to more deserving hands, occasionally stealing something, and, quite often, calling people new and old bad names. The police still arrested people for not cleaning out their courtyards or, in one case, even a newfangled water closet.[58] People were careless with fire and burned down bathhouses.[59] One man, in a tragic reminder of war's meaning, was charged at the Ignatevskii Township Court in August 1916 under Statute 109—"transportation of a corpse from abroad or . . . from one province to another . . . or from one county to another without the requisite permission."[60]

The war, in so many ways, made life for its survivors sadder, harder, and lonelier than in the past. It is a credit to rural people that when forced to deal with sudden transformations of authority and economic conditions they sought official confirmations of new property arrangements. In many—probably the most intractable—struggles over dignity in new contexts, they resorted to resolutions by legal means. It is a testimony to the quality of justice at township courts that judges recognized the needs of local households, invested women with authority when appropriate, legitimated the reallocation of property promptly, and punished violations of personal dignity by, and of, both men and women as they struggled through their new circumstances. Judges' sentences also took an empathetic turn in wartime, making it easier for convicted people to pay fines, serve short terms, and resume hard lives.

CITIZENS AND REVOLUTION

First war, then revolution. Of course, this is not how most people in the empire saw their lives in early 1917. The war was the overwhelming and ongoing transformation in rural society; who knew that a revolution—indeed two—lay ahead? One effect of looking at rural society from inside the township courtroom, with strict attention to chronology, is that the fundamental transformations demanded of and enacted by peasants during the war become visible in their own time. Before February 1917 revolution was not lurking in the corner with the waiting plaintiffs or whispering to the judges as they did their work. But revolution did arrive and, with it, both new opportunities and challenges for rural society and the law in Russia.

The Provisional Government established by Russian liberals and socialists after the fall of the monarchy set about dismantling the old regime. The new governors began this transformation immediately. Contrary to received wisdom, they did not wait for the Constituent Assembly to put their dearest objectives into law. Many of the Provisional Government's initiatives reversed defeats that liberal reformers had suffered in earlier struggles against the autocracy. Quotas on Jews were removed, along with all restrictions based on religion; press censorship was abolished; freedom of assembly was declared. Other radical measures reflected less united struggles from the past: feminists saw their moment and won from their liberal colleagues the right to vote for the Constituent Assembly and all other elected institutions. One of the Provisional Government's first reforms stemmed from a long-term demand of liberal society and addressed directly the foundations of the imperial system. This was the abolition of estates—the official division of the population into peasants, nobility, townspeople, clergy, and other legal categories.[61]

This reform, and others connected with it, was not only the embodiment of Russian liberals' dream of civic equality. It was also a radical assault on the way people had exercised their various rights in the empire and on the whole system of imperial governance. For all their lives, imperial subjects had enjoyed particular legal rights—or not—according to their estate status. The state granted these rights not to each individual but to separate status groups. By eradicating estate distinctions, the Provisional Government threw open the doors to a strange new world where rights might appear up for grabs, or even missing. In the place of estate status, with its allotment of rights, there was a void.

This void was imagined as citizenship by the Provisional Government. People would find their place in the new nation as citizens equal in rights and responsibilities, devoid of status-based privileges and disabilities, subject to the same laws and courts. This dreamworld was not reality in 1917, and it was not clear that even as a dream it was shared by all or many. From March 1917 through the October Revolution and the civil war, the inhabitants of the empire were caught up in the web of suffering, striving, and enduring that would determine the structure of their future polity and the rights survivors would have within it. Where would peasants be in the new state, without their legal rights as peasants? The township courts provided an arena for enacting and claiming the novel status of citizen.

On 9 March 1917, one week after the February Revolution, Sergei Alekseevich Chekaldin, the clerk of the Tsaritsyno court, the same person who for more than three years had meticulously categorized each accuser, defendant, and witness by her or his estate—as "peasant" so and so, *krest'ianka* Pelagea Nikolaevna Riabinina, *krest'ianin* Ivan Il'ich Levin—now identified every court participant as "citizen." This title—*grazhdanin, grazhdanka*—remained consistently in use in Chakaldin's documents, without a single slip or crossing out throughout 368 cases, from March 9 until the records of this township court broke off a year later.[62]

Chekaldin was the clerk in a village not far from Moscow; it is not surprising that he knew of the Provisional Government's decree and could put it into effect in his records immediately. The news may have taken more time to be incorporated elsewhere into township practice. In 1917 the Grebnevskii Township Court in Novaia, about fifty kilometers from Moscow in the heart of the factory and handicraft production region, was busy with the usual suits about payments, debts, and pieces of cloth, as well as the many inheritance cases of wartime. Its scribe, N. Spaskii, gradually took up the new terminology of citizenship. In May Spasskii still recorded the estate of most of the litigants at the township court as "peasant," but by July he was using the titles *"grazhdanin"* and *"grazhdanka"* with only an occasional lapse. By September the word *"krest'ianin"* had all but disappeared from records of the Grebnevskii court's decisions.[63] The title of citizen was not uniformly employed in all the courts I studied. At the Selinskii Township Court, the clerk still recorded the estate of most of the litigants in his files after March 1917. Nonetheless, even the records of this court show some changes in recorded status: in two of the eighteen cases left undecided from 1917, a party was described not as a peasant but as a "soldier."[64]

Clerk's records, no matter how well kept, do not prove that people at court thought differently about their relationship to the state. Nonetheless, the grasp at citizenship by township clerks—and their rejection of estate-based identifications—points to an important, if inadvertent, consequence of the township court system. This system empowered peasants in the governance and regulation of local matters—both through the many strands of local administrative responsibility and through the courts—but the procedures of the township courts also exposed limitations and constraints placed on rural people by the caste system. Nobles did not have to appear at township courts, and they very rarely did so. Townspeople were more likely to participate. Did their occasional victories grate on the minds of peasants? Why did Olga Vainshtein, with her literacy and her townsperson's status, receive a lesser sentence than Maria Sokolova, an illiterate peasant woman, for a reprehensible insult? Whether or not participants gave estate status much thought—something that would be very difficult to measure—the court process itself put estate on display. The registration of litigants' status, the called-out names at trials, the outgoing documents—all manifested the estate system and exposed it, perhaps, to judgment. The township courts offered peasants a chance to use and even shape the law and to make litigation a respected part of rural life. In this process some people may have learned that to be labeled a peasant was a civil disability. For such people, the title of "citizen" made sense.

The revolution meant a new egalitarian address to litigants and witnesses in the courtroom; it also meant new possibilities for conflict, and new authorities, new duties, and more reforms. Over the course of the revolutionary year rural people continued to use township courts for the same purposes and needs as in the first years of the war, but, in time, certain familiar conflicts acquired new dimensions or took on new prominence. In particular, conflicts over land emerged more often in the courts. Even more problematic were uncertainties about the laws and legal procedures to be applied in these and other cases.

In Grebnevskii Township, the summer of 1917 evoked the usual outburst of accusations of unfair harvesting,[65] but the township judges now had to contend with new questions about boundaries and rights in land. Suits brought against a fellow villager or even a family member over crops revealed themselves in court to be controversies about field allotments, household gardens, pastures, and forests. On 8 July Tatiana Nikolaevna Biriukova sued a woman in her family, Elena Sergeevna Biriukova, for one hundred rubles for cutting hay on Tatiana's land. At court it became clear that the real conflict was over rights to the section of land, which earlier had been divided off from a larger lot. To settle the case, the court referred to a decision made on 28 March 1913 by the county congress: the congress had declared that the land in question—a consolidated allotment, no longer eligible for redistribution by the commune[66]—belonged to the defendant. On the basis of this earlier decision, the court ruled that the defendant could not be charged with "illegal harvesting" since the land belonged to her, and rejected the case.[67]

In time, however, new authorities appeared claiming their right to settle land disputes. On 4 September 1917, two months after the Biriukova family case, another charge of violation of land and harvest rights was heard by the Grebnevskii judges. A plaintiff charged Mikhail Anisimovich Frolov, from Novaia, with "cutting on the household plot and seizure of part of the household plot." Frolov's response to the plaintiff's charges was to produce evidence from the township land committee "about the boundary of his household garden." The case was settled in Frolov's favor.[68] But Frolov's opponent, Prokofii Vasil'evich Shubarov, appealed the decision back to the county congress, the authority predating the new township land committee. The conflict over this parcel of land now took on a new dimension, as Shubarov and Frolov squared off over their property rights using different superior authorities to support their claims. The next legal action—after who knows how many other kinds of interventions—was a suit by Frolov against Shubarov heard on 16 October. Based on the township court's decision in favor of his claim, Frolov now required Shubarov to clear a load of brushwood off his land, presumably after Shubarov had used the territory in question as a dumping ground. Next it was Shubarov's turn to claim that the land belonged to him. With the knowledge that their earlier decision was under appeal at the county congress, the township judges decided to postpone a hearing until after the case had been resolved at the higher legal instance.[69]

Mikhail Anisimovich Frolov was a scrappy type, with at least one success behind him at the Grebnevskii Township Court. Earlier in October 1917, he had been summoned to the court in response to Avdotia Andreeva Semenova's complaint that his dog had torn up her apron. Avdotia did not show up for her hearing, but Frolov appeared to testify that the charge was "wrong," and the case was ended.[70] But Frolov could not win his case over household land, because the judges would not prioritize the land committee over the county congress. Unable to find a legal solution to their dispute, the two claimants to the same parcel of land, Shubarov and Frolov, were left to pursue their rivalry by other means.

Other tensions evident in the township courts in 1917 derived from the myriad family quarrels now given a new opening by uncertainties about legal authority. As we have seen, the share of family cases at the township courts rose dramatically in wartime; contests within families continued to be a large share (30 percent) of cases registered at the courts after 1 March 1917.[71] In the Biriukova family's controversy at the Grebnevskii court described above, a family member tried to undo the decision made by the county congress about a land allotment. This was only one of twelve civil cases between contesting family members heard by the court at Novaia between 30 May and 28 December 1917.[72] The subjects of these cases show that family members were bringing a large variety of problems before the judges: four cases were suits; two concerned family support; two requested evictions; and one each was about a harvest violation, an inheritance, a land controversy, and the right to live in a house. Such cases often involved more than one complaint: a suit could arise from a contention over harvesting or land.

These cases at the Grebnevskii court in 1917 were all civil ones. Parties were not claiming a wrong against their persons. Instead, they were asking the court, in numbers far different from those of the prewar years, to settle issues of family property and responsibility. Such requests came from people of older and younger generations, and of both sexes. Fathers sued sons; a mother sued her son; a daughter-in-law sued a mother-in-law; another daughter-in-law sued her father-in-law; a brother-in-law sued his sister-in-law; a son sued his mother. The son mentioned here was trying to evict his mother from "his" house in June 1917, but neither side showed up in court and the case was ended. On 30 May a woman sued her mother-in-law for one-half of the household plot. In this case, after hearing both parties and two witnesses, the judges decided that, since the two women were each paying one-half of the family's taxes on the land allotment and on the household plot, they must each use half the household plot. This decision underlines not only the pragmatic equity of the township court but also the economic charge on this household, now born entirely by women. On 16 October a man sued his son for refusing to support his mother and father. At the end of December 1917 a woman sued her father-in-law for selling their common property left after the death of her husband.[73]

Many of these intra-family cases at the Grebnevskii court were dropped because of the parties' absence; two ended with formal reconciliation. None of them gave the plaintiff a clear victory—as opposed to reconciliation—over the defendant. With plaintiffs coming from both sexes and generations, the judges did not seem to favor any type of family arrangement.[74] Even if a court case did not bring a clear rebuke to one's son or end with a satisfying expulsion of one's mother from a home, the registration of a case gave an official dimension to people's various notions about how to reshape their lives. As before the war and revolution, ending the case by not appearing in court was a sign that the plaintiff had decided to drop the matter. Dropped, ended with reconciliation, rejected, postponed, ended with no award—all these were lawful answers to those who demanded justice at township courts. With these answers and others, township courts continued to enable peaceful, if not amicable, resolutions of family conflicts.

During 1917 an entirely new kind of case made its appearance at the township courts. Controversies over fulfillment of and pay for political duties appeared as suits before township judges. At the Grebnevskii Township Court the first of such cases was heard on 16 October 1917. Petr Viktorovich Babaev from the village of Kostiunino sued the rural society of his own village for thirty rubles. He claimed that he was owed this for his "fulfillment of his delegate's responsibilities at the Shchelkovskii Meeting of Delegates and at the township assembly six times." (Shchelkovo, located on the railroad line to Moscow, was ten miles from Kostiunino.)[75] Representatives from the society of Kostiunino came to the hearing and testified that "the suit is not justified because [Petr Viktorovich, inserted by the clerk] Babaev was elected as a delegate, but he did not go to any of these meetings." The judges decided to postpone the case until Babaev could substantiate his suit with evidence; they wanted a "document."[76] On 30 October Babaev returned again to renew his suit against the society of Kostiunino, but once again the judges demanded evidence, this time specifying that they needed witnesses to his alleged fulfillment of these new political duties.[77]

Such cases appeared at other courts in the revolutionary year. At the Selinskii Township Court P. Saraev, the leader of the village of Pershutino, filed a suit on 23 July against his co-villager, Selivestr Sal'nikov, for "not fulfilling his public duties."[78] Before the revolution officials could be prosecuted for nonfulfillment of their duties by bringing a complaint to the county congress or to the land captain. After the February Revolution and the disappearance of the administrative ladder of the imperial administration, some rural people apparently decided that the township court was the authority that could sanction people who did not perform their official duties or, as in Babaev's case, compel the public to pay for a new kind of social service.

BREAKDOWN FROM ABOVE

Neither the leader from Pershutino in Selinskii Township nor Petr Babaev, the demanding delegate from Kostiunino in Grebnevskii Township, were able to find satisfaction at their township courts. Saraev's case was listed by the Selinskii township clerk as "unfinished" in a report sent out on 1 December 1917.[79] Try as they might to keep up with the demands from families, officials, delegates, and others for decisions of their cases, judges at township courts in the year of revolutions found themselves confronted by a critical technical problem. The documents were missing. Or going missing, or not delivered, or not drawn up.

By October 1917 the judges at Grebnevskii Township were postponing or rejecting a significant proportion of their cases for lack of adequate documentary evidence. In seven civil cases out of nineteen heard that month, the judges noted that missing documents, undelivered summonses, or the absence of a record from another instance prevented them from deciding the case. (Two more cases were cited as having insufficient evidence of an unspecified kind.) Documents—the obsession of both judges and litigants at township courts—were essential to settling the complex cases that were now being registered in the rural areas, but they were becoming harder to obtain.

Once in a while the necessary document could still be produced, as in the case of a townswoman who showed up at the Grebnevskii court on 16 October 1917 to pursue her suit against a village society for taking away land that had belonged to her mother. No village representatives appeared at the trial, an unusual occurrence. In such a circumstance the court could have made a judgment in favor of the plaintiff but, instead, the judges, Rulev, Teretin, Il'in, and Lobanov postponed the case, demanding that the plaintiff present documentary evidence of her right to inherit her mother's land. Perhaps the rural society in question knew that the judges would rule in this fashion. The townswoman was making a claim that could have been connected to the uncertainties of the period: she may have hoped that the township court would use its flexible procedures (see chapter 4) to decide her inheritance case. Two weeks later the plaintiff returned to court with the appropriate document. The judges, true to their principles, cited this 1909 decision and ruled that the village society should return the land allotment to the townswoman. It is tempting to surmise that the rural society in question had also tested the waters of the new revolutionary world by reclaiming a land allotment that had escaped from communal control at an earlier point. The court stayed with the written record and ruled for the land to be allotted according to the available legal ruling from 1909.[80]

In 1917 it seemed that everybody wanted documents. Earlier in the year the representatives of the village of Shchelkovo brought a suit against a townswoman for a map of their village. Both the village representatives and the townswoman appeared in court where they came to a peaceful agreement. The defendant agreed to return the map to the village or to buy them a new one.[81]

But what if the documents did not appear? As the year went on, documents became the objects, not the evidence, in several court cases. Some people learned fast: in October citizen Petr Viktorovich Babaev, who had been turned down in his suit against the society of Kostiunino for payment for his delegate service, sued Petr Mikhail Shokin, the village leader, for a receipt. Babaev claimed that Shokin had not given him a receipt for his payment of dues to the village of five rubles, fifty kopeks.[82] Shokin came to court and testified that he had indeed received the money but from a third party. The judges dismissed the case for lack of evidence. Babaev did not let this drop. Two weeks later he was back in court, again suing Shokin for the receipt for his money, and this time Babaev had a witness on his side. The witness, Egor Varniveevich Zarubik, testified that "he, being the leader [of a work team] received from the Arman' factory money as dues from the account of Petr Babaev-Vladimirov and this money, five rubles, fifty kopeks, he gave to the leader of the village of Kostiunino, Petr Shokin, according to a receipt." Shokin did not bother to show up for this hearing. The judges ruled in Babaev's favor and called on Shokin to provide Babaev with a receipt.[83]

This suit intimates that other kinds of conflicts may have lain behind Babaev's and Shokin's duels at court. Babaev was a factory worker, just the type to be a delegate to those newfangled meetings, and he also was a peasant owing dues to his village society, led by Petr Shokin. In October 1917 at least one of their conflicts was played out at the township court. There, the worker-peasant-delegate-citizen Babaev was granted his right to have his document.

Back at the Tsaritsynskii Township Court, documents were also becoming part of the problem. Our by now familiar clerk, Sergei Alekseevich Chekaldin, the keeper of the record books at Tsaritsyno, was himself sued in the township court on 27 July 1917. His opponent was Grigorii Ivanovich Gubantsev, citizen of the village of Shaidrovo, as judiciously recorded by Chekaldin himself in the case records. In the complaint filed on 12 June, Gubantsev claimed that Chekaldin had "lost" a document about land. The first court date had been set for 21 June, but a delay in sending out the summonses appears to have caused a postponement of the hearing. The delay itself may reflect observance of legal propriety: another clerk sent out the summons to Gubantsev, whereas Chekaldin sent one only to himself! It may not have been appropriate for Chekaldin, as both clerk and defendant, to summon Gubantsev to court. As requested by the plaintiff, a witness was also called. This was Osip Nikiforovich Kamochkin, who had served as a judge at Tsaritsyno from 1914 to February 1917.[84]

Chekaldin did not confront his challenger in court. Instead, he submitted a handwritten declaration to the court, dated 27 July 1917, the day of the case. Clearly miffed, he composed the following text:

> To the Tsaritsynskii Township Court:
>
> On 27 July I am called to the court by citizen Grigorii Ivanovich Gubantsev about some kind of document. . . . I declare to the court that during the period of my service as secretary of this court, when documents were presented by parties at the court, the court [i.e., the judges] took them personally, but not I. Besides, if a document had been presented by Gubantsev, then the whole case of documents would have been given to Secretary Dovgopolenko, for which I have certification, given me by the Tsaritsynskii Regional Committee, in return for the transfer of the matter, dated 14 June 1917, no. 655. I cannot appear in court myself on personal matters. I ask that the matter be judged in my absence and that the suit be refused as unproven.
>
> Citizen S. Chekaldin
> 27 July 1917[85]

This case was heard by a new group of judges who appeared at the Tsaritsynskii Township Court in the summer of 1917. The array of men on the bench changed several times over the course of the year. On 23 February the court turned over entirely, with the exception of one of the older judges, A. M. Kiselev, who took the place of the outgoing president, S. N. Klopov. This court—

Kiselev, A. S. Skorospelov, M. F. Barinov, and V. I. Kolotilin—had presumably been chosen for a regular three-year term by the usual election procedures and the land captain, the old judges having all served at least since 1914. This new team lasted just over two months—clearly a break with the old rules; on 10 May half of them were replaced. A new presiding judge, R. P. Soldatov from Blizhne-Beliaevo,[86] replaced Kiselev, and one new judge, I. F. Matveev, replaced one of the newly elected judges. The two other judges chosen for 1917 under the old regime, Skorospelov and Barinov, remained on the bench. Part way through the summer, another new judge, Burlakov, occasionally joined the court as a substitute. There were no further changes until 23 November, when Soldatov, the presiding judge, disappeared from the court, and one new man, Nikolaev, joined in his place. The court met eighty-three times in 1917, as usual more frequently in July, August, and September than in other months.[87]

But back to Chekaldin's case. On 27 July, in accord with Chekaldin's request, the Soldatov court ruled that the case would be ended as "unproven."[88] This was not the end of the document affair, however. Gubantsev filed a second suit against Chekaldin after the failure on 27 July. This time the court date was set for 3 August. Once again the summonses went out to Chekaldin, Gubantsev, and Osip Nikiforovich Kamochkin. When Kamochkin, the former judge, received his summons, he replied to the court by filling it out as follows: "In the circumstance of my inability to appear personally on this [case], I hereby testify in writing—about the case of Gubantsev and Chekaldin I cannot testify to anything, nothing has been admitted. Osip Kamochkin." By the time the case was heard, Gubantsev must have realized that it was hopeless. He did not come to court on 3 August. The judges in this summer month of 1917–R. P. Soldatov, M. F. Barinov, Burlakov, and I. Matveev—dismissed the case for nonappearance of the plaintiff.[89]

Chekaldin was off the hook, but this case shows how documents, and their control, had become critical to people seeking to defend their possessions or increase them during the great uncertainty unleashed by revolution. Grigorii Ivanovich Gubantsev was also involved in a dispute with his brother, Dmitri, against whom he had filed a civil suit about "hay." The two men came from a family of some stature in Shaidrovo, where a Gubantsev had been the leader in 1915. But without the precious document Grigorii Ivanovich could not pursue his suit. His second case scheduled for 3 August was also dropped for nonappearance of the plaintiff.[90]

The demand for resolution of intra-family conflicts such as Gubanstev's became acute at township courts as men of the younger generation came home from war. From March through December 1917 the percentage of cases in my survey involving sons or brothers more than doubled compared to that of the prewar years and quadrupled from that of wartime before the revolution.[91] To revise the reallocations of family and other property that had taken place during the war, these men—and their opponents—needed documents to show who had possessed what, and when. A person like Chekaldin, who knew where documents could be located, might be thought to hold extraordinary power and to be capable of abusing it.

The courts needed their own documents to function, and here, too, the revolution was wreaking havoc with the orderly resolution of cases. What if summonses were not delivered? In October 1917 the Grebnevskii judges began to postpone cases because parties had not been summoned to the court. "The summons was not delivered to the plaintiff," declared the court in a civil suit about boards on 16 October. In three cases scheduled for November 1917 the nondelivery of summonses to one or several parties meant that hearings had to be put off.[92] The Grebnevskii court was only able to decide seven of the seventeen civil cases it scheduled from 30 October 1917 through its last session of the year on 28 December. The ten other cases had to be postponed because documents were missing, summonses were not delivered, and parties—for these or other respectable reasons—did not come to court.[93]

One reason summonses were not being delivered was the ever greater institutional chaos of 1917. Some of the Provisional Government's many new initiatives were put into effect quite easily, at least in the first part of the year. In Tsaritsynskii Township, for example, the court began in April to forward its appeals not to the land captain but to the "Judicial Commissar of the Sixth District of Moscow County." On all the court's forms, the title "land captain" was crossed out and replaced with "Commissar."[94] Officials on duty in villages acquired new ranks as well; on 20 April 1917 the "Rural Commissar" of the village of Shatilovo brought an insult charge against a co-villager to the Tsaritsynskii township court.[95] Titles were the easy part. The real problems began as new institutions emerged and intersected with old ones, leaving people to guess which way to turn. The leaders of the Provisional Government, supposedly in charge of this restructuring of the state, began to panic. In their haste to put resources where they counted most—as they saw it—people in Petrograd could forget entirely about the ordinary citizen's need for legal recourse.

On 17 April 1917 the Ministry of Justice of the Provisional Government issued its "Temporary Regulation on the Police." A duty of the police, according to the new law, was to assist "governmental or social organs in fulfilling their duties." This aid "by analogy with the duties of the former police" consisted in part of "serving various institutions by delivering summonses, announcements, and other kinds of official paper." The Ministry of Justice felt compelled to prioritize these services. On 9 October 1917 a circular went out from the Second Department of the Ministry to all "Presidents and Procurors of Judicial Instances." The circular observed with anguished rationalism that

> the small number of personnel of the police, the variety and complexity of the direct responsibility laid upon it for maintaining public order and security, in connection with the extreme difficulty of carrying out duties in contemporary conditions of general disorganization, leads even without this . . . to the extraordinary burdening of police work and, as a consequence of this, . . . to a lowering of the qualitative level of such work.

Therefore the Minister of Justice, in accord with the Minister of Internal Affairs, advised all judicial institutions to use the police to deliver official papers "as little as possible," and only when no other means, such as the "post and special delivery" were available.[96] So much for summonses.

Perhaps this circular had something to do with the collapse of the summons system in Grebnevskii Township in late October.[97] Even if police were not the problem, the delivery of summonses—usually a very rapid operation—had come to a halt in the township, and with it most of the court's ability to do its job. Without the delivery of documents to get people to court and without documents to use as evidence, township justice would have to confine itself to the extremely local and the oral.[98]

Just as problematic for the township courts, and increasingly so as the year went on, was the question of which institution's documents, if they could be had, would count. People scrambled to find documents that would support their cases, but before 1917 at least they all knew the hierarchy of decision-making bodies. Rural assemblies could be trumped by township courts and township courts by the county congress or the land captain; above these institutions stood the provincial board; above that the Senate; and over it the emperor. It was not surprising that an enterprising litigant like Praskovia Aref'eva, with whom we began our judicial journey, would know the way up and down—and therefore around—the legal ladder. But what was one to do after March 1917?

DISORDERING THE LAW

The Provisional Government, with pleasure, kicked the legal ladder out from over the township courts in the early months of post-autocratic Russia. The first imperative was getting rid of what liberals and socialists regarded as repressive judicial institutions. On 4 March the chambers of the Senate, appeals instances, and circuit courts that dealt with anti-state crimes were abolished; amnesties for various kinds of political offenses were declared on 6 March. Even earlier, Alexander Kerenskii, as Minister of Justice, had begun to reform the courts with a decree establishing "temporary courts" in Petrograd to deal with "regrettable misunderstandings in the city between soldiers, the population, and workers."[99] These decrees initiated several months of abolitions, reforms, new regulations, and new institutions—in short, a nightmare for anyone seeking a clear path to state justice. Making matters even more difficult, the Provisional Government's rival for authority, the Petrograd Soviet (Council) of Workers' Deputies, and other soviets linked to it, were also issuing orders and asserting their authority in matters that earlier would have been submitted to judicial or administrative authorities.[100]

The new structures of governance asserted by various revolutionary authorities began to take their toll on the orderly business of township courts in the first months after the February Revolution. A major problem, as we have seen, was land and land-related suits about harvests, but which were the authorities that could provide the "real" documents for these cases? At the Grebnevskii

Township Court opponents such as Frolov and Shubarov could not resolve their conflict, because each resorted to a different authority. Was it the township *zemstvo* land committee, the village assembly, the new village-level "rural committee," the old county congress, or a new "soviet" at any level to whom courts and parties should turn?[101] By the fall of 1917 courts were stymied by the conflict of authorities above and around them.

At Tsaritsyno, not far from Moscow, the township court's new judges in May 1917 tried their best to integrate their work with the new non-regime. The first case heard by the new bench headed by Roman Pavlovich Soldatov was a suit from a citizen of the village of Khokhlovo brought against a citizen of the village of Shaidrovo for land. The judges' finding stated: "This case itself is not adjudicable according to the instructions of the Provisional Government." Their decision was to end the case and "send it for consideration to the Soviet of Peasants' Deputies of the Tsaritsynskii district." This was the recommended destination for three more civil cases heard at the court that day. All these cases remained undecided in the court's records at the end of the year.[102] To recognize the new authorities, the Tsaritsynskii court tried to update its record-keeping practices in 14 December 1917 by crossing out inappropriate lines in the rubrics for each case entry. Using pages printed for use in 1915, the clerk changed the announcement of parties' rights to appeal. Appeals were henceforth to go not to the outmoded land captain but to the county congress of Justices of the Peace. This change lasted for one case, after which the clerk apparently bowed to reality and simply crossed out all references to a right to appeal.[103]

One reason for the Tsaritsynskii court's early and repeated efforts to send cases on to the district's new Soviet of Peasant Deputies was the political savvy—or at least activism—of our well-connected clerk, Sergei Alekseevich Chekaldin. Chekaldin had been the clerk at Tsaritsyno since 1914 and had served the court headed by S. N. Klopov, until Klopov was replaced in February 1917. In 1917 Sergei Alekseevich leaped into the new world of unknown possibilities, while still carrying out his old duties as the township clerk. He served faithfully under Klopov's replacement and two subsequent presiding judges at the Tsaritsynskii court; at the same time, he had become the president of the "rural meeting of the village of Marino." This rural meeting (*sel'skoe sobranie*) was another reconfiguration of the revolutionary year, apparently a replacement for the rural assembly (*sel'skii skhod*) of, by then, bygone days. Chekaldin also became a member of the "Township Committee of Soviets of Peasants' Deputies," in circumstances that suggest the unraveling of old power structures in the township and the enticing possibilities open to the young and educated in 1917.[104]

On 3 August 1917, the same day the Soldatov court dismissed Gubanstev's case against Chekaldin for losing a document, Chekaldin himself was the plaintiff in a criminal case at Tsaritsyno. His charge was "insult in words and threats" against Sergei Nikitich Klopov, the former presiding judge of the Tsaritsynskii court. One word was that old favorite "scoundrel," but the others included two novel insults. In 1917 "robber" and "cheat" made their appearance as insulting terms.[105] Klopov did not appear in court and the judges decided the matter in his absence. Four men showed up as witnesses. Ilia Matveevich Chebyshev testified that

> the affair took place at a meeting at which the president of the meeting was Sergei Alekseevich Chekaldin; the question was why had Sergei Nikitich Klopov been expelled from the township committee of the group of members of Peasants' Deputies. Then, Sergei Nikitin Klopov, in a quarrel with Chekaldin, called the latter the following: cheat, scoundrel, and besides he said, that [illeg., you'd?] sell your hide to the future township *zemstvo*.

The testimony of the next witness, Sergei Grigor'evich Bakalov, retold the same story but added revealing information:

> The question they were considering related to the exclusion of Sergei Nikitin Klopov from the group of members of the . . . Committee of Soviets of Peasants' Deputies and the naming in his place of Sergei Alekseevich Chekaldin. At that time S. N. Klopov appeared at the meeting, drunk, and inflicted insult on Chekaldin, calling him [illeg.], scoundrel, cheat.

The judges decided that the case was proven by the evidence and ordered Klopov to pay the maximum fifteen-ruble fine or spend seven days in jail. Klopov paid the fifteen rubles on 27 September.[106] Was it any satisfaction to him that this incident was recorded, officially, by the township court? Chekaldin, in any case, was moving up into what appeared to be the new officialdom at the expense of the old judge.

Although civil disputes were becoming increasingly difficult to resolve as the superstructure ceased to be a structure, the township court at Tsaritsyno, as elsewhere, continued to schedule and hear cases for the whole of 1917. Even without the ability to resolve most civil matters about property, the courts were able to accommodate the demands of plaintiffs to punish others for insulting them. Procedures continued to be followed as struggles over authority heated up. The president of the court, Roman Pavlovich Soldatov, excused himself from the bench immediately after Chekaldin's insult charge was heard on 3 August. It turned out that Soldatov himself was the plaintiff in the next case. He accused three men, citizens, of course, of insulting him. This round of insults had also taken place at a meeting, and the names called included "robber," "cheat," and "fat-cat lawyer."[107] Three witnesses appeared, one woman and two men. It might appear that things were getting entirely out of hand, but the parties reconciled at court, and the next week Soldatov returned to the bench.[108]

As Chekaldin's and Soldatov's cases show, local authorities themselves turned to the court in defense of honor. And honor needed more defense than ever in late 1917. More new bad words began to be flung about, carelessly or not. In addition to the novel "robber" and "cheat," some people were called "hooligans"—new to the Tsaritsynskii court as a term of abuse.[109] On 12 October an original word appeared in a case at Tsaritsyno, but people at the court seemed unable to decide whether it was insulting. Citizen Elizabeta Grigor'evna Kashkana charged Il'ia Dmitr'evich Noskov, under Statute 130 (insult oral or written), with calling her "various words, [including] a shit."[110] Shit—*sterva*—was nothing new in 1917, but the discussion at court revealed that another term was in question. The defendant Noskov "explained that he had not pronounced any insulting words in addressing Kashkova. He had only said that she was "bourgeois." *Burzhui*—was this an insult? A witness, Maria Iakovlevna, testified, apparently in Noskov's favor, that he had "not addressed any insulting words to Elizabeta Grigor'evna Kashkina. There had only been a contradiction between them. He only said on what basis she, Kashkina, wanted to recall him to the front." The judges found the case unproven and acquitted Noskov.[111]

As before the revolution, defending one's dignity at court was not a matter reserved to any sex, generation, or occupation. The new authorities were under verbal siege by their elders, and other young men, not part of township officialdom, were turning to the courts as well. In 1917 soldiers and "comrades" appeared at township courts in insult cases—not just as defendants but also as plaintiffs charging others with violations of their dignity. Being convicted as an insulter did not go down well with these young men. On 13 July 1917 Fedor Aleksandrovich Shutkov submitted a petition to the Tsaritsynskii Township Court, requesting that he be given more time to appeal his conviction on 20 April of insulting Vasilii Grigor'ev Ereshin, his co-villager in Shatilovo. In that case, Shutkov had been sentenced to ten days of arrest for insulting Ereshin, a "civil policeman"—yet another new title—with an old bad word, "scoundrel," and a new one, "hooligan."[112] Shutkov still wanted to appeal this decision in July. Chekaldin recorded his request as follows:

> From the written declaration . . . Fedor Aleksandrovich Shutkov asks the Court to give him the right of an extension of the time for an appeal of the decision of this court from 28 April of this year, no. 8. . . . The permit for the appeal he bases . . . on the circumstance that being on the Moscow Provincial Executive Committee of the Soviet of Peasants' Deputies, he has absolutely no free time and therefore he could not appeal the court's decision of 20 April on time.

The judges found this request "worthy." Their decision noted that the defendant Shutkov had been "busy daily at the Moscow Provincial Executive Committee of the Soviet of Peasants' Deputies." He was given a second thirty-day period to appeal his case.[113]

Turnover on the bench at Tsaritsyno may have been a factor in this case. On 20 April, when Shutkov had failed to appear to defend himself against the "civil policeman," the judges had been the president, A. M. Kiselev, in addition to A. S. Skorospelov, M. F. Barinov, and V. I. Kolotilin, the men elected and chosen for the regular 1917–1920 term. By the very next session, R. P. Soldatov had replaced Kiselev as president, and I. F. Matveev had replaced V. I. Kolotilin. This was the court, half old, half new, headed by the activist Soldatov as president, that decided Shutkov's case for an extension with apparent enthusiasm on 13 July.[114]

The township court at Tsaritsyno was both sympathetic to the new politics of summer 1917 and well linked, through the clerk, to local Soviet of Peasants' Deputies. Judges and litigants seem to have found no contradiction between the justice of the township courts and the authority of "meetings," "committees," and "councils [soviets]." Residents of the township, including those newly returning, continued to seek justice at the township court. These litigants—all citizens now—included soldiers, deputies, at least one "civil policeman," and, beginning in July, "*tovarishchi* [comrades]."

Comrades could worry about their dignity, too, and with some reason. One witness in the first case brought by a comrade for insult at Tsaritsyno testified that "he heard how Koniaev [the defendant] fell upon Comrade Lunev with various insulting words, fool, swindler, and others." A second witness added that Koniaev had used the word "villain," and that Lunev, as he had claimed, had indeed been performing his "official duties" when the insult had occurred. One might think that this comrade would have won his case, but the outcome was otherwise. Koniaev and Comrade Lunev reconciled at court. Both signed the record book.[115]

This outcome was not anomalous. From postrevolutionary hindsight it may appear that things were heating up in Tsaritsynskii Township in the second half of 1917, but the court was, in fact, a place for cooling down. Litigants came to peaceful, official reconciliations in 17 percent of the criminal cases heard by the court after the February Revolution and before the end of the year. This was an increase not only over prewar times but over 1916, when less than 15 percent of cases at Tsaritsyno ended in reconciliation. In 1917, after the February Revolution, one-quarter of the intra-family criminal cases at Tsaritsyno came to a mutual and official settlement, and 15 percent of the nonrelated parties settled in this fashion. When the parties were officials, such as Judge Soldatov and Comrade Lunev, one-quarter of the cases were concluded peacefully.[116]

Hampered in the final resolution of civil cases, the judges at Tsaritsyno still managed to hear seventy-seven criminal cases between 23 March and 14 December 1917. In these hearings, fathers and sons, wives and husbands, mothers-in-law and daughters-in law, and other combinations of relatives, unrelated women, unrelated men, officials, and citizens without an office charged each other with violations of what they thought to be the correct way to live. The only kind of party who no longer appeared at court after the February Revolution was the police, with the exception of one "civil policeman" who appeared as a plaintiff in an insult case. Not a single constable brought a charge about drinking or dirt. But there were plenty of other issues to litigate about: beatings, small thievery (boards, firewood, a tablecloth), *samoupravstvo,* threats, carelessness with animals, refusal to support a family member, and above all, as usual, verbal and occasionally written insults using all those words. The township courts gave soldiers returning from the front a legal forum for their concerns, just as it had been available to women and mostly older men for the reordering of family affairs after young men left for war. The court at Tsaritsyno was flooded in the summer of 1917 with cases between spouses, and between fathers and sons, as married couples made the difficult transition to living together once again and male relatives reworked the management of family—and individual—resources. As long as the issue was not land, or documents, judges were likely to be able to come to a decision and send people on their way. Overall, at Tsaritsyno between 23 March and 14 December 1917, plaintiffs and defendants won outright almost equally (35 and 36 percent of decisions respectively), 17 percent of cases were ended with reconciliations, and 12 percent ended in other kinds of outcomes, such as postponement or shared guilt. In some kinds of cases, families and neighbors could return home from court with an official resolution of their conflicts.

There were signs—at court—of a different kind of trouble. On 13 July Vasilii Semenovich Belov charged three people, Mikhail Trofimovich Krasnoshchenkov and his son and wife with "inflicting a beating and seizing a weapon." A witness attested to the fact that there had been a fight. A gun had made its appearance during a quarrel in a garden. This was taken very seriously by the Soldatov court. The judges decided that "both sides had disturbed the social peace and order" and sentenced both the plaintiff and defendant (the father of the family) to a fine of ten rubles or five days in jail. They both paid their fines three months later on 11 October.[117]

More was to come. On 17 August Maksim Trofimovich Krasnoshchenkov (Mikhail's brother?) came to court with a countercharge against Vasilii Semenovich Belov. In his accusation, under Statute 172 (attempted theft), Krasnoshchenkov claimed that Belov had "insulted him with words and in addition taken a gun and theatened him with it." Belov pleaded not guilty. This time no witnesses appeared, and the judges, on these grounds, rejected the case.[118] In October a different kind of "threat" was cited in a criminal case: Ivan Petrovich Riabinin claimed that Emelian Vladimirovich Ivanin had threatened to kill him. Although the defendant pleaded not guilty, a female witness told the court that Ivanin had said, "he will kill Riabinin." A second female witness supported this. The defendant was a renter of quarters from the accuser, who had taken him to court for other reasons. A witnessed threat to kill someone was a misdemeanor, and Ivanin was sentenced to a four-ruble fine or two days in jail. There is no record that this sentence, delivered on 7 October, was ever fulfilled.[119]

Not until January 1918 did anyone claim at the Tsaritsynskii court that a gun had actually been fired in a dispute. The new year's first criminal case, heard on 11 January, was about a charge of "inflicting threat to kill [the plaintiff]," breaking a window, and firing a shot. The case had to be postponed. Another charge of "shooting a revolver in the vicinity of residential buildings" was heard on February 1 and dropped because an address for the defendants could not be found.[120] The records of the Tsaritsynskii Township Court end abruptly on 14 March 1918, the date meticulously noted in both old and new style by the clerk.[121]

The township courts did not collapse in 1917; they tried to do their work. Judges, scheduled for turnover in any case, were gradually and partially replaced, putting both experienced men and newcomers on the bench. Women, fathers, and affronted sons continued to come to the courts to sort out family property, to allocate responsibility, and to defend their dignity as they had done throughout the war and earlier. Returning soldiers, comrades, and political activists like Chekaldin used township courts to deal with challenges they confronted in the unprecedented uncertainty of the revolutionary year. As might be expected at a time when families had to respond to deaths, absences, and returns, the share of family cases at courts increased. Sons and brothers, perhaps considering themselves deserving of authority after their service to the polity, appeared more frequently than ever before at township courts to pursue their ideas of just deserts.

Reconciliations were more frequent in these cases after February 1917 than before, but all outcomes, especially in view of what came next, could be described as peaceful. Judges and litigants gave no sign that they wanted this system of official, legal resolution of small criminal charges and civil suits to end. Energetic men who chose to throw themselves into "official duties" in the Soviet of Peasant Deputies were also active at rural courts. There was no crisis in township jurisprudence, as it had been animated by rural people for more than fifty years. The problem, for peasants and all other citizens of the new Russia, was that the structures of government were collapsing around them. The ability to settle ordinary and extraordinary disputes legally depended on confidence that court decisions were backed by the state. Without a state, where could the majesty of law be found, no matter how good the justice at township courts?

A Different Justice?

A STORY THAT LASTS A HUNDRED YEARS

During the 1860s Russian statesmen and intellectuals regarded reform of the empire's legal system as an essential element of their various efforts to modernize the autocracy. The transformation of the courts was seen as vital to integrating peasants into the polity.[1] Countering the objection that a jury trial system could not be introduced because of the "ignorance of the people," one committee referred to the history of the jury trial in England:

> It is hardly the case that the English people of that time were more educated than ours. England introduced the jury trial everywhere its dominion was achieved, and everywhere this institution brought about beneficial consequences. The jury trial exists even in New Zealand. *Is it possible that the savages of that island are more developed than our people?* To decide about the guilt of a criminal, you need only common sense and conscience—nothing more.[2]

Confidence in the reasoning and morals of "our people" infused mid-nineteenth-century plans for legal reform. Russian peasants who were supposed to be the equivalent of English commoners of four hundred years earlier and at the same time more advanced than New Zealanders of their own day would have the "common sense and conscience" to use the law for the general good.

After the creation of the township courts, this belief in peasant legal wisdom gave way to a hegemonic view of peasants as benighted and even dangerous to the polity. As Yanni Kotsonis shows in his study of the cooperative movement, agronomists and other experts insisted that peasants had to be led by specialists, even in the most fundamental aspect of their lives—their work on the land.[3] The township courts came to be regarded as retrograde institutions, fostering peasants' inveterate traditionalism, their lack of civilization, and their adherence to customary not state law. The "small jury" principle of township jurisprudence, the representational procedures for choosing judges, the courts' strict adherence to statute law, the rendering of judgments by peasants' peers were not noticed by elite commentators. Villagers were imagined as unlettered victims of duplicitous tsarist officials, greedy local strongmen, and arbitrary rulings at township courts.[4] Separateness became a dominant element in elite discussions of peasants and the law.

The notion of a radical distinction between peasant customary law and state law, between peasant litigation in township courts and legal process in circuit courts (with their lawyers and juries), has lived on in scholarship on Russia.[5] The carryover of prerevolutionary assumptions into today's historiography is often supported by references to nineteenth-century sources—proverbs, ethnographic work by Russian scholars, and literary classics. In arguments against the apparently preposterous idea that peasants were full-fledged participants in the Russian legal system, the telling blow is often delivered by recounting a well-known short story. In my efforts to defend the proposition of peasant legal culture, I discovered—to my horror—that my strongest opponent was Anton Chekhov and, in particular, his story "The Plotter."

This very short story—four and a half pages—was first published in 1885 in a St. Petersburg newspaper. The narrative follows an encounter between a judicial investigator and a peasant accused of having stolen a nut from a railroad tie. The peasant, Denis Grigor'ev, says he needed the nut to use as a sinker to catch fish. He refuses to acknowledge that his action put people's lives in danger—this shocks him—and provides an obfuscating series of responses to the investigator's exasperated questions. At the end of the interview Denis Grigor'ev is hauled off to jail, all the while declaring his innocence of any serious crimes—he doesn't steal, he doesn't fight, he pays his taxes—and bemoaning the injustice of judges. Denis Grigor'ev claims that his former lord would have shown this judge a thing or two. "You have to judge skillfully. . . ," he mutters, "OK, so maybe you whip someone, but for something real, according to conscience."[6]

This story enjoyed widespread and long-term popularity. It was republished in a compilation of Chekhov's stories in 1886, appeared in twelve subsequent editions of this collection issued in the 1890s, and is included in Chekhov's collected works. Tolstoy was an enthusiast of the story; Gorky was an enthusiast of Tolstoy's enthusiasm.[7] In the 1990s, more than a century after its publication, "The Plotter" was cited by many of my colleagues and friends as evidence of the hopelessly naive mentality of "the" Russian peasant.[8] A historian in Moscow observed:

> Denis cannot realize that he has committed a crime, he is a malefactor only in the eyes of a magistrate but not in his own eyes. Russian peasantry and Russian authorities are quite apart, they are two distant worlds totally incomprehensible to each other.[9]

Chekhov's message, according to interpreters then and now, was that peasants lived by a different moral code, could not understand the reformed legal system, and thus constituted a threat to the public good. The idea of responsibility to society and accountability before the law were unthinkable by peasants. They lived by different rules.

SEPARATE AND LEGAL

In early twentieth-century and subsequent discussions of Russian culture, peasants' lack of legal consciousness was used as evidence, not posed as a question. An inability to understand the law served as proof of peasants' difference from "normal" people. In discussions of Russian law, the concept of peasant difference was also used as evidence, not posed as a question, to explain why peasants did not have a legal culture. They could not, because they were peasants and therefore unlike others in their ideas of justice and legality. These interlocking discourses of difference relied on a profoundly anti-democratic political demography. The purported way of being of approximately 85 percent of the population was described explicitly as exotic, while the purportedly responsible and law-abiding values of civilized elites—the "educated society" who constituted a minority of the empire's people—established norms for ordinary conduct.[10] Setting aside this upside-down conception of normality in Russian life, let us distinguish between the two ordinarily intertwined lines of argument and ask two separate questions. Did Russian peasants in the early twentieth century have a legal culture? Were Russian peasants in the early twentieth century significantly different from others in their polity?

My answer to the first question is straightforward and is based on the evidence of rural people's usage of township courts. This was the instance of the legal system made most accessible to peasants after the emancipation, and for more than half a century peasants used this legal opportunity extensively and voluntarily. The massive and increasing numbers of cases at the township courts speak for themselves. By the early twentieth century the township courts were a well-used forum for state-sanctioned resolution of small suits and misdemeanor charges. By their use of these courts, peasants demonstrated that they had a legal culture; they regarded township court decisions as a means to settle problems with their neighbors, laborers, employers, renters, buyers, sellers, and family members. A strong indicator of the significance of township courts and law in rural life is the changing usage of these courts during the war and revolution. When families fell—literally—under the stress of war, surviving members went to township courts to attain legal reallocations of household and village property. When men came home from the front, expecting to claim authority and property from the women and old folk who had managed households in wartime, families went to court to find legal ways to reconfigure power and responsibility. Men and women, young and old, appeared in township courts throughout these years to seek legal recognition of their right to live unsullied by verbal and other insults to their persons.

Formality, particularly with respect to statute law and documentary evidence, was abundant at township courts. Decisions were based strictly on imperial law, set forth in *The General Regulation on Peasants* and the *Statutes on Punishments Applicable by the Justices of the Peace.* Court procedures required adherence to basic rules of evidence: an account of the charge, testimony from both sides and witnesses, signatures on testimony and verdicts, provision of reasons for the decision, and citation of relevant statutes. Announcement of the right to appeal and provision of an opportunity for formal reconciliation were consistently part of township court hearings. Reports on all cases were forwarded to a higher authority for review. Both the land captain and the county congress were accountable for the procedural regularity of courts in their purview. That three or four judges—rather than a full-fledged jury—made decisions and issued verdicts did not make the township courts a place of "custom." Decision making at township courts, like that of other instances, was a blend of rules and content, but it was, beyond a doubt, a legal proceeding.

That township procedures were not identical to those of other instances was not inherently evidence of substandard law. Like that of most states, the empire's legal system encompassed several kinds of courts with different procedures and different jurisdictions—military, commercial, Justice of the Peace, and circuit courts, not to speak of the higher levels of judicial authority.[11] The insistence by critical elites that only the circuit court system represented law in action testifies to passions and commitments that configured reformers' assumptions: their devotion to the jury system of the circuit courts, their suspicion of the state's administrative procedures, and their low opinion of rural society. It can be argued instead that the establishment of a rural court based on imperial majesty and local authority bound together in an accessible ritual was a powerful, if unintended, way of making law attractive to peasants.

Another frequent—almost obligatory—argument against peasant legal culture is based on the unambiguous fact that peasants frequently resorted to informal, extra-legal means to resolve disputes and punish crime.[12] This point, as in Chekhov's time, is usually illustrated with horrific examples of peasants' cruelty directed at archetypal enemies: adulteresses, witches, and horse-thieves. In a variant on this theme, unofficial settlements and illegal retribution are cited to show that peasants, far from being law users, opposed the state and resisted its governance.[13]

There are two fallacies in these arguments. First, people everywhere, including those living in polities unequivocally identified as "rule-of-law states," use informal, unofficial means to settle disputes and take retribution. The law is not the first recourse for most social conflicts: quarreling neighbors in many settings try to come to terms before ending up in court. In conventionally defined law-abiding places and among citizens considered "mature," it is usually not good form to rush to court. The law rests in the background, a guarantee that ultimately parties will be able to find a legal solution to their difficulties. Settling out of court or before a case is filed—whether the settlement takes place in the family, at the tavern or the tea shop, at the school board meeting, or at the village assembly—is not a sign that people reject the power of the law. It may mean that the law has done its work: it remains a recourse and a threat and thus inclines people to come to terms.[14] This holds true for Russian peasants.

Second, incidents of gruesome violence—these fill our newspapers every day—do not mean that an entire society or status group is violent, criminal, and anti-law. The Russian press in the early twentieth century delighted in pathetic and sensationalist peasant anecdotes, but these did not tell the entire story of peasant actions or thought. Just as a murder did not mean the whole intelligentsia was homicidal, so a lethal beating of a horse thief did not mean the whole of "the peasantry" was addicted to illegal or extralegal responses to crime and preferred these means to lawful procedures. For elites, the step from a few macabre incidents to a judgment on a whole category of people was an easy one—easy but unfair and wrong.

Corruption is another long-standing argument against the proposition that peasants in the Russian Empire were legally active and aware. Charges that peasant authorities bought votes with vodka are old and persistent, appearing on Russian society's peasant screen even before the township courts were established.[15] The accusation of corruption at township courts contained the fiction that the "real" courts—the circuit courts established after 1964—were no longer subject to extra-legal pressures. Samuel Kucherov, citing V. D. Nabokov, made the extraordinary claim that the legal reforms of 1864 produced "a miracle" at the circuit courts and that "bribery disappeared from the field of administration of justice." In Kucherov's account, the reason for this wondrous transformation of the judiciary after 1864 was that judges at circuit courts were literate and trained professionals, paid a high salary, supervised by superior instances, and appointed for life.[16] The subject of my study is not the circuit courts, but such conditions have in no other country guaranteed incorruptibility of the bench. One can only imagine what Russian commentators would have said about "the" peasant judge if he, too, had been appointed for life and had received a large salary, instead of his modest stipend paid from local taxes.

A problem with arguments based on corruption is that law and corruption are not distinct ways of ordering society or alternative belief regimes. There is no corruption outside a legal system—what would there be to corrupt, whom to bribe, what laws to evade? Corruption needs a nest inside a system that is supposed to be run by rules.[17] Charges of corruption against peasant judges can be read as indications that the legal system was working in the rural areas. If people bribed the judge, and not the village leader, this would be a sign that courts mattered, more than the power of the local headman. Bribery behind the scene of township courts—invisible from court records—would not prove that peasants had an anti-law mentality. Peasants were forbidden to pay lawyers to defend their interests at the township courts, an inequity when compared to the circuit court procedures. Perhaps in some cases they paid judges. This would not indicate a lack of legal culture.

The law in Russia, as elsewhere, was not an all-or-nothing proposition. Sometimes people resorted to it; sometimes they did not. The critical and answerable questions about legal culture are these: did people use legal opportunities available to them, did they use them voluntarily, and did they, collectively, use them often? From the perspective of practice at the township courts, the answer to all three questions is yes. Peasants' massive, voluntary, and increasing use of township courts in the years before the First World War displays the practiced realm of legal culture in the Russian countryside. These legal actions are the best testimony to peasants' belief in law as a method of resolving conflicts.

Although the answer to our first question—did Russian peasants in the early twentieth century have a legal culture?—is clear, the second question about peasant difference is more difficult to resolve. A first point to make is that of course Russian peasants were different from one another.[18] In imagination, occupation, education—there was no single peasant or peasant mass in late imperial Russia. The individuality of peasants is clear in court records. Disputes at township courts were not limited to clashes between insiders and outsiders, between people of two distinct generations, or between people of different genders. Conflicts at court were almost always between individuals—parties with different aims, different interests, and, less visibly, different notions of how to make their way in life. Some were crooks, some were drunks, some were responsible daughters-in-law, some were needy fathers—a magnificent and ordinary display of human comedies and tragedies came before township judges.

A second observation with relevance to social difference is that the legal category of estate constituted a commonality, but not necessarily a common bond, among Russian peasants. There is no reason to assume that status-defined obligations and rights created ties of affinity or demand among peasants or people of other estates. When, in the late imperial period, some members of the noble estate mobilized in defense of the privileged position of the nobility, they did not act because noble status had made them all alike but rather to assert their claims as individuals with noble rights and privileges.[19] Similarly people of peasant status knew that they were peasants, but this did not mean that they consistently shared interests with other peasants or that they felt part of "a Russian peasantry."[20]

Nonetheless, because the estate system was a legal means by which the state organized its responsibilities to and demands upon its subjects, and a legal means by which people made claims on and fulfilled their duties to the state, estate-based rules had fundamental consequences for peasants and for others. Estate mattered in the question of whether peasants activated legal structures and engaged their polity in distinctive and separate ways. As various as their interests and obligations might be, litigants of peasant status appeared at township courts as holders of identical rights by virtue of their belonging to the same estate. Some of these rights were different from those of others in the polity. Under the property regime assigned to peasants, women enjoyed potentially and in many cases real control over far greater portions of family property than they would have under the regulations of the Civil Code (see chapters 4 and 6). Peasant men could aspire to judgeships at the township courts (or conspire to avoid such service) because they were members of the peasant estate attached to rural societies. Although the township courts, in theory, were open to all estates, the rules for election of judges made it highly unlikely that any person without peasant-status origins could ever be chosen as a judge.[21] A consequence of the rules on choosing judges was that, at township courts, people of peasant status—and only those of peasant status—were guaranteed judgment by their peers.

In the realm of law, rights, and conflict resolution, it is reasonable to expect that the estate system left its imprint on how Russian peasants saw the world—the world, not theirs. It would not be helpful or correct to replace the elite's illusion of a separate world with a well-meant democratic fallacy—that all people of all times and places think alike. Peasants may or may not have aspired to equality with people of other estates; equality was not part of the formative estate repertoire for any person in the empire. Peasants may or may not have hoped to enjoy rights as members of an all-inclusive citizenry in 1917; they had little but their experience of estate-based rights to work from. They may or may not have wanted to change the rules by which they were governed. Some peasants may have wanted some of these things some of the time. Payment of taxes was a normal, if compulsory, event for peasants; participation in the village assembly was a regular duty. Values shaped by these experiences would not be shared by nobles. A lifetime of exercising rights and fulfilling obligations specific to an estate could be expected to affect an individual's political and personal imagination.

THE NORMS OF TOWNSHIP COURTS

The township courts offer an opportunity to uncover shared or unshared values nourished by the estate system and expressed in case hearings. Did peasants' legal culture constitute a drag on the much desired (by reformers) transformation of the Russian Empire into a well-governed polity? Several qualities of justice at township courts suggest the opposite conclusion.

First, judges and litigants at township courts practiced a consistent set of principles concerning legal proof. Oral testimony was taken seriously by judges and figured in decisions as evidence in a case. Plaintiffs had to testify to their charges; defendants could plead guilty or not guilty. Witness testimony was often critical to a decision. Witnesses did not shirk the obligation to appear in court—if they did, they could be fined[22]—and they appeared to be cautious and precise in their declarations. They often said that "they did not know anything" about a particular accusation. Witnesses' statements were usually, although not always, consistent, perhaps because so much was known about one's neighbors in small settlements. In no record I read was an effort by the judges, or the clerk, to distort the testimony of parties or witnesses visible. One's word at court, attested to by one's own or another's signature, was treated with respect.

Oral testimony was not always clear or convincing, but all parties and judges could agree on the authority of documentary evidence. Not any document would do. Good evidence at court was a prior legal decision, recorded in an official book or copied out and stamped with a legitimating seal. The best proof of legal possession of a land allotment or of a right to rent out a parcel was a written agreement. That many people at the courts were illiterate did not undermine the significance of officially recorded decisions. On the contrary, illiterate people were adept at finding people to take down their petitions and were active participants in the veritable cult of documentation that seems to have possessed people at township courts.

What gave documents their power at township courts? One need not evoke developmentalist arguments about oral and written cultures, or distinctions between manuscript and print materials,[23] to understand why everyone at court, the literate and the illiterate, defendants and plaintiffs, judges and clerks all agreed that prior and officially recorded decisions had to be respected. Otherwise the whole system of contractual relations, so critical to carrying on economic enterprises that sustained rural and national life, would collapse. Documents wove a web of connections between the past, the present, and the future. They, better than oral agreements, could transfer local knowledge into legally recognizable forms and ensure that individuals' confidence in agreements would be binding over time.[24]

Documents, oral testimony, plaintiffs' accounts of complaints and charges, defendants' explanations of their behavior—these were the elements of township court decisions. Nowhere in these records is there any evidence that litigants resisted this kind of decision making. There are no signs of other grounds for judges' decisions. One conspicuous absence at township courts is reference to religion. There were no oaths taken at court hearings, no appeals to supernatural authority, and no issuing of verdicts in the name of god, tsar, or church. The township courts were a highly secular operation, and no one is recorded as objecting to this. The only magic worked, it seems, was the ritual formality that turned a legal proceeding into its own realm, different from life outside the courtroom. The green tablecloths, the big books, the township seal, and the signatures on testimony and verdicts—these made justice official, authoritative, tangible.

Second, peasants complied with both procedures and decisions of township courts. "Satisfied" or "not satisfied"—with these words litigants concluded their cases and recorded their own judgments on the outcome of a hearing. Justice at the township court obliged people to participate and obey. Litigants, both plaintiffs and defendants, could appeal outcomes to which they objected, but they were required to recognize—in writing—that a legal decision had been made and to record their responses to it. There was no room here for appealing to an alternative moral authority. Parties were satisfied or not; they did not denounce the standards of the court. The appeals procedures meant that judges, too, did not claim a superior ethical position. What was recognized was the legal process itself, the fact that it had taken place, and that the verdict had or had not satisfied each litigant's demand for settlement through law.

The incorporation of litigants and their desires, whether satisfied or not, into the official record may be one reason for the impressive obedience to court decisions displayed by rural people. Peasants paid their debts and fines, and served their terms of arrest with remarkable speed and regularity. The authorities responsible for delivering verdicts, collecting payments, and supervising arrests were township and village leaders. These officials were vital to the linkage of people to the courts; in the townships I studied, they carried out their duties in good time. No resistance to fulfillment of court decisions is apparent in court records except when people are back in court rehashing an old matter in a different way.[25]

The compliance of rural people with verdicts of the township courts may be related to the kinds of awards and punishments assignable at this instance. By law, township courts considered only misdemeanors, not major crimes, and, as we have seen, punishments were ordinarily limited to a maximum of fifteen days of arrest or fines of thirty rubles.[26] The judges ordinarily leaned toward the lower end of the scale of days or rubles in their sentences. As for suits, the maximum amount that could be sought at the township court was three hundred rubles. This was a considerable sum, more than the average peasant household in Moscow Province earned in a year in cash, according to a survey conducted in 1911.[27] Most suits and most awards were for much smaller amounts, and when ordered to pay, defendants did so. The pragmatic and reasonable justice of township courts encouraged obedience to its decisions.

Third, based on evidence in cases at township courts, peasants respected law-abiding behavior. In addition to their willing use of courts, litigants displayed negative attitudes toward lawbreakers in their insult cases. "Lawless woman" was an actionable insult, as was "convict." For peasants used to regimes of collective obligations, obedience to the law was expected behavior and disobedience hurt others. Peasants' responsiveness to legal authority appeared in other courts as well. A study of the circuit courts in the nineteenth century shows that peasants were more likely than elites to fulfill their jury service when called to do so.[28]

Fourth, township courts upheld and fostered responsible economic citizenship. Regulation of property rights, enforcement of contracted obligations, and wise management of resources were values evoked and nurtured by peasant legal practice. The term "civil case" used in the hundreds of such matters heard each year at each township court makes a connection between litigation and citizenship. In Russian, a civil case is *grazhdanskoe delo;* a citizen is *grazhdanin;* citizenship is *grazhdanstvennost'.* These Russian terms, like citizen, bourgeois, and *bürger,* are rooted in the word for city (*gorod, grad*). But the implication

№	СОДЕРЖАНІЕ РѢШЕНІЙ.	Когда исполнены рѣшенія.
	скать съ его на содержаніе ему съ семействомъ по десяти рублей ежемѣсячно въ теченіи одного года начиная со дня рѣшенія. МИХЫЛЪ МЫСЕЕВЪ	[illegible] 31 октября 1905 г. [illegible]
	Волостной Судъ разсмотрѣвъ настоящее дѣло и принимая во вниманіе [illegible] Михаила Чибисова [illegible] удовлетворилъ: кр-д. Спасской Слободки Григорія Михайлова Чибисова за неоказаніе родителямъ пособія подвергнуть строгому аресту при Волостномъ правленіи на пятнадцать дней, взыскать с него въ пользу отца Михаила [illegible] на содержаніе съ семействомъ по десяти рублей ежемѣсячно въ теченіи одного года считая со дня рѣшенія. Рѣшеніе можетъ быть обжаловано въ 30 дневный срокъ Земскому Начальнику 2 уч. Звенигородскаго уѣзда.	1907 года [illegible] настоящее дѣло [illegible]
	Предсѣдатель Суда [signature]	МИХ.
	Судьи [signatures]	МЫ[illegible]
	объявлено: МИХЫЛЪ МЫСЕЕВЪ	

Signatures on a case record and at the end of a case, Iaguninskii Township Court, 28 August 1905.

that urban—*bürgerlich* and bourgeois—values lay behind a Russian concept of *grazhdanstvennost'* should not prevent us from exploring the question of civic responsibility at rural township courts.

Civil cases—*grazhdanskie dela*—reveal a correspondence between rural norms and market values, despite the fact that elites thought these alien to the "backward" or "moral" economy of the village. Peasants at court had no difficulty understanding what a commodity was, and their myriad cases over sales and purchases provide exhaustive testimony of their commitment to contracts as the foundation of business arrangements. Criminal cases about debts and theft indicate that peasants wanted contractual relationships and property rights to be enforced by courts. Insult cases also provide a glimpse into Russian peasants' concern for good business practices. Many insults accused someone of deceit. "Scoundrel," "swindler," and "robber" were actionable words, prosecuted at township courts as violations of personal dignity. A person could be criticized at court for unscrupulousness. All these terms suggest the high value peasants placed on honesty in business and other relations, and their strong hostility to thieves and cheats. The minor thefts prosecuted at township courts were not of minor importance to their victims.

If we follow Habermas's notion that civil society (*bürgerliche Gesellschaft*) emerges with the development of a "commodity market . . . under public direction and supervision," then at the Russian township courts we see such a society at work. Peasants at court were engaging in governance through legalized regulation of households whose family interests intersected in a market economy.[29] Tax-paying, productive, and entrepreneurial peasants of rural Russia, arrayed in a myriad of rural societies, were participants in a market and, at the township level, in public authority.[30] In the early twentieth century their standards for ethical conduct, expressed in both civil and criminal cases at the township courts, appear very much those of civil society in its now classic definition. That peasants' values were not recognized as civil (in this definition or others) by Russian elites is a different matter to which I will return.

Fifth, the unit of responsibility and agency at township courts was the individual—male or female—and not the family. A noticeable absence in township cases—noticeable by scholars raised on peasant studies, ordinary and unremarked by peasants at court—was the family, as moral discourse and as a named collective actor. The litigants at the township courts were individuals, and they were judged as such. In no case I read was a decision based explicitly on the welfare of a family. The closest judges came to this kind of reasoning would be to censor a man for not "conducting a normal way of life" or to remove a guardianship because a man had "improved his behavior" (see chapter 4). Expanding the property of a ward was testimony to a guardian's appropriate fulfillment of his legal obligations, but nowhere do we find a case decided *because* a family was needy.

Careful readers will object that township courts heard many cases concerning inheritance and family divisions. Did these not indicate that peasants demanded a family kind of justice at township courts? A fair way to look at this question is to say that township judges took family organization for granted. It was the usual order of things. What the courts had to deal with was contentions within families, or potential contentions in the case of preemptive inheritance cases. The court was not there to preserve a family from destitution or disintegration but rather as a recourse for solving the usual family problems. These problems amounted to two major issues: control over property and personal respect. In both cases the township courts made their decisions based on evidence in the case and statute law. Never did someone win because the judges in their opinions supported the "traditional" authority of the father. No insult case at these courts was dismissed because it was immoral for daughters-in-law to insult mothers-in-law. Did she or did she not utter the insult? That was the question judges considered, for mothers, wives, and daughters, as well as for fathers, husbands, and sons, and other relatives. The answer did not depend on any established hierarchy within families or on gender.

Decisions made at township courts after the war began, when women appeared more frequently as plaintiffs and defendants, indicate clearly that the pragmatic justice of the township court was about individual responsibility within families and outside them, and not about making a family unit work according to particular rules. Daughters-in-law sometimes could inherit over fathers and brothers. Underlying such decisions may have been local knowledge about the relative responsibility and productivity of individuals, but this did not undermine the basic principle that the court was there to make decisions about who legally had the right to control property.

Township courts were surprisingly—to us but not to their participants—gender-neutral in their decisions. Overall, men did not enjoy a greater degree of success as plaintiffs than women. Perhaps behind this quantitative display of gender neutrality is the basic fact of court life: plaintiffs, if not defendants, would ordinarily be the more enterprising members of families and rural societies. It is a credit to the male judges at township courts that, in their judgments, they did not hold initiative and enterprise against female litigants.

Sixth, a major concern of peasants at court was individual honor. Rural litigants looked to the state to redress the indignities of physical and verbal violence. This was not an extraordinary or extra-legal claim.[31] Peasant litigants used statutes of the misdemeanor code applicable in other jurisdictions in their charges of insult in words, insult in deed, beating, and threats. Violence, including the threat of violence, against one's person was punishable by law, law that peasants used at township courts.

No doubt enthusiasts of "civilization" will see in these legal actions an absence of internalized morality and self-confidence. Certainly this was the position of intellectuals writing at the time these cases were taking place. A treatise translated from German to Russian and published in the Juridical Library series, J. Ekshtein's study, *Honor in Philosophy and Law,* declared that "honor is not a legal benefice" but a "psychological phenomenon." For neo-Kantian theorists at this time, the significance of law inhered in an accord between individual responsibility and absolute moral principles.[32] Peasants' use of courts for insult cases illustrates their more pragmatic and statist understanding of the law. Their charges were based on a demand for individual responsibility, judged within a framework established by the state.

Finally, among values displayed at township courts was the demand for peaceful, nonviolent ways of settling differences. Accusers who brought charges of insult in deed or beating were choosing to come to court rather than to strike back in the literal sense. The formal procedures of the court required that litigants be asked if they wanted to reconcile. If this occurred, civil cases and criminal cases ended with an official record of the parties' reconciliation. These peaceful settlements occurred rarely before the war but more frequently after August 1914 and through the revolutionary year of 1917. Even without a reconciling outcome, a case at the township court was in itself a testimonial to rural people's desire for official, legal responses to their differences. Evidence from court records cannot guarantee that a losing party in a violence case did not go back home and beat up the plaintiff once again. But the sheer numbers of cases brought by assaulted parties prove that many plaintiffs wanted court-ordered punishments for violent offenders. Criminal case records highlight the history of a massive search for nonviolent, formal, legal judgment on the part of rural people. This real past must be allowed to stand against the anecdotal, episodic, elite-generated accounts of informal and illegal violence in "the" village.

THE INTELLECTUALS' PEASANT WORLD

Paying taxes, electing peasant judges, enforcing market values, and seeking legal settlements were not the kinds of things Russian elites thought about when they worried about peasants' "different" culture. They focused most often on what appeared to be an unbridgeable gulf between peasant villages—"the village"—and "society"—their own, elite, society. "A world apart" was and remains the common metaphor for this peasant other.[33] The notion of a physical distance between peasants and others in the polity should have been untenable, if elites had looked around themselves in the cities. Peasants—people of peasant status—were everywhere; they were workers in factories, servants in grand and modest homes, sellers at markets, students at universities.[34] Something kept elite observers from seeing these peasants as part of civic life and part of their society. The strict association between peasants and the backward village had to be maintained.[35]

Consistent with the maintenance of these separate spheres, the legalism practiced at the township court remained invisible as law. Reform-minded elites were convinced that peasant customs and ideas of law were different from their own. Professionals, administrators, and journalists generally believed they knew what "peasant" values were and did not hesitate to articulate them. Political debates, anecdotes, literary masterpieces, and scholarship from late imperial Russia produced a powerful, lasting paradigm of the Russian peasant. A brief review of what I will call "the intellectuals' peasant world" as it has been passed on to our time allows a reconsideration of these attributed qualities in the light of behaviors of real peasants at township courts.

The first principle of the intellectuals' peasant world was that peasants were thought to live according to traditional rules of conduct transmitted by an oral culture, rules that guided whole villages in common activities.[36] Second, the peasants' way of making decisions was deemed to be devoid of formal procedures. The shouting, chaotic, vodka-drinking village gathering is the hegemonic representation of peasant self-governance.[37] Third, peasant society was described as conservative and authoritarian, dominated by the village patriarchs who really ran the show. Intellectuals' hostility to village elders, as well as the claim to understand how they thought, has traveled a century unscathed.[38] Fourth, the peasant world was violent. This terrible and fascinating violence was directed, in various accounts, at women (demonstrating the conservative values of the peasant family), at thieves (demonstrating a disregard for law), and at outsiders (demonstrating the insularity of the village).[39] Taken together, traditional collectivism, informal governance, authoritarianism, and violence add up to a peasant politics. The intellectuals' peasant world is ready to combat outsiders; it has external enemies, among them the state.[40]

When so many dedicated reformers and conscientious scholars insisted that the problem was a fundamental difference between peasant custom and state law, is it our prerogative to disagree with them? One attractive aspect of much recent work on peasants is precisely the empathetic relationship of today's researchers toward Russian ethnographers, jurists, geographers, and statisticians, whose irreplaceable records were achieved at the cost of physical and not infrequently psychic hardship.[41] Nonetheless, it is important to ask the same questions of these nineteenth- and early-twentieth-century scholars as we ask of our own research in these self-conscious days. Today we would not consider observations from twenty or forty years earlier to be authoritative sources about contemporary life; nor would we consider folk sayings—especially if collected by ethnographers—or short stories written by urban intellectuals as reliable sources about rural people's present-day mentality. These questions about sources do not even scratch the surface of highly applicable epistemological issues concerning the representation of other people's ideas and the ascription to these others of a "tradition."[42] Ethnographers in late imperial Russia had their categories, their selections of materials, their political antipathies and sympathies, and their deep commitment to transforming their society.[43] Their frameworks of interpretation shaped the peasants they saw into "a peasantry," with its different customary law.

It is beyond the purview of this book to explore fully why intellectuals perpetuated such misleading representations of their peasant compatriots, but a few explanations—with relevance for research today—are in order. The first and most basic point is that the material for intellectuals' descriptions of twentieth-century peasants came primarily from other intellectuals and from another time. Most of the data used to describe peasant custom and township court practice was collected in the 1870s through the 1890s, and was employed selectively thereafter.[44] Early-twentieth-century courts worked with different laws and for different peasants, but intellectuals, then and later, preferred to regard the post-emancipation peasantry as one unchanging mass.

Second, elites were not present at township courts. This fundamental reality is often lost. Evidence for peasants' use of township courts and other local practices was not only at least a generation old; it was collected from ethnographers' informants or from local correspondents for the *zemstvo*. Elites did not witness courtroom practice themselves. This nonintersection of intellectuals and peasants at township courts meant that elite analyses were always mediated by one kind of knowledge regime or by several—class politics on the left, populism and exoticism of ethnographers, nostalgic conservatism, legal idealism of liberals, or civilizing ideologies of local correspondents themselves.[45] This mediation left a huge space for imagined peasant communities.

Third, the reality that peasants were their own lawyers, even their own judges, presented a profound challenge to intellectuals' order number one: expertise belongs to experts. It was inconceivable to twentieth-century professionals that uneducated people could, on their own, reach legal decisions, pronounce them, and make them law at courts. From the 1860s on, "the peasant judge" had been a figure of controversy; after forty years of township court practice, most Russian observers still did not have a good word to say about peasant judges.[46] Without witnessing a hearing, intellectuals were sure that ignorance and corruption determined judges' decisions.

Fourth, and for jurists in particular, there were theoretical grounds on which to oppose the township courts. For jurists, township courts suffered from the absence of a general legal code applicable to all citizens, by legal specialists of course. The views of the outstanding legal scholar A. A. Leont'ev, whose work on peasant law in the early twentieth century showed a meticulous concern for uncovering peasant attitudes and practices, are a case in point. Leont'ev, unlike many others, was convinced that a "legal popular consciousness" did exist, even if it only revealed itself in "concrete cases." He wanted a government commission to collect and study peasant practices in order to establish "juridical norms in general, obligatory for all members of a given society and the subordination of the latter to these norms."[47] Here we see the imperative of positive and universal law that lay so heavily on Russian legal specialists. Leont'ev could not imagine a "real" court without a general and uniform code.[48]

Leont'ev's other major criticism of the township court concerned, once again, the absence of legal expertise:

> The main principle of a fair trial is the knowledge of the judge himself of the norms of law, which must be applied to the case. . . .
>
> To make the judge's acquaintance with the norms of law depend on the ability of the parties to demonstrate its existence—this means to burden the par-

> ties with obligations that are absolutely beyond their capacities. The parties must demonstrate the facts, but not the law.[49]

Accessing the law—that was a job for lawyers and trained judges, not for peasants. Leont'ev's opinions point back to Russian elites' insistence that only experts could define the law at proper courts.

A strong myth of peasant custom based on outdated ethnographies, the absence of professionals from township courts, an insistence that only experts could interpret the law, and an apparently democratic but highly top-down legal ideology—all these factors help to explain the glaring lack of correspondence between the customs attributed to peasants and actual litigation at township courts. The values of the intellectuals' peasant world are almost totally at odds with the legal practice of real peasants at township courts—peasants with their pragmatism, their addiction to formalism, their gender neutrality, their businesslike justice, their searches for peaceful settlements, their dignity, and legalized accommodation to a murderous war imposed on them. Let us return to Chekhov's story, which captures this harsh divide between the pragmatic responsibility of peasant life and the didactic moralism of professional elites.

We begin inside the investigator's office, listening to how this judicial official and the accused peasant address each other. The investigator calls the peasant, Denis Grigor'ev, by his name once when he opens the hearing; throughout the rest of the inquiry he uses the familiar and thus disrespectful form of "you"—"*ty*" (*tu, du*). The peasant uses the formal form of address—"*Vy*" (*vous, Sie*)—throughout and occasionally, but not initially, throws in "Your honor." The investigator loses his temper; shouts at Denis Grigor'ev; tells him repeatedly to "shut up"; calls him a "fool," a "stupid head," an infant; says "you bother me"; accuses him of lying; threatens him with exile and hard labor; and insists that he intentionally damaged the railroad in order to cause an accident. Denis Grigor'ev uses a number of strategies to counter these accusations, denies that he had lied, and insists, "by the good Lord, good gentleman, we live our lives without ever the idea of killing people entering our heads."

The investigator's accusation of lying, his name-calling and his threats would themselves be actionable as insults at a township court. But we are in a different legal setting, at the intersection between two social spheres, where only some are required to be civil. Denis Grigor'ev must bow to the superior status and authority of the investigator. His various excuses fail. As he is being hauled off to jail, he blurts out all the reasons why he should not be imprisoned. First try: "I don't have time, I have to get to the market; with Egor, to be paid three rubles for salt pork." Second try: "Prison! If it were for something, I'd go, but I'm not doing anything. . . . I didn't steal, it seems, and didn't fight . . . and if you're worrying about arrears, your honor, don't believe the village leader. . . . Ask the district supervisor." Third try: "We're three brothers. A brother isn't responsible for his brother. Kuz'ma isn't paying and he [the village leader] comes to me and says, Denis, answer for him."

None of it worked as Denis Grigor'ev, a "small, extremely skinny little peasant [*muzhichonka*]" in Chekhov's description, is dragged out by two soldiers. The investigator did not want to hear him or his reasons, but we can listen to Denis Grigor'ev's defense: "I don't lie, I don't dream of killing people, I have to go to market; I didn't steal, I didn't fight; I paid my taxes, and I'm not paying my brother's debts."[50] Confronting law determined by a bureaucrat, this fictional peasant appeals to the kind of justice we have seen enacted in many a modest, all-peasant courtroom: truth-telling; abhorrence of violent crime; recognition of market imperatives, property rights, and obligations toward the state; holding individuals, not families, responsible for paying debts. Denis Grigor'ev appears to be a member of a civil society, although this is not the way the story usually is read.

AN ALTERNATIVE TO THE TOWNSHIP COURT

Shortly after the abolition of estate distinctions in March 1917, the Provisional Government attempted to create a new administration at the township level and to replace the township courts.[51] These measures challenged the earlier distribution of power in the empire and the institutional basis for peasant legal culture. Liberal reformers wanted to destroy the administrative system that ran from peasant judges and other township officials up through the land captain to the Ministry of the Interior. The lower level of the new regime was to be a township *zemstvo,* elected by, and theoretically comprised of, rural residents regardless of their former estate status.

For years, leading figures in *zemstvo* organizations had argued that a township-level institution—a "small *zemstvo* unit"—was a requirement for progress in the countryside.[52] A township *zemstvo,* elected by people of all estates, could raise taxes from all township residents. This would be fairer than the existing system, which taxed peasants, but not nobles, for expenditures on local welfare, and distributed these funds through higher-level *zemstvo* bodies, where the township had no designated representatives.[53] A similar kind of reasoning informed liberal thought about replacing the township court with a new "local court." An all-estate court following the regulations for Justices of the Peace would mean that peasants, nobles, and all other others would be subject to the same legal authority. A controversial law on local court reform had been passed in 1912 but had not been put into effect before the beginning of the war.[54]

The February Revolution opened up the possibility of enacting these much discussed reforms. A new administrative unit, the township *zemstvo,* was established by decree in May 1917; a new local (*mestnyi*) court was to replace the township court. The local court was to be headed by a three-person college: one judge—a Justice of the Peace elected popularly by the township—and two "members of the court" elected by township assemblies. The old township court was abolished in the same decree.[55]

In the liberal press these initiatives were presented as unquestionably progressive and essential to the new democracy. Moscow's major centrist newspaper declared:

> The reorganization of the local courts is as imperative as other reforms that touch upon the arrangements of local life. The strengthening of the bases of law in local life is now one of the pressing tasks advanced by the present epoch. This task can be fulfilled only by a court that will command the complete confidence of the population. The new justice-of-the-peace court, which is close to the population and which is organized on the principle of election by a wide stratum of the population, will be able to fulfill this lofty task.[56]

Township Zemstvo, a pamphlet-sized magazine, was produced in Petrograd to popularize these initiatives and to encourage rural people to vote in township elections to the new institution. This publication, addressed to peasants and populists alike, recounted thwarted struggles under the autocracy to establish the township *zemstvo* and the great significance of this reform: "Without it [the township *zemstvo*], the village cannot stand on its legs, cannot leave its wretched life behind."[57] Elections to the township *zemstvo* began 30 July 1917 and were completed by mid-September.[58]

The results were not what reformers had expected. The editors of *Township Zemstvo* were forced to confess their disappointment. According to these enthusiasts of local power, almost everywhere peasants were indifferent to the elections—"busy with agricultural work and badly informed about what the township *zemstvo* is." One observer commented, "The general mass of the peasants is completely passive; it [the mass] is busy with the harvest and relates to the township *zemstvo* as if to something foisted on it, like a boss or a lord." Others noted that factory workers, dacha owners, and craftsmen showed interest in the elections, while the intelligentsia stayed away. According to the journal's reporters, peasants, if they voted, tried to send "useless, excess" people—those who could not work—or those with little land, in the hope that the township *zemstvo* might give them new territory.[59]

These comments can be put into a different context. These elections were organized at the peak of the year's agricultural labor, but court records show that when something mattered to peasants—such as who possessed the harvest—they were willing to spend even holidays on legal business. Moreover, the pathetic turnout for the township *zemstvo* contrasts strongly with the massive voting by peasants in the elections to the Constituent Assembly later in the revolutionary year.[60] While activists declared that the township *zemstvo* would achieve the "liberation of the peasantry from its burdensome guardianship," peasants might have had good reasons to see these elections as vastly increasing the number of their guardians. In the place of the township leader and the township clerk, the area would now be run by "twenty to fifty elected people, the township representatives," who would decide "all matters of local economy and administration" and appoint all local authorities. It was hardly likely that peasants could outmaneuver better-educated people in local elections. People were to vote by submitting a list of names to the electoral commission, an open-ended way of voting to be sure but one that guaranteed that literate, organized, and mobilized voters had a huge advantage. Elected representatives did not have to live in the same province of the *zemstvo* in question, let alone within the township they were to represent.

The fate of the township *zemstvo* and the local court reform reveals the impact of the estate system on both intellectuals and peasants. Democracy, for the editors of *Township Zemstvo,* could not be other than tutelary and collectivizing. Brochures intended to muster support for the government's reforms referred to rural people as "the benighted village."[61] Parallel but separate systems of administration had encouraged estate-like thinking on peasants' part as well. They were quite right to see the township *zemstvo* as a usurpation of their previously legitimated administrative practices. Now not just one nobleman—the land captain—would supervise their township administrations and their courts, but a raft of specialists, estate owners, teachers, and dacha renters would take over the local institutions that had been theirs to control. The axe hanging over the heads of township judges was clearly visible: they would be replaced, enthused populist propaganda, with "people who could help the peasantry carry on court affairs and understand the laws."[62] For peasants, the abolition of estate-based empowerment to elect their own judges meant the end of their right to legal judgment by their peers.

Contrary to what elite observers had anticipated, peasants did not rush to shut down the township courts and wait for new people to arrive and help them understand the laws. Township courts were in demand in the summer and fall of 1917. They provided a means for peasants to settle disputes and to allocate property—when they could obtain the necessary documents—during the uncertainties of the revolutionary year. The township courts continued their work, as the government issued orders to put new local courts in place and only gradually realized that it had graver problems to solve. As late as 14 October 1917 the Ministry of Justice was informing officials that lists of people elected to the township *zemstvo* were not to be published until complaints about the elections had been resolved by administrative courts. Loyalty oaths to the Provisional Government were signed by the new Justices of the Peace, who were to replace the township judges on 15 November 1917, the deadline that had been set for transferring authority to the new institutions. But the day before, the president of the Moscow Circuit Court had written to judges in the counties of Moscow Province, ordering them to respond to the pillage of the Moscow court headquarters by "suspending all activities in the court building, except for the activities of the Administrative Court concerning the organization of elections to the Constituent Assembly."[63] Meanwhile, at the township level, judges continued to hear cases—if the summonses were delivered and if the documents were available—and clerks continued to record them for future reference.[64]

PEASANT COURTS AND IMPERIAL THINKING

The history of township courts in the last years of the empire manifests the empowering and constraining effects of estate-based governance. Russian peasants in township courts did not face a twelve-member jury; they were judged by their peers—peasant judges elected by rural societies. An imperial principle of community self-rule fostered the inclusion of peasants in the legal system of the polity, in their separate, but very law-bound courts. A culture of respect for law could develop among Russian peasants, alongside elite society's firm conviction that peasants were devoid of legal consciousness. Both peasant legality and its critique were framed by an imperial mode of thinking. When the Provisional Government proposed to institute an all-estate court, peasants did not welcome the new institution. It would no longer be run by and for their part of the people.

Imperial politics encouraged estate-based thought, and provided the language and the laws through which claims for the distinctive rights of nobles, professionals, and others could be asserted, sustained, and seen as valid. In the last decades of the old regime, conservative nobles made an imperial political imaginary clear in their campaigns to preserve estate distinctions.[65] Their efforts to retain noble privilege reflected class interests, of course, but also mirrored a social vision particular to empire. Peasants who preferred their local courts and their local administration to elected authorities who would include nobles were expressing not just class interest—this is part of the explanation—but also a claim to status-based rights in the state.

Intellectuals, for all their discourses of equality, were also thinking imperially and could not escape the imprint of estate-based rights. In their visions the peasantry never seemed able to dissolve into individual citizens. Liberal and socialist plans for reform continued to treat rural people as a mass, with its distinctive needs, even if shorn of its distinctive rights. It is an under-examined truism that states create nations, but perhaps we should entertain a more open notion that empires create collectivities with distinctive, group-based claims upon the state. Imperial Russia created not just estates but estate-minded people. Some of these people were political leaders, who defined claims, powers, and needs in novel but still particularistic ways—the Soviets of Workers', Peasants', Soldiers', and Cossacks' Deputies, for one example. An inclusive, egalitarian democratic evolution in 1917, and later, was made difficult by the long-term practice of group-assigned rights and duties.

The discussion of estate returns us to the question of separateness. Although elites had, for the most part, a mistaken idea of peasant legal practice, there are explanations for their notions of distinctive social spheres. The estate-based principles of imperial rule did not make all nobles alike or all peasants identical, but they did structure social imaginaries. The separations maintained by including different legal communities in the empire enforced social and ideological distance between imperial groups. These communities—

established through imperial law—inspired political imagination and set its limits.

CIVIL SOCIETY IN THE COUNTRYSIDE

Throughout this book the word "society"—*obshchestvo*—has appeared in an unconventional context. Again and again we have encountered the most local administrative unit of rural Russia—the rural society. I recorded this term as it appeared in court testimony and in statute law. In the early twentieth century, at court, peasants did not describe local collectives with the terms *obshchina* or *mir.*[66] Instead, they consistently used the legal term "rural society." *Obshchestvo* is also the word that Russian elites often employed when they spoke of "society," meaning the educated people or sometimes the public. To refine the concept of public, Russian elites used the word *obshchestvennost'*, making the point that not all members of society were part of a public-spirited social sphere. The word *obshchestvo,* with its roots in the notion of something common and shared (*obshchii*), was used by both peasants and elites but in reference to two different kinds of communities—to the decision-making rural commune, composed of household heads of one or a few villages, and to the abstract notion of a public with shared interests and values. Do these notions intersect? Can they help us address one of the recent "accursed questions" of Russian political life and history, the question of civil society?[67]

To address these questions I return to the definitions and the theoretical notions of Jürgen Habermas in his seminal work, *The Structural Transformation of the Public Sphere.* Habermas's distinctions between the public (*Öffentlichkeit*) and civil society (*bürgerliche Gesellschaft*) are helpful when thinking about Russian social phenomena. The public sphere (*Öffentlichkeit*) corresponds closely in meaning to Russian elites' *obshchestvennost'*, used to describe a public sphere based in the "world of letters," the press, and clubs. *Obshchestvennost'* was imagined by its occupants as an active public intermediary between the private realm of families and the official realm of the state. Russian elites in the early twentieth century would have readily identified themselves as members of Habermas's *Öffentlichkeit.*

On the other hand, Habermas's civil society—*bürgerliche Gesellschaft*—might be unrecognizable by Russian elites as a social phenomenon. In Habermas's scheme, the formation of civil society precedes the public sphere. Civil society appears as a commodity market develops and is monitored by "depersonalized state authority." The regulation of economic activity becomes of general interest and can no longer be considered a private, family affair outside the reach of the state. In Habermas's scheme, civil society nonetheless belongs to the private realm; its *bürgerlich*—bourgeois—values are those of markets, commodity exchange, and labor. The public—*Öffentlichkeit*—is, in contrast, a space for political and social demand outside the market and the family. The public can aspire to control civil society through law and publicity—these are political demands that the public makes to the state.[68]

From this perspective, the values of Russian elites fall neatly into place in the public sphere. *Obshchestvennost'*—the engaged Russian public—did make demands on the state in the name of the common social good. It is also clear, however, that the values of the self-defined Russian public sphere were not those of "civil society" in the Habermasian sense. Most Russian elites were not defenders of the market; they generally did not merge the rights of property owners with that of humanity in the classic "civil society" way. Their paternalism extended beyond the family: they wanted a better paternalistic state, rather than the authority of individual citizens expressed in a democracy. Perhaps because the empire retained the estate system until the end and never dismantled the nobility, Russian elites retained aristocratic and imperial notions of power and of their place in the state.[69]

Peasant values expressed at township courts could well be described as bourgeois (*bürgerliche*). As taxpayers, as participants in the market economy, as producers and sellers of commodities, peasants expected their courts to enforce contractual agreements and to protect property. It was of vital importance to them that a regulatory mechanism existed outside the family to back up property transfers and to provide predictability to their economies. It is in the townships that we find a rudimentary but massive demand for legal regulation of commodified relationships. In this sense, Russian peasants did not merely create a foundation for a hypothetical future civil society: they *were* civil, and in their courts they activated a society that extended beyond the village.

Were peasants members of a Russian public (*obshchestvennost', Öffentlichkeit*) beyond the rural areas? Here the answer is no: peasants were excluded from the public, as it was understood and as it functioned in late imperial Russia. From a numerical perspective, peasants were "society" and elites were a minority, but a democratic vision of this kind was impossible for Russian elites. Their public sphere, with its canonical locations in print culture, urban sociability, and political demand, did not accommodate the civil society of the village. The political and social habits of hierarchy based on legal estates, and the profoundly aristocratic, anti-bourgeois ethos of Russian elites, shaped their ideas of citizenship in ways that excluded the homely, responsible, tax-paying, debt-fulfilling behaviors of country folk from the public sphere. It is not a paradox but a logical development of Russian imperial governance, with its preservation of estate-based rights and its elite-driven agendas of reform, that the public (*Öffentlichkeit*) in Russia was not civil (*bürgerlich,* bourgeois), while a plebian civil society with bourgeois values existed in peasant villages and courts without the ability to make itself a public.[70]

One might entertain the notion that peasants were more legally active than people ascribed to the other, "higher" estates. This is a researchable proposition; here I offer only a few observations. Many Russian radicals and artists and professionals had little but disdain for the law. Legal action was not a goal for most of educated "society," with its anti-autocratic ethos. For many nobles, conscious of their status rights, the reformed courts, with their mixed-status juries, were an abomination.[71] For peasants, on the other hand, the majesty of state-organized courts had a practical and personal significance. Township courts allowed peasants to partake of the state's power, to apply standards asserted by legal codes to local affairs. To seek a township court decision for one's own problems meant getting the state on one's side.

This interpretation of court practice and peasant values breaks not only with the traditional view of the village as the extra-legal home of custom and authenticity—in backward or nostalgic variants—but also with a sense of Russian culture as deeply un-public, informal, and unofficial. In a provocative article Edward L. Keenan argued that a formative characteristic of political culture in Russia was purposeful masking of the very principles by which the social system worked. The saying, "Don't carry rubbish out of the hut," Keenan suggested, captures the preference for settling disputes privately, inside the family, the village, or the Kremlin. In his analysis, both peasant and court cultures of Muscovite times adhered to informal practices of power, strove for at least the appearance of unanimous consensual decisions, and kept dissent and discord invisible to outsiders.[72]

The neat fit of Keenan's behavioral template to Soviet and even post-Soviet times should not obscure the strong challenges to informal, self-masking power proffered by the legal reforms of the nineteenth century, including the provision of a legal forum to the rural population. The township courts violated a fundamental principle ascribed to peasant culture: the garbage was taken out of the hut. The dirty linen could be hung on a line far enough outside the village to permit litigants to abstract their claims about character, crime, and fault from the immediate personalized conflicts of daily life. They could return home with an official resolution of their publicly declared differences—not just a settlement of accounts but a legalized definition of acceptable or unacceptable behavior. The masses of rural people who took their neighbors and drinking companions to township courts for insult made manifest the strong appeal of official yet accessible legal process in late imperial Russia. The participatory procedures of the township courts linked rural people to national legal authority, and allowed villagers and judges to elaborate together standards of civility.

If, at other times and outside township courts, empowered elites strove for secrecy, enforced unanimity, threw out dissenters, and ignored their own laws, let us not place the blame on Russian peasants. Some of the apparent unanimity of peasant governance was a consequence of administrative rules. The official document for registering a rural society's decision allowed only unanimity to be recorded (see chapter 6). Peasants may not have arrived at rural assemblies with uniform opinions; consensus emerged on paper. Rather than seeing officially recorded consensus as peasant custom, one might inquire into the origins of this imposed administrative practice. Case records of township courts reveal not only disagreements between individuals but also show that litigants accepted the notion of adversarial relations. Acknowledgment of legitimate conflict and respect for legal resolutions to them were other characteristics of civil peasant society.

PEASANTS, STATE, AND REVOLUTION

Did conflicts within families and villages mean that collective property possession and collective action were not characteristic of peasant villages and peasants?[73] Nothing in this book addresses the perennial question of whether peasants preferred communal land arrangements to individualized family farming. This study is premised on the notion that there is no single "peasant" preference. Whatever individual peasants or their families or their rural societies wished for themselves and others, they all had access to and many made use of a legal forum to settle conflicts resulting from the obstacles—usually presented by the persons of other rural people—that these wishes ran up against. Township judges recognized the voice of rural societies in property matters, but their major concern was to find documentary evidence for particular property claims. Courts did not rule for or against collective ownership as such. They responded to the vital need to know who controlled what piece of land and had the rights to its and its cultivator's products.

This book makes no broad claims about collective action: most actions at court were brought by individuals. The court was not usually the place where groups of peasants would go to carry out a village-based project, if they had one. Occasionally a whole village would be sued in court for some kind of violation of an outsider's claimed rights, but such cases were rare. Readers will be correct if they identify a skepticism in this narrative regarding notions such as "the peasant movement" or an all-Russian "peasant collective."[74] These terms should be questioned in the light (or darkness) of the intellectuals' peasant world and its totalizing assumptions.

Evidence from township courts in the early twentieth century suggests an area of ascribed collective action that should be revisited and rethought. Based on evidence in the case and conscience, can we still call peasants "makers of the revolution"? Peasants who used township courts—by the hundreds of thousands across the empire each year—demonstrated their willingness, if not their enthusiasm, for peaceful, legal means of settling disputes. They also respected state authority expressed in township courts and superior judicial instances. In 1917 peasants, including soldiers and comrades, came to court to settle property disputes, problems of power within families, and violations of dignity at meetings of newly established authorities. Litigants, as in the past, even if "unsatisfied" by a court decision, obeyed judges' rulings. Outstanding characteristics of this peasant legal culture were acceptance of legal authority and active participation in it even during the unsettling circumstances of 1917.

As the use of the status "citizen" by court participants suggests, rural people were quick to adopt the egalitarian terminology offered by the Provisional Government in March 1917. Some of them were eager to enter new political bodies appearing in the localities. To become the representative of Tsaritsynskii Township to the Soviet of Peasants' Deputies was worth a few insults from other contenders. It is hard to reconcile the values demonstrated at township courts—respect for official and participatory authority, peaceful settlements, contractual arrangements, and personal dignity—with the image of peasants' "making" the murderous upheaval that lay ahead.

Peasants were participants in many kinds of battles after 1917, combatants in contending armies as well as resistors to and supporters of the new regime.[75] It is possible that peasants' obedience to legal authority made a difference to the ability of the Red Army to command its troops and, in the end, succeed.[76] Once the whirlwind was upon them, peasants had to make their way, join sides, feed or not feed themselves, supply one or another army. But it is impossible, for me anyway, to imagine that peasants, who had suffered so much in the three years since August 1914, would have wanted to bring down the state entirely and start a civil war. Other people did that to them.

If peasants did not unleash the revolution, they were nonetheless the makers of meaningful transformations in Russian society. Historical scholarship on 1905 through 1917 has focused on discord and explicit challenges to social order in this period as causal in the empire's collapse. Disjunctures between the values of distinct social groups—classes, estates, parties, and nationalities—are considered primary factors in analyses of the late empire, an emphasis that corresponds to the often bleak views held by many elite Russians in the early twentieth century. But upsetting Bakunin's provocation, constructive actions possessed creative force, even if unacknowledged at the time. The vast legal mechanism of the township courts permitted, in much of the empire, a multitude of everyday acts of social reconfiguration, reconciliation, and orderly decision making. These were part of the empire's unconscious history.

In the regions studied in this book, serfdom for a significant percentage of the population had been a reality two generations earlier. Two generations of people—with all their overlapping continuities—had made use of institutions set in place in the reform period. By the early twentieth century another revolution in governance was taking place. New laws on land holding, taxation, and civil rights challenged the power of village elders. The township courts provided a framework in which peasants could revise the old village-based patriarchy on a case-by-case basis, where issues of responsibility, obligation, and authority could be settled by peasant judges outside the power structure of a single village.

Local knowledge exercised in this legal forum not too far from the village permitted a gradual transition from the collective patriarchy of pre-emancipation villages to a more individualized, nucleated, and flexible basis of family management. Judges at township courts were senior males, elected by rural societies; their gender-neutral decisions opened up possibilities for changes in the expected behaviors and relationships of women and men. The regulation of right and wrong, of public speech, and of inheritance through an accessible and intelligible legal process was of immense significance for the construction and adjustment of social life in villages across the empire. From 1905 to 1917 we see peasants using the township courts to shape and discipline individual and family economies, to transfer authority and responsibility when death, incapacity,

Bleaching canvas on the roof of a peasant home in winter, Moscow Province. *Photograph from the collection of Mikhail Zolotarev.*

or ambition disrupted earlier arrangements, to ensure payments of legally established debts, and to make adjustments to the horrific carnage of the world war. The opportunity to use the law to resolve local disputes and to define standards of public behavior in the countryside gave rural people a role in reshaping their society—the society of the vast majority—during what turned out to be the final decades of late imperial Russia.

Peasants were not outsiders to the official sphere of governance in Russia: the empire's time-honored resort to administration on the cheap incorporated peasant administrators. A major contribution of the township court system to the changing polity of Russia was the empowerment of peasants in the judicial system, a significant site of rule. The creation of the township courts gave peasant judges legal authority to rule on small crimes and civil cases—the vast majority of legal cases in the empire. The investiture of legal authority in peasants horrified the educated public, but it integrated great numbers of peasant men into Russian officialdom and gave them and their constituents a strong voice in the ways that civic values were enforced across a large part of the realm. Peasants, like others in the polity, could criticize officials, violate laws, and rebel against local and distant enemies, but in their everyday relations with one another they lived in a world of participatory and official regulation.

Perhaps liberal reformers who opposed separate township courts on the grounds that peasants would not grow into citizenship had won in spite of themselves. This result should not be surprising if we regard law as a practice rather than a set of rules, and if we acknowledge the lack of correspondence between intentions of rulers and interpretations of the ruled. It was the process of case hearings, the possibility of legal judgment rendered by one's peers yet legitimated by the state, that made township courts attractive to rural people. Through township courts peasants acquired a connection to the state beyond their obligations to pay taxes and provide service. They participated actively in the legal order, using courts to defend their estate-based rights. In this respect the township courts were a great, if unintended, gift of tsarist administrators to peasants and the Russian polity, a legal structure that encouraged legal culture.

This legal culture was both local and imperial. The township court was sufficiently outside the village and the family to be a site of "higher" justice, yet it was close enough to daily life to carry meaning. At the same time, the aura of state power infused the court's decisions. If we can escape the ruthlessly divisive notions of custom and peasanthood that so profoundly affected educated elites in this period, we can envision the long-term transformations of society that this inclusive legal system facilitated.

Over a few decades, the activation of law by Russian peasants changed rural society. Legal process at township courts enabled men and women to enforce contractual relationships on which trust and long-term well-being depended and thus to expand society's economic possibilities. Pragmatic, individualized, and legal reconfigurations of authority in families showed peasants' regard for merit and their commitment to responsible behavior. Their defense of personal dignity in word and deed extended a vision of individual rights and peaceful resolution of even petty quarrels. Other people, reforming the polity with a vengeance, could not see the transformation of society ongoing in the countryside, nor the possibilities that rural people's legal culture held out for the future. Lasting social revolutions are those that people make together with their states. Could common sense and conscience have been enough?

Appendix 1. Information on Data Sets

1. CASE DATA

A. Variable Information: Characteristics Recorded for Case Data

1 Township Court
2 Province
3 Archival File
4 Sample type: Inclusive Dates, Number of Consecutive Cases, Location, etc.
5 Type of Case: Civil, Criminal, Other
6 Record Book Type
7 Date Case Heard by Court: Day, Month, Year
8 Name of Presiding Judge
9 Second Judge
10 Third Judge
11 Fourth Judge, if Any
12 Clerk's Name
13 Number of Plaintiffs
14 Plaintiff's Name: Family, First, Patronymic
15 Plaintiff's Status (Office, Function, Title, etc.)
16 Plaintiff's Estate
17 Plaintiff's Sex
18 Plaintiff's Village in Township
19 Plaintiff's Location if outside Township
20 Plaintiff's Representative
21 Sex of Plaintiff's Representative
22 Plaintiff Present at Court
23 Plaintiff's Literacy (as indicated in the record)
24 Plaintiff's Family Relationship to Defendant
25 Defendant's Family Relationship to Plaintiff
26 2nd Plaintiff's Name: Family, First, Patronymic
27 2nd Plaintiff's Status (Office, Function, Title, etc.)
28 2nd Plaintiff's Sex

29 2nd Plaintiff's Village
30 2nd Plaintiff's Location if outside Township
31 2nd Plaintiff's Presence at Court
32 2nd Plaintiff's Literacy (as indicated in record)
33 2nd Plaintiff's Family Relationship to Defendant
34 Number of Defendants
35 Defendant's Name: Family, First, Patronymic
36 Defendant's Status (Office, Function, Title, etc.)
37 Defendant's Estate
38 Defendant's Sex
39 Defendant's Village
40 Defendant's Location if outside Township
41 Defendant's Representatives, Number of
42 Defendant's Representative's Sex
43 Defendant's Presence at Court
44 Defendant's Literacy (as indicated in record)
45 Defendant's Testimony
46 2nd Defendant's Name: Family, First, Patronymic
47 2nd Defendant's Status (Office, Function, Title, etc.)
48 2nd Defendant's Sex
49 2nd Defendant's Village
50 2nd Defendant's Location if outside Township
51 2nd Defendant's Presence at Court
52 2nd Defendant's Literacy (as indicated in record)
53 2nd Defendant's Testimony
54 2nd Defendant's Family Relationship to Plaintiff
55 Number of Witnesses
56 Official Testimony in Case
57 Witness 1: Sex
58 Witness 1: Literacy (as indicated in record)
59 Witness 1: Status (Collective or Individual)
60 Witness 1: Estate
61 Witness 1: Testimony
62 Witness 2: Sex
63 Witness 2: Literacy (as indicated in record)
64 Witness 2: Status (Collective or Individual)
65 Witness 2: Testimony
66 Witness 3: Sex
67 Witness 3: Literacy (as indicated in record)
68 Witness 3: Status (Collective or Individual)
69 Witness 3: Testimony
70 Primary Subject of Case
71 Secondary Subject (Amount or Object of Suit, Second Criminal Accusation)
72 Type 1st Subject Criminal Case by Chapter of *UN*
73 Type 2nd Subject Criminal Case by Chapter of *UN*
74 Type of Criminal Case (Personal Dignity, Public Welfare, Property Rights)
75 1st Statute Cited
76 2nd Statute Cited
77 3rd Statute Cited

78 Statute Numbers in Charge or Complaint
79 Document Involved in Case
80 Origin of Case (Action)
81 2nd Origin of Case (Action; Inheritance and Wardship: From/Over Whom)
82 Origin of Civil Suit
83 Primary Object(s) of Controversy
84 Second Object(s) of Controversy
85 Request in Rubles of Plaintiff or Amount of Theft in Criminal Cases
86 Request, Nonmonetary
87 Finding of Court
88 Decision/Sentence
89 Type of Civil Outcome
90 Type of Criminal Outcome
91 Type of Outcome, All Cases
92 Decision Statute
93 First Criminal Statute Cited in Decision
94 First Charge Is/Is Not Applicable Statute
95 Type of Misdemeanor, by Statute of *UN*
96 Type First Decision Statute, by Chapter of *UN*
97 Second Criminal Statute Cited in Decision
98 1st Procedural Statute Cited in Decision
99 2nd Procedural Statute Cited in Decision
100 3rd Procedural Statute Cited in Decision
101 4th Procedural Statute Cited in Decision
102 Money Amount in Rubles
103 Arrest Sentence in Days
104 Success for Plaintiff (in favor of or by agreement)
105 Fulfillment Record
106 Where Documents Sent
107 Decision Processed
108 Date Decision Acted Upon
109 Appeal
110 Date Appeal Heard
111 Appeal Result
112 Date Fulfillment Recorded
113 Authority Certifying Fulfillment of Decision
114 Amount Paid
115 Other Fulfillment of Decision

B. Variables Used in Statistical Analysis

1 Township Court
2 Province
3 Type of Case
4 Date Case Heard by Court: Day, Month, Year
5 Number of Plaintiffs
6 Plaintiff's Status
7 Plaintiff's Estate

8 Plaintiff's Sex
9 Plaintiff's Village in Township
10 Plaintiff's Location if outside Township
11 Plaintiff Present at Court
12 Plaintiff's Literacy (as indicated in record)
13 Plaintiff's Family Relationship to Defendant
14 2nd Plaintiff's Status
15 2nd Plaintiff's Sex
16 2nd Plaintiff's Village
17 2nd Plaintiff's Location if outside Township
18 2nd Plaintiff's Presence at Court
19 2nd Plaintiff's Literacy (as indicated in record)
20 2nd Plaintiff's Family Relationship to Defendant
21 Number of Defendants
22 Defendant's Status
23 Defendant's Estate
24 Defendant's Sex
25 Defendant's Village
26 Defendant's Location if outside Township
27 Defendant's Sex
28 Defendant's Presence at Court
29 Defendant's Literacy (as indicated in record)
30 Defendant's Testimony
31 Number of Witnesses
32 Official Testimony in Case
33 Witness 1: Sex
34 Witness 1: Literacy (as indicated in record)
35 Witness 1: Status (Collective or Individual)
36 Witness 1: Estate
37 Witness 1: Testimony
38 Witness 2: Testimony
39 Witness 3: Testimony
40 Primary Subject of Case
41 Document Involved in Case
42 Origin of Case (Action)
43 Request in Rubles of Plaintiff or Amount of Theft Charged in Criminal Cases
44 Finding of Court
45 Decision/Sentence
46 Money Amount in Rubles
47 Arrest Sentence in Days
48 Success for Plaintiff

2. SUBJECT SURVEY: VARIABLES

1 Township Court
2 Archival File
3 Chart ID Number (data locator)
4 Sample Type (whole month, whole year, etc.)

5	Month Cases Registered
6	Year Cases Registered
7	Type of Case (Civil, Criminal, Complaints, or Ended)
8	Subject of Case (fifty-nine subjects)
9	Second Subject of Case, if any (fifty-nine subjects)
10	Amount of Suit or Theft, in Rubles or Other Value (amount of pay, etc.)
11	Total Number of Cases of this Type
12	Number of Verdicts by Court
13	Number of Cases in Favor of Plaintiff or Convicting Defendant
14	Number of Cases Resolved against Plaintiff, Acquitting Defendant
15	Number of Cases Appealed to Higher Level
16	Number of Cases Ended because of Absence(s)
17	Number of Cases Ended by Reconciliation
18	Number of Cases Ended for Other Reasons
19	Total Number of Ended Cases

3. DATE SURVEY: VARIABLES

1	Court
2	Archival File
3	Chart ID Number (data locator)
4	Sample Type (day, month, whole year, other period)
5	Type of Case (Civil, Criminal, Complaints, or Ended)
6	Book (Type of Record Book)
7	Date of Hearing or Complaint
8	Year of Case
9	Month of Case
10	Day of Month
11	Number of Cases Heard or Registered
12	Number of Cases Canceled for Nonappearance

4. VILLAGE DATA: VARIABLES

1	Township Court
2	Province
3	Village or Settlement Name
4	Distance to District City
5	Distance to Township Court
6	Distance to Nearest Railroad Station
7	Number of Households
8	Number of Males
9	Number of Females
10	Number of Inhabitants
11	Police Station
12	Number of Churches and Chapels
13	Number of Factories and Mills
14	Number of Stores

15 Number of Taverns, Liquor Stores, and Tea Shops
16 Number of Schools
17 National and *Zemstvo* Taxes, Amount Paid
18 Local Taxes, Amount Paid
19 Village Attributes, Miscellaneous

Appendix 2. Misdemeanors to Be Adjudicated at Township Courts

All applicable statutes listed according to the 1895 edition and the 1906 continuation of the *Statutes on Punishments Applicable by the Justices of the Peace,* with number of pages of commentary in Tagantsev's 1912 publication of this code.

Statute	Description of Misdemeanor	No. of Pages
30	disobedience to police or other guards (*strazhi*) and also township and village authorities (*nachal'niki*), when they are carrying out their duties and when their demands are legal	1
31	insult to policemen or other guards, employees of legal and administrative instances, and also field and forest watchmen, while on duty	6
33	damage to official signs, insignia, advertisements, without intent of showing disrespect to authority	1
34	making a public announcement without permission when required by law, without other unlawful goals	1
37	spreading false rumors, without any political goal, but arousing anxiety in minds (*vozbuzhdaiushchie bezpokoistvo v umakh*), or intentionally causing general alarm by sounding the tocsin or in another way	1
38	quarrels, fights, fistfights, or other kinds of unruly conduct in public places (*ssori, draki, kulachnyi boi ili drugogo roda buistvo v publichnom meste*) and generally for disturbances of the social peace (*obshchestvennaia tishina*)	4
39	disturbance of order in public meetings or during popular festivals, theatrical presentations, and the like	1
41	violations of rules on sale of alcohol: opening taverns and other institutions of such type at illegal hours, allowing unpermitted amusements (*nedozvolennye uveseleniia*), disorders, etc., in such places	6

42	appearing in a public place in a condition of clear drunkenness, threatening to safety, peace, or decorum	1
42.1	taking part in collecting alcoholic beverages [lit., strong drinks] for public drinking bouts (*raspitie*) on streets and squares	1
43	for shameless acts or acts connected with seduction (*soblazn*) of others in a public place	1
43.1	causing intentional cruelty to domestic animals	3
45	public presentation or distribution of clearly corrupting devices and images	1
46	setting up forbidden games of chance, cards, dice, etc., but not in a gaming house	2
47	setting up, without permission, public lotteries, for the illegal distribution of tickets for foreign lotteries or promises, for illegal sale of any kind of promises for any kind of lottery, and of promises for tickets for credits with winnings	2
49	requesting alms out of laziness or habitual idleness (*privychka k prazdnosti*)	1
50	requesting alms rudely and crudely or using deception (*s derzost' iu i grubost' iu, ili s upotrebleniem obmanov*)	1
51	allowing children to beg, for their relatives or other guardians	1
51.13	allowing people of lower military ranks into an institution where alcoholic drinks are sold and distributing alcoholic drinks to them from this institution, for tavern proprietors	1
52	spoiling the waters of rivers, canals, springs, or wells by throwing rocks, sand, and such things into them, and equally for not fulfilling duties to clean wells and keep them in good condition	1
55	nonobservance of the rules on cleanliness and order in the street, and for letting animals roam on streets where this is not allowed	1
56	discarding dead livestock, garbage, or sewage in a place not designated for it and for an overflow or dispersal of such things while in transport; hunting without required hunting permit . . . ruining birds' nests and taking eggs and small birds from them; hunting with someone else's hunting permit, for game that is not allowed at a particular time, or by forbidden means; not presenting hunting permit on demand of a hunting supervisor; slaughtering of female elk, deer, or wild goat, or the young of these species; carrying off, carting, selling, and purchase for sale of game at a forbidden time. . . .	1
57	fishing or hunting at a forbidden time in places not	1

	allowed, by illegal means or without observing the prescribed rules	
61	absence or residence without the established permits where they are required, or with an outdated or inappropriate permit	1
65	construction or exterior reconstruction of a building without appropriate permission, when required by law	7
66	violation of technical or other construction rules, prescribed in the *Regulations on Construction,* as published in local decrees according to established procedures	4
69	incorrect maintenance of sidewalks, bridges, carriageways, and roads, after a reminder	2
70	damaging sidewalks, bridges, carriageways, and highways, or railings, ditches, posts, or trees located on them	1
72	damaging bridges, fords, dams, brushwood, etc., on roads	1
73	obstructing crossings on bridges and sidewalks, or passage along roads and streets by leaving large objects on them or in another way	1
88	construction of stoves, chimneys, smoke stacks, etc., without observing the rules established for the prevention of fire, by stove workers or others responsible [for construction]	1
89	nonobservance of prescribed rules for cleaning chimneys	1
91	carelessness with fire in settled areas, not having water container or fire-extinguishing material where required	1
92	smoking tobacco on streets and squares where this is forbidden	1
94	nonobservance of the rules established for caution with fire on boats and rafts	1
95	breaking rules on caution with fire outside residences [under various conditions]: careless use of fire near forests; leaving site of unextinguished fire; burning brush or grass in violation of established rules; employing various fuels (oil, charcoal, etc.) in violation of established rules; use of flammable materials when shooting in forests; leaving a barn unattended during heating	1
96	nonappearance at a fire with appropriate fire-extinguishing equipment in towns or settlements where this is required; for nonappearance without valid reasons when called by authorities to a forest fire, or unauthorized leaving of the place of a fire	1
98	acts described in Statutes 88–95, when a fire resulted from these	1
111	ruining water serving for people's use or for watering	2

	animals, by soaking flax or hemp, by throwing, spilling, pouring, or introducing into it substances making it unfit for use, or by another means, when there was no intent to harm public health	
115	preparation for sale, keeping in a commercial or industrial establishment, or selling of edibles or beverages harmful to health or rotten, and for the manufacture of dishes out of materials harmful to health	3
116	nonobservance of necessary cleanliness and tidiness in the preparation for sale or during the storage in a commercial or industrial establishment or during sale of edibles and beverages	1
117	keeping or carrying a forbidden weapon, shooting from a firearm or other dangerous weapon in places where this is forbidden	1
118	keeping a loaded or other dangerous weapon without necessary precaution and carrying the same where this is forbidden	1
119	nonobservance of appropriate caution during the throwing of stones or other heavy objects, while throwing out or pouring out the same, or during storage or carrying of heavy objects	1
120	keeping wild animals without observation of measures necessary for the protection of public safety, and for releasing them carelessly from their place of confinement	1
121	not taking established measures to prevent danger from domestic animals	1
122	poisoning a person, without criminal intention, by a dog or other animal [probably refers to diseases transmitted by animals, e.g., rabies]	1
123	careless driving or driving too fast in cities or villages; allowing incompetent or drunken driving of horses	2
124	not attaching supports to dilapidated fences; . . . not having warning signs or fencing around construction and other works, or around wells, cesspits, lime pits, and, in general, in those circumstances where fences or warning signs are essential for the protection of individual safety	1
125	putting cages, flowerpots, and such things in windows without requisite carefulness, and insufficient attachment of signs or shutters	1
126	transport of people in dilapidated or worn-through boats and generally for violation of the rules on safety prescribed for water transport	1
127	not safeguarding a drunk person who cannot, without obvious danger, be left on his own, by seller in drinking establishments	1
128	causing wounds or harming health of someone, but	2

	not death, through acts covered by Statutes 66, 72, 76, . . . 117, 118 pt. 1, 119, 121–127	
130	inflicting insult (*nanesenie obidy*) oral or written	14
131	inflicting insult (*nanesenie obidy*) oral or written, with forethought, or in a public place or in a popular gathering, also to a person, who, although not a direct relative of the offender, has a right in relationship to the offender to special respect, or to a person of the female sex	5
132	inflicting insult (*nanesenie obidy*) oral or written, to a direct relative	1
133	inflicting insult (*nanesenie obidy*) in deed, to a person who is not a direct relative, who himself gave grounds for the insult	4
134	inflicting insult (*nanesenie obidy*) in deed, without any grounds from the side of the offended person	2
135	inflicting insult (*nanesenie obidy*) in deed, with forethought, or in a public place or in a popular gathering, also to a person, who, although not a direct relative of the offender, has a right in relationship to the offender to special respect, or to a person of the female sex	1
136	slander (*kleveta*) oral or written	20
137	divulging, with the intention of insulting someone's honor, information communicated in secret or learned by opening another's letter or by other illegal means	1
139	threat to use force against someone, unmotivated by a mercenary or other criminal goal	4
140	threat of death or arson, unmotivated by a mercenary or other criminal goal	1
141	threat in writing, unmotivated by a mercenary or other criminal goal	1
142	*samoupravstvo*, for the use of violence, but without heavy beating or wounds or mutilation	29
143	refusal by children who have the means to provide needy parents support necessary for life	1
145	willfully being on someone else's land, but not in the manner of theft, harvesting fruits or vegetables, picking berries or mushrooms, damaging trees in gardens or pulling up garden flowers, cutting turf, digging sand, clay, etc.	5
146	willfully fishing or hunting in other ways in another's waters	1
147	walking, driving, or riding across another's meadows or fields, before the harvest of crops or of grasses on them	1
148	driving cattle through another's meadows and fields, pasturing cattle on another's lands or in another's woods	4

149	crossing or driving cattle through gardens or through meadows, fields, groves, and pastures enclosed by fences or ditches, or when there are warning signs posted about the interdiction of crossing them	1
150	dumping rocks, rubbish, dead animals, or other garbage on another's lands	1
151	resistance when animals (cattle or birds) are detained in a case of trampling, and for willfully carrying off of detained animals	1
152	damaging another's ditches, fences, or movable property	1
153	slaughtering or damaging another's animals	2
169	theft of an object worth no more than five hundred rubles, when a case of theft or swindling for the first or second time	13
170	actions covered by Statute 169 that took place in circumstances deserving increased punishment—in a church. . . , at night, breaking in, theft of essential food, through persuading several people, with the help of workers . . . or of owners of hotels and similar establishments	3
172	attempted theft, stopped through circumstances not dependent on the accused, or participation in theft and the harboring of stolen goods, concerning objects worth no more than five hundred rubles when a case of theft or swindling for the first or second time; punishment can be reduced depending on importance of the attempt or participation of the guilty	4
173	falsification in measuring or weighing during a sale, purchase, or exchange of commodities or other items, other deceptions in quantity or quality of a commodity or in calculating payments, or during exchange of money, when the price is no more than five hundred rubles and when a case of theft or swindling for the first or second time	32
174	substitution of items entrusted for keeping. . . , swindling of money or items by false communication or by enticement to profits. . . , not returning . . . a receipt or the like . . . upon payment of a debt or not indicating on such that money had been received with the intention of again demanding payment, when the amount is no more than five hundred rubles and when a case of theft or swindling for the first or second time	13
178	appropriation of found money or objects, or a treasure found on another's land, when the owner (*khoziain*) of the found object is known to the finder	4
179	not reporting found objects or money belonging	1

	to an unknown person according to established procedure within three weeks	
180	purchasing or pawning property known to be stolen or received through fraud	5
180.1	pawning government arms, clothing, or ammunition from lower military ranks	1

Source: *OPK*, 127; *UN*

Glossary

This list displays English equivalents I have chosen for Russian words. It is designed both to assist English-language readers with the occasional Russian word used in the text and to guide scholars back to the source of translated terms. The notes provide Russian terms where they might prove useful to researchers.

arshin	unit of length, 28 inches, 71 centimeters
dusha	soul, here used as a unit of taxation, applied to land allotments
dvor	court, courtyard, or household
dvoriane	nobles
dvorianin	nobleman
dvorianka	noblewoman
dvorianstvo	nobility, noble estate (from *dvor:* court, courtyard)
guberniia	province
gubernskoe prisustvie	provincial board (provincial appeals instance for township courts)
krestiane	peasants
krestianin	peasant man
krestianka	peasant woman
krestianstvo	peasantry
meshchane	townspeople
meshchanin	townsman
meshchanka	townswoman
meshchanstvo	townspeople's estate
mirskie povinnosti	collective obligations
mirskie sbory	local taxes for local obligations
pisar'	clerk
posadskii	inhabitant of trading area around a city
prigovor	decision (official, of an assembly or court)
pud	pood, unit of weight, 36 pounds
razdel	division of family property
remeslennik	artisan
sazhen'	measure of length equal to 2.13 meters, 2.3 yards, 7.1 feet

sel'skii skhod	rural assembly, village assembly
sel'skoe obshchestvo	rural society, village society
soslovie	estate
starosta, sel'skii starosta	village leader
starshina	township leader
tovar	commodity
tsekhovoi	guildsman, craftsman
uchastok	district
uezd	county
uezdnyi s"ezd	county congress (county appeals instance for township courts)
usad'ba	household plot (peasants); noble estate
veksel'	bill of exchange
versta, pl. *versty*	unit of distance: 1.06 kilometers, 3500 feet, .66 mile
volost'	township
zemskii nachal'nik	land captain, regional supervisor
zemstvo	regional council on social policy

Note on Sources

Shortened references to published and archival materials are used in the notes and text. Full citations for these materials follow in the bibliography. In a few cases, where material was only indirectly related to the topic of this book, I put full citations in the notes and omitted them from the bibliography. To facilitate locating full citations, the bibliography of published sources is divided into only two alphabetical lists of primary and secondary sources. Please consult the list of abbreviations for full names of archival collections, legal codifications, and statistical compilations.

The archival institutions on whose collections this book is based changed names, in some cases more than once, during the years of my research (1987 through 2003). Transfers of fonds (collections) from one archive to another took place in these years as they had in the past. Both renaming of institutions and transfers of files can be anticipated in the future as part of ordinary archival practice. For these reasons I decided, in most cases, to retain in my citations the names of archives and fonds that I recorded when I read each file, even if the file was subsequently renamed or moved. The bibliography provides all names of archival institutions as cited in my notes, with the fond numbers of collections. Former names of archives are given in brackets. This list should assist researchers in locating specific files and facilitate tracking the provenance of collections.

The two basic sources for legislation governing township courts in the early twentieth century are *The General Regulation on Peasants* (*Obshchee polozhenie o krest'ianakh* [*OPK*]) and the *Statutes on Punishments Applicable by the Justices of the Peace* (*Ustav o nakazaniiakh nalagaemykh mirovymi sud'iami* [*UN*]). *The General Regulation on Peasants* was issued as book 1 of *The Regulation on the Rural Estate* (*Polozhenie o sel'skom sostoianii* [*PSS*]). All eight books of *The Regulation on the Rural Estate* constitute the "Special Appendix to the Ninth Volume" of the *Collected Laws of the Russian Empire* (*Svod zakonov Rossiiskoi imperii* [*SZ*] 9, Osoboe Prilozhenie).

This project has led me to suspect that many errors of interpretation concerning legal practice in early-twentieth-century Russia may derive from using outdated materials. Laws and regulations changed significantly in the late imperial period, including legislation on the township courts. I found it both useful and imperative to consult codifications that were prepared for legal practitioners and published in the period of my research. These publications were kept up to date with new rulings; they also provide indications of which laws were changed, and when. I used the 1902 edition of *The Regulation on the Rural Estate* (*PSS*), updated to 1912, published in an edition of the *Col-*

lected Laws prepared for use by legal specialists: *Svod zakonov Rossiiskoi imperii,* ed. I. D. Mordukhai-Boltovskii, 5 vols. (St. Petersburg: Russkoe Knizhnoe Tovarishchestvo "Deiatel'," [1912]). This edition of *The Regulation on the Rural Estate* incorporates various revisions of the township court rules and peasant rights, the most substantial of which were enacted in 1889 and 1906, and includes the extensive modifications to the legal code on peasant landholding (the "Stolypin" reforms) promulgated in 1906 and 1910.

For my study of misdemeanor prosecutions and statute law at township courts, I used N. S. Tagantsev's edition of the *Statutes on Punishments Applicable by the Justices of the Peace* (*Ustav o nakazaniiakh nalagaemykh mirovymi sud'iami,* ed. N. S. Taganstev, 12th ed., exp. [St. Petersburg: Tipografiia M. Merkusheva, 1912]). This publication is based on the third (1885) edition of the *Statutes on Punishments Applicable by the Justices of the Peace,* which was issued with the regular criminal code in 1885. The expansions to the statutes incorporate changes issued in the continuations of 1906, 1908, 1909, and 1910.

For statistical reports and analysis, I compiled four data sets. The variables in each set are provided in Appendix 1. Many statistical calculations used in this book, as well as graphical displays of statistical information, can be found on my website, http://www.nyu.edu/projects/burbank/. The tables and figures in the book are based on the "Case Data" data set, described below, unless another source is given.

My most detailed data set, "Case Data," is compiled from information on 907 individual court cases. My major concern was not to select for types of cases but to let the record speak for itself. I recorded data on series of cases recorded at various courts, always proceeding sequentially for all cases recorded in the township record or for cases from a particular area within the township. Usually I read through cases over several months at a time. It was often not possible to cover all civil and all criminal cases at a particular time at a particular court, because clerks kept different books for different kinds of cases. Another variation in the source of case data is the kind of record book: civil, criminal, "ended," registered, no-show cases, all cases, and so forth. A large set of variables, 115 to be exact, allowed me to keep track of these distinctions as well as to gather information on all litigants, judges, causes, decisions, and outcomes of cases. For many of these 907 cases I was able to collect a full set of 115 variables; for others I had incomplete information. Statistical calculations of probabilities are based on 48 variables contained in this set of case data. All 907 variables and the subset of 48 variables are listed in Appendix 1.

My second data set, "Subject Survey," is based on the subjects of cases. I surveyed subjects and, in some cases, outcomes of 889 cases at three courts in 1908, 1914 (before the war), and 1916. For this material I counted and summarized long runs of cases to provide me with second readings on types of cases and case outcomes at township courts. Appendix 1 provides the list of 19 variables in this data set.

"Date Survey"—a massive compilation—looks at numbers of cases heard at a particular court at a particular time. This survey allowed me to look at the periodicities of cases at various courts. The survey covered 2,746 cases, heard at five courts from 1905 through 1916, and is used in descriptions of court activity in the text. This survey, based on 12 variables, permitted me to look at the incidence of cases that ended because of nonappearance of a party or parties.

Finally, "Village Data" is a set of characteristics for each of the settlements in the ten townships. Using published statistics and some archival information, I was able to identify population figures, geographical information such as distances to the township court or to the nearest city and railroad station, and other specifics—the presence of schools, factories, police headquarters, and drinking establishments—for most of the 253 settlements in the ten townships. In some cases I collected data on taxes paid by villages.

Discrepancies in numbers of cases appearing in tables in the text derive from the use of subsets of these data. For example, from calculations about the sex of plaintiffs I excluded cases brought by policemen where no clear plaintiff was visible. Over time I added new cases to my surveys, and made recalculations based on these larger data sets or on different subsets of cases (by area, time, type of case, etc.). I found overall that results based on around 550 or 900 cases were consistent with each other, and that calculations of percentages—on subjects of cases, for example—yielded similar results when based on different data sets.

Abbreviations

NAMES OF ARCHIVAL COLLECTIONS

LGIA	Leningradskii gosudarstvennyi istoricheskii arkhiv
RGIA	Rossiiskii gosudarstvennyi istoricheskii arkhiv
TsGAgM	Tsentral'nyi gosudarstvennyi arkhiv goroda Moskvy
TsGAMO	Tsentral'nyi gosudarstvennyi arkhiv Moskovskoi oblasti
TsGIA-L	Tsentral'nyi gosudarstvennyi istoricheskii arkhiv-Leningrada
TsGIA SPb	Tsentral'nyi gosudarstvennyi istoricheskii arkhiv Sankt-Peterburga
TsGIAgM	Tsentral'nyi gosudarstvennyi istoricheskii arkhiv goroda Moskvy
TsIAM	Tsentral'nyi istoricheskii arkhiv Moskvy

The archives cited in the text all changed names, in some cases more than once, in the 1980s and 1990s. In addition, many files I used were labeled with names of archives from before the 1980s. This list provides abbreviations for archives as I recorded them at the time of my research; these abbreviations are used in citations. See the note on sources and the archives section of the bibliography for further information.

CODIFICATIONS, STATISTICAL COMPILATIONS

OMG	*Obzor Moskovskoi gubernii*
OPK	*Obshchee polozhenie o krest'ianakh*
PSS	*Polozhenie o sel'skom sostoianii*
PSZ 3	*Polnoe sobranie zakonov Rossiiskoi imperii,* Sobranie Tretie
SURP 1917	*Sobranie uzakonenii i rasporiazhenii Pravitel'stva. 1917*
SZ	*Svod zakonov Rossiiskii imperii*
SZG	*Svod zakonov grazhdanskikh*
UN	*Ustav o nakazaniiakh, nalagaemykh mirovymi sud'iami*

See the note on sources and bibliography for full citations.

ARCHIVAL AND LEGAL CITATIONS

ch.	chast' (part)
d., dd.	delo (file), dela (files)
ed. khr.	edinitsa khraneniia (storage unit)
f.	fond (collection)
gl.	glava (chapter)
kn.	kniga (book)
o	oborotnaia storona (verso)
op.	opis' (inventory)
osob. pri.	osoboe prilozhenie (special appendix)
otd.	otdel (section)
pr.	primechanie (note)
st., sts.	statute, statutes
vyp.	vypusk (issue)

Notes

1. THE PEASANT QUESTION AND THE LAW

1. On the role of estates and the peasant estate in imperial Russia, see Wirtschafter, *Social Identity in Imperial Russia,* pp. 3–20, 101–130, 163–173. On the ideology of peasant backwardness in the late imperial period, see Kotsonis, *Making Peasants Backward.* On the Soviet re-inscription of differential status, see Fitzpatrick, "Ascribing Class"; and Vishniak, *Le régime soviétiste,* p. 26.

2. On economic policy toward the peasants in the early Soviet period, see Stanziani, *L'économie en révolution,* pp. 309–416. The issue of the Red Army and the peasant question is discussed in von Hagen, *Soldiers in the Proletarian Dictatorship.* On Stalin's campaigns, see Viola, *The Best Sons of the Fatherland.* On peasants in Stalin's time, see Fitzpatrick, *Stalin's Peasants;* Viola, *Peasant Rebels under Stalin;* and Hoffmann, *Peasant Metropolis.*

3. Lev Timofeev provides a poignant description of the condition of rural society in the last years of Soviet rule in his *Soviet Peasants; or, The Peasants' Art of Starving.*

4. Kollmann, *By Honor Bound,* p. 169.

5. On peasants' use of legal regulations to promote their interests as migrant laborers and merchants beyond the confines of their villages, see Gorshkov, "Serfs on the Move."

6. On Russian legal reform in the nineteenth century, see Adams, *The Politics of Punishment;* Wagner, *Marriage, Property, and Law in Late Imperial Russia;* Wortman, *The Development of a Russian Legal Consciousness;* and Engelstein, *The Keys to Happiness,* pp. 17–298. On the reform of corporal punishment, see Dzhanshiev, *Epokha velikikh reform,* pp. 179–247; and Schrader, *Languages of the Lash.* On peasant courts and their provenance, see Druzhinin, *Gosudarstvennye krest'iane i reforma P. D. Kiseleva,* 1:575–588; and Frierson, "Rural Justice in Public Opinion."

7. See Steven Hoch, "The Serf Economy, the Peasant Family, and the Social Order," in Burbank and Ransel, eds., *Imperial Russia,* pp. 199–209; and Hoch, *Serfdom and Social Control in Russia,* pp. 127–132.

8. On the various legal estates of peasants before 1861, see Wcislo, *Reforming Rural Russia,* pp. 6–9.

9. *OPK, PSS.* See the note on sources for descriptions of these codes. This legal code was updated in accordance with new legislation that affected rural courts. Although the status of "state peasant" ceased to exist, peasants throughout the empire were gov-

erned by a variety of statutes, according to their location, ethnicity, religion, and the kinds of lands they cultivated. This book considers peasants living in central Russian areas.

10. Many rural societies had been established at the time of emancipation from villages formally owned by a single landowner. On the functions of the commune, see Hoch, *Serfdom and Social Control in Russia,* pp. 133–159.

11. *OPK,* sts. 47, 48.

12. Much of the literature on Russian peasants neglects the rural societies or does not use the term; one source claims that the *sel'skoe obshchestvo,* "was a fictitious unit" (Macey, *Government and Peasant in Russia,* p. 261 n. 24). In analyses of peasant institutions, historians have prioritized the peasant commune—the *mir* or *obshchina*-rather than the *sel'skoe obshchestvo.* The vast literature on the commune, however, rarely justifies this choice of terminology. As Macey observes, the "history of these Russian terms [*mir, obshchina, sel'skoe obshchestvo*] is both complex and confusing and is concerned more with the misconceptions of capital-city society and the aspirations of government legislators than with either rural realities or peasant consciousness" (ibid., p. 258 n. 40). According to Macey, the concept of the peasant commune was introduced into Russian discourse by Baron von Haxthausen (ibid., p. xvii). In records generated by township courts from 1905 through 1917, peasants used the term *sel'skoe obshchestvo,* and not *mir* or *obshchestvo,* to refer to their village organizations. For an account of the significance of village-level institutions, see Gaudin, "Les zemskie načal'niki au village," pp. 263–265.

13. *OPK,* sts. 50–52. For the parish model and exceptions to it, see st. 50, pr. 2. On the size of townships, see S. Latyshev, "Volost'," in *Entsiklopedicheskii slovar',* 13:95. The word *volost'* is associated with the Russian word for power—*vlast'*—and was used since Muscovite times to delineate administrative regions. Translating *volost'* as township suggests correspondences between Russian, British, and American history. Townships were administrative units modeled on parishes in ancient England; they are also administrative divisions of counties in many areas of the United States; see *Webster's Third International Dictionary of the English Language,* 3 vols. (Chicago: Encyclopedia Britannica, 1986), 3:2418.

14. *OPK,* sts. 124–129.

15. On the origins of the township court, see Frierson, "Rural Justice in Public Opinion," pp. 526–529. On the reform of the courts for the state peasants, see Druzhinin, *Gosudarstvennye krest'iane i reforma P. D. Kiseleva,* 1:572–588.

16. *OPK,* sts. 77, 113–115, 124–131, 135.

17. On the effort to replace the township court with an all-class local court in the early twentieth century, see Zyrianov, "Tret'ia duma i vopros o reforme mestnogo suda i volostnogo upravleniia." A reform of township administration was finally attempted in the spring of 1917; on this subject, see chapter 8.

18. For nineteenth- and early-twentieth-century views on the township courts, see Frierson, "Rural Justice in Public Opinion."

19. On the transmission of nineteenth-century and fin de siècle constructions of peasant character and legal ideas to twentieth-century historiography, see my article, "Legal Culture, Citizenship, and Peasant Jurisprudence," in Peter Solomon's edited volume, *Reforming Justice in Russia, 1864–1994,* pp. 85–94. On the construction of long-lasting images of Russian peasants, see Frierson, *Peasant Icons.* An example of the customary law approach to peasant legal culture is Stephen P. Frank's "Popular Justice, Community, and Culture among the Russian Peasantry, 1870–1900," in Eklof and Frank, *The World of the Russian Peasant,* pp. 133–153. See also Frierson, "'I Must Always Answer

to the Law . . .'"; Frierson contrasts "peasant" and "national, formal legality" (p. 334). For an unusually positive assessment of the township courts, but one still situated in the tradition of peasant backwardness, see Tarabanova, "Sudebno-pravovaia kul'tura krest'ian poreformennoi Rossii," pp. 40–54. This article is based on descriptions of the township courts from 1862 to 1872.

20. Disdain for the law has a long pedigree in histories of Russia; an anti-law mentality has been traced to the Slavophiles' search for a native non-Western tradition and connected to the revolutionary opposition to the tsarist state. On the anti-law tradition, see Walicki, *Legal Philosophies of Russian Liberalism,* pp. 9–104. Richard Pipes described Russian governance as patrimonial, and attributed a lack of law and courts to the absence of Western-style feudalism in Russia (*Russia under the Old Regime,* pp. 50–57). For Pipes's view of law in the Soviet period, see his essay, *Legalized Lawlessness: Soviet Revolutionary Justice* (London: Institute for European Defense and Strategic Studies, 1986).

21. For studies of Russian legal philosophy, see Walicki, *Legal Philosophies of Russian Liberalism;* and Heuman, *Kistiakovsky.* For the Soviet period and for a more social focus, see Berman, *Justice in the U.S.S.R.;* and Solomon, *Soviet Criminal Justice under Stalin.*

22. Burbank, "Discipline and Punish in the Moscow Bar Association," pp. 45–48. This article focuses on the paternalistic and didactic culture of the Russian bar.

23. On the origins of legal reform in the mid-nineteenth century, see Wortman, *The Development of a Russian Legal Consciousness.* Excellent sources for the legal pathos of the early twentieth century are *Velikaia reforma;* and Koni, *Otsy i deti sudebnoi reformy.*

24. See Piers Beirne, *Revolution in Law: Contributions to the Development of Soviet Legal Theory, 1917–1938* (Armonk, N.Y.: M. E. Sharpe, 1990).

25. This polemic reinforced the orientation of scholarly inquiry around the significance of "bourgeois" or European law for Russian development. See, for example, *Soviet Legal Philosophy,* trans. Hugh W. Babb, intro. John N. Hazard (Cambridge, Mass.: Harvard University Press, 1951); Bierne, *Revolution in Law;* Pipes, *Legalized Lawlessness;* and Leonard Schapiro's introduction to his *Origin of the Communist Autocracy: Political Opposition in the Soviet State, First Phase 1917–1922,* 2nd ed. (Cambridge, Mass.: Harvard University Press, 1977).

26. A new attention to legal issues in post-Soviet Russia has elicited a new wave of scholarship on law in Russia. For a comprehensive perspective on the late imperial period, see Baberowski, *Autokratie und Justiz.* Among recent works that take a long-term perspective, see Solomon, *Reforming Justice in Russia;* and on the late Soviet period, see Barry, *Toward the "Rule of Law" in Russia.*

27. Tenishev, *Pravosudie v russkom krest'ianskom bytu,* p. 4. On the increase in the use of the courts in the late nineteenth century, see Frierson, "'I Must Always Answer to the Law,'" pp. 327–329.

28. On the empire's legal pluralism, see Jane Burbank, "Narodnye sudy, imperskoe zakonodatel'stvo i grazhdanstvo v Rossii," in Miller, *Rossiiskaia imperiia v sravnitel'noi perspektive.* On legal pluralism, see the discussions in Dupret, Berger, and al-Zwaini, *Legal Pluralism in the Arab World,* pp. vii–xviii, 3–40.

29. On the ideology of Russian legal reform, see Wortman, *Development of a Russian Legal Consciousness;* and Wagner, *Marriage, Property, and Law,* pp. 1–58.

30. On distinctions between the civil law and common law traditions, see Merryman, *The Civil Law Tradition;* on regulation's appeal, see Foucault, *Discipline and Punish,* esp. pp. 298–303; and on liberal legal theory in Russia, see Engelstein, "Combined Underdevelopment," pp. 338–353.

31. The work of Russian statisticians has been analyzed critically by Alessandro

Stanziani, in, among other works, his "Les Enquêtes Orales en Russie, 1861–1914." On the impact of agronomists and other specialists on policy toward peasants, see Kotsonis, *Making Peasants Backward.* Teodor Shanin's influential work, *The Awkward Class* (1972), made explicit the connections between early twentieth-century scholarship and later peasant studies with his attention to Chaianov's theory of peasant economy.

32. On the debates over customary law, see Frierson, "Rural Justice in Public Opinion." On the peasant question in the nineteenth century, see Michael B. Petrovich, "The Peasant in Nineteenth-Century Historiography," in Vucinich, *The Peasant in Nineteenth-Century Russia,* pp. 191–230; and Frierson, *Peasant Icons. Peasant Icons* reveals how both questions and answers concerning Russian peasants were established in the post-emancipation period. As late as 1909 A. A. Leont'ev, an outstanding specialist on peasant law, called for a systematic codification of customary law (Leont'ev, *Krestianskoe pravo,* pp. 399–401).

33. Most influential among peasant-resistance scholars remains Scott, particularly his *Weapons of the Weak.* For a critique of resistance studies, see Cooper, "Conflict and Connection." Resistance regains its power when it is applied to peasants' opposition to collectivization, as in Viola's *Peasant Rebels* and Fitzpatrick's *Stalin's Peasants.*

34. An influential text here is Moore, *Law as Process.* The premises of a processual approach are set out in her introduction, pp. 1–31.

35. This perspective is articulated by Margaret Somers; see her articles, "Rights, Relationality, and Membership: Rethinking the Meaning of Citizenship"; and "Citizenship and the Place of the Public Sphere." An important early work in this tradition was Douglas Hay's "Property, Authority, and the Criminal Law," in Hay et al., *Albion's Fatal Tree,* pp. 17–63.

36. See the provocative and persuasive work of Ewick and Silbey, *The Common Place of Law;* Merry, *Getting Justice and Getting Even;* and Greenhouse, "Interpreting American Litigiousness." I thank Mark Suchman for his discussion of these sources.

37. For a summary of approaches to legal pluralism, see John Griffiths's preface to Dupret, Berger, and al-Zwaini, *Legal Pluralism in the Arab World,* pp. vii–ix, 3–19; and Gordon R. Woodman, "The Idea of Legal Pluralism," in ibid., pp. 3–19.

38. Here is where I differ from Christine Worobec, whose otherwise excellent book, *Peasant Russia,* assumes that there is a peasant culture that extends over the whole post-emancipation period. Stephen Frank's book, *Crime, Cultural Conflict, and Justice,* makes frequent use of analogies with peasants in distant times and places, and with colonialism.

39. On the historical connection of legal culture and citizenship, see Somers, "Rights, Relationality, and Membership," pp. 63–112.

40. On the influence of prerevolutionary ideas, see Jane Burbank, "Legal Culture, Citizenship, and Peasant Jurisprudence," pp. 85–94. Peter Gatrell provides an account of the transmission of Russian theories to other areas in his "Historians and Peasants," pp. 22–50.

41. For an excellent overview of the historiography and a comprehensive study of the topic, see Moon, *The Russian Peasantry, 1600–1930.* Among other perspectives on the field, see Eklof, "Ways of Seeing"; Burbank and Ingerflom, "Paysans et intellectuels en Russie"; Moon, "Women in Rural Russia from the Tenth to the Twentieth Centuries"; and Gromyko, "Kul'tura russkogo krest'ianstva XVIII–XIX vekov kak predmet istoricheskogo issledovaniia."

42. Kotsonis, *Making Peasants Backward;* Stanziani, "Les enquêtes orales en Russie"; and Stanziani, *L'économie en révolution.*

43. Field's notion that peasants were "naive monarchists" offered an answer to the apparent contradiction between peasant interest (presumed to be the overthrow of autocracy) and peasant behavior; see Field, *Rebels in the Name of the Tsar.*

44. Frierson's article described family divisions—the breakup of extended families into smaller ones—as a "normal element in the cycle of rural family life," p. 50; see Frierson, "*Razdel:* The Peasant Family Divided." Analysis of Russian public opinion as representation and not reality remained a hallmark of Frierson's later studies of elite images of peasants and peasant activism; see her *Peasant Icons* and *All Russia Is Burning!*

45. Several of Hoch's conclusions about peasant labor and social organization under serfdom did not fit with conventional wisdom about the Russian economy. His research demonstrated that the serf diet was more adequate than that of Western European peasants (*Serfdom and Social Control,* pp. 28–51). Two classic books on peasant agriculture are Michael Confino's *Domaines et seigneurs en Russie vers la fin du XVIIIe siècle* (Paris, 1963); and Jerome Blum's *Lord and Peasant in Russia from the Ninth to the Nineteenth Century* (Princeton, N.J.: Princeton University Press, 1961).

46. Brooks, *When Russia Learned to Read.*

47. Eklof, *Russian Peasant Schools.*

48. Note the collectivizing titles of collective volumes appearing in the post-Soviet wave of peasant studies: *The World of the Russian Peasant; Peasant Economy, Culture, and Politics of European Russia, 1800–1921; Russian Peasant Women.* In the post-Soviet period, scholars have returned to topics raised in the late 1960s and early 1970s—ethnography, peasant economy, and peasant politics. The most comprehensive of these new studies is Worobec's *Peasant Russia.* Worobec adheres closely to ethnographic investigations produced in mid- to late-nineteenth-century Russia and describes a long-lasting "mind-set of the Russian peasant" (p. 221), but other recent works challenge the conventional historiography. Esther Kingston-Mann has argued that communal land arrangements did not preclude agricultural innovation and improvement; Elvira Wilbur's research questioned the long-held thesis of peasant impoverishment in the late nineteenth century. Stephen Wheatcroft disconnected peasant rebellion from the causality of economic crisis. See Kingston-Mann, "Peasant Communes and Economic Innovation"; Wilbur, "Peasant Poverty in Theory and Practice"; and Wheatcroft, "Crisis and the Condition of the Peasantry in Late Imperial Russia," in Kingston-Mann and Mixter, *Peasant Economy, Culture, and Politics of European Russia,* pp. 23–51, 101–127, and 128–172, respectively. Other prominent contributions to this field are Eklof and Frank, *The World of the Russian Peasant;* Farnsworth and Viola, *Russian Peasant Women;* and Frank, *Crime, Cultural Conflict, and Justice.*

49. See David Moon's thoughtful address to this question in his *Russian Peasantry,* pp. 11–36. On native categories and their uses, as well as a critique of identitarian scholarship, see Brubaker and Cooper, "Beyond 'Identity.'"

50. The category "peasant economy" was a fundament of *zemstvo* studies. An example is the ten-part study concerning the "influence of fodder cultivation on various aspects of peasant economy," published by P. A. Vikhlaev, head of the Statistical Bureau of the Moscow Provincial Zemstvo, between 1912 and 1915. Vikhlaev's series, *Vliianie travoseianiia na otdel'nie storony krest'ianskogo khoziaistva,* included the following "peasant" titles, all from Moscow—Vol. 4: *Travoseianie i krest'ianskie postroiki,* 1913; Vol. 6: *Krestianskoe zemlevladenie pri polevom travoseianii,* 1914; Vol. 10: *Krest'ianskoe khoziaistvo Moskovskogo uezda pri polevom travoseianii.*

51. On "*kustar',*" see Mogul, "In the Shadow of the Factory."

52. N. Rubakin, *Rossiia v tsifrakh.* Following the arguments of a leading jurist, Rubakin argued that the estate system was an eighteenth-century import from Western Europe (pp. 52–53). See Gregory L. Freeze's discussion of the liberal attack on *soslovie* in his provocative article, "The *Soslovie* (Estate) Paradigm and Russian Social History."

53. Among many works on the multiplicity of peasant occupations at this time, see Engel, *Between the Fields and the City;* Johnson, *Peasant and Proletarian;* and Burds, *Peasant Dreams and Market Politics.*

54. For a summary of the legal position of ex-serfs after the emancipation, see Daniel Field, "The Year of Jubilee," in Eklof, Bushnell, and Zakharova, *Russia's Great Reforms,* pp. 40–53.

55. *Rightful obligation* is my term.

56. All eight books of *The Regulation on the Rural Estate* (*PSS*) constitute the "Special Appendix to the Ninth Volume" of the *Collected Laws of the Russian Empire* (*SZ* 9, *Osoboe Prilozhenie*). Book 1 of *The Regulation on the Rural Estate* was addressed specifically to "peasants." See the note on sources about this codification.

57. *OPK,* sts. 1–7.

58. Unless they were on the lam, of course, and even then they would need to find new fake credentials. On runaways and status, see Schrader, *Languages of the Lash,* pp. 84–103.

59. TsIAM, f. 749, op. 1, d. 33.

60. On entry into the townspeople's estate, see Wirtschafter, *Social Identity,* pp. 132–136. For an example of merchant ambition, see David L. Ransel, "An Eighteenth-Century Russian Merchant Family in Prosperity and Decline," in Burbank and Ransel, *Imperial Russia,* pp. 256–280.

61. Alexander K. Afanas'ev, "Jurors and Jury Trials in Imperial Russia, 1866–1883," in Eklof, Bushnell, and Zakharova, *Russia's Great Reforms,* p. 225.

62. A stark expression of this approach is the following sentence from René Beerman, "Prerevolutionary Russian Peasant Laws," in Butler, *Russian Law: Historical and Political Perspectives,* p. 184: "The *volost'* courts were a most essential institution which, however, testified to the extent to which the peasantry were divorced from the rest of society."

63. A farsighted forerunner of this new wave of interest in the township court was Czap, whose article, "Peasant Class Courts and Peasant Customary Justice in Russia, 1861–1912," introduced these courts and the question of peasant custom to Anglophone scholars in 1967. An influential article in the collectivist tradition was Lewin's "Customary Law and Russian Rural Society in the Post-Reform Era." A major innovation was Beatrice Farnsworth's use of materials on the township courts to study daughters-in-law in peasant families ("The Litigious Daughter-in-Law"). See also Farnsworth's "Soldatka: Folklore and Court Record."

64. Frierson, "Rural Justice in Public Opinion," and "'I Must Always Answer to the Law . . .'"

65. Popkins, "Popular Development of Procedure in a Dual Legal System"; "Code *versus* Custom"; and "Peasant Experiences of the Late Tsarist State."

66. In his 1907 handbook on peasant jurisprudence, V. V. Tenishev defined *samosud* as "the implementation of legal [*sudebnyi*] authority that is not stipulated by the law and is carried out in an unauthorized way [*samovol'no*] and moreover whose judgments, established in an unauthorized way, are put into effect in a way not stipulated by the law, in most cases violently" (*Pravosudie,* p. 33). The major scholarly encyclopedia of the time defined *samosud* with a specific reference to the United States: "*Samosud* over criminals, corresponding to the American Lynch court . . . is quite widespread

in peasant society" (*Entsiklopedicheskii slovar'*, 28:231). (The origins of the American term are disputed.) See also Dal', *Tolkovyi slovar' velikorusskogo iazyka,* 4:135. In this dictionary, from an earlier period, the folkloric sayings cited about *samosud* are negative in tone: "*Samosud* is not a court," "*Samosud* is crooked justice," and so on. These "sayings," expressing a critical attitude toward unofficial justice, have been ignored in elite commentaries.

67. For an example, see Steven Frank's article, "Popular Justice, Community, and Culture, 1870–1900," in a collection with the revealing title *The World of the Russian Peasant.* In this book, whose goal was to address the "material life, society, and culture of the late nineteenth-century Russian peasantry," the single article on law focuses on extralegality. Frank's application of the term *charivari,* derived from Western legal studies, leaves peasant legal practice in the realm of ritual; see Frank, "Popular Justice," in Eklof and Frank, *The World of the Russian Peasant,* pp. 137–144; and idem, *Crime, Cultural Conflict, and Justice,* pp. 249–261. For another analysis of *samosud* that avoids the resistance paradigm, see Frierson, "Crime and Punishment in the Russian Village." On the influence of subaltern studies on historical theory, see the following articles in the AHR Forum: *American Historical Review* 99, no. 5 (December 1994): Gyan Prakash, "Subaltern Studies as Postcolonial Criticism," pp. 1475–1490; Florencia E. Mallon, "The Promise and Dilemma of Subaltern Studies: Perspectives from Latin American History," pp. 1491–1515; and Frederick Cooper, "Conflict and Connection: Rethinking Colonial African History," pp. 1516–1545. See also Frederick Cooper and Ann Laura Stoler, "Colonial Studies in the 1990s: Rethinking an Agenda," in Cooper and Stoler, *Tensions of Empire,* pp. 1–56; and Guha and Spivak, *Selected Subaltern Studies.*

68. See Giovanni Levi's discussion of the tendency to focus on the "contradictions of normative systems," in his essay, "On Microhistory," in Burke, *New Perspectives on Historical Writing.* David Ransel provides a more inclusive view of microhistory; see his "Eighteenth-Century Russian Merchant Family in Prosperity and Decline," in Burbank and Ransel, *Imperial Russia,* pp. 256–257.

69. Erich Auerbach, *Mimesis: The Representation of Reality in Western Literature,* trans. William Trask (New York: Doubleday, 1957 [1946]), p. 488.

70. Tenishev, *Pravosudie,* pp. 185–192.

71. Ibid., pp. 185, 188, 192. Translation of "*sovershenno khladnokrovno otnessia k svei spine.*"

72. See, for example, *Iuridicheskii kalendar' dlia volostnykh i dolzhnostnykh lits;* and *Iuridicheskii kalendar' dlia zemskikh nachal'nikov 1904 g.*

73. For most citations of court regulations I use an edition of the *Collected Laws* prepared for use by legal specialists: *Svod Zakonov Rossiiskoi Imperii,* ed. I. D. Mordukhai-Boltovskii, 5 vols. (St. Petersburg: Russkoe Knizhnoe Tovarishchestvo "Deiatel'," [1912] [*SZ*]). This includes the 1902 edition of *The Regulation on the Rural Estate* [*PSS*]), updated to 1912. It incorporates preceding revisions of the township court rules and peasant rights, the most substantial of which were enacted in 1889 and 1906, and includes the extensive modifications to the legal code on peasant landholding (the "Stolypin" reforms) promulgated in 1906 and 1910. See the note on sources.

74. Record books were not always kept for separate calendar years. In addition, some clerks kept separate books for criminal, civil, and closed cases. These practices, combined with the uneven survival of the township records, mean that it is not possible to find exactly equivalent long runs of cases for different courts.

75. See the note on sources and Appendix 1.

76. See Appendix 1.

77. For displays of calculations, graphs, and other illustrative material not published in this book, but relevant to the topic, see http://www.nyu.edu/projects/burbank/.

78. I also read a few records from a court in Novgorod Province, Tikhvin County, Anisimovskii Township and from a court in Olonetsk Province, Lodeinopol'skii County, Zaostrovskii Township. These courts did not figure in the numerical surveys.

79. Both words refer to villages: a *selo* has at least one church, a *derevnia* has none. In principle, a *selo* should be a bigger settlement, but this was not always the case. *Derevnia* has the stronger association with peasants and a peasant way of life. Adjectives from both words—*derevenskii* and *sel'skii*—can simply mean rural.

80. There were two estates in the township that had no peasants living on them and were thus not included in the "peasant settlements" (*Naselennye mesta Moskovskoi gubernii* [1913], pp. 242–243). On the Savvinskaia sloboda, see *Odintsovskaia zemlia*, pp. 370–377.

81. For a list of trades, see *Moskovskoe gubernskoe zemstvo v poluvekovuiu godovshchinu osnovaniia zemskikh uchrezhdenii, 1864–1914*, pp. 76–83.

82. The *zemstvo* was a provincial or county-level organization of local representatives, elected according to the estate principle, and delegated by the imperial government to provide social services to a region. On *zemstvo* schools, see Eklof, *Russian Peasant Schools*, pp. 70–96.

83. *Naselennye mesta Moskovskoi gubernii* (1913), p. 243. In 1904 a taxation record book attributed 231 taxable male "souls" to Iagunino (TsIAM, f. 748, op. 1, d. 117a). A local record book lists 60 heads of household for Iagunino on 3 January 1905 (TsIAM, f. 748, op. 1, d. 32, l. 3o), which is consistent with a population of around 430 at the beginning of the period under study. The number of people registered in a settlement can be approximated by multiplying households by about seven, or by doubling the number of male "souls." This technique is, of course, inexact. A specialist on Moscow province calculated that the average family size was 6.3 people in 1910 (P. A. Vikhlaev, *Naselenie i promysli travopol'nogo raiona*, Vol. 9: *Vliianie travoseianiia na otdel'nye storony krest'ianskogo khoziastva*, p. 1). Another source indicates that, in 1890, Iagunino had 699 inhabitants and that in 1926 its population was 467 (*Odintsovskaia zemlia*, p. 466). The population may have contracted and expanded more than once between these dates.

84. The official title of the county's central city is *uezdnyi gorod*.

85. *Pamiatnaia kniga Moskovskoi gubernii na 1908 god*, p. 302.

86. *Naselennye mestnosti Moskovskoi gubernii . . . na 1912 god*, pp. 239–242.

87. Ibid, pp. 239–242.

88. Wheels were produced throughout Moscow Province. *Moskovskoe gubernskoe zemstvo*, pp. 76, 81, 83.

89. Klin was a town in the thirteenth century, part of the principality of Tver' until 1482. The town was made a county center in 1781; see *Rossiia: Polnoe geograficheskoe opisanie nashego otechestva*, 1:230; Shramchenko, *Spravochnaia knizhka Moskovskoi gubernii*, p. 235.

90. Orlov, *1905 v Klinskom uezde*, p. 3.

91. *Otchet Klinskoi uezdnoi zemskoi upravy po ekonomicheskoi chasti za 1903 g.*, pp. 7–55; *Doklad Klinskoi uezdnoi upravy po ekonomicheskoi chasti* (Klin: Klinskoe uezdnoe sobranie, 1905), pp. 2–26. In 1905 the Klin district *zemstvo* ordered plows and other items from local artisans (*Obzor Moskovskoi gubernii za 1905*, 1906, p. 15).

92. Gorshkov, "Serfs on the Move," p. 648.

93. Orlov, *1905*, pp. 3–4.

94. Orlov, *1905*, pp. 3–5; *Naselennye mestnosti Moskovskoi gubernii . . . na 1912 god*, pp. 285–287. Selinskoe was a *selo*.

95. Gorshkov, "Serfs on the Move," pp. 639, 643, 649.

96. *Rossiia: Polnoe geograficheskoe opisanie,* 1:291; "Gorod Bogorodsk," *Istochnik,* no. 3 (1994): 113–118; *Uezdnyi gorod Bogorodsk na starykh fotografiiakh,* pp. 4, 13, 30–33; Mikhail Drozdov, "Bogorodsk na starykh fotografiiakh," *Pamiatniki otechestva* 34, nos. 3–4 (1995): 98–101. A silk-making instrument figured in the coat of arms of Bogorodsk, the capital city of the county (Tokmakov, *Istoriko-statisticheskoe i arkheologicheskoe opisanie goroda Bogorodska,* p. 13).

97. Zhukova, *Staryi Pavlovskii posad,* pp. 11–14, 34–62. This is an excellent study of Pavlovskii posad and its surroundings before 1917.

98. *Statisticheskii ezhegodnik Moskovskoi gubernii za 1908 god,* p. 3.

99. The connection between peasant enterprise and education can be seen from various perspectives. Boris Gorshkov argues that participation in trade and production stimulated not only demand for education but the opening and financing of schools. See Gorshkov, "Serfs on the Move," pp. 652–653. Contemporary statisticians complained of the negative effect of the widespread home workshop system on girls' education, claiming that parents kept their female children out of school for the sake of their labor (Vikhlaev, *Ekonomicheskie usloviia narodnogo obrazovaniia v Moskovskoi gubernii,* pp. 5–40).

100. Elizavetino was a *sel'tso.*

101. *Naselennye mestnosti Moskovskoi gubernii* (1913), pp. 79–81; Zhukova, *Staryi Pavlovskii posad,* pp. 3, 11–14, 39.

102. *Naselennye mestnosti Moskovskoi gubernii* (1913), pp. 95–98; *Rossiia: Polnoe geograficheskoe opisanie,* 1:159, 291; *Istorichesko-statisticheskoe opisanie sela Grebneva,* pp. 9, 15–20. In the early eighteenth century Novaia belonged to the Trubetskoi family (*Istorichesko-statisticheskoe opisanie Sela Grebneva,* p. 11). Shchelkovo was itself the location of several major factories; see *Pamiatnaia kniga Moskovskoi gubernii na 1914 god,* pp. 114–115.

103. From the sixteenth century, peasants had occupied themselves with "ogorodnichestvo and sadovodchestvo"; see *Ekonomichesko-statisticheskii sbornik,* vyp. 3 (Moscow, 1911), pp. 35–44, for a critical and detailed overview of the region's economy in 1910. For the nineteenth century, see *Rossiia: Polnoe geograficheskoe opisanie,* 1:137, 320–321.

104. In the 1930s a workers' settlement of small-scale apartment buildings was constructed in Tsaritsyno, by then renamed Lenino. The big housing projects, characteristic of these areas in the late Soviet period, were begun only in the 1960s, when Lenino and Nagatino were incorporated into Moscow city (personal communication, Sergei Romaniuk).

105. *Moskovskoe gubernskoe zemstvo,* pp. 78, 79, 83.

106. *Opisanie Moskovskogo uezda, s ukazaniem v onom stanov, volostei, uriadov i selenii,* p. 55; *Novaia karta okrestnostei Moskvy; Naselennye mestnosti Moskovskoi gubernii . . . na 1912 god,* pp. 42–44.

107. *Rossiia: Polnoe geograficheskoe opisanie,* 1:137, 320–321; *Pamiatniki otechestva* 32, nos. 3–4 (1994): 163–166. *Opisanie Moskovskogo uezda,* p. 50; *Novaia karta okrestnostei Moskvy; Naselennye mestnosti Moskovskoi gubernii . . . na 1912 god,* pp. 44–46.

108. To give some sense of the population shifts in the late imperial period: in the 1880s forty peasant households were registered in the village of Tsaritsyno, and the population was ninety-three males and ninety-nine women of all ages (*Opisanie Moskovskogo uezda,* p. 50).

109. Note the changes in administration of this region. According to *Tikhvinskii krai,* ed. V. I. Ravdonikis (Tikhvin: Tikhvinskii uispolkom, 1926), p. 192, Zaborovskii Township changed jurisdictions as follows:

1917	1918	1919
Tikhvinskii uezd	Tikhvinskii uezd	Malovisherskii uezd
Novgorodskaia guberniia	Cherepovetskaia guberniia	Cherepovetskaia guberniia

110. *Spisok naselennykh mest Novgorodskoi gubernii,* vyp. 7: *Tikhvinskii uezd,* pp. 50–51. My hesitancy about the population derives from a smaller figure recorded in the rural society's decision regarding the change in their land tenure arrangements. In the words of a court case: the villagers chose a *"perekhod ot obshchinnogo k poddvornomu nasledstvennomu pol'zovaniiu nadel'noi zemli"* (TsGIA-L, f. 1807, op. 1, ed. khr. 54, ll. 1–2). On peasants' *"udel'noe"* status, see TsGIA-L, f. 1807, op. 1, ed. khr. 31, ll. 11–11o), which also contains a list of seventeen out of twenty-five heads of household, the village *starosta* and the township *starshina,* recorded by the scribe on 8 April 1909. According to this document, the village was home to sixty-eight souls and twenty-five household heads in April 1909. Out-migration for employment may explain these disparities in population figures.

111. *Pamiatnaia knizhka Novgorodskoi gubernii na 1913 god,* p. 321.

112. *Rossiia: Polnoe geograficheskoe opisanie nashego otechestva,* 3: *Ozernaia oblast'; Statisticheskii sbornik po Petrogradskoi gubernii 1913 god,* vyp. 2: *Nachal'noe narodnoe obrazovanie v 1912–1913 uchebnom godu,* pp. XVII, XX–XXI, 5, 19, 38.

113. *Rossiia: Polnoe geograficheskoe opisanie nashego otechestva,* 3:366–367; *Pamiatnaia kniga S.-Peterburgskoi gubernii na 1914–1915 gg.,* p. 79.

114. *Obzor S.-Peterburgskoi gubernii za 1909 god,* pp. 12, 16, 17, 25; *Statisticheskii sbornik po Petrogradskoi gubernii 1913 god.,* vyp. 2: *Nachal'noe narodnoe obrazovanie v 1912–1913,* pp. XX–XXI.

115. An official handbook from 1864 observes that the entire county was 47.2 percent Finnish (*Spiski naselennykh mest Rossiiskoi imperii, XXXVII. Sankt-Peterburgskaia guberniia.* Spisok naselennykh mest po svedeniiam 1862 goda, p. XLIII).

116. *Rossiia: Polnoe geograficheskoe opisanie,* 3:110.

117. Their names, respectively, were Ivan Semenovich Khaigonen and Mikhail Nikitin Lisitsin. The teachers at the *zemstvo* school in Toksovo were Mikhail Andreevich Kosolainen and Mariia Nikolaevna Smirnova, another Finnish-Russian pair (*Pamiatnaia knizhka S.-Peterburgskoi gubernii na 1914–1915 gg.,* pp. 388, 403). For place names, see *Spiski naselennykh mest Rossiiskoi imperii, XXXVII. Sankt-Peterburgskaia guberniia,* pp. 196–197.

118. *Kratkii statisticheskii ocherk krest'ianskogo zemlevladeniia i promyslov v Tsarskosel'skom uezde SPb. gub.,* pp. 1, 8; *Materialy k otsenke zemel' v S.-Peterburgskoi gubernii,* Vol. 6: Tsarskosel'skii uezd, pp. 2, 5. A later study suggested different figures, namely, that 50 percent of the "workers" (not households) in Sosnitskii Township were engaged exclusively in agriculture (*Promysly krest'ianskogo naseleniia S-Peterburgskoi gubernii. Tsarskosel'skii uezd,* p. 7).

119. On the subject of out-migration for work (*otkhod*), see Burds, *Peasant Dreams and Market Politics.*

120. *Promysly S-Peterburgskoi gubernii. Tsarskosel'skii uezd,* pp. 7, 36–40, 80–81.

121. For descriptions of this area, see Moon, *The Russian Peasantry,* pp. 38–43.

122. On the reforms and for interpretations of their significance, see Wcislo, *Reforming Rural Russia,* pp. 119–242; Macey, *Government and Peasant,* pp. 214–249; Stanziani, *L'économie en révolution,* pp. 23–147; and Kotsonis, *Making Peasants Backward,* pp. 13–134.

123. See Macey, *Government and Peasant,* pp. 76–77, on the relation of this law to the reform process. The abolition of collective responsibility of 1903 applied to peasants

possessing communal property. Earlier, collective responsibility was abolished for peasants holding individual allotments, and later, in 1906, collective responsibility was abolished universally; see A. A. Leont'ev, "Zakonodatel'stvo o krest'ianakh posle reformy," in *Velikaia reforma,* 6:188–190.

124. Leont'ev, "Zakonodatel'stvo," *Velikaia reforma,* 6:188; Frank, "Emancipation and the Birch," pp. 401–416; Schrader, *Languages of the Lash,* pp. 153–155.

125. *PSZ* 3, vol. 26 (1906), otd. 1, no. 28392; Leont'ev, "Zakonodatel'stvo," *Velikaia reforma,* 6:188–191; Macey, *Government and Peasant,* pp. 129, 233–234. Macey observes that the law of 5 October 1906 "might well be considered the most revolutionary" of the government's reforms. See also Wcislo, *Reforming Rural Russia,* pp. 210–211.

126. On the 1906 "Stolypin" reform, see Macey, *Government and Peasant,* pp. 234–238; and Atkinson, *The End of the Russian Land Commune 1905–1930,* pp. 57–60.

127. *PSZ* 3, vol. 26 (1906), otd. 1, no. 28392.

128. On the division of power between peasantry and the state at the time of the emancipation, see Hoch, "The Serf Economy," p. 206. As Hoch notes, the emancipation "attached the peasants to the land even more firmly than serfdom had done."

129. On this point, see Macey, *Government and Peasant,* p. 234.

130. See Atkinson, *The End of the Russian Land Commune,* p. 59; and Macey, *Government and Peasant,* p. 237. The second "Stolypin" law of 1910 reinforced male dominance by defining property of households headed by females as common property, whereas male heads of household were given individual control of their family's holdings (Atkinson, *The End of the Russian Land Commune,* p. 61).

131. Macey, *Government and Peasant,* p. 238; Atkinson, *The End of the Russian Land Commune,* pp. 41–55.

132. For a discussion of the ways that crisis has been read back over the history of imperial Russia, see Confino, "Present Events and the Representation of the Past," pp. 851–853; and Burbank and Ransel, introduction to Burbank and Ransel, *Imperial Russia,* pp. xi–xii.

133. For an example of a careful Soviet-era usage of the notion that "contradictions" can be seen as shaping history but are not in themselves fatal in the short (historical) run, see the conclusion to N. M. Druzhinin's magisterial study of the Kiselov reform in his *Gosudarstvennye krest'iane i reforma P. D. Kiseleva,* 2:577. For provocative treatments of ways that conflicting ideas of the law can be sustained in a legalistic society, see Ewick and Silbey, *The Common Place of Law,* pp. 45–53; and Greenhouse, "Interpreting American Litigiousness," pp. 252–273.

2. A LITIGIOUS PERSON AND HER POSSIBILITIES

1. Sosnitskii Township was in Tsarskosel'skii County, Petrograd Province; the province, like the capital city, was renamed from St. Petersburg during the war. See the description of this area in chapter 1.

2. The source for this case is RGIA, formerly TsGIA, f. 1344, op. 306, d. 215: Delo po predstavleniiu i. d. Petrogradskogo komisara s zhaloboi kr-ki Praskovoi Aref'evoi o nasledii. . . , dated 28 July 1917. Unfortunately the pages of the file are not sequentially numbered, so a general reference will have to suffice for citations to the case. I indicate names of subdocuments in the file where appropriate.

3. Her characterization in the record is *krest'ianka devitsa* (peasant spinster).

4. There are inconsistencies in the spelling of the village's name. A 1913 source records the name as Lemozha (*Alfavitnoi spisok naselennykh mest S.-Peterburgskoi gubernii*, p. 62). Two other spellings—Lemozhi and Limozhi—are given in *Spiski naselennykh mest Rossiiskoi imperii, XXXVII. Sankt-Peterburgskaia guberniia.* Spisok . . . 1862 goda (p. 175). The Lemozha rural society consisted of thirty-seven household heads in 1901 and forty-three household heads in 1911, according to the various records of meetings of the rural assembly (RGIA, f. 1344, op. 306, d. 215).

5. N. 22 kopiia s resheniia Sostnitskogo volostnogo suda po grazh. N. 22–1908g., RGIA, f. 1344, op. 306, d. 215.

6. Elena was described as *bezumnaia* (insane). On Iamburg, see *Rossiia: Polnoe geograficheskoe opisanie,* 3:292; P. Zhulev, *Ocherk istorii Kingissepskogo uezda i goroda Kingissepp (byvshego Iama-Iamburga);* and *Materialy k otsenke gorodskikh nedvizhimykh imushchestv v S.-Peterburgskoi gubernii,* vyp. 4: *Gorod Iamburg.*

7. Posemeinyi spisok, RGIA, f. 1344, op. 306, d. 215.

8. See no. 3, Prigovor, kopiia, [1901 goda aprelia 25 dnia . . .], RGIA, f. 1344, op. 306, d. 215. Here Elena is described as *idiotka* (idiot).

9. The resolution cites Statute 51 of the Law of 19 February 1861 (the Emancipation Decree). This statute was subsequently incorporated into the post-1906 edition of *The General Regulation on the Peasants* as statute 62 (*OPK,* st. 62; *SZ* 9, osob. pri., st. 62).

10. N. 6, Prigovor kopiia, RGIA, f. 1344, op. 306, d. 215.

11. Kazennaia palata, 18 November 1906, RGIA, f. 1344, op. 306, d. 215. The land captain was the official charged with oversight of the township administration. On the land captains' supervision of the courts, see chapter 6; also see Popkins, "Peasant Experiences of the Late Tsarist State"; and Gaudin, "Les zemskie načal'niki au village."

12. On the law of 9 November 1906, see Macey, *Government and Peasant,* pp. 226–238. Macey notes that "the head of household now achieved recognition as the legal owner of all forms of peasant property" (p. 237). Dorothy Atkinson argues that the 1910 legislation made it impossible for women to hold the household property as private property (*The End of the Russian Land Commune,* p. 61). The regulations on "peasants' right to private property on sections of allotment land" in the 1910 version of the Stolypin laws indicate that a *"domokhoziain"* can own such property as *"sobstvennost',"* and that if women and children possess undivided property, they hold it in collective ownership (*OPK,* sts. 37^4, 37^5).

13. See Praskovia Aref'eva's petition of 28 June 1917 to the Senate (RGIA, f. 1344, op. 306, d. 215), in which she provides the information for the higher authorities.

14. N. 22 kopiia s resheniia Sosnitskogo volostnogo suda po grazh N. 22–1908g., RGIA, f. 1344, op. 306, d. 215.

15. Ibid.

16. Ispolnitel'nyi list, RGIA, f. 1344, op. 306, d. 215.

17. On the county congress as an appeals institution, see Popkins, "Peasant Experiences of the Late Tsarist State," pp. 90–114; and on appeals from the township courts, see Popkins, "Code *versus* Custom."

18. Kopiia iz resheniia Sosnitskogo volostnogo suda . . . 21 aprelia 1911, RGIA, f. 1344, op. 306, d. 215.

19. On the elections of township court judges, see chapter 6.

20. Kopiia iz resheniia Sosnitskogo volostnogo suda . . . 21 aprelia 1911, RGIA, f. 1344, op. 306, d. 215.

21. See Prigovor . . . 1911 goda 9 oktiabria, sel'skii skhod Lemozhi, RGIA, f. 1344, op. 306, d. 215.

22. The value of the joint movable property of Frol Grigor'ev and Elena Ivanova, now to be formally managed by Frol Grigor'ev, was estimated at 565 rubles, and included one horse, one sheep, several buildings, and farming implements. Cows no longer figured in the inventory (Prigovor . . . 1911 goda 9 oktiabria, sel'skii skhod Lemozhi, RGIA, f. 1344, op. 306, d. 215).

23. Kopiia resheniia Sos. vol. suda po grazhdan. dela 1911, No. 172, RGIA, f. 1344, op. 306, d. 215.

24. Ibid.

25. *The Regulation on Land Captains* is part of *The Regulation on the Rural Estate* (*PSS*, Polozhenie o zemskikh uchastkovykh nachal'nikakh, sts. 2–135).

26. RGIA, f. 1344, op. 306, d. 215.

27. On Sosnitskii township, see chapter 1.

28. RGIA, f. 1344, op. 306, d. 215.

29. Ibid. The word for restrictions based on expired time is *davnost'*.

30. Zhaloba, 24 avgusta 1916, RGIA, f. 1344, op. 306, d. 215.

31. Defending the statute of limitations, the board cited decrees of the Second Department of the Senate from 10 March 1908, 15 October 1910, and 26 November 1912, and noted, "complaints about the resolutions of a village assembly that have violated the property rights of individual members may be submitted before the expiration of the ten-year term [*zemskaia davnost'*]."

32. Petrogradskoe gubernskoe prisutstvie, 2 iunia 1917, RGIA, f. 1344, op. 306, d. 215.

33. Zhaloba, 28 iiunia 1917, RGIA, f. 1344, op. 306, d. 215.

34. See the section, "O pravakh krest'ianakh," in *OPK*, esp. sts. 1, 2, and 4, and chap. 1.

35. On *soslovie*, compare Freeze, "The *Soslovie* (Estate) Paradigm and Russian Social History."

36. Wirtschafter, *Social Identity in Imperial Russia*, p. 169.

37. *OPK*, st. 4.

38. Ibid.

39. Noble demands for privilege did not mean that the nobility was a uniformly thinking group. Individual, clan, class, and other divides crisscrossed this estate as well. The difficulty nobles had in developing a sense of corporate interest in Russia displays the powerfully individualizing way that status rights connected people to the state. For two perspectives on nobility and collectivity, see Kivelson, *Autocracy in the Provinces*, esp. pp. 52–57; and Becker, *Nobility and Privilege in Late Imperial Russia*.

40. From the Emancipation Statutes: "Vo poriadke nasledovaniia imushchestvom krest'ianam dosvoliaetsia rukovodstvovat'sia mestnymi svoimi obychaiami" (*OPK*, st. 13).

41. Cathy Frierson's insightful book, *Peasant Icons*, shows us how the nineteenth-century intelligentsia fell into these collectivist traps.

42. On the ways that criticism of the law's malfunctioning is part of legal culture, see Ewick and Silbey, *The Common Place of Law*, pp. 35–36.

43. On legal assistance, see Pomeranz, "Legal Assistance in Tsarist Russia"; and Neuberger, "Shysters or Public Servants?"

44. If Praskovia had had noble status, her inheritance would have been regulated by the Civil Code. In the absence of a will, she would have received one-seventh of her father's land and her brother would have received the rest (*SZ* 10, ch. 1, *Svod zakonov grazhdanskikh* [*SZG*], st. 1128).

45. Friedrich Nietzsche, *The Genealogy of Morals*, trans. Francis Golffing (Garden City, N.Y.: Doubleday, 1956 [1887]), p. 157.

3. A DAY AT COURT

1. On the question of fees, see Popkins, "Peasant Experiences," p. 97.

2. LGIA, f. 1807, op. 1, ed. kh. 50, l. 1.

3. TsIAM, f. 10, op. 1, ed. khr. 109, ll. 1–1o.

4. The name for this book is *nastolnyi reestr.*

5. Nastol'nyi reestr Zaborovskogo volostnogo suda Tikhvinskogo uezda, LGIA, f. 1807, op. 1, d. 24.

6. On the Tikhvin region in the early twentieth century, see *Spisok naselennykh mest Novgorodskoi gubernii,* vyp. 7: *Tikhvinskii uezd.* The town of Tikhvin, connected by railroad to St. Petersburg and by water route to Lake Ladoga, had two printing establishments at this time (p. 7).

7. A copy of a summons form can be found in TsGIA-L, f. 1807, op. 1, d. 26.

8. For an example of a dossier prepared for an inheritance case, see TsIAM, f. 749, op. 1, d. 27.

9. *OPK,* st. 133. A party in township cases was called a "side" (*storona*).

10. *OPK,* st. 134; and st. 77, pr. 1.

11. *OPK,* st. 77, pr. 1.

12. For these rules on people of other status (*litsa drugikh sostoianii*), see *OPK,* sts. 128, 162; on the Justices of the Peace and their jurisdiction, see Neuberger, "Popular Legal Cultures: The St. Petersburg *Mirovoi Sud.*"

13. *OPK,* st. 125, pr. 1 and 2.

14. See Frierson, "I Must Always Answer to the Law. . . ," pp. 327–330, on the expanding use of township courts in the late nineteenth century. My cautious figure of 85 percent is calculated on the estate breakdown of the empire's population provided in Rubakin, *Rossiia v tsifrakh,* p. 54. Peasants and townspeople constituted 87.7 percent of the empire's population, according to Rubakin's figures, based on the 1897 census.

15. TsGIAgM, f. 1112, op. 1, d. 16, ll. 29o–45. The significance of no-show cases is considered in chapter 6.

16. See the criminal cases for 1913 in TsGIAgM, f. 10, op. 1, d. 91. For a fuller discussion of the Nagatinskii Township Court, see chapter 5.

17. For example, in Grebnevskii Township in the mixed textile-producing and agricultural region of Bororodskii County in Moscow Province, there were 1,880 peasant households and only 3 private estates in the area of peasant settlement, and 1 dacha settlement and 13 more private estates outside the area of peasant settlement (*Naselennye mesta Moskovskoi gubernii,* pp. 95–98). Peasant households constituted an overwhelming majority in the township, as they did in most rural areas.

18. *OMG,* 1910, pp. 117, 123.

19. This un-gendered aspect of the codes governing peasant life was noted by Prince V. N. Tenishev, the major expert on peasant legal practice in the nineteenth century. He notes that nothing in the law prevented a woman from participating in the village assembly either as a head of household (*zhenshchina-domokhoziaka*) or as a substitute for her husband, or from being elected to the township-level assembly (Tenishev, *Administrativnoe polozhenie russkogo krest'ianina,* p. 7).

20. *OPK,* st. 50; st. 50, pr. 1.

21. Some plaintiffs and more defendants were registered outside the township at which cases were heard, and for these I do not have comparable data.

22. TsGIAL, f. 1807, op. 1, d. 26.

23. LGIA, f. 1807, op. 1, d. 24 (1906–1907), l. 169, cases 7 and 9; l. 176, case 20; l. 179, case 57; l. 180, case 62. Several cases initiated by Smetanin as early as 1900 can also be found in this file.

24. LGIA, f. 1807, op. 1, d. 42, ll. 1–2.

25. *OPK*, st. 118.

26. TsGIAgM, f. 849, op. 1, dd. 8, 9.

27. For court sessions see TsIAM, f. 749, op. 1, dd. 20, 21; for 1914 holidays, see *Pamiatnaia knizhka Moskovskoi gubernii na 1914 g.*, pp. V–VIII.

28. On the judges' medallions, see *OPK*, st. 198. On the selection of judges at the township courts, see chapter 6 below.

29. See the statutes on the court (*OPK*, sts. 119, 121; and Tenishev, *Pravosudie v russkom krest'ianskom bytu*, p. 75). See also the description of courtroom procedures in Frierson, "'I Must Always Answer to the Law. . . ,'" pp. 318–319.

30. This description of procedure is derived from the court records of township courts in four provinces and from a cautious reading of the account in Tenishev, *Pravosudie*, p. 75.

31. The original regulations on the township court forbade the township leader from "interfering in the process of the Township Court" and from being present during the "consideration of a case." This restriction was abolished in the 1889 revision of court regulations, much to the dissatisfaction of critics of the reform; see Leont'ev, *Krest'ianskoe pravo*, pp. 124–127.

32. See Tenishev, *Pravosudie*, pp. 75, 167–168. In his account of township court procedure, which is based on nineteenth-century observations, Tenishev notes that all participants stood when the judges' decision was read out. This is impossible to verify from the clerk's record books, but it is not unlikely that this nineteenth-century practice continued into the twentieth century.

33. TsIAM, f. 749, op. 1, d. 8, ll. 51o–52o. This award of thirty rubles was confirmed by the land captain on 6 October of the same year.

34. This award was collected on 11 October 1906—more than a year later—an unusually long delay for cases at the township courts (TsIAM, f. 749, op. 1, d. 8, ll. 53–54).

35. *UN*, sts.143, 144. The subject of family support is discussed further in chapters 4 and 5.

36. TsGIAgM f. 849, op. 1, d. 9, ll. 41–42.

37. TsGIAgM f. 849, op. 1, d. 9, ll. 43–43o.

38. TsGIAgM f. 849, op. 1, d. 9, ll. 44–44o.

39. TsGIAgM f. 849, op. 1, d. 9, ll. 45–45o. This case is discussed further in chapter 5.

40. TsGIAgM f. 849, op. 1, d. 9, ll. 46–46o.

41. *OPK*, st. 120.

42. TsGIAgM, f. 849, op. 1, d. 8, ll. 112–112o. The name Gordiono may raise some speculation about ethnic origins or pretensions of the owner of this shop; this name is clearly entered in the case record.

43. *OPK*, sts. 137, 138.

44. *OPK*, st. 125.

45. On the history of corporal punishment in Russia, see Schrader, *Languages of the Lash*.

46. Even nineteenth-century ethnographers on the alert for evidence of pre-capitalist practices in the village did not find evidence of payments made in kind at the township court; see Tenishev, *Pravosudie*, p. 186.

47. *OPK*, st. 153.

48. *OPK*, sts. 143, 148, 150; see also Tenishev, *Pravosudie*, pp. 185–187. Before 1906 community service was also an option as a punishment for misdemeanors. On its abolition, see Czap, "Peasant Class Courts and Peasant Customary Justice in Russia, 1861–1912." In all cases I examined, community service was never an option, although nineteenth-century observers noted that peasants convicted to jail terms in some areas carried out tasks for the township administration during their arrests (Tenishev, *Pravosudie*, p. 187).

49. More than 90 percent of all civil payments in my survey were set at 100 rubles or less. There is a strong correspondence between the amounts of payments assessed by the township courts and the amounts sought by plaintiffs in civil cases. For a discussion of this point and of civil case payments generally, see chapter 4.

50. Action was to be taken *"nemedlenno"* (*OPK*, st. 139).

51. TsGIAgM, f. 10, op. 1, d. 99, ll. 95–96.

52. Tenishev, *Pravosudie*, p. 187. Tenishev's account, drawn from his father's earlier survey, observes that peasants submitted "calmly" to arrest and provides descriptions of the variety of township jails; see *OPK*, st. 143, for the regulation on harsh arrest.

53. TsGIAgM, f. 849, op. 1, d. 8, l. 53. It was also unusual, as discussed above, for a nobleman to bring a case to the township court.

54. TsGIAgM, f. 849, op. 1, d. 8, l. 12

55. TsGIAgM, f. 849, op. 1, d. 8, ll. 44o–45.

56. TsGIAgM, f. 74, op. 1, d. 52, ll. 1–2.

57. On mercy and its importance for legal authority, argued in a very different forum, see Douglas Hay's classic article, "Property, Authority and the Criminal Law," in Hay et al., *Albion's Fatal Tree*, pp. 17–63.

58. On this point, see Jeffrey Burds's discussion of the use of distraint (confiscation of property) to compel compliance with local obligations, rather than as a source of revenue through actual sale of confiscated items (*Peasant Dreams and Market Politics*, p. 62).

59. Stephen P. Frank suggests that the state was insufficiently concerned with crime in rural areas in his book, *Crime, Cultural Conflict, and Justice in Rural Russia, 1856–1917*, and that peasants turned to illegal violence to protect themselves (pp. 268–269). The widespread and growing popularity of township courts would seem to contradict his thesis of increasing dissatisfaction with state justice. At the same time, the promptness with which local officials punished misdemeanors suggests that rural people indeed took crime seriously.

60. Wages varied not just by individual, by task, region, and sex, but also by the time of year. Pay for work was highest during the harvesting seasons, when labor was scarce for the short period of bringing in the crops. According to the annual report published by the governor's office, the average pay for one day of agricultural labor with food provided by the employer in the areas of Moscow Province where township courts in my survey were located was between 41 and 60 kopeks a day at the time of spring sowing in 1908. If the laborer provided a horse, this average wage increased to 120 to 141 kopeks a day, depending on the region (*Statisticheskii ezhegodnik Moskovskoi gubernii za 1908 god.*, ch. 1, p. 124). On the politics of statistical compilations, see Stanziani, "Les statistiques des récoltes en Russie."

61. TsIAM, f. 1112, op. 1, d. 19.

62. The township clerk, Vasilii Andreevich Tunin, was the local correspondent for the statistical yearbook published for Moscow Province (*Statisticheskii ezhegodnik Moskovskoi gubernii za 1908 god*, ch. 1, pp. 124, 199). For a critical examination of how reports

were generated and correspondents selected for various statistical projects, see Stanziani, "Les enquêtes orales en Russie, 1861–1914."

63. For an example of a half-ruble fine and a whole day in jail, set in 1913 by the Nagatinskii Township Court, see TsGIAgM, f. 10, op. 1, d. 91, ll. 379–380.

64. *Statisticheskii ezhegodnik Moskovskoi gubernii za 1908 god,* ch. 1, p. 124. A sense of the disparities of local life can be measured in the difference in the prices cited for "peasant" animals and those of "landlord [*vladel'cheskii*]" horses and cows: the average price of a landlord's horse in 1908 was fifty-five or sixty rubles (winter vs. summer) and a landlord's cow cost an average of fifty or sixty-four rubles.

65. In my survey of all ten courts for all years, 15.7 percent of cases were appealed.

66. *OPK*, st. 137.

67. See the reorder form, addressed to the "Fabrika kontornykh knig. Otto Kirkhner," in the archives of the Toksovskii Township Court in St. Petersburg Province (LGIA, f. 1934, op. 1, d. 4).

68. TsGIAgM, f. 74, op. 1, d. 53.

69. For examples of other records books, see, for Iaguninskii Township, TsGAgM, f. 849, op. 1, dd. 8, 9; for Ignatevskii Township, see TsIAM, f. 1112, op. 1, d. 19; for Toksovskii Township, see LGIA, f. 1934, op. 1, d. 4.

70. TsGIAgM, f. 10, op. 1, dd. 91, 99.

71. In Russian, *istets, otvetchik, obvinitel'* or *poterpevshii,* and *obviniaemyi.*

72. For an example, see a 1916 record book of the Nagatinskii Township Court (TsGIAgM, f. 10, op. 1, d. 114).

73. TsGIAgM, f. 74, op. 1, d. 50.

74. For an excellent example, see the record book of criminal cases at the Nagatinskii Township Court in the first half of 1913 (TsGIAgM, f. 10, op. 1, d. 91).

75. At the Nagatinskii and Tsaritsynskii township courts near Moscow, record books provided four pages per case. At the Zaborovskii court in Novgorod Province, a court that apparently practiced economies while keeping excellent records, the decision books offered the clerk two pages per case. If the account of a case required more than two pages, the clerk of this court would indicate a continuation at a page assigned to a different, conveniently short case record. For Nagatinskii Township Court, see TsGIAgM, f. 10, op. 1, dd. 91, 99, 114; for Tsaritsynskii Township Court, see TsGIAgM, f. 74, op. 1, d. 50, for 1914; and for Zaborovskii Township Court, see LGIA, f. 1807, op. 1, dd. 20, 21.

76. For examples of these books, see the Iaguninskii Township court records for 1905 and 1906 in TsGIAgM, f. 849, op. 1, d. 8; and the Ignatevskii Township court records for 1908 in TsIAM, f. 1112, op. 1, d. 19.

77. *Kniga dlia zapisi reshenii* for civil cases, and *Kniga dlia zapisi prigovorov* for criminal ones; see examples for Nagatinskii Township Court in TsGIAgM, f. 10, op. 1, dd. 91, 99, 114. At the Iaguninskii Township Court, the court considered criminal cases only at seven of its thirty-one sessions in 1905, civil cases only at another seven sessions, and both kinds of cases at seventeen sessions. Nonetheless, in accord with the record-keeping habits of this court, the decisions in civil and criminal cases were always recorded separately. See TsGIAgM, f. 849, op. 1, dd. 8, 9.

78. *Kniga no. 6 dlia zapiski reshenii Zaborovskogo volostnogo suda* (LGIA, f. 1807, op. 1, d. 20); *Kniga na zapisi reshenii Zaborovskogo volostnogo suda po grazhdanskim i ugolovnym delam na 1911 god* (TsGIA-L, f. 1807, op. 1, d. 21).

79. TGIAgM, f. 849, op. 1, dd. 8, 9.

80. TGIAgM, f. 849, op. 1, d. 12.

81. See Ignatevskii court records for 1908 (TsIAM, f. 1112, op. 1, d. 19) for an example of a book of criminal case records, each one signed by the judges and all participants.

82. For a very different argument that claims peasants were increasingly hostile to official justice in these years, see Frank, *Crime, Cultural Conflict, and Justice.*

83. V. V. Tenishev cites the observation that the township courts "solved 80 percent of the cases of 80 percent of the whole population of the empire" as evidence of the importance of reforming this institution (Tenishev, *Pravosudie,* p. 4). Alessandro Stanziani's work on statistical information in late imperial Russia explores the profound divisions among state institutions and between central and *zemstvo* institutions. He suggests that rivalries among these institutions prevented them from sharing their results; see Stanziani, "Enquêtes orales," p. 238. In the case of the court statistics gathered by the governor's office and by the Ministry of Justice, figures on usage of the various judicial instances were published annually in such compilations as *Obzor Moskovskoi gubernii* [*OMG*] and *Sbornik statisticheskikh svedenii Ministerstva iustitsii* but were ignored in discussions of peasant legal culture.

84. Frierson, "Official Culture," pp. 10–13; see also Gareth Popkins's article on inheritance cases at the township courts for examples of the courts' widespread usage ("Popular Development of Procedure in a Dual Legal System," pp. 57– 87).

85. *OMG* 1905, pp. 79–131.

86. N. P. Eroshkin described this ladder as the system of *"pravitel'svenno-dvorianskii nadzor"* (Eroshkin, *Istoriia gosudarstvennykh uchrezhdenii Rossii,* pp. 267–268).

87. *OMG* 1905, pp. 80–81, 84–85.

88. There are slight discrepancies in numbers of cases heard at each instance related to the ways that cases were processed, deriving from the difference between numbers of cases available for processing in a single year, some of which might have been left over from an earlier year, and the number of cases submitted to an instance in a single year. See the rubrics in the statistical compilations in *OMG* 1905, pp. 80–131, and in subsequent years. These reports are the source for my calculations.

89. See Peter Solomon's discussion of the significance of appeal and appeal results in his *Soviet Criminal Justice under Stalin,* pp. 53–54.

90. Popkins, "Peasant Experiences," p. 113. Popkins's statistics on the percentages of cases appealed in a county of Tambov Province in 1892—from 9 to 15 percent—are consistent with my figure of 14.4 percent from my case survey for 1905–1914. See also Popkins, "Code vs. Custom," based on appeals from St Petersburg, Tambov, and Vologda provinces.

91. On the structure of the various institutional hierarchies of the imperial government, see the excellent diagrams in Eroshkin, *Istoriia gosudarstvennykh uchrezhdenii,* Prilozhenie, Karty-Skhemy.

92. These numbers represent all cases, not just those brought by peasants. Peasants would have been the vast majority of litigants at township courts. Because of their proportion of the population, peasants would also have comprised a significant percentage of the users of other courts, where, in some cases, they could bring complaints and where they could have been compelled to appear as defendants or witnesses.

93. The commercial courts were established to enhance economic development in a few big cities of the empire in the early nineteenth century; see Eroshkin, *Istoriia gosudarstvennykh uchrezhdenii,* pp. 167, 169.

94. *OMG* 1909, pp. 122–131. Of the 284 cases per court, 254, or 89 percent, were

decided in that calendar year. The 168 courts "decided," as opposed to processing, 18,381 criminal cases and 24,266 civil cases in this calendar year. On the rate of processing cases, see chapter 6.

95. If we compare the 44,947 cases at township courts in 1905 to the population of 2,433,356 for the province in the 1897 census (this was the practice of the Ministry of Justice) and assume each case is brought by a different person, 1.96 percent of the population of the province brought cases to the township court that year. This is obviously a rough estimate, based on the year with the lowest number of cases and on a population figure that was nine years old. For the Ministry of Justice's calculation of the provision of judicial instances for the population of a region, see *Sbornik statisticheskikh svedenii Ministerstva iustitsii,* vyp. 21, ch. 1: "Svedeniia o lichnom sostave i o deiatel'nosti sudebnykh ustanovlenii evropeiskoi Rossii za 1905," pp. 16–37. Popkins's work on civil cases also suggests that a high proportion of the rural population was involved in legal actions. He finds that from 4 to 8 percent of households in Saratov, Vladimir, and Kherson provinces were involved in appeals to county congresses, and that these numbers increased over time (Popkins, "Peasant Experiences, p. 93).

96. For examples see the tables of contents of *Sbornik statisticheskikh svedenii Ministerstva iustitsii,* vyp. 21, ch. 1: "Svedeniia o lichnom sostave i o deiatel'nosti sudebnykh ustanovlenii evropeiskoi Rossii za [1905–] and *OMG* [1905–]. For a study of how statistical categories were generated by other institutions, see Stanziani, "Les statistiques des récoltes en Russie, 1905–1928."

97. *UN.* See my note on sources. On the intersection of the Justice of the Peace regulations with township court criminal proceedings, see chapter 5.

98. Special forms for reporting on the fulfillment of sentences for theft were issued to the courts; see, for example, the form filled out for the Zvenigorod County Congress in TsGIAgM, f. 846, op. 1, d. 4, ll. 6–9.

99. Statutes 35 and 36 of *UN* were cited in the statistical compilations issued for Moscow Province until at least 1914, but they had been abolished by the law of 14 March 1906; see *UN,* sts. 35, 36.

100. For 1910 statistics, see *OMG* 1910, Vedomost' no. 18, pp. 114–117.

101. *OMG* 1910, pp. 122–123.

102. Vasil'ev had attained the rank of Hereditary Honorable Citizen; on the rank, see Wirtschafter, *Social Identity in Imperial Russia,* pp. 73, 193 n. 35; and Fedosiuk, *Chto neponiatno u klassikov,* p. 170.

103. TsGIAgM, f. 846, op.1, d. 4, ll. 1–5.

104. The category in the code is *"vsiakogo roda spory i tiazhby"* (*OPK,* st. 125, ch. 2).

105. *UN,* sts. 28, 31, 33, 34.

4. ALL SORTS OF SUITS AND DISPUTES

1. My use of the controversial term, *civil society,* derives from Habermas's definition of *bürgerliche Gesellschaft,* in his *Structural Transformation,* p. 19. This issue will be discussed at greater length in chapter 8. For a summary of recent approaches to civil society with direct relation to Russian history, see Bradley, "Subjects into Citizens."

2. In one of the cases heard at the Iaguninskii Township Court on 28 August 1905, the judges advised a successful plaintiff in a criminal family support case that he could bring a civil suit for damages (TsGIAgM, f. 849, op. 1, d. 9, ll. 41–42). Even if clerks used

the same record book to register both kinds of cases, the type of case was made explicit. See chapter 3 on these issues.

3. See *OPK*, st. 124, which provides the most general description of the kinds of cases that could be settled by the township courts: "The Township Court adjudicates . . . disputes and suits over property, as well as cases concerning misdemeanors of peasants and other people under the jurisdiction of this Court."

4. *OPK*, st. 125. Property is translated from *imushchestvo*, ownership from *sobstvennost'*.

5. "The disputes that arrive at courts can be seen as the survivors of a long and exhausting process," notes Marc Galanter in his definitive article on the question of measuring litigiousness ("Reading the Landscape of Disputes," p. 12). The pyramid of injuries, grievances, claims, disputes, and legal cases is used by Galanter and other specialists on litigiousness. For a summary of work on litigation and its meaning, see Friedman, "Litigation and Society." See also Felstiner et al., "The Emergence and Transformation of Disputes."

6. On inheritance cases and procedures, see Popkins, "Popular Development of Procedure in a Dual Legal System."

7. In my survey of subjects of cases based on hundreds of cumulated records, land without a specified value was the object of 16 percent of prewar suits. In my more finely tuned survey of case records, land was usually given a value, and only 5 percent of requests in such suits were for land measured in taxation units or just as an allotment. These disparities suggest that the monetary value of land appeared in the course of the vast majority of case hearings.

8. TsGIAgM, f. 849, op. 1, d. 8, ll. 47–47o.

9. Ibid.

10. TsGIAgM, f. 849, op. 1, d. 8, ll. 13o–18o.

11. TsGIAgM, f. 849, op. 1, d. 8, ll. 13o–14.

12. On guildsmen, see Elise Wirtschafter's discussion in her *Social Identity in Imperial Russia*, pp. 131–140. This is an example of what Wirtschafter identifies as an unstudied problem—how people of the various townspeople's ranks fared in courts (p. 140).

13. TsGIAgM, f. 849, op. 1, d. 8, ll. 15o–16.

14. TsGIAgM, f. 849, op. 1, d. 8, ll. 17o–18o.

15. TsGIAgM, f. 849, op. 1, d. 8, ll. 2o–3.

16. This compromise (*mirovaia sdelka*) on losses resulting from the bulls' poor performance was fulfilled by the villagers of Iagunino (TsGIAgM, f. 849, op. 1, d. 8, ll. 14o–15).

17. TsGIA-L, f. 1807, op. 1, d. 21, ll. 37o–38.

18. For examples of work and commodity cases at the Nagatinskii Township Court, see TsGIAgM, f. 10, op. 1, d. 114, ll. 1–4, 45–46.

19. TsGAMO, f. 5170, op. 1, d. 5, l. 22. The court used the term *primirenie* for the settlement.

20. For a detailed discussion of cabbage, as well as potatoes and cucumbers, in Tsaritsynskii Township, and for a study of the market conditions in the region in the early twentieth century, see *Ekonomichesko-statisticheskii sbornik*, vyp. 3 (Moscow, 1911), pp. 25–44.

21. TsGIAgM, f. 74, op. 1, d. 52, ll. 241–242.

22. Enforcement of sales of agreed-on commodities at agreed-on prices occurred at all the township courts I surveyed. The case of the twice-sold barn heard at the Ia-

guninskii Township Court on 28 August 1905 was another example of judges' concern to establish clearly the conditions of a sale. No one had a right to sell the same object to two different buyers, as discussed in chapter 3; see TsGIAgM, f. 849, op. 1, d. 8, ll. 51o–52o. For other sales cases, see TsGIAgM, f.74, op. 1, d. 55, l. 4; TsGAMO, f. 5170, op. 1, d. 5, ll. 42o, 45–45o; and cases discussed below in this chapter.

23. The percentage of documents involved in prewar civil suits was much higher than in later years, an issue discussed in chapter 7. The percentages of documents cited in cases under-represent documents both because their presence in the court record could easily have been missed when data were collected and because the clerk may not have recorded documents not cited in the decision.

24. TsGIA-L, f. 1807, op. 1, d. 21, l. 42.

25. TsGIA-L, f. 1807, op. 1, d. 21, ll. 57o–58.

26. TsGIAgM, f. 849, op. 1, d. 8, ll. 13o–14. For another debt case at Bol'shoe Zaborov'e, see LGIA, f. 1807, op. 1, d. 24, l. 158o.

27. For examples, see cases at the Ignatevskii Township Court in 1906 (TsGIAgM, f. 1112, op. 1, d. 16, ll. 29o–45) and at the Tsaritsynskii township court in 1915 (TsGIAgM, f. 74, op. 1, d. 52, ll. 3–4).

28. The importance of documents to legal judgments about debts has a long history in Russia; see Weickhardt, "Due Process and Equal Justice in the Muscovite Codes," p. 471.

29. TsGIA-L, f. 1807, op. 1, d. 21, ll. 7o–8.

30. He was from Borovichi. On this town, see *Pamiatnaia knizhka Novgorodskoi gubernii na 1913 god,* pp. 4, 26–27.

31. LGIA, f. 1807, op. 1, d. 24, ll. 160–164o, cases 23, 24, 25, 66, 68, 70, 72. Trampling from *potrava;* trepass from *khod.*

32. LGIA, f. 1807, op. 1, d. 24, l. 160. This case was heard on March 23 and later on April 13, earlier than the hearings of townsman Antonov's suits.

33. TsIAM, f. 749, op. 1, d. 8, ll. 35o–36o.

34. TsIAM, f. 749, op. 1, d. 8, ll. 39o–40o.

35. TsIAM, f. 749, op. 1, d. 8, ll. 43–44. The term used at court was *slomannaia trava.*

36. TsIAM, f. 749, op. 1, d. 8, ll. 48o–51.

37. TsIAM, f. 749, op. 1, d. 8, ll. 48–49.

38. On the Stolypin reforms, see David Macey's clear exposition in his article, "'A Wager on History,'" and, on the disruption of these policies, see Gaudin, "No Place to Lay My Head."

39. Gaudin, "No Place to Lay My Head," p. 755.

40. TsGIA-L, f. 1807, op. 1, d. 54, ll. 1–3. The text of the petition was included in the record of this case brought in December 1909. Act translated from *akt.*

41. For an example at the Ignatevskii Township Court in 1906, see TsGIAgM, f. 1112, op. 1, d. 16, ll. 29o–46, case 91/77.

42. TsGIA-L, f. 1807, op. 1, d. 21, ll. 15o–16. This decision was appealed and overturned by the county congress later in the year.

43. TsGIA-L, f. 1807, op. 1, d. 31.

44. Ibid.

45. TsGIA-L, f. 1807, op. 1, d. 31, ll. 10–10o.

46. TsGIA-L, f. 1807, op. 1, d. 31, ll. 11–11o.

47. TsGIA-L, f. 1807, op. 1, d. 31, ll. 15–30.

48. The county congress's recognition of all three brothers as possessors of the property in question again suggests that the transfer to household ownership had not taken

place. If it had, one person, the head of household, would have been legally in charge of the family's allotment. Dmitrii Chudin may have understood this rule when he made his deal with Dmitrii Nikitin for the land in question.

49. TsGIA-L, f. 1807, op. 1, d. 31, ll. 20–20o.

50. TsGIA-L, f. 1807, op. 1, d. 35, ll. 1–1o.

51. TsGIA-L, f. 1807, op. 1, d. 35, ll. 6–6o. The township clerk E. Zaozerskii had gone back fifteen years to the township's "Book No. 7" to copy out this contract "concluded on the basis of statute 21 of the General Regulation on Peasants . . . of the verbal agreement, made and recorded on 31 March 1897." A note entered on 10 January 1910, signed by Nikita Kutin, testified that the rent for the land had been reduced to five rubles because of the reduction of redemption dues.

52. TsGIA-L, f. 1807, op. 1, d. 22, ll. 66o, 67, 69, 88o.

53. On inheritance cases at the township courts from 1889 to 1912, see Popkins, "Popular Development of Procedure in a Dual Legal System."

54. On family divisions, see Frierson, "*Razdel:* The Peasant Family Divided."

55. *OPK*, st. 125.

56. *OPK*, st. 135.

57. According to *"mestnye svoi obychai"* (*OPK*, st. 13).

58. Burbank, "Narodnye sudy, imperskoe zakonodatel'stvo i grazhdanstvo v Rossii."

59. Major concerns for jurists were the impact of the Stolypin reform of 1906 on peasant inheritance, possible conflicts between local property arrangements and the rights of newly empowered peasant land owners, and the intersection between village custom and the civil code. For detailed discussions of peasant inheritance at this period, see Vorms, "Zakon i obychai v nasledovanii u krestian"; and Leont'ev, *Krest'ianskoe pravo,* pp. 353–379. See Vorms's strong defense of the orderliness of inheritance law on peasant property. He argues that the Stolypin laws of 9 November 1906 and 14 June 1910 had little impact on the dominant principle of local custom in deciding such cases ("Zakon i obychai," pp. 97–100).

60. He also noted that some peasant customs were close to the customary law of "Western European peoples" (Leont'ev, *Krest'ianskoe pravo,* p. 361). On female inheritance under the civil code, see Wagner, *Marriage, Property, and Law,* esp. pp. 332–336.

61. Gareth Popkins explores this kind of inheritance case in his article, "Popular Development of Procedure," pp. 57–87. He found the confirmation of inheritance cases to constitute between 1.7 and 9.3 percent of cases at township courts in Orel', Khar'kov, and Saratov provinces between 1910 and 1915. The increase in the war years is discussed in chapter 7.

62. TsGIAgM, f. 849, op. 1, d. 8, ll. 11o–12.

63. Ibid. The case could be appealed within thirty days to the land captain of the second district of Zvenigorod County, by submitting a complaint, in two copies, to the township court.

64. LGIA, f. 1807, op. 1, d. 42, ll. 1–2.

65. Ibid.

66. *SZ* 10, st. 1148.

67. LGIA, f. 1807, op. 1, d. 42, ll. 1–2. Historians of peasant legal practice have observed that women were frequent users of the township courts; see Beatrice Farnsworth's two influential articles, "The Soldatka: Folklore and Court Record" and "The Litigious Daughter-in-Law." Corinne Gaudin examines women's claims to property in the context of the Stolypin legislation in her article, "'No Place to Lay My Head.'" Gareth Pop-

kins observes that women were "over-represented" in court confirmation cases ("Popular Development of Procedure," pp. 72–75). My survey of court cases suggests that women's disproportionate share of inheritance cases at the township courts began only during the war; on this point, see chapter 7.

68. TsGIA-L, f. 1807, op. 1, d. 26, ll. 1–2. The timing of this case was discussed in chapter 3 above.

69. LGIA, f. 1807, op. 1, d. 4, ll. 4–4o; d. 24, cases 7, 9, 20, 33, 34, 35, 38, 57 (l. 179), 62.

70. Evdokiia Alekseevna Kolchina had died on 21 August 1915 at the age of fifty-eight. Her four children, two women and two men—Natalia, Akulina, Andrei, and Ivan—brought this case to the Zaborovskii Township Court on 30 August (LGIA, f. 1807, op. 1, d. 50, ll.1–2, 3–6).

71. LGIA, f. 1807, op. 1, d. 50, ll. 3–6.

72. Ibid.

73. TsGIAgM, f. 74, op. 1, d. 5, ll. 3–4.

74. As Cathy Frierson notes, these observers were dismayed and puzzled by the irrationality of family divisions, dismayed because of what they perceived to be disastrous consequences for peasants and puzzled because they viewed the peasant as driven by economic considerations and hence aware of the misfortune that probably awaited them after an extended family had broken up; see Frierson, "Razdel," p. 45.

75. *Rossiia: Polnoe geograficheskoe opisanie nashego otechestva,* Vol. 1, *Moskovskaia promyshlenaia oblast',* p. 106.

76. At least one ethnographer in the nineteenth century, Aleksandra Efimenko, took what we might call a feminist position on family divisions; she argued that husbands would better recognize the value of their wives in a nuclear family with only two adult laborers. See her *Issledovaniia narodnoi zhizni,* ch. 1: *Obychnoe pravo,* pp. 122–123.

77. Frierson's article emphasizes the normality of *razdel* and its role in the ordinary cycle of family growth, division, and regrowth ("Razdel," pp. 35–36, 50–51).

78. See *OPK,* sts. 38–46, 62 (7).

79. TsGIAgM, f. 1112, op. 1, d. 16, ll. 29o–45.

80. Note 1 to the first statute, first chapter, first division of the regulation asserts that the care of orphans devolved upon village or township communities of the children's place of residence or the place where their immovable property was located. Property was to be assigned to "guardians and trustees" (*opekuni i popechiteli*). The Orphan's Court was also mentioned as subject to this "obligation" (*OPK,* razdel 1, glava 1, st. 1, pr. 1). The word *guardianship* is used to translate *opeka.*

81. *OPK,* razdel 1, glava 1, st. 1, pr. 1, 2. Appeals could also be made to land arbitrators (*mirovye posredniki*), where and when these existed.

82. See Worobec, *Peasant Russia,* pp. 70–74, for a discussion of practices and regulations concerning orphans; see also Ransel, *Mothers of Misery.*

83. See the "no. 3, Prigovor, kopiia," [1901 goda aprelia 25 dnia . . .], in RGIA, f. 1344, op. 306, d. 215.

84. TsGIAgM, f. 74, op. 1, d. 52, ll. 5–6. The guardian, Maria's uncle Petr Tolmazov, appeared in court. He testified that "the minor in his guardianship had died and that the expenses presented to him for the funeral of the ward were fair."

85. Ibid. From the record book: "The plaintiff requested the recovery from the *opeka* over the minor Mariia Tolmazova, thirteen years old, who died on 15 December 1914, 293 rubles 46 kopeks spent on the funeral of the minor ward, Mariia Tolmazova, [he] presented justificatory documents for the indicated sum and certification of the death

of the ward." Copies of the decision were sent on 9 February and the receipt of the full 293 rubles 46 kopeks was recorded.

86. I had read the court case in Soviet days, without access to archival catalogs. In the mid-1990s, after restrictions on foreign scholars' use of archival catalogs were lifted, I was able to locate the file on the *opeka:* TsGIAgM, f. 74, op. 1, d. 52, ll. 9–10. A note appeared in the record to indicate that seventy-six rubles, ninety-nine kopeks, was indeed transferred from the "Tsaritsynskoe kreditnoe tovarishchestvo [Tsaritsynskii Credit Association]."

87. The document was registered at the township administration on 24 May 1908 (TsIAM, f. 378, op. 1, d. 387).

88. The inventory was signed by several of the Tolmazovs' co-villagers and by the village leader, and stamped with the village leader's official seal (TsIAM, f. 378, op. 1, d. 387, l. 2).

89. A "decision" from 12 December 1909 attested that "Petr Pavlov Tolmazov, guardian over . . . Mariia seven years old," had shown 802 rubles, 34 kopeks, of profit and 802 rubles, 34 kopeks, of expenditures from the ward's property. Out of seventy-five household heads, fifty-six signed the following declaration: "To recognize the activity of the guardian Tolmazov concerning the wardship over the minor Mariia as correct [*pravil'nyi*]" (TsIAM, f. 378, op. 1, d. 387, l. 4).

90. Possibly the buildings had been overvalued earlier or transferred at less than 3,000 rubles, for her property at that point amounted to 1,270 rubles, 2 kopeks, held in two banks—900 rubles, 2 kopeks, in the State Savings Bank, Book no. 997, and 370 rubles in the Tsaritsynskii Credit Association, Book no. 18. That year the guardian received income of 434 rubles, 70 kopeks (TsIAM, f. 378, op. 1, d. 387, ll. 9–11o). Different numbers of householders signed each yearly account, and the specific amounts of income and their allocation were always noted.

91. The expenses were recorded on the printed form in a space provided for reporting these costs. The report concluded with a printed rubric indicating a standard for a satisfactory performance: "Having read the income and expenses, the village assembly observes that the guardian does not have the orphan's money in his possession [*na rukakh*] and the expenditures we recognize as correct, i.e., justifying documentation of them has been provided. The property of the orphaned wards is available [*na litso*]. We do not observe abuses and negligence on the part of the guardian. To this we sign, peasant heads of household" (TsIAM, f. 378, op. 1, d. 387, l. 13).

92. TsIAM, f. 378, op. 1, d. 387, ll. 1–17o.

93. TsIAM, f. 378, op. 1, d. 387, ll. 17–17o.

94. These village-level decisions were not signed by Pavel Tolmazov, Maria's grandfather, which could be a sign of his reputation in the village and perhaps explain why he felt obliged to bring two cases to the township court against Maria's property. The amount claimed for funeral expenses—more than the annual expenditures on Maria's upkeep—may also suggest why Pavel Tolmazov was not chosen to be her guardian in the first place. The last note on the Tolmazov cases indicates that seventy-six rubles, ninety-nine kopeks, were indeed transferred from the Tsaritsyno Credit Association and received by Maria's grandfather (TsIAM, f. 74, op. 1, d. 52, ll. 9–10).

95. See *OPK*, st. 124, on *opeka po rastochitel'nosti*. The law of 18 May 1911 specifically assigned the township court the power to establish guardianships for wastefulness (*PSZ* 3, otd. 1, no. 35218.

96. TsGIAgM, f. 74, op. 1, d. 52, ll. 17–18.

97. Ibid.

98. TsGIAgM, f. 74, op. 1, d. 52, ll. 19–20.

99. TsIAM, f. 749, op. 1, d. 38, ll. 27–28. In Russian, the critical terms are *"samostoiatel'no vedet krest'ianskoe khoziaistvo"* and (for economically) *"khoziaistvenno."*

100. Ibid.

101. The word *"ispravit'sia"* used in the Shcherbakov case suggests this quality of recovering from being a wastrel, as after an illness. Peasant economy—*"krestianskoe khoziaistvo"*—is a positive term for litigants.

102. The last case offers a hint of what might disrupt that normal productivity. The township judges observed that "the cause" that gave rise to the guardianship in 1912 "had been removed." Possibly they refer to the effects on the former wastrel of the wartime temperance regulations, but this was not part of the official record (TsIAM, f. 749, op. 1, d. 38, ll. 27–28).

103. For another perspective on rural patriarchy, see Worobec, *Peasant Russia,* pp. 175–216. Worobec treats the whole post-emancipation years as a single period, an approach that cannot reveal shifts in values that occurred over this long—three generations—and dynamic time.

104. *Rossiia: Polnoe geograficheskoe opisanie,* 1:104.

105. Ibid., 1:105.

106. See chapter 3 for annual statistics of civil cases in the township courts of Moscow Province. See Burds, *Peasant Dreams and Market Politics,* esp. pp. 143–185, for an examination of peasant participation in the market before 1905.

107. People with the same last name could be members of separate households who were making claims against each other. This would increase the number of households represented at court. On the other hand, in the official population statistics, households in this area were large, with about fifteen individuals registered in each household. This would mean that these forty people at the township court were probably distributed between fewer than twenty households.

108. This calculation is based on the very conservative estimate that half the villagers listed in the official statistics would have been children.

109. *Spisok naselennykh mest Novgorodskoi gubernii,* vyp. 7: *Tikhvinskii uezd,* pp. 50–51.

110. See Munger, "Law, Change, and Litigation," on the lack of correspondence between economic transformation and litigation rates; and, on the meaning of litigiousness, see Galanter, "Reading the Landscape of Disputes."

111. See the Kutin brothers' case above (TsGIA-L, f. 1807, op. 1, d. 22, ll. 66o, 67, 69, 88o).

112. See *OPK,* sts. 17–23, 37, 46, for the major revisions of peasant land rights.

113. For example, Chekhov's one-act play, *Predlozhenie* (Chekhov, *Sobranie sochinenii,* 9:300–320.

114. See Macey, "'A Wager on History,'" pp. 154–161.

5. SMALL CRIME AND PUNISHMENT

1. In 1906, 24,425 criminal cases were heard in the township courts of Moscow Province—an upsurge that merits further study. Criminal charges fell back to 23,218 in 1907 and then began a steady climb. See Table 3.6.

2. *OPK,* sts. 77, 124, 128. This jurisdictional ruling applied to areas in which the supervision of the land captain had been introduced.

3. *OPK,* st. 128.

4. *OPK*, st. 132.

5. The clerk did not record the estate of lower-level officials. A policeman, like a judge, was acting in his capacity as an official, rather than exercising rights as a member of an estate. These recording conventions display how state service neutralized estate and how estate status gave people rights as subjects.

6. *OPK*, st. 127.

7. On the Justices of the Peace and their courts, see *Mirovoi sud: Prakticheskii kommentarii po pervuiu knigu Ustava grazhdanskogo sudoproizvodstva*. In rural areas these courts were abolished in 1889 in connection with the reform of the township courts; see Neuberger, "Popular Legal Cultures: The St. Petersburg *Mirovoi sud*," p. 232. Neuberger's article explores the ways that Justice of the Peace courts functioned in St. Petersburg.

8. The code was designed to move judicial matters out of the hands of the police and to overcome arbitrariness and conflicts over jurisdiction. See the discussion of the history of the misdemeanor code in N. C. Tagantsev's introduction to *UN*, pp. V–VIII.

9. Other nonstatutory violations listed in earlier versions of *The General Regulation on Peasants* were no longer in effect after 1906; see *OPK*, st. 127, and notes and observations. The notes clarify the impact of the law of 5 October 1906.

10. *OPK*, st. 127, ch. 2, note; ch. 3, note (p. 28); *PSZ* 3, 26 (1906), otd. 1:28392. Peter Czap made the important point that the law of 5 October 1906 gave peasants civil rights equal to those of nonpeasants. The elimination of punishments and of misdemeanor charges not covered by statute law for other people were part of this equalization of status in matters of criminal justice; see Czap, "Peasant-Class Courts and Peasant Customary Justice in Russia, 1861–1912," p. 177; and Macey, *Government and Peasant in Russia*, pp. 233–234.

11. *OPK*, sts. 143, 144. I use the term *arrest* to refer to a verdict sentencing a person to confinement in the local jail. Arrest meant confinement rather than detention before a case was heard.

12. *UN*, sts. 30, 31, 34, 38, 42, 45, 72, 88, 95, 111, 121, 124.

13. *UN*, sts. 130–136.

14. *UN*, sts.145, 169, 173, 174.

15. This calculation is based on cases in which I recorded statute numbers from the court's record, in all years and for all courts in my survey.

16. TsGIAgM, f. 74, op. 1, d. 53, ll. 7–8.

17. The Ignatevskii court in Moscow Province heard several criminal cases about driving animals over fields; see TsIAM, f. 1112, op. 1, d. 107.

18. The full text reads: "hunting at forbidden times, in places not permitted, by illegal means, or without observing established rules, likewise for the destruction of birds' nests or for the sale of game, obtained at a time not permitted, likewise for willful hunting on another's lands or in another's forests and waters" (*OPK*, st. 127).

19. For a study of hunting and poaching violation in another context, see Schulte, *The Village in Court: Arson, Infanticide, and Poaching in the Court Records of Upper Bavaria, 1848–1910.*

20. My research on this point contrasts strongly with the assumptions of peasant "resistance" or dissatisfaction with state law. Resistance provides the framework for much of Stephen Frank's *Crime, Cultural Conflict, and Justice.*

21. See TsIAM, f. 849, op.1, d. 39, l. 4. A criminal charge of violation of statute 48, concerning fraudulent sales of various things, but not applicable by the township court, was dropped.

22. TsGIAgM, f. 74, op. 1, d. 53.

23. *OPK*, st. 127; *UN*, st. 130–142.

24. *UN*, st. 138.

25. Lutsino lay on the right bank of the Moscow River, one verst from the township administration. In 1912 there were 76 households in the village (*Naselennye mesta Moskovskoi gubernii* [1913], p. 242), suggesting a population of around 600. The village had 550 inhabitants in 1890. The basic economic activity of the settlement was agriculture. An earlier wood-transporting occupation was dying out, as the forests were depleted, but handicrafts still flourished. At the end of the nineteenth century people in the settlement began to make wooden musical instruments for sale, including guitars and balalaikas. See *Odintsovskaia zemlia*, pp. 278–281.

26. TsIAM, f. 749. op. 1, d. 39, ll. 9o–10.

27. Appeals were initiated by bringing two copies of the complaint to the township court; these would be forwarded to the land captain who could send them on to a higher instance.

28. TsIAM, f. 749, op. 1, d. 39, ll. 9o–10.

29. I am basing my view that Prokhor Ivanov did not go to jail on the assumption that the court would follow the regulations for the timing of sentences, as it did in other cases. A township court decision was to go into effect only after the appeal period had expired, unless, in the case of misdemeanors, both parties explicitly refused their right to appeal and had the refusals recorded in the book of decisions (*OPK*, st. 139).

30. TsIAM, f. 749, op. 1, d. 39, ll. 9o–10.

31. TsIAM, f. 849, op.1, d. 39.

32. The *Statutes on Punishments* made distinctions between "violence" and "insult." Both misdemeanors were described in chapter 11 of the code, "On Insults to Honor, Threats, and Violence." The township judges could have chosen to use Statute 142, which included "the use of violence but without heavy beatings, wounds, or mutilations" for their charge, but instead they chose Statute 134 and its formulation of "insult through action" without provocation (*UN*, sts. 134, 142).

33. See Kollmann, "Honor and Dishonor in Early Modern Russia," *Forschungen zur Osteuropäischen Geschichte* 46 (1992): 131–146; and her magisterial work, *By Honor Bound*. Kollmann argues that the defense of honor was a major function of state power that served the interests of both rulers and ruled.

34. The 1912 Tagantsev edition of the *Statutes* adds to the text of the 1889 code—with interpellated revisions from 1906, 1908, 1909, and 1910—excerpts from the supreme criminal cassation department of the Senate, from the general sessions of the cassations departments, and from arguments presented to the Senate and the main military court (*UN*, p. III). Statute 138 is not a description of a misdemeanor but a procedural statute dealing with mutuality of insults.

35. *UN*, sts. 130–142, and commentaries. In the 1912 edition of the *Statutes* chapter 11 is eighty-two pages long, the longest of the sections of the code, with the exception of the section on general regulations and the enormous chapter on "misdemeanors against another's property." I am translating both *oskorbleniia* and *obida* as "insult." Foul language is from *grubost'*; slander from *kleveta*.

36. *UN*, st. 136, p. XIII, commentaries 96–102.

37. *OPK*, st. 127, lists by number the statutes in the *Statutes on Punishments* under which township inhabitants could be prosecuted or could themselves take others to court.

38. Tagantsev's 1912 edition of the 181 statutes of the *UN* is 624 pages long. The bulk of the text is citations from decisions and commentaries.

39. *UN*, st. 142, II, ii, commentary 177 on *poboi*.

40. *UN,* st. 142, II, ii, commentary 180. "Man" in this commentary is from *chelovek;* "person" is from *lichnost'.*

41. *UN,* st. 142, II, ii, commentaries 182, 183.

42. *UN,* sts. 133–135. Statute 135 was for insults that were "intentional, or in a public place, or a crowded meeting, to a person, who, although not a direct senior relative of the insulter, has the right according to a particular relation to particular respect, or to a person of the female sex."

43. *OPK,* sts. 143, 144.

44. *UN,* sts. 133–135.

45. As one of myriad examples of the peasant separatism approach, see Boris Mironov, writing in 1985 and citing an observer from 1902: "As a result of the juridical, social, and cultural isolation of the peasantry, it [the peasant commune] represented not simply a social estate, but 'a completely separate world, in the very foundations of its civic order profoundly distinct from all other social groups in the Russian population.'" The internal quotation is from A. Nikolskii, *Zemlia, obshchina i trud: Osobennosti krest'ianskogo pravoporiadka, ikh proiskhozhdenie i znachenie* (St. Petersburg, 1902). Mironov's 1985 article is republished in Eklov and Frank, *The World of the Russian Peasantry;* for the quotation, see pp. 25, 39 n. 86.

46. *Naselennye mesta Moskovskoi gubernii* (1913), p. 242.

47. Complaints against employers for verbal insult have been interpreted as demands for dignity by scholars of the labor movement and working class; see, among others, Smith, "The Social Meanings of Swearing." In this article the author makes a distinction between insult and foul language per se. Swearing could be used for a variety of purposes, not all of them insulting, and insults did not always involve swearing (pp. 183–185).

48. *UN,* st. 130, I, 1.72/284, Shishkin. "Person" is translated from *litso.*

49. *UN,* st. 130, I, 3.

50. See, for example, *UN,* st. 130, I, 4, 5, 6.

51. *UN,* st. 130, I, 5.

52. *UN,* st. 130, VI, 30. This was one of many "Examples of Personal Insults" provided under Statute 130.

53. *UN,* st. 130, VI, 30, 33, 34.

54. Statute 130 designated punishments "for the carrying out of insult, in words or in writing," a formula that makes oral words and writing into distinct processes (*UN,* st. 130). "Words" here could be understood as in the English, "they had words."

55. *UN,* st. 130, VI, 31, 32, 39.

56. *UN,* st. 130, VI, 37, 38. The Russian is more reticent: *liubov'naia sviaz'* (love tie).

57. TsIAM, f. 74, op. 1, d. 57, ll. 3–4.

58. *Naselennye mesta Moskovskoi gubernii* (1913), p. 242.

59. TsIAM, f. 749, op. 1, d. 39, ll. 10o–11.

60. Ibid. *"Blizkie otnosheniia"* was the term used in the record.

61. Ibid.

62. Kollmann, "Honor and Dishonor," pp. 140–141.

63. *UN,* st. 130, VI, 33. The opinion about the word *"lgun"* was that of Stasov.

64. See Burbank, "Discipline and Punish in the Moscow Bar Association."

65. TsIAM, f. 846, op. 1, d. 4, ll. 1–5.

66. Exact population counts are, as always, difficult to come by. In a statistical description of Moscow Province published in 1890, the population of Savvinskaia sloboda was registered as 717 (Shramchenko, *Spravochnaia knizhka Moskovskoi gubernii,* p. 226).

In 1904 300 male tax souls were registered in Savvinskaia sloboda, with 1,004 land allotments—the largest population and taxed land area in the township (TsIAM, f. 748, op. 1, d. 117a). A 1913 source indicates that Savvinskaia sloboda had 136 households (*Naselennye mesta Moskovskoi gubernii* [1913], p. 243). For information on the village's history, see *Odinstovskaia zemlia,* pp. 370–378.

67. TsIAM, f. 749, op. 1, d. 9, l. 80o. Convict is translated from *"arestant."*

68. TsIAM, f. 749, op. 1, d. 9, ll. 80o–81.

69. Ibid.

70. TsIAM, f. 749, op. 1, d. 9, ll. 81–81o.

71. The ruling in this case accords with the sense of Statute 138 that prohibited punishment of defendants who had suffered equal or worse insults. The statute was not assigned to the township courts, and thus the judges were not compelled to let the defendant off. See *UN,* st. 138.

72. *OPK,* st. 119.

73. The Kvardakovs were clearly important people in the township and in Savvinskaia sloboda. N. A. Kvardakov served as president of the township court in 1905 and 1906 (TsIAM, f. 749, op. 1, d. 9); Aleksei Kvardakov was the township leader from 1914 to 1916 (TsIAM, f. 749, op. 1, d. 39). No first name is provided for the owner of the tea shop.

74. The rules governing "no-shows [*neiavki*]" were printed on the forms used by the Iaguninskii court to summon parties to a hearing. If a plaintiff did not appear, the case was to be dropped; if a defendant did not appear, the court would make a decision in absentia; a witness who did not appear was to be fined (TsIAM, f. 749, op. 1, d. 24, ll. 2–3).

75. TsGIAgM, f. 10, op.1, d. 91, ll. 353–354. The charge was *nanesenie poboi.*

76. Ibid.

77. *UN,* st. 133, II, 17, 18.

78. TsGIAgM, f. 10, op.1, d. 91, ll. 353–354.

79. TsGIAgM, f. 10, op.1, d. 91, ll. 369–370.

80. *Naselennye mesta Moskovskoi gubernii* (1913), p. 42.

81. TsGIAgM, f. 10, op. 1, d. 91, ll. 369–370.

82. *UN,* st. 139, I, 1. "The same expression cannot be recognized simultaneously as an insult and a threat," opined a commentary on Statute 139 (*UN,* st. 139, III, 13). The ambiguous title of chapter 11, "Insults to Honor, Threats, and Violence," seems to draw a distinction between insults, threats, and the use of force, but force was part of the other two categories. An early opinion cited in the statute book notes: "Statute 139 [on threats] concerns a threat to carry out a violent act against someone, i.e., an announcement to the threatened person in words or writing of an intention to infringe his personal inviolability." As with insults, the statute law addressed the threat itself, not its motives or the probability of its being carried out. A threat to use violence to demand money, for example, would not be a misdemeanor but a crime and would have been prosecuted as extortion or robbery by a higher court.

83. TsGIAgM, f. 74, op. 1, d. 53, ll. 57–58. In their decision the judges cited Statute 135—"inflicting insult in deed with forethought"—apparently interpreting Alekseev's multiple charges of threatening violence and making noise under the more general rubric of intentional insult in deed.

84. TsGIAgM, f. 74, op. 1, d. 53, ll. 55–56.

85. TsGIAgM, f. 74, op. 1, d. 53, ll. 59–60. Again, the judges used the harshest insult statute in their verdict—"insult in deed with forethought." The chicken "*propala* [croaked]."

86. TsGIAgM, f. 74, op. 1, d. 53, ll. 23–24, 55–60, 63–64.

87. TsGIAgM, f. 10, op. 1, d. 91, ll. 175–176o. The sentence was originally ten rubles, but it was reduced in accord with a general amnesty. See the discussion of this case in chapter 6.

88. TsGIAgM, f. 10, op. 1, d. 91, ll. 341–342.

89. TsIAM, f. 749, op. 1, d. 9, ll. 36o–37.

90. Ibid.

91. *UN*, sts. 20, 22; *OPK*, st. 145.

92. TsGIAgM, f.10, op.1, d. 91, ll. 167–168o.

93. The statute had emerged from the heated debates and controversies over the role of the courts after the emancipation and, like most elements of the misdemeanor code, it derived from recombinations and reinterpretations of the 1857 misdemeanor regulations (*UN*, pp. V, 358–387; and st. 142).

94. *UN*, st. 142, 1. This commentary was based on a selection of rulings from 1869 through 1885.

95. *UN*, st. 142, 23.

96. *UN*, st. 142, 22.

97. TsGIAgM, f. 849, op. 1, d. 9, ll. 46–46o. See chapter 3.

98. See TsGIA-L, f.1807, op. 1, d. 24, l. 160, for another conflict over a fence. For a claim to hay, see TsGIAgM, f. 1112, op. 1, d. 16, ll. 29o–45.

99. TsIAM, f. 1112, op. 1, d. 107. Over the year criminal cases increased in the late spring, peaked in the summer, and fell off in October. This July outburst of *samoupravstvo* cases may have been connected to conflicts arising during the war. See chapter 7 on this issue.

100. For cases of brothers charging their brothers with *samoupravstvo*, see TsGIA-L, f. 1807, op. 1, d. 24, l. 160; and TsGIAgM, f.10, op. 1, d. 91, ll. 36–37o.

101. TsGIAgM, f. 1112, op. 1, d. 16, case 126/108. The plaintiff died before the case was heard.

102. In Nagatino, with its active constabulary, in at least one case the local police opened a case of *samoupravstvo* against a peasant couple; see TsGIAgM, f. 10, op. 1, d. 91, ll. 193–194.

103. In a case at the Nagatino Township Court, a record seven witnesses from the same village came to testify in a 1913 *samoupravstvo* case (TsGIAgM, f. 10, op. 1, d. 91, ll. 42–43o). The village leader testified in TsGIAgM, f. 10, op. 1, d. 91, ll. 36–37o.

104. The typology was an artifact of the way the misdemeanor code was produced; see *UN*, st. 142 n. 3.

105. Chapter 3 of the *Statutes on Punishments* lists violations *"protiv blagochiniia, poriadka, i spokoistviia"* (*UN*, sts. 35–51).

106. *UN*, st. 38, condemns *"ssori, draki, kulachnyi boi ili drugogo roda buistvo v publichnykh mestakh."*

107. On campaigns against alcohol and use of alcohol before the revolution, see Herlihy, *The Alcoholic Empire;* and White, *Russia Goes Dry: Alcohol, State, and Society*, pp. 3–15.

108. TsGIAgM, f. 10, op. 1, d. 91.

109. TsGIAgM, f. 10, op. 1, d. 91, ll. 369–370.

110. For these rare cases of convictions under Statute 42, see TsGIAgM, f. 10, op. 1, d. 99, ll. 99–100; and TsGIAgM, f. 10, op. 1, d. 91, ll. 191–192o.

111. In TsGIAgM, f. 849, op.1, d. 9, ll. 38–39, a man was convicted under Statute 42, but beating was part of the charge in addition to intoxication.

112. On the tea shop as a place for the consumption of alcoholic beverages, see Herlihy, *The Alcoholic Empire,* 6.

113. For examples of confessions of intoxication, see TsGIAgM, f. 74, op.1, d.53, ll. 7–8, 9–10, 11–12.

114. TsGIAgM, f. 849, op. 1, d. 9, ll. 45–45o.

115. TsGIAgM, f. 10, op. 1, d. 91, ll. 179–180o.

116. TsGIAgM, f. 10, op. 1, d. 91, ll. 283–284. The defendant confessed to being "*p'ian sil'no* [strongly drunk]." Repin went to jail from 22 June to 7 July.

117. TsGIAgM, f. 74, op. 1, d. 53, ll. 7–21. The relevant terms are *buistvo* and *bezobrazie.*

118. TsGIAgM, f. 849, op. 1, d. 9, l. 38.

119. See examples at TsGIAgM, f. 849, op. 1, d. 9, ll. 45–45o; and TsGIAgM, f. 10, op. 1, d. 91, ll. 283–284.

120. TsGIAgM, f. 849, op. 1, d. 9, ll. 44–44o. See the discussion in chapter 3. In a case at the same court from 1906, the charge of Statute 43 was changed by the judges to Statutes 38 and 42, when unruly conduct and drinking were proven but "the use of vulgar and insulting words" did not meet the judges' notion of "shameless acts" (TsGIAgM, f. 849, op. 1, d. 9, ll. 79–80).

121. See Nagatino, TsGIAgM, f. 10, op. 1, d. 91, ll. 55–56o, for a prosecution under Statute 46.

122. TsGIAgM, f. 74, op. 1, d. 53, ll. 27–28.

123. For examples, see TsIAM, f. 849, op. 1, d. 9, ll.7o–8. This case is discussed in chapter 6.

124. The Simonovskii District was outside the boundaries of Moscow but under the authority of Moscow city in police matters; see *PSZ* 3:26, no. 27817. The constable of the Simonovskii District was frequently called on to bring cases to the Nagatinskii Township Court.

125. TsGIAgM, f. 10, op. 1, d. 91, ll. 103–104o, 149–150o, 153–154o, 277–278o, 347–348o. The policeman who brought these charges was the constable of the Simonovskii district.

126. At the Nagatinskii Township Court, 54 percent of all defendants were residents outside the township; at the Tsaritsynskii court, 24 percent of all defendants were from outside the township.

127. TsGIAgM, f. 74, op. 1, d. 53, ll. 17–18. The insulting word in question was *zhulik.*

128. These were the topics of chapters 3, 6, 7, 8, 9, and 10 in *UN.*

129. See Engel, *Between the Fields and the City,* pp. 207–210, on the sanitation difficulties faced by newcomers to cities and, perhaps not to the same degree, by people living in rural areas bordering cities.

130. This statute was used in 74 percent of all health and safety cases at Nagatino.

131. TsGIAgM, f. 10, op. 1, d. 91, ll. 243–244.

132. *Naselennye mestnosti Moskovskoi gubernii,* p. 41.

133. TsGIAgM, f. 10, op. 1, d. 91, ll. 293–294. Police testified in 30 percent of criminal cases in Nagatino in 1913, and defendants appeared in 74 percent of criminal case hearings. But defendants showed up less frequently for public health violations—in 57 percent of cases of this type at Nagatino.

134. TsGIAgM, f. 10, op. 1, d. 91, ll. 293–294.

135. TsGIAgM, f. 10, op. 1, d. 91, ll. 323–324.

136. TsGIAgM, f. 10, op. 1, d. 91, ll. 325–326; see a similar case at TsGIAgM, f. 10, op. 1, d. 91, ll. 217–218.

137. See other cases in TsGIAgM, f. 10, op. 1, d. 91.

138. Arson would be tried in the circuit courts if charged. On fire and arson, see Frierson, *All Russia Is Burning!*

139. For fire-prevention misdemeanors, see *UN,* sts. 88–98.

140. TsGIAgM, f. 74, op. 1, d. 53, ll. 31–32.

141. TsGIA-L, f.1807, op. 1, d. 24, l. 158o; TsGIAgM, f.10, op. 1, d. 91, ll. 313–312o.

142. LGIA, f. 1807, op. 1, d. 24, l. 159.

143. TsGIAgM, f. 10, op. 1, f. 91, ll. 353–354, 317–318.

144. *UN,* st. 43.1.

145. TsGIAgM, f. 10, op. 1, d. 91, ll. 26–27, 93–94, 131–132, 137–138.

146. *UN,* sts. 145–153, 169, 170, 172–174, 178–180.1. The chapter heading is "On Violations of Another's Property [*sobstvennost'*]." Clerks often just entered *"krazha"* as a charge.

147. *OPK,* sts. 143, 148; TsGIAgM, f. 1112, op. 1, d. 16, case 125/75.

148. TsGIAgM, f. 1112, op. 1, d. 16, case 108/91.

149. TsIAM, f. 1112, op. 1, d. 107, ll. 26o–27.

150. TsIAM, f. 849, op. 1, d. 39, ll. 4o–6.

151. TsGIA-L, f.1807, op. 1, d. 24, l. 158o; TsGIAgM, f. 10, op. 1, d. 91, ll. 305–306.

152. TsGIAgM, f. 10, op. 1, d. 91, ll. 223–224. The plaintiff testified that the thief *"pokhitil"* these *"shtiblety."*

153. TsGIAgM, f. 10, op. 1, d. 91, ll. 311–312.

154. TsGIAgM, f. 10, op. 1, d. 91.

155. Ibid. For particular examples of female defendants and their perhaps stolen goods, see TsGIAgM f. 10, op. 1, d. 91, ll. 229–230, 233–234, 267–268, 271–272.

156. On female labor in cities, see Barbara Engel's superb book, *Between the Fields and the City.*

157. TsGIAgM, f. 10, op. 1, d. 91, ll. 271–272; TsGIAgM, f. 10, op. 1, d. 99, ll. 95–96o. This last unfortunate got away for a time but was finally arrested. This case was discussed in chapter 3.

158. See Engelstein, *The Keys to Happiness,* pp. 96–127; and Schrader, "Containing the Spectacle of Punishment."

159. TsGIAgM, f. 10, op. 1, d. 91, ll. 379–380.

160. *OPK,* st. 9, on the right to *"priobretat' v sobstvennost'."*

6. PEASANT JURISPRUDENCE

1. This bifurcated image of the township judge emerged in the public discourse of late-nineteenth-century Russia; see Frierson, *Peasant Icons,* 54–75. For a right-wing defense of township judges, see *Rech' V. A. Obraztsova v Gosudarstvennoi dume 4 noiabria 1909,* pp. 2–11.

2. On the debate over the peasant judge and the 1889 reform, see Frierson, "Rural Justice in Public Opinion," pp. 536–541. The representation of the 1889 reform and the land captaincy as hallmarks of reaction is still standard in most historical scholarship.

3. *OPK,* st. 114, reads: "Each rural society elects one Candidate for the Township Judges; however, the whole number of elected people must not be fewer than eight. If a township comprises less than eight rural societies, then the missing number to make up the indicated list of Candidates is elected by those societies proposed by the County Conference. From the list of chosen people, the land captain confirms four in the positions of Township Judges for three years, and the rest are appointed as Candidates for

these [positions] for the same term. The Candidates take the place of the Township Judges in the case of their leaving their positions before the end of the three-year term or of a temporary absence, for which process the order and list established for this purpose by the land captain is observed."

4. TsIAM, f. 747, op. 1, d. 66, l. 1. The land captain was probably Viktor Vasil'evich Panov; see his signature on the file cited above; see also *Pamiatnaia knizhka Moskovskoi gubernii na 1912 god,* p. 229. He refers to the absence of any *"tsenzovoe trebovanie"* in his letter.

5. The statute also refers to the abolition of corporal punishment and a restoration of the right to be elected for people who had been condemned to corporal punishment but were of good behavior (*OPK,* sts. 115, 182).

6. *Pamiatnaia knizhka Moskovskoi gubernii na 1909 god,* p. 363; *Pamiatnaia knizhka Moskovskoi gubernii na 1912 god,* p. 245; TsIAM, f. 747, op. 1, d. 66.

7. TsIAM, f. 747, op. 1, d. 66. The elections were recorded as *"prigovory"* (verdicts) made by each assembly.

8. See *OPK,* gl. 2, "O sel'skom obshchestvennom pravlenii," otd. 1, "O sel'skikh skhodakh," esp. sts. 65, 66, 67.

9. *OPK,* st. 64.

10. Some societies united several villages, and others consisted of one big or one small village; see *OPK,* st. 48.

11. *OPK,* sts. 116, 189.

12. TsIAM, f. 747, op. 1, d. 66, ll. 1, 3.

13. TsIAM, f. 747, op. 1, d. 66, l. 3.

14. Ibid.

15. TsIAM, f. 747, op. 1, d. 66. A careful reading of the resolution from the Chasovinskoe meeting suggests that this figure for the size of the village is probably exact. The village leader had made a mistake when he filled in his mimeographed form and listed 124 householders present out of 76 eligible to vote; later this mistake had been caught, the numbers reversed in red ink. The number of households in the village of Chasovnia listed in the 1913 edition of statistics on settlements for Moscow Province was 142, probably representing an increase in population of this factory town since the 1911 elections (*Naselennye mestnosti Moskovskoi gubernii* [1913], p. 240).

16. *Naselennye mestnosti Moskovskoi gubernii* (1913), p. 240.

17. TsIAM, f. 747, op. 1, d. 66.

18. These population figures were gathered by township authorities (TsIAM, f. 747, op. 1, d. 49, l. 9).

19. TsIAM f. 747, op. 1, d. 66.

20. On paternalism and authority in Russian governing practice, see Wirtschafter, "The Ideal of Paternalism in the Prereform Army."

21. TsIAM, f. 747, op. 1, d. 49, ll. 29–30.

22. *OPK,* st. 117.

23. TsIAM, f. 747, op. 1, d. 66.

24. *OPK,* st. 198.

25. TsIAM, f. 8, op. 1, d. 183.

26. For the Klopovs, see TsIAM, f. 74, op. 1, dd. 36, 50, 52, 53. The Kamochkin family figures in these records, as both clerks and judges.

27. On the image of clerks in the late nineteenth century, see Frierson, *Peasant Icons,* pp. 152–153. See Frank, *Crime, Cultural Conflict, and Justice,* pp. 49–50, for a summary of earlier views and a harsh criticism of clerks as manipulators of information.

28. On peasants' views of literacy, see Eklof, *Russian Peasant Schools,* pp. 251–282.

29. See Bruno LaTour's provocative and suggestive discussion of networks that combine objects, humans, and practices over time in *We Have Never Been Modern,* esp. pp. 55, 81–82, 120–122.

30. On the township administration's members, see *OPK,* st. 105; on the court's membership, see *OPK,* st. 113; on the clerk's qualifications, see *OPK,* sts. 179–183. He was a *dolzhnostnoe litso.*

31. *OPK,* sts. 195, 196.

32. *OPK,* st. 112.

33. See *Iuridicheskii kalendar' dlia volostnykh i dolzhnostnykh lits* for 1904 and other years. The land captain's version was very similar to the calendar for township authorities (*Iuridicheskii kalendar' dlia zemskikh nachal'nikov 1904 g.*) Other convenient publications included Fedoseev, *Iuridicheskii spravochnik dlia krest'ian i melkikh sobstvennikov-zemlevladel'tsev,* and, at a later time, Rozenshtein, *Iuridicheskaia entsiklopediia.* In 1914 I. M. Tiutriumov published a compilation of all Senate opinions on peasant affairs since 1882 (Tiutriumov, *Pratika Pravitel'stvuiushchego Senata*). This might have been used by an exceptionally diligent clerk.

34. See TsGIAgM, f. 10, op. 1, d. 99, for the use of a stamp to routinize the recording of cases where the plaintiff did not appear in court.

35. See summonses in the Zaborovskii court records (TsGIA-L, f. 1807, op. 1, d. 31).

36. TsGIAgM, f. 74, op. 1, d. 52, ll. 253–270.

37. For Akimov's assumption of the post of *"zavedyvaiushchii deloproizvodstvom volostnoi pisar',"* see TsGIAgM, f. 849, op. 1, d. 8, which shows some changes in August 1905, and the records of the decisions of the Iaguninskii township assembly for 1907–1910 (TsIAM, f. 748, op. 1, d. 34). At this court, one clerk filled in for two months in the beginning of January 1914, and then the long-term occupant of the office, Lanin, took over at the beginning of March (TsIAM, f. 749, op. 1, d. 20).

38. This court heard twenty-three civil cases in three sessions at this time. Of these cases, eleven were miscellaneous suits and six were inheritance cases (TsGIAgM, f. 10, op. 1, d. 114, ll. 1–46). See chapter 7 for the context of these cases.

39. TsGIAgM, f. 10, op. 1, d. 91, ll. 175–176. The insult was *"zhulik."*

40. *OPK,* st. 133; see also V. V. Tenishev, *Pravosudie v russkom krest'ianskom bytu,* pp. 91–105. Tenishev's account includes a long description of informal peasant lawyers, in accord with his ethnographic exoticism, but he concludes that "real lawyers" were inaccessible for peasants.

41. The role of lawyers in enhancing legal access is disputed by contemporary legal theorists, who do not share Russian jurists' confidence in the superior justice to be attained through legal expertise; see Galanter, "Reading the Landscape of Disputes," pp. 18–21.

42. On the peasant economy at this time, see Stanziani, "Organisations familiales et marché du travail en Russie, 1861–1922," pp. 121–162. On the fluidity of imperial society, see Wirtschafter, *Social Identity in Imperial Russia,* and her *Structures of Society: Imperial Russia's "People of Various Ranks."* Gorshkov's "Serfs on the Move: Peasant Seasonal Migration in Pre-Reform Russia, 1800–1861," describes the extensive and enterprising labor migration of peasants under serfdom. See Engel, *Between the Fields and the City,* on women's employment in this period. For a study of migration, mobility, and aspiration, see Burds, *Peasant Dreams and Market Politics.*

43. On regional and other variations, see Stanziani, "Organisations familiales." On

peasant family arrangements in the post-emancipation period, see Frierson, "*Razdel:* The Peasant Family Divided," pp. 35–52; and Worobec, *Peasant Russia,* pp. 76–117. For a contemporary's view of shifts in power in the family, see Efimenko, *Issledovaniia narodnoi zhizni,* esp. pp. 122–123.

44. Gorshkov's article on the serf economy observes that, in the mid-nineteenth century, women entrepreneurs owned 11 percent of Moscow regional enterprises. The majority of these women would have been of peasant background but had already acquired the status of townspeople or merchants. Many of the legal matters involving richer women would have been considered at other courts because of either the woman's place of residence or the amount of the case. See Gorshkov, "Serfs on the Move," p. 649.

45. See Brooks, *When Russia Learned to Read,* p. 13.

46. Clerks did not always record the family relationships involved, presumably because these were well known to the parties.

47. TsGIAgM, f. 10, op. 1, d. 91, ll. 115–116

48. TsGIAgM, f. 74, op. 1, d. 53, ll. 37–38.

49. Both parties and all witnesses were obligated by the rules on the township court to appear at a hearing in response to a summons (*OPK,* sts. 133, 134). The rules governing "no-shows [*neiavki*]" were printed on the forms used by the Iaguninskii court to summon parties to a hearing. If a plaintiff did not appear, the case would be dropped; if a defendant did not appear, the court would make a decision in absentia; a witness who did not appear would be fined (TsIAM, f. 749, op. 1, d. 24, ll. 2–3).

50. See TsGIAgM, f. 10, op. 1, d. 99. Under the rubric "decided," he would use another stamp to enter "to end the consideration of this case."

51. It is possible that records of "ended" cases were kept separately in some areas, and this would then underrepresent the proportion of cases ended by absence of parties. For Tsaritsynskii Township, I have found a separate record book for cases that were ended without a decision by the judges (TsGIAgM, f. 74, op. 1, d. 55). Because this book was for 1917, however, it should not be assumed that, in other years, records were kept in this way.

52. *OPK,* st. 136. The introductory section of a court record registered the composition of the court, the charge, and the parties and witnesses in the case, and concluded with a printed rubric: "The township court proposed reconciliation to the sides, but this did not take place." For examples, see the record books of the Tsaritsynskii Township Court for 1914 (TsIAM, f. 74, op. 1, d. 50).

53. On the relations of disputes to litigation in the United States, see Galanter, "Reading the Landscape of Disputes," pp. 11–18.

54. TsGIAgM, f. 74, op. 1, d. 50. In addition to the ended cases (*prekrashchennye dela*) mentioned here, two were illegible and one was ended without a recorded reason.

55. *OPK,* st. 135.

56. In 1 percent of cases the meaning of the defendant's testimony was unclear.

57. It is important to remember that in these trials most witnesses would know the people they were called on to testify about. The question of identification of a defendant never occurred at the township courts; people were simply asked to testify about whether a particular person—presumed to be known to all—had, in fact, done or said something. This situation contrasts sharply with courtroom evidence in areas where parties did not know each other. Thus one of the major questions of criminal justice—the ability of witnesses to identify culprits—was moot for the township courts.

On the debate over such testimony in the twenty-first century, see Atul Gawande, "Under Suspicion: The Fugitive Science of Criminal Justice," *The New Yorker,* 8 January 2001, pp. 50–53.

58. Documents might not have been mentioned in the official record of a case, even if they were indeed employed during the hearing. For this reason, my survey, based on reading case records, may underestimate their use.

59. TsGIAgM, f. 10, op. 1, d. 91, ll. 169–170o.

60. TsGIAgM, f. 849, op. 1, d. 12, ll. 96o–97. Mozhukin asked for *"posobie na pitanie"* from his son.

61. TsGIAgM, f. 849, op. 1, d. 9, ll. 79–80. The charge was *buistvo s upotrebleniem ploshchadnykh i oskorbitel'nykh slov.* See *UN,* sts. 43, 38 (*"Za ssori, draki, kulachnyi boi ili drugogo roda buistvo v publichnykh mestakh"*) and 42 n. 2. I cite the text of Statute 42 before the 1906 revision, which I assume would not have reached Iagunino by March of that year.

62. *UN,* st. 16 n. 2. This 1885 version is most likely the text available at the Iaguninskii Township Court in March 1906.

63. TsGIAgM, f. 849, op. 1, d. 9, ll. 79–80.

64. For an example of "heartfelt repentance" in a drinking case, see chapter 5 and TsGIAgM, f. 849, op. 1, d. 9, ll. 45–45o.

65. TsGIAgM, f. 849, op. 1, d. 9, ll. 39o–40o.

66. On judicial revisionism in the civil law in Russia, see Wagner, *Marriage, Property, and Law,* pp. 206–223, 337–377.

67. TsGAMO, f. 5170, op. 1, d. 5; case 10/36.

68. Ibid. Nastasia's name was officially registered as Anastasia.

69. Ibid. Signatures of both parties—Ivan and Anastasia—and those of all the judges and the clerk were recorded on this decision.

70. TsGIA-L, f. 1807, op. 1, d. 48, l. 4o.

71. On transfers of property under the Stolypin rules, see Macey, "'A Wager on History,'" pp. 149–173; and Atkinson, *End of the Russian Land Commune,* pp. 56–100.

72. *OPK,* st. 118, describes the usual Sunday or holiday meeting time.

73. For individuals whose behavior "threatened local well-being and safety," see *OPK,* st. 62, ch. 3.

74. Each year provincial administrators recorded the numbers of civil and criminal cases that had been registered for processing at circuit courts—including cases new in a particular year and those left over from previous years—as well as the number of cases (both new and those left over) that courts had resolved. Similar statistics were kept at the county level for township courts. My figures were calculated on the basis of statistics compiled in *Sbornik statisticheskikh svedenii Ministerstva iustitsii,* vyp. 21, ch. 1: "Svedeniia o lichnom sostave i o deiatel'nosti sudebnykh ustanovlenii evropeiskoi Rossii za [1905–1914]"; and *OMG za [1905–1913].*

75. The circuit courts in Moscow Province processed less than half the number of cases heard at township courts in this province in 1905; see chapter 3.

76. For population figures, see A. G. Rashin, *Naselenie Rossii za 100 let.* The population of Moscow city, second only to that of St. Petersburg, is calculated, in this now classic source, to have been 1,762,700 for 1 January 1914 (p. 90). In all counties of the province, township courts decided a higher percentage of civil cases than criminal cases within any given year.

77. The statistics on township courts in Moscow Province were calculated on the basis of the appropriate volumes of *OMG,* 1905–1913.

78. These sums and often the exact days of arrest were recorded by the township clerk, thus completing a case and leaving a record for historians and others.

79. TsIAM, f. 849, op. 1, d. 9, ll. 70–8.

80. *OPK*, sts. 153, 363, 368.

81. *OPK*, sts. 359–361. The term for this local fund was *mirskie povinnosti*. On firefighting measures, see Frierson, *All Russia Is Burning!*

82. This is the mean percentage paid by a single village society, calculated from the record book of tax accounts for Iaguninskaia Township for twenty villages represented at the Iaguninskii Township Court (TsIAM, f. 748, op. 1, d. 117a). Dues are *mirskie sbory*.

83. For examples, see Iaguninskaia Township records for 1904 (TsIAM, f. 748, op. 1, d. 117a). Only a small fraction of the rural societies were in arrears and for small amounts. For a very detailed record of tax payments from larger communities closer to Moscow, see the tax collection books for the *Kolomenskoe obshchestvo sadovshchikov* for 1908 (TsIAM, f. 8, op. 1, d. 149); and for *Kolomenskoe obshchestvo* for 1913, see TsIAM, f. 8, op. 1, d. 183 (1913).

84. On the elite debate over taxation, see two articles by Kotsonis, "'Face-to-Face': The State and the Individual in Russian Taxation, 1863–1917"; and "'No Place to Go': Taxation and State Transformation in Late-Imperial and Early Soviet Russia."

85. *OPK*, sts. 196–199.

86. *OPK*, sts. 200–207; *PSS*, kn. 3, st. 58. The land captain, on his own authority, could sequester an official's property and begin court proceedings.

87. Frierson, *Peasant Icons*, pp. 71–74.

7. LEGAL RECOURSE IN A TIME OF TROUBLES

1. On the crisis perspective on Russian history, see Burbank and Ransel, introduction to idem, *Imperial Russia: New Histories for the Empire*, pp. xi–xiii. Michael Confino has pointed out the illogicalities of the notion of a century-long Russian crisis; see his "Present Events and the Representation of the Past," pp. 851–853.

2. On the First World War in Russia, see Lincoln, *Passage through Armageddon;* and with particular relevance to the disruption of peasants' lives, see Gatrell's superb study of refugees, *A Whole Empire Walking*.

3. Of the areas I studied, only in Iaguninskii Township was there an unusual interruption of the clerk's term at this period. The clerkship was vacant officially in 1914, and at least two different clerks served that year. See *Pamiatnaia knizhka Moskovskoi guberniia na 1914 god*, p. 277; and TsIAM, f. 749, op. 1, d. 20.

4. See his suits heard on May 24 for three rubles, seven rubles and ten kopeks, and two rubles, one against a relative from his village of Pokrovskoe. The court found in his favor in two of these cases (TsIAM. f. 749, op. 1, d. 38, ll. 52–54).

5. TsIAM. f. 749, op. 1, d. 38, ll. 44–45.

6. Ibid.

7. Ibid.

8. On appeals from township courts, see Popkins, "Peasant Experiences of the Late Tsarist State." Appeals results are difficult to analyze from the perspective of lower courts, in part because outcomes may not have been consistently reported back to townships and recorded in case hearing books by clerks. In my survey very few responses to wartime appeals were recorded in court records; all reported appeals, however, ultimately upheld the lower court. This low rate of response to appeals from the townships may be

a consequence of the institutional breakdown described later in this chapter. Before the war, appeals were upheld wholly or in part in 82 percent of reported outcomes in my survey. This matter deserves fuller study.

9. The classic statement of the argument is Florinsky's *The End of the Russian Empire.*

10. Statistics on the numbers of court cases at the township courts of Moscow Province displayed in chapter 6, Chart 6.1, show the beginning of a radical drop in cases in 1914.

11. Statistics for 1913 and 1914 are from *OMG 1913–1914.* This publication did not appear after 1915. My figures for cases at the Ignatevskii and Iaguninskii courts are derived from TsIAM, f. 1112, op. 1, dd. 16, 107; and TsGIAgM, f. 849, op. 1, dd. 8, 20/1, 38.

12. Calculated from case data in TsGIAgM, f.1112, op. 1, d. 1.

13. Statistics on civil cases calculated from TsIAM, f. 749, op. 1, d. 38; numbers of criminal cases recorded from TsIAM, f. 749, op. 1, d. 39.

14. TsGAMO, f. 5170, op. 1, d. 5, ll. 8–9.

15. Historians of peasant legal practice have observed that women were frequent users of the township courts. Beatrice Farnsworth discusses this issue for an earlier period in her articles, "The Soldatka: Folklore and Court Record" and "The Litigious Daughter-in-Law." Corinne Gaudin examines women's claims to property in the context of the Stolypin legislation in her article, "'No Place to Lay My Head,'" pp. 764–772. Gareth Popkins observes that women were "over-represented" in court confirmation cases (Popkins, "'Protective Litigation,'" pp. 72–75). In my survey of court cases based on township records, women brought 15 percent of all civil cases before the war, and their disproportionate share of inheritance cases began only during the war.

16. TsIAM, f. 749, op. 1, d. 38, ll. 56–58o. On the impact of the war on peasant households, see Stanziani, "War and the Disintegration of Economic Space," pp. 183–187. Stanziani observes the increased participation of women in the industrial sector and notes that "women and adolescents seized the opportunity presented by the war to increase their economic power within the household unit" (p. 187).

17. TsIAM, f. 749, op. 1, d. 38, ll. 24o–25o, 59–61.

18. Ibid.

19. TsIAM, f. 749, op. 1, d. 38, ll. 50o–51.

20. Ibid.

21. TsIAM, f. 378, op. 1, d. 387, ll. 1–17o.

22. Refugees might also be part of this story, although they were more present in towns and cities than in villages; see Gatrell, *A Whole Empire Walking,* p. 3. Worobec, *Peasant Russia,* pp. 175–216, discusses female authority in households and villages as exceptional and describes the township court as relentlessly enforcing patriarchy for the entire post-emancipation period.

23. TsIAM, f. 74, op. 1, d. 53, ll. 9–10. Eremin confessed to being *sil'no p'ian* after drinking *odekolon.*

24. Before the war, charges of public inebriation accounted for only 1 percent of all cases against male defendants; during the war this shifted to 9 percent of all such cases.

25. See *Derevnia i zapreshchenie prodazhi pitei v Moskovskom uezde,* pp. 9–12, 66–93. Nagatinskii and Tsaritsynskii townships are singled out as "much-drinking regions" (*mnogop'iushchie regiony*).

26. On the wartime temperance rules and their effects, see Herlihy, *Alcoholic Empire,* pp. 138–145. The creativity of Russians' search for alcohol should not be underestimated. See the homage to such behavior in Venedikt Erofeev's Soviet-era masterpiece, *Moscow to the End of the Line,* trans. H. William Tjalsma (Evanston, Ill.: Northwestern University Press, 1994).

27. On the relation between age, gender, and crime (and alcohol), see Sampson and Laub, *Crime in the Making,* pp. 6–24, 179–203; the controversial article by Hirschi and Gottfredson, "Age and the Explanation of Crime"; and Gottfredson and Hirschi, *A General Theory of Crime,* pp. 111–120, 123–149.

28. The Russian legal term is *kleveta.*

29. TsIAM, f. 849, op. 1, d. 39, ll. 1–11o.

30. TsIAM, f. 74, op.1, d. 53, ll. 1–70.

31. The court at Tsaritsyno heard a total of thirty-four criminal cases from January through August 1916 (TsIAM, f. 74, op.1, d. 53, ll. 1–70). As in my survey generally, this number represents a fall from the number of cases in the prewar period. In 1909, for example, for the same months, the Tsaritsyno court heard forty-one cases (TsIAM, f. 74, op.1, d. 36).

32. TsIAM, f. 74, op.1, d. 53, ll. 1–2.

33. TsIAM, f. 74, op.1, d. 53, ll. 21–22.

34. TsIAM, f. 74, op.1, d. 53, ll. 33–34.

35. TsIAM, f. 74, op.1, d. 53, ll. 41–42. Bad faith is translated from *nedobrosovestnost'.*

36. TsIAM, f. 74, op.1, d. 53, ll. 43–44. The defendant said that the case was brought *"nedobrosovestno."* The witness noted an insult of *"bezzakonnitsa."*

37. TsIAM, f. 74, op.1, d. 53, ll. 53–56, 59–60.

38. TsIAM, f. 74, op.1, d. 53, ll. 59–60. See chapter 5 for details.

39. O. N. Kamochkin had been on the bench since at least 1914. The Kamochkin family figures in the records of the Tsaritsynskii Township Court from the prewar years. S. N. Klopov was probably the son of N. Klopov, the president of the court at Tsaritsyno in 1909 and 1910. See TsIAM, f. 74, op.1, dd. 36, 50, 52, 53.

40. TsIAM, f. 74, op.1, d. 53.

41. TsIAM, f. 74, op.1, d. 53, ll. 17–18.

42. TsIAM, f. 74, op.1, d. 53, ll. 51–52.

43. TsIAM, f. 74, op.1, d. 53, ll. 37–38. The problem was an *ozornoe pis'mo.*

44. TsIAM, f. 74, op.1, d. 53, ll. 45–46.

45. The major work on this transformation is Brooks, *When Russia Learned to Read.*

46. TsIAM, f. 74, op. 1, d. 53, ll. 19–20; *OPK,* sts. 127, 128. The request was *"ee vdont'."* The defendant responded: *"zhit' s nim sovmestno nepopast'."*

47. TsIAM, f. 74, op. 1, d. 53, ll. 23–24.

48. TsIAM, f. 74, op. 1, d. 53, ll. 3–4.

49. See Gatrell, *A Whole Empire Walking,* pp. 65–68, on refugees in the countryside.

50. TsIAM, f. 749, op. 1, d. 38, ll. 84o–85.

51. Ibid.

52. This figure is provided in *Naselennye mesta Moskovskoi gubernii,* p. 242.

53. TsIAM, f. 749, op.1, d. 38, ll. 43–43o, 45–48, 48o–49, 49o–50.

54. Ibid.

55. The subject of criminality throughout the war period, and not just in 1917, remains uninvestigated. Two recent works on crime, peasants, and other people end in 1914: Neuberger, *Hooliganism: Crime, Culture, and Power in St. Petersburg, 1900–1914;* and Frank, *Crime, Cultural Conflict, and Justice in Rural Russia, 1856–1914.* On other kinds of shifts in behavior during the war, see Jahn, *Patriotic Culture in Russia during World War I.*

56. She had also been a plaintiff at the Tsaritsynskii Township Court in 1915 (TsIAM, f. 74, op. 1, d. 52, ll. 141–142).

57. TsIAM, f. 74, op. 1, d. 53, ll. 65–68. "Depraved widow" is the translation of *razvratnaia vdova;* sworn at and attacked, *"rugali, napadali."*

58. TsGAIgM, f. 74, op. 1, d. 53, ll. 29–30. A witness testified that it had been his job to clean the *"vater,"* and the defendant was let off.

59. TsGAIgM, f. 74, op. 1, d. 53, ll. 31–32.

60. TsIAM, f. 1112, op. 1, d. 107; *UN,* st. 109. This was an exceptional case in my survey in that the judges applied a statute listed as inapplicable at township courts. Perhaps this misdemeanor had been added under wartime procedures.

61. Volume 1 of the collection of documents edited by Robert Paul Browder and Alexander F. Kerensky, *The Russian Provisional Government 1917,* provides a sense of the radical nature of the Provisional Government's first months. For the texts of civil rights and local court decrees, see pp. 226–238. On the feminists' victory, see Edmondson, *Feminism in Russia, 1900–1907,* pp. 165–168.

62. TsGIAgM, f. 74, op. 1, dd. 55, 57, 58; for this transition in status, see d. 55, ll. 6–6o, d. 57, ll. 9–10; and d. 58, ll. 5–6.

63. TsGAMO, f. 5170, op. 1, d. 5, ll. 1–51. In October 1917 the description reappeared exceptionally in a case brought by a woman against the "peasants" of a village, presumably all of them, for seizure of her mother's land (an *otdel*), but individual plantiffs and respondents were not labeled peasants (l. 36).

64. TsGAgM, f. 1656, op. 1, d. 5, ll. 75–76.

65. TsGAMO, f. 5170, op. 1, d. 5. ll. 1–51. For harvesting and border conflicts, see cases 20/78, 24/56, 29/71, 32/86, 36/100, 37/98, 40/103, 41/105, 42/106, 49/113, 50/114, 51/112, and 51/136. For land conflicts, some of which were connected with the above crop controversies, see cases 14/76, 24/56, 36/100, 38/104, 40/103, 41/105, 42/106, 47/110, 48/111, 49/113, 51/103, and 51/110.

66. On the significance of this kind of consolidated allotment (*otrub*) and the shifts in the land reform at this time, see Macey, "The Stolypin Reforms as Process," pp. 151–153, 164–165.

67. TsGAMO, f. 5170, op. 1, d. 5, ll. 19–19o. The charge was *pokos.*

68. TsGAMO, f. 5170, op. 1, d. 5, ll. 27–27o. The land committee was recorded as *"Zemel'nyi [Volost'noi] komitet."*

69. TsGAMO, f. 5170, op. 1, d. 5, ll. 37–37o.

70. TsGAMO, f. 5170, op. 1, d. 5, l. 29. "Wrong" in this testimony was *nepravil'nyi.*

71. The percentage of contested intra-family cases fell from 31 percent to 30 percent in my survey after 1 March 1917, an insignificant change.

72. Family cases accounted for 27 percent of the cases heard at this township court in this period.

73. See TsGAMO, f. 5170, op. 1, d. 5, ll. 10–51.

74. Ibid.

75. *Naselennye mesta Moskovskoi gubernii,* p. 95.

76. TsGAMO, f. 5770, op. 1, d. 5, l. 34o.

77. TsGAMO, f. 5770, op. 1, d. 5, l. 40.

78. TsGAgM, f. 1656, op. 1, d. 5, l. 75. Public (*obshchestvennyi*) duties were concerned.

79. Ibid.

80. TsGAMO, f. 5170, op. 1, d. 5, ll. 36, 41o–42. The suit was for *otniatie otdel;* the decision states that the *nadel* (allotment land) should be returned to the plaintiff.

81. TsGAMO, f. 5170, op. 1, d. 5, l. 3o.

82. This was a payment of *obrok,* dues in money, probably dues Babaev owed as a member of the village society.

83. TsGAMO, f. 5170, op. 1, d. 5, ll. 41o–42.

84. TsIAM, f. 74, op. 1, d. 136, ll. 1–3; on Kamochkin, see TsIAM, f. 74, op.1, dd. 50, 52, 53, 55.

85. TsIAM, f. 74, op. 1, d. 136, ll. 4–5.

86. D. Soldatov testified as a representative of the Blizhne-Beliaevo obshchestvo in 1915 (TsIAM, f. 74, op. 1, d. 52, ll. 143–144). Several Soldatovs appear in various documents from this village; see the Tolmazov guardianship case in TsIAM, f. 378, op. 1, d. 387, ll. 1, 6.

87. TsIAM, f. 74, op. 1, d. 57. A similar gradual transformation leaving two "old" judges in place along with two new men took place at the Grebnevskii Township Court (TsGAMO, f. 5170, op. 1, d. 5, ll. 1–51).

88. TsIAM, f. 74, op. 1, d. 136, l. 10.

89. TsIAM, f. 74, op. 1, d. 138, ll. 4–20.

90. TsIAM, f. 74, op. 1, d. 55, l. 38o. Gubantsev testified at the Tsaritsynskii Township Court in a civil case involving claims to potatoes in Shaidrovo on 24 September 1915 (TsIAM, f. 74, op. 1, d. 52, ll. 199–200).

91. The share brought by sons or brothers had fallen during the war years—from 3.9 percent to 1.6 percent of cases—and rose after 1 March 1917 to 7.1 percent.

92. TsGAMO, f. 5170, op. 1, d. 5, ll. 42o, 44o, 46, 47o.

93. TsGAMO, f. 5170, op. 1, d. 5, ll. 39–51.

94. See TsIAM, f. 74, op. 1, d. 58, ll. 15–20.

95. TsIAM, f. 74, op. 1, d. 57, ll. 13–14.

96. TsGAgM, f. 1696, op. 1, l. 31.

97. The circular was received by the not too distant Klinskii county congress on 10 November 1917 (TsGAgM, f. 1696, op. 1, l. 31).

98. This localization took place to some extent at the Selinskii and Grebnevskii courts, where parties in late 1917 were almost exclusively from local areas (TsGAgM, f. 1696, op. 1, l. 75; TsGAMO, f. 5170, op. 1, d. 5, ll. 1–51).

99. For the texts of civil rights and local court decrees, see Browder and Kerensky, *The Russian Provisional Government 1917,* pp. 226–238.

100. On the "dual power" period, see Galili, *The Menshevik Leaders in the Russian Revolution,* esp. pp. 69–155.

101. See TsGAMO, f. 5170, op.1, d. 5, ll. 11–51, for examples of resort to each of these authorities in Grebnevskii Township. The "rural committees" were to replace the old "rural societies." On the township *zemstvo,* see chapter 8.

102. TsIAM, f. 74, op. 1, d. 55, ll. 10, 13b, 14, 16.

103. TsIAM, f. 74, op. 1, d. 55, ll. 164–166.

104. TsIAM, f. 74, op. 1, d. 57, ll. 69–70.

105. *Grabitel'* is the term used in this case. This was the first usage in my survey of cases. The word was used by Lenin in the Bolsheviks' slogan, *"Grab nagrablennogo"* (Rob what was robbed). Cheat—*obarokh,* possibly *oborokh*—is more difficult to translate. The probable reference is to *obrakhovat'.*

106. TsIAM, f. 74, op. 1, d. 57, ll. 69–70.

107. Translation of *briukho iurist.*

108. TsIAM, f. 74, op. 1, d. 57, ll. 70–72.

109. TsIAM, f. 74, op. 1, d. 57, ll. 13–14, 15–16, 57–58. On hooliganism as a phenomenon before the war, see Neuberger, *Hooliganism: Crime, Culture, and Power;* and Weissman, "Rural Crime in Tsarist Russia." Weissman claims, with no evidence, that "hooligans often enjoyed the sympathy of the entire village" (p. 239). I found no cases

using the word in township courts until 1917. This is another area in which a reading of local court records seems to provide an entirely different perspective on local attitudes toward crime than interpretations based on elite categories.

110. TsIAM, f. 74, op. 1, d. 57, ll. 139–140. *Sterva,* female form of *stervets,* roughly translates as "shit, stinker, carrion." We heard this word before, in 1906 to be precise, at the Iaguninskii Township Court; see chapter 5, and TsIAM, f. 749, op. 1, d. 9, ll. 80o–81.

111. TsIAM, f. 74, op. 1, d. 57, ll. 139–140. Between them there was a *prekoslovie.*

112. TsIAM, f. 74, op. 1, d. 57, ll.15–16.

113. TsIAM, f. 74, op. 1, d. 57, ll. 57–58. The request was found to be *uvazhitel'nyi.*

114. TsIAM, f. 74, op. 1, d. 57.

115. TsIAM, f. 74, op. 1, d. 57, ll. 51–52. Swindler (*moshennik*) and villain (*merzavets*) were among the insults in this case.

116. TsIAM, f. 74, op. 1, d. 57.

117. TsIAM, f. 74, op. 1, d. 57, ll. 55–6.

118. TsIAM, f. 74, op. 1, d. 57, ll. 85–86.

119. TsIAM, f. 74, op. 1, d. 57, ll. 135–136.

120. TsIAM, f. 74, op. 1, d. 57, 11.167–168; d. 55, l. 70.

121. TsIAM, f. 74, op. 1, d. 57, l. 184; d. 58, l. 300; d. 55, l. 71o.

8. A DIFFERENT JUSTICE?

1. At mid-century it was argued that the emancipation of serfs required a reform of the court. Later, after the 1864 court reform, it was argued that the emancipation of 1861 had been the impetus behind the government's decision to recast the legal system. On this point and for the goals of reformers, see Dzhanshiev, *Epokha velikikh reform,* pp. 121–125.

2. Ibid., pp. 122–123.

3. Kotsonis, *Making Peasants Backward.*

4. See Cathy A. Frierson's "Rural Justice in Public Opinion," and *Peasant Icons.*

5. Two major and recent histories of the Russian Revolution incorporate ideas of peasant difference with regard to law. Richard Pipes refers to the peasants' "poorly developed legal sense" in his *Russian Revolution,* pp. 114–117; Orlando Figes analyzes peasant justice as based on customary moral norms; see his *People's Tragedy,* pp. 98–101. Two common modes of peasant difference in recent peasant studies are obstinate traditionalism—see Moshe Lewin's classic works, especially his influential article "Customary Law and Rural Society in the Postreform Era"—and resistant colonial subalternity, as in Stephen Frank's *Crime, Cultural Conflict, and Justice in Rural Russia.*

6. Chekhov, *Sobranie sochinenii,* 3:180–184. The title in Russian is "*Zloumyshlennik*" and is difficult to translate with all its nuances.

7. Ibid., 3:508–509.

8. The story was recounted to me in numerous settings, with its meanings explicated in identical fashion, by Russian intellectuals. But the story is also a favorite for translation into English—an attractive example of peasant exoticism—and thus is well known among students of Russian culture generally. "The Culprit" appears in *The Portable Chekhov,* ed. Avrahm Yarmolinsky (New York: Viking, 1965), pp. 103–108; in 1965 this collection was in its fourteenth printing. For a recent citation in a formidably respectable source, see Figes, *A People's Tragedy,* p. 101.

9. Sergei Romaniuk, personal correspondence, 4 March 2001.

10. Educated society—*obrazovannoe obshchestvo*—was a common usage; see Dzhanshiev, *Epokha velikikh reform,* p. 120, for an example.

11. See the concise description of the court system in Kazantsev, "'Sudebnaia respublika' tsarskoi Rossii," *Sud prisiazhnykh v Rossii,* pp. 4–6.

12. Stephen Frank's *Crime, Cultural Conflict, and Justice* makes an extended argument along these lines, although his major point is that peasants had to rely on themselves because of the state's inadequate attention to rural criminality. For other examples, see Frierson, "Crime and Punishment in the Russian Village," pp. 55–69.

13. Figes finds, based on Chekhov's story, "moral subjectivity" to have been "the root of the peasant's instinctive anarchism" (*A People's Tragedy,* p. 101).

14. On these issues of disputes and the resort to law, see Galanter, "Reading the Landscape of Disputes"; Greenhouse, "Interpreting American Litigiousness"; and Ewick and Silbey, *The Common Place of Law,* pp. 15–32.

15. Moon, *The Russian Peasantry 1600–1930,* pp. 234–236; Frierson, *Peasant Icons,* pp. 73–74.

16. Kucherov, *Courts, Lawyers and Trials under the Last Three Tsars,* p. 92.

17. Moral corruption can be defined against an ethical rather than a legal system, but here, too, the existence of a code—in this case a moral one—is essential for the notion of decay or decline.

18. See David Moon's observations on this issue in his *Russian Peasantry,* p. 3.

19. On the emergence of a "gentry" opposition, headed by noblemen but not including all nobles, see Manning, *The Crisis of the Old Order in Russia,* pp. 25–64. On the nobility in this period, see Becker, *Nobility and Privilege in Late Imperial Russia.* For a fascinating account of the noble elite and its role in governance, see Lieven, *Russia's Rulers under the Old Regime.*

20. David Moon likewise finds it "unlikely" that peasants in the imperial period "had a concept of a 'Russian peasantry'" (*Russian Peasantry,* p. 17). These considerations are related to the discussions of identity in Russia. Too often this category has been used to imply that interests or self-representations were shared by people of the same status ascription. Questions are asked about what "peasant" interests or attitudes were, as if status was, in fact, a category around which people collectively organized their aspirations, actions, and ideas. For a critique of the identity concept itself, see Brubaker and Cooper, "Beyond 'Identity.'"

21. The one exception would be a person formerly of non-peasant status who had been accepted into a rural society and thus acquired peasant status, including the possibility of election to the township bench. See chapter 2 for an example of this procedure.

22. *OPK,* st. 134.

23. Ong, in *Orality and Literacy,* makes a strong distinction between print and manuscript cultures, claiming that manuscript cultures remained "marginally oral," even when words were recorded (p. 119). The recorded testimony of the township court hearing records does have this oral quality, but the mix of literacy, illiteracy, print, and handwriting at the township courts does not neatly fit into an "oral" or "literate" category.

24. The intersection of documents and human subjects in making law together and extending it over time could be seen as an example of a network, in Bruno Latour's formulation. Township court practice satisfies his description of "networks of practices and instruments, of documents and translations." See his *We Have Never Been Modern,* esp. pp. 120–122.

25. The cases submitted by the troubled Khrushchev family about their family division are examples of resistance to a court decision addressed by returning to the court; see chapter 7.

26. Exceptionally "important" property crimes could be punished by a fine of up to thirty rubles and an arrest of up to thirty days (*OPK,* st. 148).

27. Anfimov, *Rossiisskaia derevnia v gody pervoi mirovoi voiny,* p. 252, from a survey conducted by Chaianov in 1911.

28. A. M. Afanas'ev, "Jurors and Jury Trials in Imperial Russia, 1866–1883," p. 225.

29. Habermas, *The Structural Transformation of the Public Sphere,* p. 19.

30. On the impact of the market economy on peasant values, see Brooks, *When Russia Learned to Read,* p. xxi. Brooks draws similar conclusions about peasant aspirations from his study of what peasants read in this period.

31. The Russian state, since its Muscovite beginnings, had taken on the task of punishing those who offended the honor of Russian subjects; see Kollmann, *By Honor Bound.*

32. *Chest' v filosofii i v prave,* pp. 81, 78. Three editions of this work appeared between 1895 and 1899. Benefice is translated from *blago.*

33. See Figes, *A People's Tragedy,* p. 84. Another variant is in the title of Eklof and Frank, *The World of the Russian Peasant.*

34. See, from the extensive literature on peasant workers, Engel, *Between the Fields and the City;* Johnson, *Peasant and Proletarian;* and Zelnik, *A Radical Worker in Tsarist Russia,* pp. xv–xxiv. On peasant enrollments in universities, see Eklof, *Russian Peasant Schools,* pp. 467–469; and Leikina-Svirskaia, *Russkaia intelligentsiia v 1900–1917 godakh,* pp. 123–23. Enrollments in universities in the empire by students whose parents were of peasant estate increased from 5.5 percent to 13.3 percent of all enrollments between 1906 and 1914 (Leikina-Svirskaia, *Russkaia intelligentsiia v 1900–1917 godakh,* p. 24).

35. Cathy Frierson concluded that educated society's self-produced relationship to the peasantry in the 1890s was essentially the same as that of the 1860s: the village was a world apart, the peasant was "other," and the intelligentsia alone was capable of modernizing initiatives (*Peasant Icons,* p. 194).

36. In the words of a recent historian of the Russian Revolution: "This was still an oral culture, where the customs of the past, passed down through generations, served as a model for the collective actions of the village in the present and the future" (Figes, *A People's Tragedy,* p. 91).

37. Ibid., p. 90; Moon, *Russian Peasantry,* pp. 234–235.

38. "On the whole the peasant patriarchs had an inbred mistrust of any ideas from the world outside their own experience. They aimed to preserve the village traditions and defend them against progress. The 'old way of life' was always deemed to be better than the new" (Figes, *A People's Tragedy,* p. 92).

39. Maksim Gorky's memoirs and other writings were influential purveyors of the image of peasant cruelty, although much of the action in *My Childhood* takes place outside villages. See the large literature on *samosud;* recent examples are in Frank, *Crime, Cultural Conflict, and Justice,* pp. 243–275; and Frierson, "Crime and Punishment in the Russian Village."

40. Figes describes a "functional logic of peasant self-organization in the struggle for survival against the harsh realities of nature and powerful external enemies, such as the landlords and the state" (*A People's Tragedy,* p. 90).

41. See, for example, the following life stories: Ravich, *Evgenii Ivanovich Iakushkin;* Ransel, introduction to Tian-Shanskaia, *Village Life in Late Tsarist Russia,* pp. xi–xxi;

and Frierson, introduction to *Aleksandr Nikolaevich Engelgardt's Letters from the Country,* pp. 3–20.

42. From a huge literature on these issues, see Hobsbawm and Ranger, *The Invention of Tradition;* Clifford and Marcus, *Writing Culture: The Poetics and Politics of Ethnography;* and the opening salvoes of the subaltern school in Guha and Spivak, *Selected Subaltern Studies.*

43. On this subject, see Stanziani, "Les Enquêtes Orales en Russie, 1861–1914," and "Les statistiques des récoltes en Russie, 1905–1928"; and Kotsonis, *Making Peasants Backward,* pp. 135–184.

44. The major source for township court practice still remains the volumes published in the 1870s by a commission studying the effects of the recently introduced courts; see *Trudy komisii po preobrazovaniiu volostnykh sudov,* vols. 1–7 (St. Petersburg, 1873–1874). Prince V. V. Tenishev's influential *Pravosudie v russkom krest'ianskom bytu,* published in 1907, is a compilation and interpretation based on the materials collected by his father, V. N. Tenishev, from local correspondents in the late nineteenth century (pp. 3–5). Nonetheless, it is considered a source for peasant legal practice in the early twentieth century. See Engel, *Between the Fields and the City,* p. 246, for a description of the Tenishev archive in St. Petersburg.

45. See Stanziani, "Les statistiques des récoltes," pp. 94–96, on the relationship between bureaucracy, knowledge, and anti-democratic governance.

46. I must note one exception. This is V. A. Obraztsov's anti-lawyer and anti-Semitic speech of 4 November 1909 in which he praises peasant judges and township courts: *Rech' V. A. Obraztsova v Gosudarstvennoi dume,* pp. 1–11. However, Obraztov would not be considered an intellectual by Russian intelligentsia standards.

47. Leont'ev, *Krestianskoe pravo,* p. 391.

48. Despite the insistence of Russian specialists on the need for a single code, codification is not a necessary condition for a civil law system; see Merryman, *The Civil Law Tradition,* pp. 26–27. Merryman observes that one should think of "codification not as a form, but as the expression of an ideology," a remark very appropriate to the Russian case.

49. Leont'ev, *Krest'ianskoe pravo,* p. 395.

50. Chekhov, *Sobranie sochinenii,* 3:180–184.

51. For the texts of civil rights and local court decrees, see Browder and Kerensky, *The Russian Provisional Government 1917,* 1:226–238. For the law replacing the township courts with new local courts, see *SURP 1917,* otd. 1, no. 577, 6 May 1917, pp. 909–913. The law was signed on 4 May 1917. On the abolition of estates and its significance at township courts, see chapter 7.

52. On the township *zemstvo,* see Shingarev, *Melkaia zemskaia edinitsa ili volostnoe zemstvo;* and Count Uvarov's passionate plea in *Moskovskoe gubernskoe zemstvo v poluvekuiu godovshchinu,* pp. 28–34.

53. For an example of this pleading, see *Volostnoe zemstvo,* no. 3 (1917): 85. On taxation in the townships, see chapter 6.

54. On the *mestnyi sud* debates, see *Ob uchastii narodnogo elementa v mestnom sude;* M. M. Mogilianskii, "Zemstvo i mestnyi sud," in *Iubeleinyi zemskii sbornik, 1864–1914,* pp. 86–96; and Kots, *Mestnyi sud i ego reforma.* The law on reform of the local court was issued by the imperial government on 15 June 1912, but a decree putting the law into effect in some regions of the realm did not follow until 16 September 1914 (*Ustav grazhdanskogo sudoproizvodstva,* comp. I. M. Tiutriumov, p. 1 [st. 1, pr. 2]). On the law, see Rudin, *Zakon 15 iiunia 1912 o preobrazovanii mestnogo suda.* For an analysis of

how this law was produced, see Zyrianov, "Tret'ia duma i vopros o reforme mestnogo suda."

55. *SURP 1917,* otdel 1, no. 577, 6 May 1917, pp. 909–913. Browder and Kerensky, *Provisional Government,* 1:234–235.

56. Browder and Kerensky, *Provisional Government,* 1:236; translated from *Russkie vedomosti,* no. 106 (13 May 1917): 3.

57. *Volostnoe zemstvo,* no. 3 (1917): 83.

58. Ibid., no. 17–18 (1917): 343.

59. Ibid., pp. 343–345.

60. See Radkey, *Elections to the Consitutuent Assembly,* pp. 60–61. Radkey's fascinating study shows that a higher percentage of the population voted in the countryside than in the cities. See also Protasov, *Vserossiiskoe uchreditel'noe sobranie,* pp. 224–239. Protasov describes the large turnout in disparaging terms typical of the intellectuals' peasant world discussed above.

61. For the term *derevenskaia temnota,* see *Volostnoe zemstvo,* no. 17–18 (1917): 343.

62. *Volostnoe zemstvo,* no. 9–10, pp. 262, 263, 266, 267.

63. TsGAgM, f. 1656, op. 1, d. 5, ll. 19, 32, 33, 34, 56, 58.

64. Problems with the delivery of summonses begin to appear at the Grebnevskii court in late October 1917 (TsGAMO, f. 5170, op. 1, d. 5, ll. 42o, 47o, 51).

65. On gentry politics in the late imperial period, see Lieven, *Russia's Rulers;* and Manning, *The Crisis of the Old Order.*

66. The terms *obshchina* and *mir* continue to be used by scholars writing about the peasantry in this period. For one among many examples, see the title of Zyrianov, *Krest'ianskaia obshchina evropeiskoi Rossii, 1907–1914 gg.*

67. For a summary of the literature and an approach to the concept, see Joseph Bradley, "Subjects into Citizens."

68. Habermas, *The Structural Transformation of the Public Sphere,* pp. 1–56.

69. For a suggestive reading on this issue, see Vishniak, *Le régime soviétiste,* p. 26. Vishniak argues that the Bolsheviks carried the estate principle into Soviet governance.

70. Habermas mentions, but then sets aside, the "plebian public sphere" in his introduction to *The Structural Transformation of the Public Sphere.* But his description suggests that he had in mind a proletarian formation (pp. xviii–xix).

71. See Afanas'ev, "Jurors and Jury Trials," pp. 218–225. Afanas'ev notes that peasants were the majority of defendants at the circuit courts (p. 227).

72. "Muscovite Political Folkways," see, esp., pp. 116, 119, 123–136.

73. See Figes, *A Russian Tragedy,* p. 91.

74. A single "peasant *obshchina*"—of all Russian peasants—figures as the subject of Zyrianov's work, *Krest'ianskaia obshchina evropeiskoi Rossii 1907–1914 gg.*

75. See, among many other works, Oliver Henry Radkey, *The Unknown Civil War in Soviet Russia* (Stanford, Calif.: Hoover Institution, 1976); and Figes, *A People's Tragedy.* Radkey is one of few who, before 1991, called the Tambov peasant revolt against Bolshevik rule a "civil war."

76. The Bolsheviks both claimed, and were, the government in the years of civil war; this would be important to many peasants with the statist ideologies I describe. On the army leaders' views of "the peasant question," as they in good intellectual tradition saw it, see von Hagen, *Soldiers in the Proletarian Dictatorship,* esp. pp. 60–63, 231–239.

Bibliography

ARCHIVES

Moscow

Tsentral'nyi gosudarstvennyi arkhiv Moskovskoi oblasti (TsGAMO)
f. 5170 Grebnevskii volostnoi sud

Tsentral'nyi istoricheskii arkhiv Moskvy (TsIAM)
[Tsentral'nyi gosudarstvennyi arkhiv goroda Moskvy (TsGAgM)]
[Tsentral'nyi gosudarstvennyi istoricheskii arkhiv goroda Moskvy (TsGIAgM)]

f. 8 Nagatinskoe volostnoe upravlenie
f. 10 Nagatinskii volostnoi sud
f. 54 Moskovskoe gubernskoe upravlenie
f. 74 Tsaritsynskii volostnoi sud
f. 184 Moskovskaia gubernskaia zemskaia uprava
f. 378 Tsaritsynskoe volostnoe upravlenie
f. 747 Sharapovskoe volostnoe upravlenie
f. 748 Iaguninskoe volostnoe upravlenie
f. 749 Iaguninskii volostnoi sud (TsIAM)
f. 846 Sharapovskii volostnoi sud
f. 849 Iaguninskii volostnoi sud (TsGIAgM)
f. 1112 Ignatevskii volostnoi sud
f. 1656 Klinskii uezdnyi s"ezd (TsGAgM)

St. Petersburg

Rossiiskii gosudarstvennyi istoricheskii arkhiv (RGIA)
[Tsentral'nyi gosudarstvennyi istoricheskii arkhiv (TsGIA)]

f. 1344 Senat. Vtoroi departament (krest'ianskii)

Tsentral'nyi gosudarstvennyi istoricheskii arkhiv Sankt-Peterburga (TsGIA SPb)
[Leningradskii gosudarstvennyi istoricheskii arkhiv (LGIA)]

[Tsentral'nyi gosudarstvennyi istoricheskii arkhiv Leningrada (TsGIA-L)]

f. 244	Petrogradskii uezdnyi mirovoi sud'ia
f. 1050	Tikhvinskii volostnoi sud
f. 1807	Zaborovskii volostnoi sud
f. 1815	Zaostrovskii volostnoi sud
f. 1934	Toksovskii volostnoi sud
f. 2036	Anisimovskii volostnoi sud

PUBLISHED SOURCES, PRIMARY

Agishev, N. M., and V. D. Bushen, eds. *Materialy po obozreniiu gorskikh i narodnykh sudov kavkazkogo kraia.* St. Petersburg: Senatskaia tipografiia, 1912.

Alfavitnoi spisok naselennykh mest S.-Peterburgskoi gubernii. St. Petersburg: Gubernskaia tipografiia, 1913.

Browder, Robert Paul, and Alexander F. Kerensky. *The Russian Provisional Government 1917.* Stanford, Calif.: Stanford University Press, 1961.

Chayanov, A. V. *The Theory of Peasant Economy.* Edited by Daniel Thorner, Basile Kerblay, and R.E.F. Smith. Foreword by Teodor Shanin. Madison: University of Wisconsin Press, 1986.

Chekhov, A. P. *Sobranie sochinenii.* 12 vols. Moscow: Gosudarstvennoe izdatel'stvo khudozhestvennoi literatury, 1961.

Dal', Vladimir. *Tolkovyi slovar' velikorusskogo iazyka.* 2nd ed. 4 vols. St. Petersburg: Knigoprodavets-tipograf M. O. Vol'f, 1880–1882. [Fascimile edition: Moscow: Russkii iazyk, 1991.]

Derevnia i zapreshchenie prodazhi pitei v Moskovskom uezde. Moscow: Pechatnia S. P. Iakovleva, 1915.

Doklad Klinskoi uezdnoi upravy po ekonomicheskoi chasti. Klin: Klinskoe uezdnoe sobranie, 1905.

Doklad Redaktsionnogo komiteta Otdeleniia obychnogo prava S Pb iuridicheskogo obshchestva o predstoiashchei emu deiatel'nosti. St. Petersburg, 1898.

Dzhanshiev, G. A. *Epokha velikikh reform.* 10th rev. ed. St. Petersburg: Tipo-litografiia V. M Vol'fa, 1907.

Efimenko, A. Ia. *Issledovaniia narodnoi zhizni.* Vyp. 1, *Obychnoe pravo.* Moscow: Russkaia tipo-litografiia, 1884.

Ekonomichesko-statisticheskii sbornik. Vyp. 3. Moscow, 1911.

Ekshtein, J. *Chest' v filosofii i v prave.* Translated by B. L. G-ch. St. Petersburg: Izdanie Ia. Kantorovich, 1899.

Engelgardt, Aleksandr Nikolaevich. *Letters from the Country, 1872–1887.* Translated and edited by Cathy A. Frierson. New York: Oxford, 1993.

Entsiklopedicheskii slovar'. Edited by F. A. Brokgaus and I. A. Efron. 51 vols. St. Petersburg: Tipo-litografiia I. A. Efrona, 1890–1907.

Fedoseev, P. I. *Iuridicheskii spravochnik dlia krest'ian i melkikh sobstvennikov-zemlevladel'tsev.* Moscow: P. K. Komisarenko, 1914.

Iakushkin, E. I. *Obychnoe pravo.* Vyp. 1. 2nd rev. ed. Moscow: Tovarishchestvo tipografii A. I. Mamontova, 1910.

Imperskoe vol'noe ekonomicheskoe obshchestvo. *Trudy.* 1904, 2, kn. 4–5.

Istorichesko-statisticheskoe opisanie sela Grebneva. Edited by I. O. Tokmakov. Moscow: Gorodskaia tipografiia, 1903.

Iubileinyi zemskii sbornik 1864–1914. St. Petersburg: O. N. Porova, 1914.

Iuridicheskii kalendar' dlia volostnykh i dolzhnostnykh lits. Sumy: N. T. Volkov, 1904.

Iuridicheskii kalendar' dlia zemskikh nachal'nikov 1904 g. Sumy: N. T. Volkov, 1903.

Iuridicheskii kalendar na 1910 god. St. Petersburg: Novoe zakonodatel'stvo, 1910.

Koni, A. F. *Otsy i deti sudebnoi reformy (K piatidesiatiletiiu Sudebnykh Ustavov) 1864 10 noiabria 1914.* Moscow, Izd. T-va I. D. Sytina, 1914.

Kovalevskii, V. I., ed. *Rossiia v kontse XIX veka.* St. Petersburg: Tipografiia Brokhaus-Efron, 1900.

Kots, E. S. *Mestnyi sud i ego reforma.* St. Peterburg: Zemledelets, 1913.

Kratkii statisticheskii ocherk krest'ianskogo zemlevladeniia i promyslov v Tsarskosel'skom uezde SPb. gub. St. Petersburg: Tipo-litografiia K. L. Penkovskogo, 1907.

Latkin, V. N. *Uchebnik istorii russkogo prava perioda imperii (XVIII i XIX st.).* 2nd rev. ed. St. Petersburg: Montvida-Goncharnaia, 1909.

Leont'ev, A. A. *Krest'ianskoe pravo. Sistematicheskoe izlozhenie osobennostei zakonodatel'stva o krest'ianakh.* St. Petersburg: Izdanie knizhnogo magazina "Zakonovedenie," 1909.

Materialy k otsenke gorodskikh nedvizhimykh imushchestv v S.-Peterburgskoi gubernii. Vyp. 4: *Gorod Iamburg.* St. Petersburg: Tipografiia K. S. Antokol'skogo, 1905.

Materialy k otsenke zemel' v S.-Peterburgskoi gubernii. Vyp. 6: *Tsarskosel'skii uezd.* St. Petersburg: Tipografiia K. S. Antokol'skogo, 1906.

Mirovoi sud: Prakticheskii kommentarii po pervuiu knigu Ustava grazhdanskogo sudoproizvodstva. Compiled by V. L. Isachenko. St. Petersburg: Tipografiia M. Merkusheva, 1913.

Moskovskoe gubernskoe zemstvo v poluvekuiu godovshchinu osnovaniia zemskikh uchrezhdenii, 1864–1914. Moscow, 1917.

Naselennye mestnosti Moskovskoi gubernii. Moscow: Gubernskaia tipografiia, 1913.

Naselennye mestnosti Moskovskoi gubernii. Prilozhenie k Pamiatnoi knizhke Moskovskoi gubernii na 1912 god. Moscow: Gubernskaia tipografiia, 1911.

Novaia karta okrestnostei Moskvy. Moscow: Knigoizdatel'stvo I. A. Maevskogo, 1915.

Ob uchastii narodnogo elementa v mestnom sude. St. Petersburg: tip. M. M. Stasiulevicha, 1911.

Ob'iasnitel'naia zapiska k proektu Ministerstva iustitsii o vvedenie v deistvie zakona 15 iiunia 1912 g. o preobrazovanii mestnogo suda. n.p., 1913.

Obzor Moskovskoi gubernii za [1905–1914]. Moscow: Gubernskaia tipografiia, [1906–1915].

Obzor S.-Peterburgskoi gubernii za 1909 god. St. Petersburg: St. Peterburgskaia gubernskaia tipografiia, 1910.

Opisanie Moskovskogo uezda, s ukazaniem v onom stanov, volostei, uriadov i selenii. Edited by B. P. Afanias'ev. Moscow, 1884.

Otchet Klinskoi uezdnoi zemskoi upravy po ekonomicheskoi chasti za 1903 g. Klin: Klinskoe uezdnoe sobranie, 1904.

Pamiatnaia kniga S.-Peterburgskoi gubernii na 1914–1915 gg. St. Petersburg: Gubernskaia tipografiia, 1914.

Pamiatnaia knizhka Moskovskoi gubernii na [1908, 1909, 1912, 1913, 1914] god. Moscow, Gubernskaia tipografiia, [1907, n.d., 1911, 1912, 1913].

Pamiatnaia knizhka Novgorodskoi gubernii na 1913 god. Novgorod: Gubernskaia tipografiia, 1913.

Pervaia vseobshchaia perepis' naseleniia Rossiiskoi imperii, 1897 g. Vol. 37: *S. Petersburgskaia guberniia.* St. Petersburg: Izdanie Tsentral'nogo statisticheskogo komiteta Ministerstva vnutrennikh del, 1903.

Polnoe sobranie zakonov Rossiiskoi imperii. Sobranie tretie. 33 vols. St. Petersburg/Petrograd, 1885–1916.

Praktika Pravitel'stvuiushchego senata po krest'ianskim delam. Compiled by I. M. Tiutriumov. St. Petersburg: Zakonovedenie, 1914.

Promysly krest'ianskogo naseleniia S-Peterburgskoi gubernii. Tsarskosel'skii uezd. St. Petersburg: Tipografiia K. S. Antokol'skogo, 1910.

Rech' V. A. Obraztsova v Gosudarstvennoi dume 4 noiabria 1909 goda v zashchitu volostnogo (krest'ianskogo) suda. Ekaterinoslav: tip. byvsh. Bratstva Sv. Vladimira, n.d.

Rossiia: Polnoe geograficheskoe opisanie nashego otechestva. Edited by V. P. Semenov. Vyp. 1: *Moskovskaia promyshlennaia oblast'.* St. Petersburg: A. F. Devrien, 1899. Vyp. 3: *Ozernaia oblast'.* St. Petersburg: A. F. Devrien, 1900.

Rossiia 1913 god. Statistiko-dokumental'nyi sbornik. St. Petersburg: Blits, 1995.

Rozenshtein, M. L. *Iuridicheskaia entsiklopediia.* Petrograd: Zhizn' i sud, 1916.

Rubakin, N. *Rossiia v tsifrakh.* St. Petersburg: Vestnik Znaniia, 1912.

Rudin. N. *Zakon 15 iiunia 1912 g. o preobrazovanii mestnogo suda.* St. Petersburg: Sotrudnik, 1912.

Russkaia gruppa Mezhdunarodnogo soiuza kriminalistov. *Ob uchastii narodnogo elementa v mestnom sude.* St. Petersburg: Tipografiia M. M. Stasiulevich, 1911.

Sbornik statisticheskikh svedenii Ministerstva iustitsii. Vyp. 21, ch. 1: "Svedeniia o lichnom sostave i o deiatel'nosti sudebnykh ustanovlenii evropeiskoi Rossii za [1905–1914]." St. Petersburg: Senatskaia tipografiia, [1907–1915].

Sbornik ukazov i postanovlenii Vremennogo pravitel'stva. Vyp. 1. 27 fevralia–5 maia 1917 g. Petrograd: Gosudarstvennaia tipografiia, 1917.

Shingarev, A. *Melkaia zemskaia edinitsa ili volostnoe zemstvo.* St. Petersburg: Narodnoe pravo, 1907.

Shramchenko, A. P., ed. *Spravochnaia knizhka Moskovskoi gubernii.* Moscow: Gubernskaia tipografiia, 1890.

Sobranie uzakonenii i rasporiazhenii Pravitel'stva, izdavaemoe pri Pravitel'stvuiushchem senate. 1917. Petrograd: Senatskaia tipografiia, 1917.

Spiski naselennykh mest Rossiiskoi imperii, XXXVII. Sankt-Peterburgskaia guberniia. Spisok naselennykh mest po svedeniiam 1862 goda. St. Petersburg: Tsentral'nyi statisticheskii komitet Ministerstva vnutrennikh del, 1864.

Spisok naselennykh mest Novgorodskoi gubernii. Vyp. 7: Tikhvinskii uezd. Novgorod: Gubernskaia tipografiia, 1911.

Statisticheskii ezhegodnik Moskovskoi gubernii za 1908 god. Ch. 1. Moscow: T-vo Pechatnia S. P. Iakovleva, 1909.

Statisticheskii sbornik po Petrogradskoi gubernii 1913 god. Vyp. 2: *Nachal'noe narodnoe obrazovanie v 1912–1913 uchebnom godu.* Petrograd: Tip. K. S. Antokol'skogo, 1915.

Svod zakonov Rossiiskoi imperii v piati knigakh. Edited by I. D. Mordukhai-Boltovskii. St. Petersburg: Deiatel', 1912.

Tenishev, V. V. *Pravosudie v russkom krest'ianskom bytu.* Briansk: Tipografiia L. I. Itina, 1907.

———. *Administrativnoe polozhenie russkogo krest'ianina.* St. Petersburg: Tipografiia A. S. Suvorina, 1908.

Tian-Shanskaia, Olga Semyonova. *Village Life in Late Tsarist Russia.* Edited by David L. Ransel. Translated by David L. Ransel, with Michael Levine. Bloomington: Indiana University Press, 1993.

Tokmakov, I. O. *Istoriko-statisticheskoe i arkheologicheskoe opisanie goroda Bogorodska (Moskovskoi gubernii) s uezdom i sviatyniiami.* Moscow: Pechatnia A. I. Snegirovoi, 1899.

Ukazateli uzakonenii, otnosiashchikhsia k ustroistvu sel'skogo sostoianiia s 1858 po 1896 god. St. Petersburg: Zemskii otdel Ministerstva vnutrennikh del, 1897.

Ustav grazhdanskogo sudoproizvodstva. Compiled by I. M. Tiutriumov. St. Petersburg: Zakonovedenie, 1916.

Ustav grazhdanskogo sudoproizvodstva dlia mestnostei, v kotorykh zakon o preobrazovanii mestnogo suda vveden v nepolnom ob"eme. Compiled by K. P. Zmirlov. St. Petersburg: Pravo, 1914.

Ustav o nakazaniakh, nalagaemykh mirovymi sud'iami. Edited by N. S. Tagantsev. 12th exp. ed. St. Petersburg: Tipografiia M. Merkusheva, 1912.

Velikaia reforma. Edited by A. K. Dzhivelegov, S. P. Mel'gunov, and V. I. Picheta. 6 vols. Moscow: Sytin, 1911.

Vikhlaev, P. A. *Ekonomicheskie usloviia narodnogo obrazovaniia v Moskovskoi gubernii.* Moscow: Pechatnaia S. P. Iakovleva, 1910.

———. *Vliianie travoseniami na otdel'nye storony krest'ianskogo khoziaistva. Naselenie i promysli travopol'nogo raiona.* Vyp. 9. Moscow: Petchatnia S. P. Iakovleva, 1915.

Vishniak, Marc. *Le régime soviétiste: Étude juridique et politique.* Paris: Imprimerie Union, 1920.

Vladimirskii-Budanov, M. F. *Obzor istorii russkogo prava.* 6th ed. St. Petersburg: N. Ia. Ogloblin, 1909.

Volostnoe zemstvo. 1917.

Vorms, A. "Zakon i obychai v nasledovanii krestian." *Iuridicheskii vestnik* (1913): 97–125.

Zakony o sostoianiiakh. Compiled by Ia. A. Kantorovich. 2nd ed. St. Petersburg: Pravo, 1911.

Zapiska Chlena Soveshchaniia Senatora N. A. Khvostova po voprosu o volostnom sude i o primenenii obychnogo prava po delam podsudnym volostnomu sudu. n.p., n.d. [1905].

Zhulev, P. *Ocherk istorii Kingissepskogo uezda i goroda Kingissepp (byvshego Iama-Iamburga).* Kingissepp, 1924.

PUBLISHED SOURCES, SECONDARY

Adams, Bruce F. *The Politics of Punishment: Prison Reform in Russia, 1863–1917.* DeKalb: Northern Illinois University Press, 1996.

Anfimov, A. M. *Rossiiskaia derevnia v gody pervoi mirovoi voiny (1914–fevral' 1917).* Moscow: Sotsial'no-ekonomicheskaia literatura, 1962.

———. "On the History of the Russian Peasantry at the Beginning of the Twentieth Century." *Russian Review* 51 (July 1992): 396–407.

Ascher, Abraham. *P. A. Stolypin: The Search for Stability in Late Imperial Russia.* Stanford, Calif.: Stanford University Press, 2001.

Atkinson, Dorothy. *The End of the Russian Land Commune, 1905–1930.* Stanford, Calif.: Stanford University Press, 1983.

Baberowski, Jörg. *Autokratie und Justiz: Zum Verhältnis von Rechsstaatlichkeit und Rückständigkeit im ausgehenden Zarenreich, 1864–1917.* Frankfurt am Main: V. Klostermann, 1996.

Barry, Donald D. *Toward the "Rule of Law" in Russia: Political and Legal Reform in the Transition Period.* Armonk, N.Y.: M. E. Sharpe, 1992.

Becker, Seymour. *Nobility and Privilege in Late Imperial Russia.* DeKalb: Northern Illinois University Press, 1985.

Benton, Lauren. *Law and Colonial Cultures: Legal Regimes in World History, 1400–1900.* Cambridge: Cambridge University Press, 2002.

Berman, Harold. *Justice in the U.S.S.R.* Rev. ed. New York: Vintage, 1963.

———. *Law and Revolution: The Formation of the Western Legal Tradition.* Cambridge, Mass.: Harvard University Press, 1983.

Bobrovnikov, V. O. "Sud po adatu v dorevoliutsionnom Dagestane (1860–1917)." *Etnograficheskoe obozrenie,* no. 2 (March–April 1999): 31–32.

———. *Musul'mane severnogo kavkaz: Obychai pravo nasilie.* Moscow: Vostochnaia literatura, 2002.

Bourdieu, Pierre. *Outline of a Theory of Practice.* Translated by Richard Nice. New York: Cambridge University Press, 1977.

———. *Distinction: A Social Critique of the Judgement of Taste.* Translated by Richard Nice. Cambridge, Mass.: Harvard University Press, 1984.

Bradley, Joseph. "Subjects into Citizens: Societies, Civil Society, and Autocracy in Tsarist Russia." *American Historical Review* 107, no. 4 (October 2002): 1094–1123.

Brooks, Jeffrey. *When Russia Learned to Read: Literacy and Popular Literature, 1861–1916.* Princeton, N.J.: Princeton University Press, 1985.

Brubaker, Rogers, and Frederick Cooper. "Beyond 'Identity.'" *Theory and Society* 29 (2000): 1–47.

Burbank, Jane. *Intelligentsia and Revolution: Russian Views of Bolshevism, 1917–1922.* New York: Oxford University Press, 1986.

———. "Discipline and Punish in the Moscow Bar Association." *Russian Review* 54, no. 1 (January 1995): 44–64.

———. "Legal Culture, Citizenship, and Peasant Jurisprudence: Perspectives from the Early Twentieth Century." In Peter Solomon, ed., *Reforming Justice in Russia, 1864–1994: Power, Culture, and the Limits of Legal Order,* pp. 82–106. Armonk, N.Y.: M. E. Sharpe, 1997.

———. "Narodnye sudy, imperskoe zakonodatel'stvo i grazhdanstvo v Rossii." In Aleksei Miller, ed., *Rossiiskaia imperiia v sravnitel'noi perspektive.* Moscow, Novoe izdatel'stvo, 2004.

Burbank, Jane, and Claudio Ingerflom. "Paysans et intellectuels en Russie." *Études rurales* 149–150 (January–June 1999): 173–180.

Burbank, Jane, and David L. Ransel, eds. *Imperial Russia: New Histories for the Empire.* Bloomington: Indiana University Press, 1998.

Burds, Jeffrey. *Peasant Dreams and Market Politics: Labor Migration and the Russian Village, 1861–1905.* Pittsburgh: University of Pittsburgh Press, 1998.

Burke, Peter, ed. *New Perspectives on Historical Writing.* University Park: University of Pennsylvania Press, 1991.

Butler, William E., ed. *Russian Law: Historical and Political Perspectives.* Leyden: A. W. Sijthoff, 1977.

Cherkasova, N. V. *Formirovanie i razvitie advokatury v Rossii: 60–80 gody XIX v.* Moscow: Nauka, 1987.

Clements, Barbara Evans, Barbara Alpern Engel, and Christine C. Worobec, eds. *Russia's Women: Accommodation, Resistance, Transformation.* Berkeley: University of California Press, 1991.

Clifford, James, and George E. Marcus, eds. *Writing Culture: The Poetics and Politics of Ethnography.* Berkeley: University of California Press, 1986.

Clowes, Edith W., Samuel D. Kassow, and James L. West. *Between Tsar and People: Educated Society and the Quest for Public Identity in Late Imperial Russia.* Princeton, N.J.: Princeton University Press, 1991.

Confino, Michael. "Russian Customary Law and the Study of Peasant Mentalités." *Russian Review* 44 (January 1985): 27–33.

———. "Present Events and the Representation of the Past." *Cahiers du Monde russe,* 35, no. 4 (October–December 1994): 839–868.

Cooper, Frederick. "Conflict and Connection: Rethinking Colonial African History." *American Historical Review* 99 (1994): 1516–1545.

Cooper, Frederick, and Ann Laura Stoler, eds. *Tensions of Empire: Colonial Cultures in a Bourgeois World.* Berkeley: University of California Press, 1996.

Crisp, Olga, and Linda Edmondson, eds. *Civil Rights in Imperial Russia.* Oxford: Clarendon, 1989.

Czap, Peter. "Peasant Class Courts and Peasant Customary Justice in Russia, 1861–1912." *Journal of Social History,* no. 1 (1967): 149–178.

Druzhinin, N. M. *Gosudarstvennye krest'iane i reforma P. D. Kiseleva.* 2 vols. Moscow: Akademiia Nauk SSSR, 1958 [1946].

Dupret, Baudouin, Maurits Berger, and Laila al-Zwaini, eds. *Legal Pluralism in the Arab World.* The Hague: Kluwer Law International, 1999.

Edelman, Robert. *Gentry Politics on the Eve of the Russian Revolution: The Nationalist Party, 1907–1917.* New Brunswick, N.J.: Rutgers University Press, 1980.

Edmondson, Linda Harriet. *Feminism in Russia, 1900–1907.* Stanford, Calif.: Stanford University Press, 1984.

Eklof, Ben. *Russian Peasant Schools: Officialdom, Village Culture, and Popular Pedagogy, 1861–1914.* Berkeley: University of California Press, 1986.

———. "Ways of Seeing: Recent Anglo-American Studies of the Russian Peasant (1861–1914)." *Jahrbücher für Geschichte Osteuropas* 36, no. 1 (1988): 57–79.

Eklof, Ben, and Stephen P. Frank, eds. *The World of the Russian Peasant.* Boston: Unwin Hyman, 1990.

Eklof, Ben, John Bushnell, and Larissa Zakharova, eds. *Russia's Great Reforms, 1855–1881.* Bloomington: Indiana University Press, 1994.

Engel, Barbara. *Between the Fields and the City: Women, Work, and Family in Russia, 1861–1914.* Cambridge: Cambridge University Press, 1995.

Engelstein, Laura. *The Keys to Happiness: Sex and the Search for Modernity in Fin-de-Siecle Russia.* Ithaca, N.Y.: Cornell University Press, 1992.

———. "Combined Underdevelopment: Discipline and Law in Imperial and Soviet Russia." *American Historical Review* 98 (April 1993): 338–353.

Eroshkin, N. P. *Istoriia gosudarstvennykh uchrezhdenii dorevoliutsionnoi Rossii.* 4th rev. ed. Moscow: Tretii Rim, 1997.

Ewick, Patricia, and Susan S. Silbey. *The Common Place of Law: Stories from Everyday Life.* Chicago: University of Chicago Press, 1998.

Farnsworth, Beatrice. "The Litigious Daughter-in-Law: Family Relations in Rural Russia in the Second Half of the Nineteenth Century." *Slavic Review* 45, no. 1 (spring 1986): 49–64.

———. "The Soldatka: Folklore and Court Record." *Slavic Review* 49, no. 1 (spring 1990): 58–73.

Farnsworth, Beatrice, and Lynne Viola, eds. *Russian Peasant Women.* New York: Oxford University Press, 1992.

Fedosiuk, Iu. A. *Chto neponiatno u klassikov, ili Entsiklopediia russkogo byta XIX veka.* Moscow: Flinta, Nauka, 1999.

Felstiner, William L. F., Richard L. Abel, and Austin Sarat. "The Emergence and Transformation of Disputes: Naming, Blaming, Claiming . . ." *Law and Society Review* 15, no. 3–4 (1980–1981): 631–654.

Field, Daniel. *Rebels in the Name of the Tsar.* Boston: Unwin Hyman, 1989.

Figes, Orlando. *A People's Tragedy: The Russian Revolution, 1891–1924.* New York: Penguin, 1998.

Fitzpatrick, Sheila. "Ascribing Class: The Construction of Social Identity in Soviet Russia." *Journal of Modern History* 65 (December 1993): 745–770.

———. *Stalin's Peasants: Resistance and Survival in the Russian Village after Collectivization.* New York: Oxford University Press, 1994.

Florinsky, Michael. *The End of the Russian Empire.* New York: Collier, 1961.

Foucault, Michel. *Discipline and Punish: The Birth of the Prison.* Translated by Alan Sheridan. New York: Vintage, 1979 [Paris: Gallimard, 1975].

Frank, Stephen P. "Emancipation and the Birch: The Perpetuation of Corporal Punishment in Rural Russia, 1861–1907." *Jahrbücher für Geschichte Osteuropas* 45 (1997): 401–416.

———. *Crime, Cultural Conflict, and Justice in Rural Russia, 1856–1914.* Berkeley: University of California Press, 1999.

Frank, Stephen P., and Mark D. Steinberg, eds. *Cultures in Flux: Lower-Class Values, Practices and Resistance in Late Imperial Russia.* Princeton, N.J.: Princeton University Press, 1994.

Freeze, Gregory. "The *Soslovie* (Estate) Paradigm and Russian Social History." *American Historical Review* 91, no. 1 (1986): 11–36.

Friedman, Lawrence. "Litigation and Society." *Annual Review of Sociology* 15 (1989): 17–29.

Frierson, Cathy A. "Rural Justice in Public Opinion: The *Volost'* Court Debate." *Slavonic and East European Review* 64, no. 4 (October 1986): 526–545.

———. "Crime and Punishment in the Russian Village: Rural Concepts of Criminality at the End of the Nineteenth Century." *Slavic Review* 46, no. 1 (1987): 55–69.

———. "*Razdel:* The Peasant Family Divided." *Russian Review* 46 (1987): 35–52.

———. *Peasant Icons: Representations of Rural People in Late Nineteenth-Century Russia.* New York: Oxford University Press, 1993.

———. "'I Must Always Answer to the Law . . .': Rules and Responses in the Reformed *Volost'* Court." *Slavonic and East European Review* 75, no. 2 (April 1997): 308–334.

———. *All Russia Is Burning! A Cultural History of Fire and Arson in Late Imperial Russia.* Seattle: University of Washington Press, 2002.

Galanter, Marc. "Reading the Landscape of Disputes: What We Know and Don't Know (and Think We Know) about Our Allegedly Contentious and Litigious Society." *UCLA Law Review* 31, no. 1 (October 1983): 4–71.

Galili, Ziva. *The Menshevik Leaders in the Russian Revolution: Social Realities and Political Strategies.* Princeton, N.J.: Princeton University Press, 1989.

Gatrell, Peter. "Historians and Peasants: Studies of Medieval English Society in a Russian Context." *Past and Present,* no. 96 (1982): 22–50.

———. *A Whole Empire Walking: Refugees in Russia during World War I.* Bloomington: Indiana University Press, 1999.

Gaudin, Corinne. "Les zemskie načal'niki au village: Coutumes administratives et culture paysanne en Russie 1889–1914." *Cahiers du monde russe* 36, no. 3 (juillet–septembre 1995): 249–272.

———. "Tribunaux paysans en Russie, 1889–1914." *Histoire sociale/Social History* 30, no. 59 (May 1997): 109–126.

———. "'No Place to Lay My Head': Marginalization and the Right to Land during the Stolypin Reforms." *Slavic Review* 57, no. 4 (winter 1998): 747–773.

Gordon, Robert. "Critical Legal Histories." *Stanford Law Review* 36 (January 1984): 57–125.

Gorshkov, Boris B. "Serfs on the Move: Peasant Seasonal Migration in Pre-Reform Russia, 1800–61." *Kritika: Explorations in Russian and Eurasian History* 1, no. 4 (fall 2000): 27–56.

Gottfredson, Michael, and Travis Hirschi. *A General Theory of Crime.* Stanford, Calif.: Stanford University Press, 1990.

Greenhouse, Carol J. "Interpreting American Litigiousness." In Jane Collier and June Star, eds., *History and Power in the Study of Law: New Directions in Legal Anthropology,* 252–273. Ithaca, N.Y.: Cornell University Press, 1989.

Gromyko, M. M. "Kul'tura russkogo krest'ianstva XVIII–XIX vekov kak predmet istoricheskogo issledovaniia." *Istoriia SSSR,* no. 3 (1987): 39–60.

———. *Mir russkoi derevni.* Moscow: Molodaia gvardiia, 1991.

Guha, Ranajit, and Gayatri Chakravorty Spivak, eds. *Selected Subaltern Studies.* New York: Oxford University Press, 1988.

Habermas, Jürgen. *The Structural Transformation of the Public Sphere.* Translated by Thomas Burger, with the assistance of Frederick Lawrence. Cambridge, Mass.: MIT Press, 1991.

Haimson, Leopold H., ed. *The Politics of Rural Russia, 1905–1914.* Bloomington: Indiana University Press, 1979.

Hay, Douglas, et al. *Albion's Fatal Tree: Crime and Society in Eighteenth-Century England.* New York: Pantheon, 1975.

Herlihy, Patricia. *The Alcoholic Empire: Vodka and Politics in Late Imperial Russia.* New York: Oxford University Press, 2002.

Herrup, Cynthia B. *The Common Peace: Participation and the Criminal Law in Seventeenth-Century England.* Cambridge: Cambridge University Press, 1987.

Heuman, Susan. *Kistiakovsky: The Struggle for National and Constitutional Rights in the Last Years of Tsarism.* Cambridge, Mass.: Harvard University Press and Harvard Ukrainian Research Institute, 1998.

Hirschi, Travis, and Michael R. Gottfredson. "Age and the Explanation of Crime." *American Sociological Review* 89 (1983): 552–584.

Hobsbawm, E. J. *Primitive Rebels: Studies in Archaic Forms of Social Movement in the 19th and 20th Centuries.* New York: Norton, 1965.

Hobsbawm, Eric, and Terence Ranger, eds. *The Invention of Tradition.* Cambridge: Cambridge University Press, 1983.

Hoch, Steven L. *Serfdom and Social Control in Russia: Petrovskoe, a Village in Tambov.* Chicago: University of Chicago Press, 1986.

———. "On Good Numbers and Bad: Malthus, Population Trends and Peasant Standard of Living in Late Imperial Russia." *Slavic Review* 52, no. 3 (spring 1994): 41–75.

Hoffmann, David. *Peasant Metropolis: Social Identities in Moscow, 1929–1941.* Ithaca, N.Y.: Cornell University Press, 1994.

Humphreys, Sally. "Law as Discourse." *History and Anthropology* 1 (1985): 241–264.

Jahn, Hubertus F. *Patriotic Culture in Russia during World War I.* Ithaca, N.Y.: Cornell University Press, 1995.

Johnson, Robert Eugene. *Peasant and Proletarian: The Working Class of Moscow in the Late Nineteenth Century.* New Brunswick, N.J.: Rutgers University Press, 1979.

Kazantsev, S. M., ed. *Sud prisiazhnykh v Rossii: Gromkie ugolovnye protsessy 1864–1917 gg.* St. Petersburg: Lenizdat, 1991.

Keenan, Edward L. "Muscovite Political Folkways." *Russian Review* 45 (1986): 115–181.

Kenez, Peter. *The Birth of the Propaganda State: Soviet Methods of Mass Mobilization, 1917–1929.* Cambridge: Cambridge University Press, 1985.

Kingston-Mann, Esther, and Timothy Mixter, eds. *Peasant Economy, Culture and Politics of European Russia, 1800–1921.* Princeton, N.J.: Princeton University Press, 1991.

Kivelson, Valerie A. *Autocracy in the Provinces: The Muscovite Gentry and Political Culture in the Seventeenth Century.* Stanford, Calif.: Stanford University Press, 1996.

———. "Merciful Father, Impersonal State: Russian Autocracy in Comparative Perspective." *Modern Asian Studies* 31, no. 3 (1997): 635–663.

———. "Muscovite 'Citizenship': Rights without Freedom." *Journal of Modern History* 74 (September 2002): 465–489.

Kollmann, Nancy Shields. *By Honor Bound: State and Society in Early Modern Russia.* Ithaca, N.Y.: Cornell University Press, 1999.

Korotkikh, M. G. *Sudebnaia reforma 1864 goda v Rossii (Sushchnost' i sotsial'no-pravovoi mekhanizm formirovaniia).* Voronezh: Izdatel'stvo Voronezhskogo universiteta, 1994.

Kotsonis, Yanni. *Making Peasants Backward: Agricultural Cooperatives and the Agrarian Question in Russia, 1861–1914.* New York: St. Martin's, 1999.

———. "'Face-to-Face': The State and the Individual in Russian Taxation, 1863–1917." *Slavic Review*, forthcoming 63, no. 2 (summer 2004).

———. "'No Place to Go': Taxation and State Transformation in Late-Imperial and Early Soviet Russia." *Journal of Modern History*, forthcoming September 2004.

Kucherov, Samuel. *Courts, Lawyers, and Trials under the Last Three Tsars.* New York: Praeger, 1953.

LaTour, Bruno. *We Have Never Been Modern.* Translated by Catherine Porter. Cambridge, Mass.: Harvard University Press, 1993.

Leikina-Svirskaia, V. R. *Russkaia intelligentsiia v 1900–1917 godakh.* Moscow: Mysl', 1981.

Lewin, Moshe. "Customary Law and Rural Society in the Postreform Era." *Russian Review* 44, no. 1 (January 1985): 1–19.

Lieven, Dominic. *Russia's Rulers under the Old Regime.* New Haven, Conn.: Yale University Press, 1989.

Lincoln, Bruce. *Passage through Armageddon: The Russians in War and Revolution.* New York: Oxford University Press, 1994.

Macey, David A. J. *Government and Peasant in Russia, 1861–1906.* DeKalb: Northern Illinois University Press, 1987.

———. "'A Wager on History': The Stolypin Agrarian Reforms as Process." In Judith Pallot, ed., *Transforming Peasants: Society, State and the Peasantry, 1861–1930,* pp. 149–173. New York: St. Martin's, 1998.

Manning, Roberta Thompson. *The Crisis of the Old Order in Russia: Gentry and Government.* Princeton, N.J.: Princeton University Press, 1982.

Martin, Virginia. "Barimta: Nomadic Custom, Imperial Crime." In Daniel R. Brower and Edward J. Lazzerini, eds., *Russia's Orient: Imperial Borderlands and Peoples, 1700–1917,* pp. 249–270. Bloomington: Indiana University Press, 1997.

Merry, Sally Engle. *Getting Justice and Getting Even: Legal Consciousness among Working-Class Americans.* Chicago: University of Chicago Press, 1990.

Merryman, John Henry. *The Civil Law Tradition: An Introduction to the Legal Systems of Western Europe and Latin America.* 2nd ed. Stanford, Calif.: Stanford University Press, 1985.

Mogul, Jonathan M. "In the Shadow of the Factory: Peasant Manufacturing and Russian Industrialization, 1861–1914." Ph.D. dissertation, University of Michigan, 1996.

Moon, David. "Peasants into Russian Citizens? A Comparative Perspective." *Revolutionary Russia* 9, no. 1 (June 1996): 44–81.

———. "Women in Rural Russia from the Tenth to the Twentieth Centuries." *Continuity and Change* 12, no. 1 (1997): 129–138.

———. *The Russian Peasantry, 1600–1930*. London: Longman, 1999.

Moore, Sally Falk. *Law as Process: An Anthropological Approach*. London: Routledge and Kegan Paul, 1978.

Munger, Frank. "Law, Change, and Litigation: A Critical Examination of an Empirical Research Tradition." *Law and Society Review* 22, no. 1 (1988): 57–101.

Neuberger, Joan. *Hooliganism: Crime, Culture, and Power in St. Petersburg, 1900–1914*. Berkeley: University of California Press, 1993.

———. "Popular Legal Cultures: The St. Petersburg *Mirovoi Sud*." In Ben Eklof et al., eds., *Russia's Great Reforms, 1855–1881*, pp. 231–246. Bloomington: Indiana University Press, 1994.

———. "Shysters or Public Servants? Uncertified Lawyers and Legal Aid for the Poor in Late Imperial Russia." *Russian History*, nos. 1–4 (1996): 295–310.

Odintsovskaia zemlia. Moscow: Entsiklopediia rossiiskikh dereven', 1994.

Ong, Walter J. *Orality and Literacy: The Technologizing of the Word*. London: Routledge, 1982.

Orlov, V. I. *1905 v Klinskom uezde*. Moscow-Leningrad: Moskovskii rabochii, 1931.

Orlovsky, Daniel T. *The Limits of Reform: The Ministry of Internal Affairs in Imperial Russia, 1802–1881*. Cambridge, Mass.: Harvard University Press, 1981.

Pallot, Judith, ed. *Transforming Peasants: Society, State, and the Peasantry, 1861–1930*. New York: St. Martin's, 1998.

Pipes, Richard. *The Russian Revolution*. New York: Vintage, 1991.

———. *Russia under the Old Regime*. 2nd ed. London: Penguin, 1995.

Pomerantz, William E. "Justice from Underground: The History of the Underground Advokatura." *Russian Review* 52, no. 3 (July 1993): 321–340.

———. "Legal Assistance in Tsarist Russia: The St. Petersburg Consultation Bureaus." *Wisconsin International Law Journal* 14, no. 3 (summer 1996): 586–610.

Popkins, Gareth. "Popular Development of Procedure in a Dual Legal System: 'Protective Litigation' in Russia's Peasant Courts." *Journal of Legal Pluralism and Unofficial Law*, no. 43 (1999): 57–87.

———. "Peasant Experiences of the Late Tsarist State: District Congresses of Land Captains, Provincial Boards and the Legal Appeals Process." *Slavonic and East European Review* 78, no. 1 (January 2000): 90–114.

———. "Code *versus* Custom: Norms and Tactics in Peasant *Volost'* Court Appeals, 1889–1917." *Russian Review* 59, no. 3 (July 2000): 408–424.

Protasov, L. G. *Vserossiiskoe uchreditel'noe sobranie: Istoriia rozhdeniia i gibeli*. Moscow: Rosspen, 1997.

Radkey, Oliver. *The Election to the Russian Constituent Assembly of 1917*. Cambridge, Mass.: Harvard University Press, 1950.

Ransel, David. *Mothers of Misery: Child Abandonment in Russia*. Princeton, N.J.: Princeton University Press, 1988.

Rashin, A. G. *Naselenie Rossii za 100 let*. Moscow: Gosizdat, 1956.

Ravich, L. M. *Evgenii Ivanovich Iakushkin (1826–1905)*. Leningrad: Nauka, 1989.

Razumov, L. V. *Rassloenie krest'ianstva tsentral'no-promyshlennogo raiona v kontse XIX–nachale XX veka*. Moscow: Institut rossiiskoi istorii RAN, 1996.

Romaniuk, S. K. *Po zemliam moskovskikh sel i slobod*. Moscow: ZAO "Svarog i K," 1998.

Sampson, Robert, and John Laub. *Crime in the Making: Pathways and Turning Points through Life*. Cambridge, Mass.: Harvard University Press, 1993.

Schrader, Abby M. "Containing the Spectacle of Punishment: The Russian Autocracy and the Abolition of the Knout." *Slavic Review* 56, no. 4 (1997): 613–644.

———. *Languages of the Lash: Corporal Punishment and Identity in Imperial Russia.* DeKalb: Northern Illinois University Press, 2002.

Schulte, Renate. *The Village in Court: Arson, Infanticide and Poaching in the Court Records of Upper Bavaria, 1848–1910.* Translated by Barrie Selman. Cambridge: Cambridge University Press, 1994.

Scott, James C. *Weapons of the Weak: Everyday Forms of Peasant Resistance.* New Haven, Conn.: Yale University Press, 1985.

Seregny, Scott J. *Russian Teachers and Peasant Revolution: The Politics of Education in 1905.* Bloomington: Indiana University Press, 1989.

Shanin, Teodor. *The Awkward Class: Political Sociology of a Developing Society, Russia 1910–1925.* Oxford: Oxford University Press, 1972.

———. *Russia as a "Developing Society."* Vol. 1, *The Roots of Otherness: Russia's Turn of Century.* New Haven, Conn.: Yale University Press, 1985.

Shepelev, L. E. *Chinovnyi mir Rossii XVIII–XX v.* St. Petersburg: Iskusstvo-SPB, 1999.

Smith, S. A. "The Social Meanings of Swearing: Workers and Bad Language in Late Imperial and Early Soviet Russia." *Past and Present* 160 (August 1998): 167–202.

Solomon, Peter. *Soviet Criminal Justice under Stalin.* Cambridge: Cambridge University Press, 1996.

———, ed. *Reforming Justice in Russia, 1864–1996.* Armonk, N.Y.: M. E. Sharpe, 1997.

Somers, Margaret. "Citizenship and the Place of the Public Sphere: Law, Community, and Political Culture in the Transition to Democracy." *American Sociological Review* 58, no. 5 (October 1993): 587–620.

———. "Rights, Relationality, and Membership: Rethinking the Making and Meaning of Citizenship." *Law and Social Inquiry* 19, no. 1 (winter 1994): 63–112.

Sotsial'no-politicheskoe i pravovoe polozhenie krest'ianstva v dorevoliutsionnoi Rossii. Voronezh: Voronezhskii universitet, 1983.

Stanziani, Alessandro. "Les statistiques des récoltes en Russie, 1905–1928." *Histoire et Mesure* 7, nos. 1–2 (1992): 73–98.

———. *L'économie en révolution: Le cas russe, 1870–1930.* Paris: Albin Michel, 1998.

———. "War and the Disintegration of Economic Space." In Judith Pallot, ed., *Transforming Peasants: Society, State, and the Peasantry, 1861–1930,* pp. 174–193. New York: St. Martin's Press, 1998.

———. "Organisations familiales et marché du travail en Russie, 1861–1922." *Histoire et Mesure* 14, no. 1/2 (1999): 121–162.

———. "Les Enquêtes Orales en Russie, 1861–1914." *Annales HSS,* no. 1 (January–February 2000): 219–241.

Steinwedel, Charles Robert. "Invisible Threads of Empire: State, Religion, and Ethnicity in Tsarist Bashkiria, 1773–1917." Ph.D. dissertation, Columbia University, 1999.

Tarabanova, T. A. "Sudebno-pravovaia kul'tura krest'ian poreformennoi Rossii (po materialam volostnykh sudov)." In *Rossiia i reformy,* vyp. 2, pp. 40–54. Moscow: Medved', 1993.

Timofeev, Lev. *Soviet Peasants; or, The Peasants' Art of Starving.* Edited by Armando Pitassio and Viktor Zaslavsky. Translated by Jean Alexander and Alexander Zaslavsky. New York: Telos, 1985.

Uezdnyi gorod Bogorodsk na starykh fotografiiakh. Compiled by M. S. Drozdov and M. V. Zolotarev. Bogorodsk: Bogorodskii pechatnik, 1994.

Viola, Lynne. *The Best Sons of the Fatherland: Workers in the Vanguard of Soviet Collectivization.* New York: Oxford University Press, 1987.

———. *Peasant Rebels under Stalin: Collectivization and the Culture of Peasant Resistance.* New York: Oxford University Press, 1996.

Von Hagen, Mark. *Soldiers in the Proletarian Dictatorship: The Red Army and the Soviet Socialist State, 1917–1930.* Ithaca, N.Y.: Cornell University Press, 1990.

Vucinich, Wayne S., ed. *The Peasant in Nineteenth-Century Russia.* Stanford, Calif.: Stanford University Press, 1968.

Wagner, William. *Marriage, Property, and Law in Late Imperial Russia.* Oxford: Clarendon, 1994.

Walicki, Andrzej. *Legal Philosophies of Russian Liberalism.* Oxford: Clarendon, 1987.

Wcislo, Francis William. "Soslovie or Class? Bureaucratic Reformers and Provincial Gentry in Conflict, 1906–1908." *Russian Review* 47 (1988): 1–24.

———. *Reforming Rural Russia: State, Local Society, and National Politics, 1855–1914.* Princeton, N.J.: Princeton University Press, 1990.

Weber, Max. *Economy and Society: An Outline of Interpretive Sociology.* Edited by Guenter Roth and Claus Wittich. 2 vols. Berkeley: University of California Press, 1978.

Weickhardt, George G. "Due Process and Equal Justice in the Muscovite Codes." *Russian Review* 51 (October 1992): 463–480.

Weissman, Neil B. "Rural Crime in Tsarist Russia: The Question of Hooliganism, 1905–1914." *Slavic Review* 37, no. 2 (1978): 228–240.

———. *Reform in Tsarist Russia: The State Bureaucracy and Local Government, 1900–1914.* New Brunswick, N.J.: Rutgers University Press, 1981.

Werth, Paul W. "Changing Conceptions of Difference, Assimilation, and Faith in the Volga-Kama Region, 1740–1870." In Jane Burbank and Mark von Hagen, eds., *Geographies of Empire: Ruling Russia, 1700–1930.* Unpublished manuscript.

Wirtschafter, Elise Kimerling. "The Ideal of Paternalism in the Prereform Army." In Ezra Mendelsohn and Marshall Shatz, eds., *Imperial Russia 1700–1917: State Society Opposition—Essays in Honor of Marc Raeff,* pp. 96–114. DeKalb: Northern Illinois University Press, 1988.

———. *Structures of Society: Imperial Russia's "People of Various Ranks."* DeKalb: Northern Illinois University Press, 1994.

———. *Social Identity in Imperial Russia.* DeKalb: Northern Illinois University Press, 1997.

———. "Legal Identity and the Possession of Serfs in Imperial Russia." *Journal of Modern History* 70 (September 1998): 561–563.

Worobec, Christine. *Peasant Russia: Family and Community in Post-Emancipation Russia.* Princeton, N.J.: Princeton University Press, 1991.

Wortman, Richard. *The Development of a Russian Legal Consciousness.* Chicago: University of Chicago Press, 1976.

Yaney, George. *The Systematization of Russian Government: Social Evolution in the Domestic Administration of Imperial Russia, 1711–1905.* Urbana: University of Illinois Press, 1973.

———. *The Urge to Mobilize: Agrarian Reform in Russia, 1861–1930.* Urbana: University of Illinois Press, 1982.

Zelnik, Reginald E., ed. and trans. *A Radical Worker in Tsarist Russia: The Autobiography of Semen Ivanovich Kanatchikov.* Stanford, Calif.: Stanford University Press, 1986.

Zhukova, E. V. *Staryi Pavlovskii posad.* Moscow: Kniga, 1994.

Zyrianov, P. N. "Tret'ia duma i vopros o reforme mestnogo suda i volostnogo upravleniia." *Istoriia SSSR,* no. 6 (1969): 45–62.

———. *Krest'ianskaia obshchina evropeiskoi Rossii 1907–1914 gg.* Moscow: Nauka, 1992.

Index

Page numbers in italics refer to illustrations and tables. In subentries, the word "courts" generally refers to township courts. For subjects of indexed statutes of the *Statutes on Punishments Applicable by the Justices of the Peace,* see Appendix 2.

JANE BURBANK is Professor of History and Russian and Slavic Studies at New York University. Her publications include *Intelligentsia and Revolution: Russian Views of Bolshevism, 1917–1922* and *Imperial Russia: New Histories for the Empire* (co-edited with David Ransel).

www.ingramcontent.com/pod-product-compliance
Lightning Source LLC
LaVergne TN
LVHW011204090826
844660LV00058B/268

* 9 7 8 0 2 5 3 3 4 4 2 6 7 *